Yankel's Tavern

Yankel's Tavern
Jews, Liquor, and Life in the Kingdom of Poland

Glenn Dynner

OXFORD
UNIVERSITY PRESS

Oxford University Press is a department of the University of Oxford.
It furthers the University's objective of excellence in research, scholarship,
and education by publishing worldwide.

Oxford   New York
Auckland   Cape Town   Dar es Salaam   Hong Kong   Karachi
Kuala Lumpur   Madrid   Melbourne   Mexico City   Nairobi
New Delhi   Shanghai   Taipei   Toronto

With offices in
Argentina   Austria   Brazil   Chile   Czech Republic   France   Greece
Guatemala   Hungary   Italy   Japan   Poland   Portugal   Singapore
South Korea   Switzerland   Thailand   Turkey   Ukraine   Vietnam

Oxford is a registered trade mark of Oxford University Press
in the UK and certain other countries.

Published in the United States of America by
Oxford University Press
198 Madison Avenue, New York, NY 10016

© Oxford University Press 2014

First issued as an Oxford University Press paperback, 2015.

All rights reserved. No part of this publication may be reproduced, stored in a
retrieval system, or transmitted, in any form or by any means, without the prior
permission in writing of Oxford University Press, or as expressly permitted by law,
by license, or under terms agreed with the appropriate reproduction rights organization.
Inquiries concerning reproduction outside the scope of the above should be sent to the Rights
Department, Oxford University Press, at the address above.

You must not circulate this work in any other form
and you must impose this same condition on any acquirer.

Library of Congress Cataloging-in-Publication Data
Dynner, Glenn, 1969– author.
Yankel's tavern : Jews, liquor, & life in the Kingdom of Poland / Glenn Dynner.
pages cm
Includes bibliographical references and index.
ISBN 978-0-19-998851-8 (hardcover : alk. paper); 978-0-19-020414-3 (paperback : alk. paper)
1. Jews—Poland—Social conditions—19th century.   2. Hotelkeepers—Poland—History—
19th century.   3. Bars (Drinking establishments)—Poland—History—19th century.
4. Alcohol (Jewish law)   5. Poland—Politics and government—19th century.
6. Poland—Ethnic relations.   I. Title.
DS134.55D96   2013
647.9543809'034—dc23
2013019941

Dedicated to my father, Alan Dynner

CONTENTS

Author's Preface   ix
A Note on Translations, Foreign Terms, and Names   xi

Introduction   1
1. Entrance: Myths and Countermyths   14
2. Rural Jewish Prohibition in the Kingdom of Poland   47
3. The Urban Jewish Liquor Trade in the Kingdom of Poland   82
4. Soldiers, Smugglers and Spies: Jewish Tavernkeepers during the Polish Uprisings of 1830 and 1863   103
5. The Tavernkeepers Speak: Polish Jewish Tavernkeeping in the Wake of Peasant Emancipation   131
6. Farmers, Soldiers, and Students: Reforming Jewish Tavernkeepers   153
Conclusion   175

Notes   179
Bibliography   225
Index   241

AUTHOR'S PREFACE

On a chilly March evening I made my way across downtown Manhattan towards the new brick building that houses the Center for Jewish History. I was nervous. Tonight, for the very first time, I was to present the results of my archival research on the Polish Jewish liquor trade before the general public. One of the world's most prominent historians of Polish Jewry was to serve as the respondent. To add to my nervousness, I had to wonder how many people appreciated the importance of the topic. Would anyone show up?

As I entered the building, I was met by the program coordinator and YIVO archivist, Fruma Mohrer. "There are almost a hundred people expected tonight," she said.

"What?"

"Apparently, everyone has a grandfather who ran a tavern back in the Old Country."

Soon, audience members began to file into the pre-lecture reception area. I stood off in a corner sipping my coffee. "Glenn!" called Fruma, approaching me with a smile. "They want to know who you are!" She began introducing me to people. Then I heard someone call out, "There he is!" A tide of people waving genealogical documents of various kinds—birth records, newspaper clippings, and so on—began to make its way towards me. "My grandfather ran a tavern in Bielsko-Biala," announced one woman. "Mine ran a tavern in Zhitomir," another informed me. After answering as many questions as I could, I was led into the large lecture hall.

My first public lecture on Jewish tavernkeeping felt strange for several reasons. Strange that so many people would turn out to hear a talk on what I had thought was a relatively unknown topic. Stranger still because East European Jewish historians of the postwar period had unanimously pronounced the Jewish liquor trade dead by the late nineteenth century, yet here were living people claiming that their grandparents had run taverns in Eastern Europe. Even stranger because their memories so stubbornly repudiated the broader picture of East European Jewry that recent historians have given us, a picture that is dominated by secularizing, urban, cosmopolitan types—*maskilim*, Zionists, Bundists, university students, and so on. Tonight's audience members nourished an image of their grandfathers that is more akin to the Jewish grandfather in Joseph Roth's great novel *Radetzky March*: "an orthodox Jewish tavernkeeper . . . [who] used to sit at the huge arched entrance to his border tavern at all hours of the day."[1] Some even had documents to back it up. This lecture experience, as well as many subsequent ones, reinforced my sense of an enormous divide between the general public's memories of the East European Jewish past and the reconstructions of professional historians.

Among historians, the main response to this divide has been resignation: Jewish history and Jewish memory must inevitably exist in opposition, many historians conclude, since the latter amounts to little more than myth. This book resists that notion, arguing that historians' reconstructions of the East European Jewish past have, in their own way, been as distorting as those of Jewish memory.[2] Recent historians of the region may have provided an important corrective to the Chagall-esque image of shtetl naiveté, piety, and insularity that still dominates the popular imagination. But by selectively emphasizing East European Jewry's most avid modernizers, they have gone too far in the other direction. This book by no means disregards secularizing urban elites—to the contrary, we will learn a good deal about their struggles and aspirations. But we will learn even more about the hundreds of thousands of workaday city, shtetl, and village Jews who have usually been consigned to the realm of popular memory. And as so many were engaged in the production and sale of liquor, the quest for a more representative East European Jewish history requires spending some time in their taverns.

A NOTE ON TRANSLATIONS, FOREIGN TERMS, AND NAMES

As the renowned scholar of Jewish mysticism Elliot Wolfson once noted, translation entails a "double bind." To translate is necessary; but to translate is also to deform.³ Though wary of this dilemma, I have made an effort here to translate more rather than less. My feeling is that when I render the Hebrew term *halakha* as "Jewish law," the Yiddish term *kvitlekh* as "petitions," or the Polish term *arenda* as "lease," the nonspecialist reader's task is significantly eased. I have also supplied well-known English equivalents for Polish town names (e.g., Warsaw instead of Warszawa), and refer to Polish nobles by the honorific "Lord" instead of "*Pan*."

In this same spirit, I have Anglicized Hebrew first names but, on the advice of several Polish historians, left Polish first names in the original, as is standard in the field of Slavic studies. It may help non-Polish speakers to know, however, that "sz" is pronounced "sh" (e.g., Szymon = Shimon); that the "ł" is pronounced like an English "w"; and that the Polish "w" is pronounced like a "v" (e.g., Walenty = Va-WEN-te). A related dilemma is how to identify figures after their first mention—whether by their first or last name alone. In employing first names of unknown figures, I hope to reduce the number of multisyllabic, consonant-freighted Polish surnames. Even Jewish surnames, as they appear in the Polish archives, can be thorny: Zelka Wigdorowicz, I feel, is more easily discussed as "Zelka." The same is true of Hebrew names, which appear no less exotic for non-Hebrew speakers: Moshe ben Rivka is rendered as "Moses ben Rebekah." On the other hand, famous or official figures are designated by their surnames (e.g., Moses Montefiore becomes "Montefiore"; Adam Czartoryski becomes "Czartoryski") for easy identification in other works.

Yankel's Tavern

Introduction

"All the towns, large and small, are filled with nobody but Jews, who also run the village breweries, roadside taverns, and inns, so that our Poland is more like Jerusalem than a Polish state."[1] Such was the assessment of Polish chronicler Stefan Garczyński (1690–1756), and many a traveler would have been tempted to agree. A journey along the mud-choked roads of Poland-Lithuania was relieved only by a stop at a tavern, where one could drink, feed oneself and one's horses, purchase necessities, exchange news, and finally get some sleep. And as the nobles who owned the taverns preferred to lease them to Jews, the weary traveler was almost invariably received by an exotic Jewish proprietor. Few observers, and certainly not Garczyński, gave much thought to the vital contributions made by these Jewish tavernkeepers. But their omnipresence reflected a centuries-old modus vivendi between Poles and Jews that may surprise those accustomed to viewing Polish-Jewish relations through the lens of anti-Semitism and violence. The Jewish-run tavern was a constant, iconic fixture of the Polish landscape, though pulsing with "intersections of mobile elements," to borrow a phrase from Michel de Certeau.[2]

Soon after Garczyński's chronicle appeared, Poland-Lithuania was no more. In three successive stages, in 1772, 1792, and 1795, her neighbors helped themselves to enormous chunks of territory and then swallowed her up completely. Although Prussia and Austria gained substantial territories, it was Tsarist Russia that took the lion's share. Russia's portion grew even larger when the Napoleonic Duchy of Warsaw became, as a result of the 1815 Congress of Vienna, the tsarist-ruled "Congress" Kingdom of Poland. The Polish Jewish community was now divided among three absolutist empires—Prussian, Habsburg, and Tsarist (see figure 0.1). But each regime pursued the same goal of modernizing and integrating its suddenly substantial Jewish population by trying to eliminate glaring Jewish economic niches like tavernkeeping, differing only in method and pace.

(2) *Yankel's Tavern*

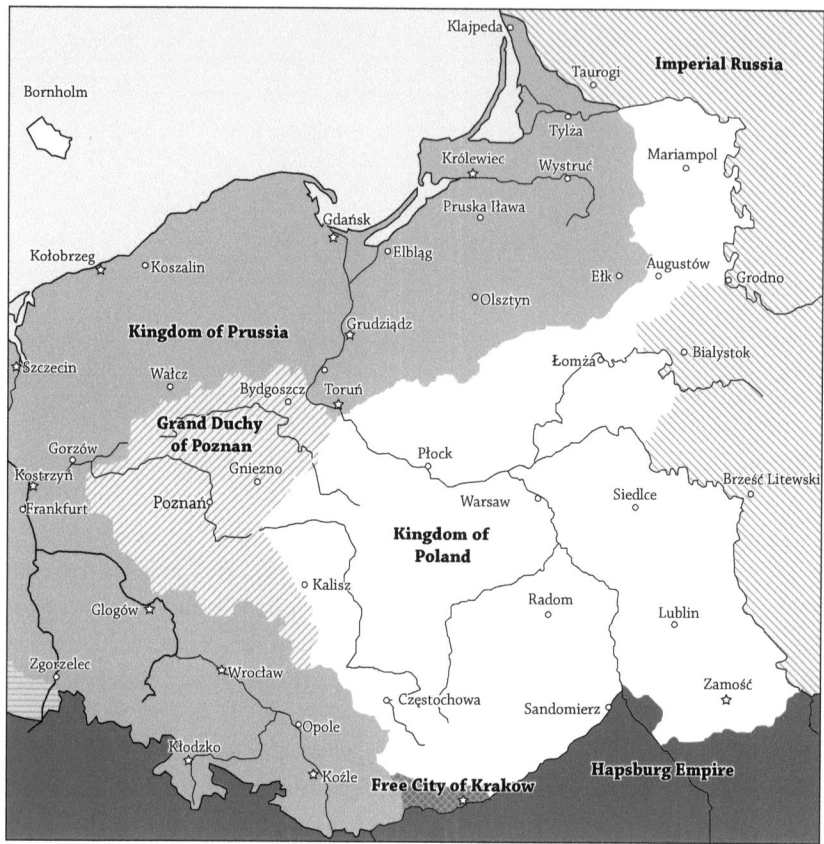

Figure 0.1 Partitioned Poland, 1815.

The most cautious and gradual changes occurred in the Congress Kingdom of Poland (henceforth, the Kingdom of Poland), the region's most industrialized and urbanized section. Tsar Alexander might have wanted to unify policies here with those in the Russian Empire proper, where Jewish tavernkeeping had already been outlawed in 1804, but he treated his new prize delicately. There was a recent tradition of Polish autonomy under the Napoleonic Duchy of Warsaw regime (1807–15), and it was here that Polish nationalism burned brightest—a fact that would eventually be borne out in two major insurrections (1830 and 1863). Tsar Alexander only arrogated for himself the title of "king" here and even agreed to a constitution. He seemed to think it best to avoid for the time being any abrupt reforms that might alienate local elites. So the Polish nobleman continued to run affairs on his own estates, including the management of his lucrative liquor monopoly; the peasant remained a serf, compelled to work the nobleman's land for free and drink only in his taverns; and the Jew remained disenfranchised and subjected to special taxation and fees yet able to benefit from unique opportunities to serve the nobleman, most importantly by leasing and operating his taverns and distilleries. This scenario prevailed throughout all the tsar's formerly Polish and Lithuanian lands. When Adam Mickiewicz (pronounced mitz-kee-EV-itch) penned his classic epic poem *Pan Tadeusz* ("Lord Thaddeus," 1834), set in historic Lithuania, it was only natural for him to anchor the plot in a tavern owned by a Polish nobleman and leased by a Jew, Yankel the tavernkeeper.

The old social structure formally endured in the kingdom down to the eve of the 1863 Polish uprising against the tsar, at which point the regime, despairing of ever co-opting the Polish nobility, began the process of emancipating the peasantry. But even after peasant emancipation in 1864, the old structure effectively remained intact for another generation. Peasants made only modest gains in land ownership at the nobility's expense, and Jews continued to ply the countryside with their merchandise, lend money, and serve as the nobility's factors and leaseholders. Historian Arno Mayer's observation that late-nineteenth-century Continental Europe was "still predominantly rural and agrarian rather than urban and industrial" and that its "traditional and heavily landed elite was inordinately absorbent and resilient" was particularly germane to this part of Europe.[3]

THE EAST EUROPEAN ERA OF JEWISH HISTORY: A NEW DIRECTION

By 1880, on the eve of the first mass Jewish emigration to America, the vast majority of the world's Jews resided in a region loosely termed "Eastern Europe" (more precisely, Eastern and East Central Europe), and were concentrated mainly in the formerly Polish lands (see figure 0.2). Jews composed around 10 percent of the general population in Eastern Europe but a much larger proportion of its urban centers, ranging from around 30 percent in cities like Warsaw and Lodz to 70, 80, and sometimes 90 percent in small to mid-sized market towns, the so-called shtetls. Even rural Jews, who ran multipurpose taverns along the web of dirt roads connecting the region's thousands of villages, may be said to have inhabited urban-like spaces. Just as Garczyński had complained, Jews were found almost anywhere that travelers gathered and commerce occurred.[4]

Of course, any feeling of hegemony was illusory. "True," the pioneering Yiddish writer S. Y. Abramovitsh (1835–1917) recalled of his town,

(4) *Yankel's Tavern*

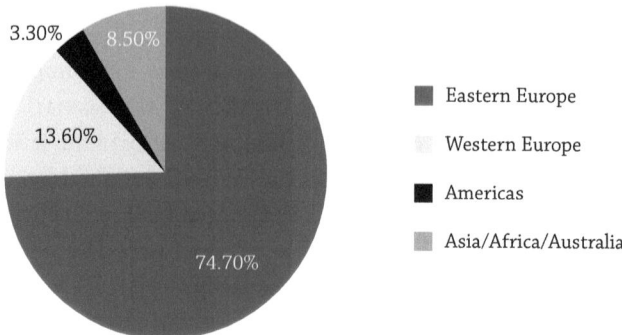

Figure 0.2 Source: Jacob Lestschinsky, "Die Umsiedlung und Umschichtung des jüdischen Volkes im Laufe des letzten Jahrhunderts," *Weltwirtschaftliches Archiv*, 30. Bd. (1929), 136.

Kapulye (now Kapyl, Belarus), "the market and the shops, the merchants and middlemen, the taverns and inns, were all Jewish; but land, and the fields round about the town—all belonged to the Gentiles!"[5] Even this was an overstatement—Count Wittgenstein actually owned Kapulie and its "Jewish" taverns and inns; a Polish nobleman owned the surrounding towns, villages, and taverns; and most commerce occurred only at their pleasure. Still, Jews were valued by such landowners, who for centuries had made efforts to attract them to their towns and villages by offering them privileges, economic opportunities, and physical protection, allowing Jews to predominate within certain economic niches.

All this is a sign of just how deeply Jews were integrated into the noble-dominated economy. Yet if we were to identify the one concern that has driven most studies of nineteenth-century East European Jewry, it would be the failure of *social* integration—that is, why most Jews failed to become Poles or Russians of the Mosaic persuasion in the way that their West European coreligionists succeeded in becoming Frenchmen, Germans, and so on. Such a line of inquiry has tended to rivet our attention on the cadre of urbanized Polish and Russian Jewish elites who adopted the kinds of cultural reforms embraced by their West European counterparts, but who had to navigate a much more daunting labyrinth of legal obstacles, social barriers, and anti-Semitic attacks. Even when they failed, their adoption of Polish or Russian (and in some cases German)[6] language, dress, manners, and secular education reflects an openness to non-Jewish culture that belies the reigning image of insularity. As anti-Semitism became politicized and the first pogrom waves spread across the region in 1881, many of these same Jewish elites began espousing creative, secular political solutions to the Jewish predicament (Zionism, Jewish socialism, and diaspora nationalism). By focusing on this vanguard we achieve an inspirational, whiggish tale of secularism triumphant in the face of endemic intolerance.

But this reconstruction, which we might term a "secularization narrative," has certain shortcomings. For one thing, it is quite problematic to invoke as a reference point the much smaller Jewish communities of Western Europe, where early emancipation helped foster the spread of Jewish Enlightenment-oriented ideas and cultural reforms (Haskalah), religious reform (Reform Judaism), acculturation, and more extensive social integration.[7] As the historian Paula Hyman once noted, "The East European model derived from the political and cultural environment of multiethnic east European states that rejected Western-derived notions of civic equality. These states contained relatively large, and overwhelmingly non-middle-class Jewish populations that retained such significant markers of distinctiveness as the Yiddish language and aspects of traditional Judaism."[8] The Jewish population of nineteenth century Eastern Europe was in fact about six times larger than that of Western Europe; its emancipation process was much slower and spottier; its adoption of non-Jewish languages was much less extensive; and its industrialization was much more modest, at least until the 1890s. This combination of factors ensured that the Western-influenced Jewish acculturated elites who have attracted the attention of recent historians remained very much in the minority during most of the nineteenth century. Most East European Jews were still what scholars would call "traditionalist," a somewhat ambiguous term that implies attunement to the rhythms of Jewish ritual law (*halakha*) and an increasingly conscious resistance to social integration and secularization. While not every nineteenth-century Jew in Eastern Europe lived up to this in practice, few rejected it as a model. To highlight only those who made a conscious break with tradition is to risk succumbing to a kind of secular parochialism that reduces the great majority of East European Jews to an undifferentiated mass.[9]

What if we were to invert the current schema, with its emphasis on interethnic integration and conflict, and highlight the more normative experience of Jewish-Christian commercial coexistence? Instead of integration, we would find social *interaction* between Jews and non-Jews within heavily prescribed roles. In normal circumstances, nineteenth-century peasants encountered Jews as petty merchants, tavernkeepers, and creditors; nobles encountered Jews as their factors, lessees, and moneylenders; and Christian townspeople encountered Jews mainly as competitors but also as renters of their apartments and storefronts. Few sought either their social company or their physical destruction; most merely accepted Jews as a fact of life.[10] To view the history in this way is not to omit the crucial story of the rise of new social configurations and discursive strategies among urban Jewish elites, nor the appearance of more virulent forms of anti-Semitism near the end of the century, but rather to cast these novelties into sharper relief. Such an approach, it is argued here, better enables us to appreciate East European Jewry on its own terms.

The Jewish-Christian interaction in pre-twentieth-century Eastern Europe is most observable within four distinct but overlapping economic systems that had roots in the largely feudal and agrarian Polish-Lithuanian Commonwealth (Poland-Lithuania for short).

The mercantile system. The first, an interethnic mercantile system, involved a symbiosis between the landowning nobility and Jewish merchants. Polish landowners had long been keen on attracting Jewish merchants to settle their towns and frequent their trade fairs on account of the Jewish reputation for industriousness, taxability, and a capacity to procure luxury goods and provide easy credit. In addition, as landowners floated their grain down the Vistula River toward the port city of Gdańsk (Danzig), they rented out space on their barges to Jewish merchants, who dealt in secondary items like forest products, in order to help finance the ventures. Jewish traders, from humble peddlers to international merchants, were so numerous and active that foreign travelers from this period often gained the impression that all of Poland's trade was in "Jewish hands." Such observers missed the predominance of Polish magnates and the important endeavors of ethnic Germans and other Christian townspeople. But the Jewish role in trade was certainly outsized and impressive, particularly in private, noble-owned towns.

The leaseholding system. This mercantile system came to be accompanied by an even stronger noble-Jewish symbiosis, the nonagricultural leaseholding (*arenda*) system. Within this second system, noble landowners leased their mills, tolls, and taverns almost exclusively to Jews. As the grain export trade slackened in the eighteenth century and landowners felt compelled to turn more and more of their grain into liquor, tavern leases became more numerous and important. Landowners who experimented with Christian peasants as tavernkeepers often found they could not cope with the record keeping and reinvestment involved in running a profitable tavern, while minor gentry proved too quarrelsome and demanding.[11] So they turned to Jews, who seemed to possess the requisite skills, industry, literacy, and most importantly, sobriety without the exasperating status consciousness or political aspirations of their peers.[12] Jewish-run taverns were soon found everywhere, from sleepy villages to booming metropolises. The Jewish-Christian interaction was arguably played out more in taverns, open every day and at all hours, than even in market squares.

The two systems generally complemented each other. It was vital, for example, that traveling Jewish merchants have access to hospitality, information, and kosher food, all of which was available in Jewish-run taverns. The eighteenth-century memoirist Solomon Maimon depicted Jewish merchants as "continually moving about from place to place; and as there was a great traffic at our village, they were frequently passing through it, and of course they had to stop at my grandfather's inn."[13] Tavernkeepers cherished this steady flow of nonlocal clientele, most of whom paid in cash. Local Christians, for their part, gained access to regional markets through both systems, though the benefits accrued by peasants and nobles differed vastly.

The state-Jew system. Jewish merchants also benefitted monarchs and their noble appointees (starostas), settling in royal towns, supplying the army with meat, leather, and textiles, loaning large sums to the government, and leasing state monopolies on products like salt. A small cadre residing in the capital city of Warsaw gradually transitioned from these pursuits into banking and industry, attaining extraordinary levels of wealth but little social or legal parity with Christian elites. This lopsided situation caused many Jewish mercantile elites to turn inward and become patrons of the popular mystical movement known as Hasidism.[14]

The partitions of Poland-Lithuania, the transformation to absolutist rule, the nobility's loss of its autonomous city enclaves, and the slow rise of urbanization and industrialization brought many other Jewish merchants into a more direct relationship with the state, resulting in an enhanced state-Jew system. This system is also justifiably described as symbiotic, considering the benefits Jews could offer the state by providing vital goods and services, military supplies, tax revenue, liquor concession fees, and so on. But absolutist state officials did not often see it that way, and took steps to minimize what they saw as Jewish overrepresentation in certain trades, especially liquor. Their attempt to drive Jews out of the liquor trade naturally came into conflict with the older leaseholding system, and as state power was decisive, open conflicts were usually resolved at the expense of the leaseholding system. Nevertheless, the state could not be everywhere at once, and one gets the impression that in private, noble-owned towns and villages it was barely anywhere at all. Many Jewish tavernkeepers found they could easily dodge state officials with the help of noble landowners, who tended to resent outside interference in their estate management and who continued to believe that Jews were uniquely suited to run their taverns. In addition, during periods of political instability such as the aftermath of insurrections, state officials seemed too shaken to prosecute illegal Jewish tavernkeeping. The result was an underground Jewish liquor trade so extensive and so widely tolerated as to ambiguate the entire notion of criminality. The service sector of Eastern Europe's most important commercial enterprise was now to a large extent underground.

The black market. Alongside these three systems there functioned a smaller, less visible, and less ambiguously criminal system, the black market. The greater part of this system, smuggling, was also very much an outgrowth of the partitions of Poland, since new borders with steep tariff barriers now sliced through the middle of the old Polish-Lithuanian Commonwealth. Extensive smuggling commenced immediately along the new Prussian and Austrian borders and spread to the Russian border after the tsar imposed a punitive tariff in the wake of the Polish uprising of 1830. Smuggling, like underground Jewish tavernkeeping, entailed both a strong Jewish presence and a strong interethnic symbiosis, since most ventures involved merchants spiriting goods over borders with the assistance of corrupt border guards of various religions, ethnicities, and nationalities, and tavernkeepers willing to stash the contraband. And like underground Jewish tavernkeeping, smuggling clashed with state prerogatives because it undercut state revenues and made a mockery of state authority. Yet even smuggling was criminalized only inconsistently. During insurrections, Polish and Russian officers alike readily enlisted smugglers to procure tobacco, coffee, tea, and other products for their troops. At such times, smuggling was only a crime when it benefited the wrong side.

Truth be told, absolutist state officials tended to look upon virtually all Jewish economic endeavors as criminal. They may not have openly criminalized legitimate Jewish mercantile endeavor or moneylending, but they did seek to counteract what they regarded as Jewish aggressiveness and overrepresentation in trade through residential restrictions, entry tickets into cities, and other Jewish-specific penalties. In the case of Jewish tavernkeeping, one can speak of outright criminalization, as officials sought to penalize, restrict, and ban what most believed to be the cause of peasant drunkenness and ruin. In the case of smuggling, of course, criminalization occurred even more consistently, apart from periods of military conflict. This prevailing criminal-but-necessary attitude toward Jewish economic endeavor may have seemed logical to officials who understood and accepted the moral economy of enlightened absolutism (discussed in chapter 2). But it seemed rather arbitrary to everyone else.

THE FOCUS OF THIS STUDY

One of the most important achievements of Polish historians writing from behind the Iron Curtain was to gather voluminous economic data about the Polish past. We have, thanks to them, a much clearer picture of nineteenth- and early twentieth-century developments, from the slow emergence of industrialization to the vicissitudes of trade in grain and its most lucrative byproduct, liquor.[15] Yet in Poland, particularly under Communist rule (1945–1989), it was not easy to write about the key role played by Jews. Even those few Jewish historians who proved able to continue researching in Poland tended to avoid confronting the almost ubiquitous phenomenon of Jewish tavernkeeping during the nineteenth century, apart from charting the alleged demise of this embarrassing feudal relic.[16]

In the post-Communist era, the subject of Jewish economic history became less touchy, and scholars from Poland and abroad were granted renewed access to rich archival collections. For the first time, one could focus on the "lords' Jews," the title of Moshe Rosman's pioneering study on Jews in pre-partition Poland-Lithuania.[17] Yet the new studies do not take us beyond the pre-partition era. For the partition era itself (1772–1918), we remain trapped in an improbable loop of recurring tavernkeeper expulsions: Jewish tavernkeepers are evicted or taxed out of existence once, twice, and three times over; yet there they are again. Their (repeated) demise has been used by historians to illustrate the allegedly rapid breakdown of the age-old noble-Jewish alliance and the ruthless inefficiency of absolutist regimes that now ruled over Poland. The fact that Jewish tavernkeepers keep popping up in late romantic Polish literature as a natural part of the social landscape remains something to be explained away.

The first step necessitated by the current project was to retrace the archival footsteps of some of the post-war pioneers of nineteenth-century Polish Jewish history, who unanimously posited the Jewish liquor trade's demise. During my first trip back to the Polish archives, as I began thumbing through the heavy leaves of official correspondence, it became apparent that most of these historians were guided by a heavy positivist bias: official data, legislation, and policy pronouncements were considered the stuff of history, while case studies and individual petitions, even the most elaborate, were shunted aside. The problem with such an approach is that government officials usually invoked data, legislation, and policy goals to reassure each other that the problem of Jewish tavernkeeping—and thus epidemic Polish drunkenness—had been solved, or nearly solved. Such sources are often merely a gauge of official aspirations, and are repeatedly belied by exposés of clandestine tavernkeeping and petitions by

Jewish tavernkeepers, in addition to inadvertent descriptions in internal Jewish sources like rabbinical literature and memoirs.

Taken together, the new sources uncovered here suggest that the rise of the bureaucratic state and its social engineering projects did not, in the end, significantly alter the way most people lived. Nobles ensured that Jewish men and women remained central to the liquor trade as lessees of liquor monopolies, excise taxes, taverns, and distilleries throughout most of the nineteenth century, in villages, towns, and cities, both legally and illegally. While it is difficult to gauge the extent of Jewish tavernkeeping in particular, the available data suggest that at the beginning of the partition era Jews leased approximately 85 percent of all taverns, and that officially-recognized tavernkeepers and their families constituted as much as 37 percent of the Jewish population. To be specific, there were 19,749 registered taverns in the Duchy of Warsaw in 1808 (the majority of which, 13,157, were in villages). The official figure for Jewish tavernkeeping closest to that date is 17,561 families.[18] The number of registered Jewish tavernkeepers had plummeted to 2,329 families by 1828 as a result of expensive, Jewish-specific liquor concession fees. However, over the next fifty years, officials continued to dole out liquor concessions to those Jews perceived as loyal or economically important, while helplessly noting that "Jews everywhere" simply ignored concessions and bans and evaded detection by hiring Christians to sell the liquor in their taverns.[19] Internal Jewish sources only bolster those claims, revealing, in addition, the widespread Jewish practice of setting up impromptu taverns in private homes on Christian holidays and other occasions.[20] The impression is that Jewish tavernkeepers did not really decline in number at all. They just became less visible to the state.

The Jewish men and women who continued to lease taverns from the nobility usually distilled the liquor themselves from rye (often grown on the tavern's plot) and sold it to customers on credit via their Christian fronts. They also lent their customers money on the side, cooked their meals, offered them business advice, absorbed their curses and impotent rage, sold them supplies, played music for them, put up the mostly Jewish travelers for the night, and drove them to their destinations in their carriages the next day. They leased taverns because there were not many alternatives for East European Jews, who were usually denied permission to purchase land, join artisan guilds and professions, and study in secular institutions of higher education. But they also leased taverns because the occupation was lucrative and accessible.

There are indications that it was prestigious, too. A tavernkeeper, according to S. Y. Abramovitsh, was thought "respectable; in fact they made excellent in-laws, and their opinion carried weight everywhere from the bathhouse to the synagogue." Much of their prestige derived from their "frequent business dealings with the rich, with noblemen, and government ministers," dealings which "enabled such people to intercede for individual Jews or for the whole community in time of crisis." Many communities "escaped disaster" thanks to their intervention.[21] However, later accounts suggest a diminishing prestige. The Yiddish writer Sholem Aleichem (1859–1916), for example, recalls that he and his siblings were "astonished and embarrassed that their parents were now innkeepers.... They couldn't imagine a greater comedown or humiliation."[22]

The first chapter of this book constitutes an overview of Jewish tavernkeeping throughout pre- and postpartition Poland-Lithuania, focusing especially on the myths that sustained and threatened it. For Christian and Jewish observers alike, taverns were not only valued as economic enterprises and gathering spots; they were feared as sites of physical and spiritual pollution. Each set of observers merely had different ideas about the source of the pollution—whether it was the sober, sinister Jewish tavernkeeper or the drunken, crude gentile clientele. The second chapter focuses in on Jewish tavernkeeping in the Kingdom of Poland, following attempts to restrict Jewish tavernkeeping within Polish archival documents and rabbinic literature. In this chapter, we uncover a flourishing underground Jewish liquor trade in the countryside based on a surprising degree of Jewish-Christian collusion. The government only summoned the will to crack down on the underground Jewish liquor trade (as well as introduce Jewish military conscription, agricultural initiatives, and clothing decrees) in the 1840s, when the political situation in the kingdom seemed to have stabilized. The third chapter considers the situation in towns and cities where, despite a more lenient official policy, tavernkeepers faced higher concession fees, residential restrictions, and expulsions from choice streets. Some urban Jews—especially women—responded by attempting to appeal to government officials' professed Enlightenment ideals and economic pragmatism. The lesson imparted from these various cases, both rural and urban, seems to be that the reigning climate of discrimination made "business as usual" unviable for Jews. Survival was possible only by circumventing discriminatory legal barriers one way or another. While Jewishness per se is no explanation for such distinctive behavior, it does appear that Jewish status necessitated greater adaptability and persistence.[23] The inadequacies of tsarist rule helped, too: instead of the cruelly effective, heavily repressive regime portrayed throughout the older Polish and Jewish historiographies, we will find a regime weakened and at times paralyzed by its internal inconsistencies. Jews and Poles alike were left with a great deal of room to maneuver if they kept their nerve.

The fourth chapter confronts the loaded question of espionage, smuggling, and other black market endeavors by Jewish tavernkeepers during the period of Polish uprisings against the tsar (1830–1865). Here, we will seek to move beyond the highly selective debates over questions of Jewish loyalty and criminality by considering spies and smugglers of all backgrounds, including Polish Christians. The fifth chapter affords rare glimpses of the interior lives of Jewish male and female tavernkeepers during the decade following peasant emancipation, thanks to an enormous cache of petitions (*kvitlekh*) to the non-Hasidic miracle worker Rabbi Elijah Guttmacher (1796–1874). These petitions show that, despite dramatic changes to the social structure on paper, Jewish tavernkeeping continued in full force during the 1870s. The final chapter assesses the record of government social engineering initiatives aimed at normalizing Jews, and in particular, Jewish tavernkeepers. Needless to say, efforts to push Jews out of tavernkeeping and into agriculture and military service, which would have destroyed the kingdom's surrogate middle class had it actually succeeded, seldom achieved the intended results. In some cases, Jewish farmers and soldiers came full circle, returning finally to the production and sale of the kingdom's most lucrative and accessible commodity, liquor.

This project was made possible thanks to numerous people and institutions. It began with a trip, courtesy of a Sarah Lawrence College faculty travel grant, to Archiwum Główne Akt Dawnych (the Central Older Archives) in Warsaw. There, I received extremely generous help and support from Małgorzata Koska and Hanna Węgrzynek, who continued to help me over the next few years beyond all expectations. They are true colleagues. At the Herbert D. Katz Center for Advanced Judaic Studies at the University of Pennsylvania, under the direction of David Ruderman, I benefited enormously from discussions with fellows, in particular Adam Teller. I was also fortunate enough to discover, in the center's library, Rabbi Sol Cohen, who was kind enough to set up a regular "*hevruta*" with me for studying rabbinic responsa and decrees (*takanot*). As the Hans Kohn Member at the Institute for Advanced Study, at Princeton University, I benefitted from the advice of two faculty members in particular, Jonathan Israel and Avishai Margalit. I was also fortunate to meet Menachem Fisch, a fellow member who proved willing to advise and challenge me on an almost daily basis. I received additional support from the Hadassah-Brandeis Institute and the YIVO Emanuel Patt Visiting Scholar fellowship. The staff of the YIVO archives during my exploration of the Guttmacher collection was extremely helpful and supportive. Rabbi Shmuel Klein went so far as to help me decipher some of the less legible *kvitlekh*. A portion of chapter 2 appeared in the journal *Jewish Social Studies*.

During my year at the Institute for Advanced Study, my father, Alan Dynner, made me an offer I could not refuse: he would fly me to Poland if I would show him around the country for a week. This not only gave me the opportunity to tour Poland's towns, cities, and sites of memory with my father, but allowed me to tack on another week in the archives, which yielded abundant new material on Jews during the Polish uprisings. This is only one instance of my father's generosity throughout my scholarly career. He also read over my manuscript to provide an educated layperson's perspective, and had valuable suggestions about how to achieve greater accessibility. I have attempted to show my deep gratitude by dedicating this book to him.

Several colleagues and mentors helped me in important ways and supported me throughout this project: Gershon Hundert, Jonathan Karp, Olga Litvak, Yohanan Petrovsky-Shtern, Antony Polonsky, Moshe Rosman, Timothy Snyder, Scott Ury, and Elliot Wolfson. My student Anastasiya Novatorskaya was of great help in proofreading and compiling the bibliography and index. During the final stages of preparing the manuscript, I was dazzled by the generosity of several colleagues who agreed to read it over completely and provide detailed suggestions: Natalia Aleksiun, Allan Arkush, Jeremy Dauber, Brian Porter, and Carol Zoref. They impressed me most of all with what they were not supposed to know, each demonstrating enormous intellectual reach. It almost goes without saying, however, that any errors here are mine.

Throughout this project, my extended family made it possible to live a truly full life. I would like to thank, in addition to my father, my loving and supportive mother Nancy Smith, who has always believed in me; and Ron Smith, Lisa Dynner, Susan Dynner, Karin and Christopher Petersen, and Marsha and Barry Cohen, for their continued support and encouragement. My wife, Heather, my secret strength, was always there for me, encouraging me, reading chapters, advising me, and drawing me out of my seclusion and into the world. Together, we have raised our precious daughters Ela and Lyla, who continue to amaze us with their humor, affection, curiosity, and many gifts. I cannot imagine this project without them. May they all obtain free liquor concessions.

CHAPTER 1

Entrance

Myths and Countermyths

It was Sunday, and from church after morning Mass,
They came to Yankel's to drink and relax
In everyone's cup grey vodka swished
'Round with a bottle the barmaid rushed
Yankel, the tavernkeeper, stood in the midst.
    Adam Mickiewicz, *Pan Tadeusz* (1834), Book 4.

Yankel ("Jankiel" in Polish), the iconic Jewish tavernkeeper in Adam Mickiewicz's *Pan Tadeusz*, actually runs two taverns. He leases one from the noble Horeszko family and another, newer one from the rival Soplica clan. But it is the older tavern that captures the poet's imagination. Built in the Tyrian architectural style replicated in taverns throughout the Polish lands, its front resembles Noah's ark, its rear Solomon's Temple. Judaism itself seems etched onto the Polish landscape: "From a distance the rickety old tavern looked/ like a Jew rocking in prayer/ the roof like a hat, the thatch spilling down like a beard/ the sooty walls like a gabardine/ in front, carvings protruding like *tzitzit* [ritual fringes] down his body."[1]

For Mickiewicz, the Jew and his tavern are not only a natural part of the landscape, they are a unifying force in fractious postpartition Poland-Lithuania. As Lord (*Pan*) Tadeusz and company enter the older tavern after church services, they find peasants, wives, gentry, and a priest drinking and chatting harmoniously under Yankel's auspices. Yankel, for his part, seems to unite all of Polish Jewry in his person—sage rabbi, shrewd business advisor, just mediator, melancholy singer, rapt dancer, and, of course, tavernkeeper. He is also, implicitly, everything that Polish Jewry is not (yet). He speaks Polish with good pronunciation, is "a loyal Pole by reputation" who embraces the cause of independence, and is even an honest tavernkeeper: "Neither peasants nor gentlemen ever complained; why complain? / He had good, choice drinks / kept his accounts strictly and without any trickery." True, Yankel is rumored to have suspicious nocturnal meetings with Father Robak. But those meetings, we are reassured, have nothing to do with smuggling.[2]

Scholars often regard the Jewish tavernkeeper as anachronistic by the very period during which Yankel's character was conceived. Although historians agree that the vast majority of Polish taverns and distilleries were leased to Jews by the end of the eighteenth century,[3] the rapid modernization narrative they often espouse assumes that most Jews—no matter how honest or patriotic—would have already been driven out of the liquor trade by the 1830s. In the Kingdom of Poland (1815–1918), the focus of much of this study, the fees, restrictions, and eventual bans imposed on Jewish tavernkeepers allegedly sparked mass urbanization and an economic transformation.[4] Many Polish polemics against Jewish tavernkeepers, according to this schema, would have been published, oddly enough, *after* most Jews had been forced out of tavernkeeping. And most depictions of Jewish tavernkeepers in Polish Romantic literature, of which Mickiewicz's Yankel is but an early example, would have appeared after the eviction process was supposedly completed. One literary scholar, no doubt puzzled by this disjuncture, has felt compelled to dismiss the ubiquitous Jewish tavernkeeper in nineteenth-century Polish literature as a mere echo from an earlier time, an indication that the folk-type "managed to survive most of its prototypes in real life."[5]

These conclusions turn out to be too hasty. For one thing, in the Kingdom of Poland undisguised Jewish tavernkeeping continued to be legally tolerated in towns and cities, where competition from Christian townspeople was believed to mitigate its public harm.[6] As for restrictions and all-out bans in villages, they were implemented only gradually and enforced sporadically, and they ultimately proved unsustainable. Rural Jews held on tenaciously, continuing to fulfill historical tavernkeeper functions like supplying liquor, providing hospitality, and serving in the capacity of the nobleman's clerk (i.e., collecting his debts and taxes, and processing payments drawn on outstanding lease payments [*assignacja*]).[7] Rural Jewish tavernkeepers were able to hold on despite the opposition of nearly every powerful group in Polish society—reform-minded and enterprising nobles, government officials, Christian clergy, Jewish integrationists, even Jewish religious leaders—because one crucial group continued to provide them with cover: the very Christians they were accused of victimizing.[8]

Foremost among their Christian enablers were local nobles, whose subterfuges and interventions on behalf of their Jewish lessees reflected their belief that only Jews were capable of running an orderly and profitable tavern. This belief was a product of a powerful, dual myth that will be explored in the current chapter: the myth of Jewish sobriety and gentile (usually peasant) drunkenness. Belief in this dual myth was shared by nobles, Jews, and Christian social reformers alike, and thus helps explain not only the astonishing staying power of the Jewish tavernkeeper but also the fierce opposition from those who thought they saw a sober Jewish conspiracy behind the region's rampant drunkenness.

The origins and nature of the lord-Jew alliance in the prepartition era have already been subjected to fruitful scholarly analysis and debate. Moshe Rosman has deemed the lord-Jew relationship a "marriage of convenience" in which each side felt a mutual responsibility that transcended mere utility.[9] But Adam Teller cautions that the relationship remained at base an exploitative, feudal one in which Jews were valued and protected only insofar as they were perceived to be uniquely equipped to provide vital services and enhance estate revenues.[10] Either way, the available data reflect an extraordinary degree of Jewish participation in the liquor trade by the eighteenth century. In seven towns in Bielsk County (Podlaskie District) between 1772 and 1779, 94 percent of tavernkeepers (*karczmarzy*) and 53 percent of bartenders (*szynkarzy*) were identifiably Jewish. In the county's fifty-one villages, 78.7 percent of tavernkeepers and bartenders were identifiably Jewish, though the proportion was likely higher since not a single tavernkeeper or bartender on the Bielsk County inventory bears a Christian-sounding name. Similarly, in the town of Opatów, 88 percent of the liquor sellers over the course of the eighteenth century were Jews, while leases on the surrounding villages' mills, breweries, distilleries, and taverns were "regularly held by the town's Jews," according to one study.[11] Tavernkeeping had become what sociologists would term an "ethnic economy"; yet ethnic protectionism was enforced not by the Jewish lessees themselves but by Christian landowning elites.[12]

This extraordinary Jewish presence in the liquor trade was in part a natural outgrowth of the rise of Jewish leaseholding in general in the early modern period. Leases on immovable property other than real estate, known as *arendas*, came increasingly to denote taverns and distilleries as landowners found liquor to be the most profitable and expedient way to monetize their grain. The word *arendarz* (lessee) became synonymous with "Jew."[13]

During the next period, the partition era, historians have assumed the collapse of Jewish tavernkeeping and the lord-Jew alliance in general. Polish landowners, they argue, became increasingly reform-minded and entrepreneurial by the nineteenth century, rendering the Jewish middleman dispensable in their eyes and giving rise to a newly aggressive anti-Jewish discourse. The anti-Jewish liquor legislation of the period is attributed to the influence of those landowners on ostensibly naïve, uninformed absolutist leaders.[14] Yet careful scrutiny of the planning, composition, and implementation of legislative initiatives reveals that such landowners constituted only a small, albeit vocal, group, and that their actual impact on policy was limited. The great majority of landed nobility struggled to preserve life as it had been, with Jews serving liquor, peasants drinking much of it, and nobles enjoying a steady flow of lease payments within their hundreds of small towns. The state's experiments in social engineering were an impediment to the cherished inertia, and legislative assaults on the Jewish liquor trade tended to drive nobles and Jews into a defensive formation. Time and again, the lord felt constrained to intervene with officials on behalf of "his" Jew or simply flout restrictive decrees, if only to maintain the profitability of his enterprises. For who else, he reasoned, could cater to traveling Jewish merchants, handle basic bookkeeping, and remain sober enough to run a successful tavern?

The presence of an absolutist state bureaucracy in the wake of the partitions of Poland could, it is true, undermine the noble-Jewish relationship, since it offered Jews a court of appeal when they felt ill-used by their lords. But the most common result of state initiatives was a closing of ranks in a common effort to evade disruptive legislation.[15] The survival of the Jewish liquor trade even in villages, which as we will see had taken on such a monstrously negative symbolism, suggests that the addition of the absolutist state to the equation in many instances shored up traditional economic relationships. It also suggests a need to take more seriously the many nineteenth-century literary portrayals of Jewish tavernkeeping since, notwithstanding their polemical elements, they often reflect the imperfect sphere of everyday life more accurately than government statistics and legislation, which deny the Jewish tavernkeeper's ubiquity and, sometimes, his very existence.

THE POLISH TAVERN

As any traveler through partitioned Poland knew, a tavern was more than a tavern. It often constituted a bar, distillery, country store, hotel, stable, post office, and bank wrapped into one. Like the famed caravansary found along the Silk Road, it supported the flow of commerce, news, and people. It was frequently the sole entertainment venue within miles and the only place that one could take care of problems incurred on the roads: "a broken axle, hub or linchpin, or a torn yoke thong. If a man became ill along the way or something harmed his horse, the innkeeper was like a brother and his wife was like a mother. Where else could one wait out a heavy downpour or a blizzard, when continuing 'without a road' in pitch darkness meant risking one's life?"[16] Many goods could be acquired in a tavern besides vodka, including buns, doughnuts, cottage-cheese cakes, pickled herrings, salt, tobacco, matches, needles, ribbons, and edgings for girdles. One could, it is true, buy these notions from one of the Jewish peddlers who roamed the countryside with their bundles. But the tavern occupied a more fixed position in the social topography. Peasants spent almost anything they earned there; even their ill-gotten gains were eventually funneled back to the nobleman through his Jewish tavernkeeper.

The tavern was also a place where prostitutes plied their trade, soldiers celebrated their freedom from society's strictures, and smugglers and thieves planned their expeditions and stashed their contraband.[17] Ordinary citizens turned criminal there as well. According to a lurid deposition from 1780, a group of men entered a tavern in Opatów one Sunday night, found a "trollop" drinking there, and took her upstairs. Suddenly, a peasant in the next room was awakened by a loud scream and tumult, and proceeded to eject the unruly men from the tavern. The following Sunday, they returned and spied the woman and, after a futile chase, returned to the tavern. On their way home, full of drink and unfulfilled lust, four of the men encountered a different woman coming down the path through a field. Matteusz, a glazier, "seized her, threw her on the ground, and fornicated

Figure 1.1: Józef Chełmoński, *In Front of the Tavern* (*Przed karczmą*), 1877.

with her." Walenty and Stefan raped her next. Jakub, "a married man," watched. The woman finally extricated herself and ran sobbing into the tavern, pleading with the customers, "Have mercy, my people! Come quickly to Pogorzelski's field.... The four men who raped me and barely let me go have caught another woman and are fornicating with that woman!" The tavernkeeper's wife urged the customers to come with her, but nobody wanted to get involved. So she went herself and spied the fourth man, Stefan, raping a woman while the others stood nearby. She reported the incident to the authorities.[18]

During the ensuing investigation, the culprits "voluntarily confessed to fornicating on a Sunday." One man, Jan, who had only been involved the first evening, was sent to a monastery for having "engaged in fornication upstairs in Wyworkowski Tavern with a trollop." Jakub was fined for observing fornication, a violation of his marital oaths. The three rapists were ordered to publicly donate roses to the church on the next five consecutive Fridays, a shaming ritual intended to deter as much as punish. In these sentences, extremely light from our vantage point, we glimpse how "tavern" and "church" constituted opposing yet mutually dependent spatial categories, for sins committed in the former were expiated by rituals performed in the latter. This juxtaposition between tavern (unstable/temporal/sinful/Jewish) and church (fixed/spiritual/expiatory/Christian) became prominent in Polish Romantic literature over the next century.[19]

Taverns were sites of religious tension and transgression, as well. Drunken theological debates between Christian and Jewish customers could occur there, with fatal consequences for the latter.[20] Sabbateans, members of the banned Jewish messianic movement, could attempt to sway the tavernkeeper's children with their eccentric interpretations of classical Jewish texts.[21] Taverns were also the hunting grounds of Christian missionaries. According to Michael Solomon Alexander (1799–1845), a Jewish convert to Christianity and future Anglican bishop of Jerusalem, the fact that "most of the inns in Poland and West Prussia" were kept by Jews and attracted Jewish customers meant that a missionary was "at once introduced to many, with whom he wishes to converse, who are to be met with in the traveler's room, and of their own accord often inquire for the stranger who has visited their town. This harmless curiosity often leads to conversation, and with a frank, sociable, intelligent people like the Jews, presents a favourable opening for cultivating intercourse."[22]

Taverns thus both strengthened and destabilized their communities, and tavernkeepers, who straddled several worlds—local and foreign—were regarded with a blend of trust and mistrust. This might be said of taverns and tavernkeepers throughout the whole of nineteenth-century Europe.[23]

But in the Polish-Lithuanian case, where the tavernkeeper was typically a Jew, the owner a nobleman, and the clientele a mix of local Christians and traveling Jewish merchants, the tavernkeeper also straddled rival religious cultures. Nevertheless, it was this volatile border zone and not the stable, homogenous church that formed the epicenter of village and small town life.

SPIRITUAL POLLUTION

Of course, the primary draw was liquor. In contrast to wine-producing parts of Europe, where wine was affordable, inhabitants of Poland-Lithuania of all social strata drank rye-based, un-aged liquor called "vodka." They drank it to socialize, celebrate, seal a deal, warm themselves during their travels, and, in the case of the peasantry, to escape the drudgery of a life dedicated to cultivating someone else's land. Liquor was celebrated in Polish drinking songs and exalted in Polish poetry.[24] It was, according to Polish rabbinic commentators, the true "wine of the land" (ḥemer medinah). But the parallel to wine had its limits. Whereas Jews in medieval wine-producing areas like France often engaged in its cultivation and sale, Polish Jews had cornered the much larger market on a much more intoxicating and addictive beverage, including its production, distribution, sale, excise tax, and monopoly management (propinacja).[25]

Figure 1.2: Henryk Rodakowski, *Karczmarz Jasio*, from the series *Album Pałahickie*, 1867.

Foreign travelers in the Polish lands considered this situation an affront to their Christian sensibilities. On his tour of Galicia, where "all the inns" were kept by Jews, British visitor Adam Neale was scandalized by the Jewishness of his accommodations: "From the centre of the roof of these *Golgothas*, I always observed suspended, a large brass chandelier with seven branches! This is the Sabbath lamp, and is regularly lighted every Friday evening at sun-set, when all the fires are carefully extinguished, and not re-lighted till the same hour on the next evening."[26] Below this brazen symbol of Jewish triumph (Neale had in mind the candelabra of the ancient Temple) lay representations of Jewish filth: "A long wooden table soiled with grease stands beneath, occupying the middle of the apartment, around which are ranged several wooden benches, with one or two rotten chairs and a cushion stuffed with hay." The furs that Neale and his companions had brought to sleep on were inadequate, for "the noisome smells from the damp earthen floors of these Jewish *hostels* were frequently so powerful and disgusting as to keep us awake." No less offensive was the food, the best of which was "stewed veal of calves, two days old perhaps, floating in a sour paste called *Barszcz* [borsht] . . . beet root or cucumbers stewed and fermented like sour-crout, called *buraszki*, with *rosoli*, a gruel made of flesh and oatmeal, or *pirogy*, a soup or pottage made of barley, rice, and millet, or manna." The bread was "black, gritty, and ill tasted, generally composed of every grain except that of wheat," and they also served "large, overgrown cucumbers fermented with salt and fennel leaves," which we may recognize as pickles.[27] The liquor, drunk straight and in enormous quantities, was "rendered more palatable and destructive by the addition of the essential oils of fennel and caraway seeds, which are mixed with the wash previously to distillation."[28] Jews, he added, leased all the nobility's distilleries, paying them large sums for "the privilege of poisoning and intoxicating their serfs."[29]

Descriptions of central Polish taverns, "all kept by Jews" according to British tourist George Burnett, are similar. "On entering the house, you are assailed by the most abominable host of stinks which ever conspired to war against the nose. . . . Frequently, the house is half full of the wretched peasants and peasant women, getting drunk upon *schnaps* (a sort of whisky)." When it was time to go to sleep, pallets of straw or hay were merely strewn upon the earthen floor. Travelers often slept in the stable, where the odor was less offensive—but then there was the fear of being trampled by horses. When Burnett finally lucked upon a rare interior room with a small couch, he was rudely awakened by "an unusual humming noise," which turned out to be "a Jew on his knees [!] muttering his orisons, at which he continued for at least half an hour."[30] William Wraxall described his tavern as "a wretched hovel inhabited by Jews," admittedly "a race of people to whom, notwithstanding their extortions, the traveler is under the greatest obligation, when passing through this inhospitable portion of Europe." He spent the night "stretched on dirty straw, among ducks, pigs, Poles, and Jewesses; devoured by vermin, and unable to sleep on account of the heat, as well as the smells which annoyed me."[31] Ukrainian taverns were certainly no better. British philosopher Jeremy Bentham (1748–1832), on his way to visit his brother in Cricheff (Krichev), felt compelled to leave his attendant to "bask in the straw inhaling the fumes of Judaism." He preferred to spend the chilly winter night in his carriage.[32]

Native Christians only heightened the rhetoric of spiritual and physical pollution. Galician ethnographer Józef Mączyński, saw the tavern as a veritable antichurch: "The largest room, called a barroom, is the sanctuary. Its altar is the cupboard where the drinks are stored, behind wooden railings..., and the priest of this altar is a bearded Jew, called *arendarz*, (except in villages in the Kingdom of Poland, where Jews aren't allowed, fortunately for the peasants there), or a Catholic, called 'innkeeper' (*karczmarz*)."[33] The drinking songs, he noted, were like diabolical hymns, with one song praising God for creating the tavern as much as for creating the sun (the latter sustained life, the former leisure).[34] Jan Slomka (1842–1927), mayor of Tarnobrzeg (Galicia), likewise sensed the tavern's perverse sanctity. Masses for dead relatives and funeral and wedding receptions commemorated in the church were followed by a migration to the tavern. After a wedding ceremony in the church, the wedding party descended directly to the tavern, where the Jewish proprietor appeared with a bottle, ceremoniously blessed the couple, wished them luck, and treated everyone to a drink. Then the music erupted, and everyone made their way into the main room. Throughout the joyous proceedings, the Jew remained suspiciously sober.[35]

Józef Ignacy Kraszewski (1812–87) allowed that the tavern was "the heart of a village," where locals sinned, married, grieved, fought, and loved.[36] Yet he conjured a macabre description of a Polesian tavern: a goat was being slaughtered in one corner, a gloomy Jewish boy sat studying in another, a cat slinked along with her kittens, and wild Jewish children crawled between his legs. His nostrils were assailed by pipe smoke, vinegar, burning fat, fish, tar, mud, mildew, vodka, and the sour peasant brew, kvass; his ears by the shrieks of children and poultry, the clinking of glasses, and raucous peasant songs. Kraszewski was certain that "nothing in the world is more abominable than a Polesian tavern."[37]

Jewish observers agreed that taverns were physically and spiritually polluted spaces, but identified a different source of the pollution.

Modern Yiddish author S. Y. Abramovitsh's description is strikingly similar to Kraszewski's and no less grotesque, but it deftly inverts the polemic. As his alter ego Mendele enters a local tavern, he is "hit by a shot of the mixed reeks of strong spirits, cheap shag-smoking tobacco, and excesses of human perspiration, all of which vapors had concocted themselves into one tremendous goaty smell." Next comes the assault on his ears, "a sudden violent discord of ear-killing shrill shrieks and coarse throaty roarings, and assorted raucous cacklings and windy bleats that I could scarcely credit were human voices at all." Finally, his eyes behold the drunken Christian patrons: "disembodied human features [that] emerged glistening out of the obscure fogs and hazes within." It is they, not the Jewish proprietors and their families, who are the defilers.[38]

Maimon's account of his stint as a tutor for the children of a rural Jewish tavernkeeper exudes a similar disgust for the peasant customers, who "guzzle their whiskey and make an uproar, while the people in the house [i.e., the Jews] sit in the corner."[39] His description of members of the upper nobility is equally grotesque. Lord Karol Radziwiłł, whose list of drunken exploits included arbitrarily maiming Jews, destroying synagogue artifacts, and urinating on a church altar, once spent the night in Maimon's mother-in-law's tavern. The drunk, unconscious magnate was thrown upon a bed fully clothed while the retinue continued its carousing all night long. Upon waking the next day, Radziwiłł held a sumptuous feast and lusted after Maimon's young wife, who had to be spirited away. In Maimon's estimation, Radziwiłł's faults "deserve rather our pity than our hatred or contempt."[40]

The preeminent modern Hebrew poet, H. N. Bialik, raised in the Volhynian town of Radi, reified the conventional polemic of disgust in a poem about his father's tavern: it was a "den of piglike men and tavern filth / In foul vapors of libations and hazes of base incense," a perverse anti-Temple. Bialik, at that time a boy of less than seven years, clung to his father as to a rock in a sea of corruption:

> Silently I stood between his knees, my eyes hanging on his lips,
> Drunks rumbled around and drinkers sated themselves amid vomit,
> Monstrous faces corrupted and tongues flowing with invectives.
> The walls shrank from hearing, the windows hid their faces,
> Only to my ears alone, the ears of an uncorrupted child,
> Did the holy lips spout and gush a secret whisper,
> A whisper of Torah and prayer and words of the living God.[41]

The polluted stream of liquor, vomit, and invectives issuing from the carousing gentile patrons contrasts starkly with the pure stream of Torah and prayer imbibed by the innocent child.

Some Jewish commentators worried that tavern proprietors would inevitably become contaminated by their debased clientele. Tzevi Hirsch Kaidanover (d. 1712), author of the popular ethical treatise *Kav ha-yashar* ("A Just Measure"), warned his readers against "building a house and designating a special room for the uncircumcised to come and drink, party, and fornicate, a common sin, which many have committed in Poland and Lithuania and which no one prohibits." Kaidanover believed that after a while "the spirit of defilement will certainly settle upon the house, and the one who built it will not leave this world until he is punished through that very house."[42] But most rabbis reconciled themselves to economic reality and perhaps understood on some level that the constant spectacle of gentile misbehavior only improved Jewish self-perception, a point to which we will soon return.[43]

THE MYTH OF JEWISH EXPLOITATION

Polish reformers argued that Jewish tavernkeepers were not merely spiritually defiling; they were the direct cause of widespread drunkenness and ruin in the countryside, in particular, where Christians seldom ran taverns.[44] Stanisław Staszic, a proponent of Enlightenment, warned darkly that "to grant Jews the provisioning of spirits of such terrible consequences is to entrust the property of our farmer to people without faith, who are inimical to Christians, and thus to place in their hands a weapon by which they can with impunity make whatever use they please of the farmer's property."[45] During Poland-Lithuania's last-ditch effort at reform in the parliamentary session known as the "four-year Sejm" (1788–92), and again in the wake of the establishment of the Kingdom of Poland (1815), writer after writer called for the eviction of Jews from the countryside to save the peasant from ruin. This polemical backdrop makes Mickiewicz's creation of the rather likeable Yankel the tavernkeeper all the more remarkable.[46]

Many reformers were noblemen themselves, and thus disinclined to blame their peers for placing the "weapon" of liquor in Jewish hands. But some, at least, seemed to genuinely believe that Christian lessees would be disinclined to sell drinks on credit and more likely to have social bonds with their clientele. "The fewer Jewish tavernkeepers there are," reasoned one reformer, "the less inclined peasants are to get drunk, because the Jewish tavernkeeper sees only the sale of vodka, not his buddy, mate, and best friend with whom he spends time."[47] Such reformers were probably unaware of the numerous complaints issued against rural Christian tavernkeepers. To cite but a few examples, Jędzej Herenczyk, who was both the tavernkeeper and mayor, was fined and expelled for using false measures, failing to meet payments, accepting bribes, selling off silverware belonging to the castle, and allowing a thief, bandit, and prostitute to reside in his tavern. The tavernkeepers Łukacz and Wojciech Janasko were accused of beating peasants' sons, insulting customers, rarely having beer for sale, and generally neglecting their tavernkeeping duties.[48] Other peasant petitions accused Christian tavernkeepers of falsifying measures and forcing them to purchase spoiled beer.[49] By the second half of the nineteenth century, reformers were complaining that Christian tavernkeepers sold liquor on credit, trafficked in stolen goods, and had contacts with criminals "just like Jews."[50]

But beyond any moral concerns was the maddening profitability of a trade in which members of an out-group had assumed such a central role. Most complaints against Jewish tavernkeeping appeared, suspiciously enough, only after liquor had become the region's boom industry. Liquor sales accounted for over 40 percent of revenues from royal properties by 1789.[51] The proportion may have been even higher on noble estates: we know, for example, that in 1791 liquor accounted for 46.2 percent of revenues on the vast Zamoyski estates.[52] Maimon describes the centrality of liquor production within the network of villages that his grandfather leased from Lord Radziwiłł: the produce of arable lands was "sufficient, not only for the wants of his own family, but also for brewing and distilling." In addition, "his bee-hives were sufficient for the brewing of mead.[53] On this, as on other estates, most surplus grain and all honey were diverted into alcohol production.

The Polish nobility could at this point be described in economic terms as liquor producers, the Polish peasantry as the main liquor consumers, and Jews as the liquor trade's service sector. In the Kingdom of Poland, the collapse of the international grain trade and the loss of the port of Gdańsk (Danzig) to Prussia in 1793 only increased landowner reliance on alcohol production and solidified those economic roles. Noblemen wishing to export grain had to contend with both high Prussian tariffs and the British Corn Laws (1825–45), while profits from rye sold for export no longer even covered transit costs. Turning that same rye into alcohol, on the other hand, yielded almost 50 percent more profit.[54] Liquor had saved Polish landowners from collapse.

Improvements in distilling, thanks to the importation of the Pistorius liquor still in the 1820s and the cultivation of potatoes, elevated the potency of drink fourfold and, along with it, chronic drunkenness among the peasantry.[55] But business is business. The Zamoyski holdings, a network of around one hundred estates in the southern Kingdom of Poland containing thirty-eight distilleries, 101 bars, and 140 taverns, saw a net increase in liquor profits of 49 percent between 1833 and 1839.[56] Kingdom-wide, the number of legal distilleries *doubled* between 1830 and 1840.[57] Only gradually would it dawn on landowners that a drunken peasantry meant a drunken labor force, another drag on the already sluggish estate productivity. In the meantime, there was too much money to be made. Agricultural surveys praised villages for their "extremely well-ordered distillery, in which there was a steam-driven Pistorius still that derived twelve quarts of liquor from one bushel of potatoes."[58] Beer was displaced by vodka.[59]

Accusations that Jews induced peasants to drunkenness and cheated them thus served to justify efforts to exclude Jews from the liquid gold rush. However, some complaints may have been merited. The monopolistic nature of the production and sale of the nobleman's liquor virtually ensured that the quality remained low—it was illegal to buy liquor anywhere else or to produce one's own—and purchase of the vile substance was sometimes made compulsory. As tavernkeepers had to sell off every bottle, some would bring them to the huts of delinquent peasants and demand payment whether they wanted liquor or not.[60] This rather shocking practice of compulsory consumption had a grim logic: it allowed the lord to siphon off any surplus money that peasants had managed to obtain by ensuring that they spent their profits in a noble-owned enterprise rather than in the general marketplace.[61] Jewish tavernkeepers may not have been the architects of this ghastly enterprise nor even its main beneficiaries, but they were fully complicit.

Of course, Jewish tavernkeepers may be said to have been coerced by circumstances. How else was a member of an unemancipated people, barred from viably engaging in agriculture, crafts, and professions, to make a living? Polish Jewry may justly be described as a captive service sector, surviving mainly at the landowners' pleasure. But one does not have to accept the anti-Jewish claims of the day to perceive how readily the business lent itself to unscrupulousness. High liquor concession fees, applicable only to Jews, could make tavernkeepers feel justified extracting the greatest possible profit from drunken, illiterate customers. Perhaps they really did make it their business to know about everything the peasants possessed—"every sheaf in the field, every head of cattle in the herd"—so as to be able to recoup their drinking debts. A Polish proverb warned, rather dramatically, "the peasant drinks at the inn and the Jew does him in."[62]

It did not help that the peasants behaved so rudely. According to the memoirist Slomka, a culture of mutual contempt prevailed in which the tavernkeeper was content to let his non-Jewish customers repeatedly laugh at his expense because, after the money had "all been sucked out, he can laugh too."[63] Slomka recalls how Jewish tavernkeepers took every opportunity to exploit a certain well-to-do peasant who "loved to sneer at the Jews, but would go to the tavern regularly." One day, when a tavernkeeper refused the peasant a drink until he paid off his tab, the peasant struck him in the face. The tavernkeeper took him to court, but then withdrew the charge after the peasant "promised to spend five guilders in his shop for vodka." True to his word, the peasant came back to his tavern, but "when he wanted more drink and the innkeeper demanded his money in advance, [the peasant] hit him again in the face, and shouted: 'I hit you before on one side; now you have it on the other. If I didn't your nose would be crooked, but now I have straightened it!'" Once again, there were proceedings; yet "nothing came of it, for the Jew again let him off on the promise of his keeping on with his drinking parties." While this particular peasant was apparently worse than others, the situation was always volatile. Members of a denigrated out-group were, after all, being expected to police themselves in a situation of moral ambiguity.[64]

Yet the relationship between the Jewish tavernkeeper and his Christian customers was not reducible to one of mutual contempt and suspicion. To more fully understand the relationship, it is crucial to see beyond the grotesque polemics that so often overwhelm historians' interpretations of Jewish-Christian relations. Yiddish writer I. L. Peretz's interview with his coachman, Matthew, during his ethnographic expedition captures some of the grudging trust that accompanied the tensions and occasional ruptures:

"And the Jew used to write down what you owed?"

"Of course he did. Would you expect him to make me a present of it [the liquor]? Doesn't he have a wife and children too? Everyone has to look out for himself."

"Did he chalk up twice as much as you really owed?"

"Who knows? My wife used to say so, but that didn't stop her. She kept drinking on credit."

"Your wife?"

"Her too. You have to, often you have to. Once when she was drunk, she wanted to burn down Moshke's place."

"Moshke?"

"Moshke was the one with the tavern. Now he trades with us. An honest man, Moshke. Does he cook his accounts? I don't know, but otherwise he's a good man.

A jack-of-all-trades: first aid, medicine, law. He knows everything, and he does business everywhere."

"So she didn't burn him out?"

"Of course not. She was running with a lighted torch in her hand to burn the tavern down when she tripped and fell in the street. Her hand was burnt in the fire, and she still has the scars to show for it. How she screamed! Later she asked Moshke to forgive her, and you know what? He did forgive her. He's a good person, Moshke."[65]

Matthew's responses transport us into the combustible mix of alienation, suspicion, dependence, admiration, and respect that constituted a peasant-Jewish relationship in the mid-nineteenth-century Kingdom of Poland. Whether or not the anecdote is completely accurate (the incident likely occurred a couple of decades earlier), it conveys ambiguity—an oscillation between distance and relative closeness rather than the static dualism reflected in so many literary constructions.

In fact, what social reformers invariably failed to mention was that peasants usually considered the Jewish tavernkeeper and his wife unique and vital resources. Moshke's function as a "jack-of-all-trades" surely derived from his former, tavernkeeping career. "Let it be as Sarah said," went one folk saying, alluding to the tavernkeeper's wife; "When in trouble, turn to the Jew," went another. They relied on their Jewish tavernkeepers for news, loans, supplies, advice, matchmaking, redress, prescriptions, remedies, information, and mediation—including mediation with the landowners. The latter relied on them, too, considering them the most sober, dependable, and pliant lessees, and they strove to protect them from peasant wrath.[66]

In the end, we witness an astonishing degree of local coexistence, if not actual intimacy. Within demarcated boundaries—i.e., between the tavern walls and behind the bar—the Jewish tavernkeeper had come to be not only valued but considered indispensable, and this perception served as a check on anti-Jewish violence. Most Jewish tavernkeepers were also probably careful not to push things too far. Perhaps few felt bound by their lease contracts' pro forma moral stipulations, according to which they promised never to cheat customers.[67] And perhaps few were deterred by the risk of fines and prison sentences for serving liquor that was less than the regulation 45 percent alcohol. But each was constrained by the knowledge that there was a limit to what the peasant was willing to endure in terms of watered-down vodka, usurious loans, cooked books, and so on.[68]

As the field of ethnography emerged as an important part of the Polish nationalist project by the mid-nineteenth century, Jewish-run taverns came to be valued as receptacles of precious folk customs. Some Polish ethnographers let themselves be riveted and charmed by all the "folk" songs and "folk" dances, accompanied by violins, pipes, and, less often, fifes and drums, played by traveling or local musicians, the latter often the Jewish tavernkeepers themselves. The tavern not only helped villagers make it through the long winter months, when there was no work to be done in the fields, but also facilitated local and regional self-expression. Here, Polish folk culture blossomed in all its splendid variety. Particularly colorful were "Forefathers" celebrations (analogous to Halloween) and the heady carnival days preceding Lent, which were celebrated with dances and rituals allotted according to gender and generation. On these holidays, we again witness the time-honored tension between church and tavern, for the entire village would eventually proceed to the tavern, where the Jew had set up a large poplar log in the center of the main room. The older women would attach the younger married women to the log until they bought bottles of vodka, one for themselves and two for their husbands, while the older landowners fashioned whips and went around the village driving older farmhands toward the tavern to buy drinks for unmarried men. Elderly men and women went house to house collecting eggs to bring to the tavern in exchange for vodka, which they then drank together. The tavern—and hence the Jew—was as central to certain Christian celebrations as the church and the priest.[69]

The renditions of Polish folk life by Gustaw Pilatti (1874–1931) include an idyllic tavern scene in which local Christians in holiday garb dance to a Jewish fiddler's tunes while another Jew serves drinks. A young peasant family with an infant is seated off to the side, lending the scene an almost domestic air [figure 1.3]. The portrait of interethnic and interreligious

Figure 1.3: Gentiles dancing and drinking in a Jewish tavern. Lithograph by Gustaw Pillati published by A. Chlebowski in the journal "Swit," and printed by B. Wierzbicki and Sons, Warsaw, n.d. (Moldovan Family Collection). Courtesy of the Moldovan family.

Figure 1.4: W. Grabowski, *After a Quart of Vodka* (1883). Courtesy of Professor Hillel Levine.

coexistence here contrasts starkly with the more sinister depictions of that era, such as in W. Grabowski's *After a Quart of Vodka* [figure 1.4]. We are prone to favor Pilatti's more positive image. But we have to be cautious—the ethnographic conception of the Jewish tavernkeeper as facilitator of an authentic Polish peasant folk culture through musical accompaniment is tendentious in its own way. Recent research on Yiddish performances suggests a much more complex intercultural dynamic in taverns, in which Yiddish and Slavic songs alike were played before mixed audiences. Although the languages and the messages of the songs differed, with the Yiddish songs tending to bemoan the vicissitudes of mercantile life, both were apparently heard and at least partially understood by peasants and Jews alike. The conception of Jewish taverns as incubators of a pure Polish folk culture should be seen as an artifact of the nineteenth-century Polish ethnographers' nationalist project, even if it does serve as a corrective to the exploitation image.[70]

Not surprisingly, the exploitation image finds even less support in Jewish accounts. In fact, Jewish observers often reversed the accusation: Christian customers allegedly stole liquor and reneged on their debts. Maimon reports that his grandfather was regularly robbed by his Christian customers, who would break into the tavern's store room, get drunk, and flee at the slightest noise while liquor ran out of the opened casks. Others refused to pay their tabs. Maimon relays a chilling tale about a local priest who was accustomed to drinking copiously in his grandfather's tavern without paying. One day, Maimon's grandfather finally refused to serve him. In retaliation, the priest did something monstrous: he persuaded a beaver trapper to plant the corpse of an infant in Maimon's grandfather's house. That night, the priest arrived with some of his parishioners, made a search of his house, and, sure enough, found the infant corpse in a sack that was supposed to contain a beaver pelt. Maimon's grandfather was hauled to the nearby town of Mir in chains and questioned under torture. Fortunately, the beaver trapper later confessed to his part in the blood libel, and Maimon's grandfather was set free.[71]

Jewish memoirist Dov Ber Birkenthal (1723–1805) and his Jewish partners were undone by selling drinks on credit. At first, "every single gentile of our town, along with his wife and children, came in great glee because I was the lessee, and drank a lot and paid in cash, and the liquor brought in several hundred zlotys." But Birkenthal's partners became suspicious on account of his careful record keeping, "which no other Jew employs in this business," and transferred the tavern from Birkenthal's house to that of his neighbor. As a result, liquor was offered to the gentiles on credit that went unrepaid, and profits dwindled, failing to cover even half of the lease payment.[72] One episode in Birkenthal's account does, however, bolster the stereotype of the dishonest Jewish tavernkeeper. Jacob Johan Labadie, a Christian merchant who had swapped Hebrew for German lessons with Birkenthal, was able to read his Hebrew bill and discover that his tavernkeeper was trying to overcharge him.[73]

THE MYTH OF JEWISH SOBRIETY

If the Jewish tavernkeeper was widely believed to be exploiting his drunken peasant customers, it is all the more intriguing that noble tavern owners should have continued to insist on appointing Jews as lessees. Though landowners were seldom inclined to empathize with their serfs, they surely knew that it was they who would ultimately have to bail them out, lending them any farm equipment or draught animals they had lost to drinking debts so that they might continue to work the manor land.

The most important reason for their continued preference for Jewish lessees was, it turns out, inherent in the exploitation myth itself: Jews, they believed, were able to extract maximum profit from the peasantry (as well as refrain from drinking up the product) because they themselves did not drink. While there were additional considerations, the decisive factor seemed to be Jewish sobriety. It had come to be considered a veritable law of nature in the land of liquor. According to the nobleman Antoni Ostrowski, Jews were "always sober, and this virtue should be conceded: drunks are rare among Jews."[74] The memoirist Slomka declared that Jews "never drank themselves, and it was the greatest rarity to see a Jew drunk."[75] A British report to Parliament described Polish Jews as "acute, temperate, economical," in stark contrast to the drunken Polish peasantry.[76] Polish folk idioms mocked Jews for having so much liquor at their disposal yet being so stupid as to not drink it themselves. And when they did drink, it was only in moderation: to "drink Jewishly" meant to remain calm.[77]

Not surprisingly, Jewish sobriety was frequently cast in a sinister light: Jewish tavernkeepers were staying shrewdly sober while their naïve peasant customers ran up their tabs and became too drunk to notice deliberate miscalculations. Even Ostrowski, usually a sympathetic observer, assumed that Jewish tavernkeepers only remained sober in order to take advantage of their Christian customers. Similarly, Slomka described Christians spending hours in the taverns, "making themselves at home, taking their drink: while the [Jews] got more out of them, exploiting their weaknesses." Whenever Solomon, the village's Jewish tavernkeeper, brought drinks around to customers' homes in exchange for gifts in accordance with local custom, "all the folk were more or less befuddled with the liquor. Solomon alone was sober, and he left the village with a wagon full of good things."[78]

But not every observer regarded Jewish sobriety suspiciously. Father Karol Mikoszewski, a preacher in Saint Alexander's Church in Warsaw and future Polish insurrectionist, often invoked it to shame his audiences.[79] In his *Kazania o pijaństwie* (Sermons on Drunkenness, 1862), he identified liquor as the single greatest obstacle to the revival of Polish nationhood, since it had stupefied the masses and entrenched them in poverty, hunger, immorality, superstition, ignorance, wickedness, and crime. Workers and craftsmen were abandoning the churches on Sundays in droves to go to taverns, and were becoming weakened in body and spirit. Polish villages and towns were in a lamentable state. Warsaw, the former seat of monarchs, now presented a pathetic scene, its inhabitants crammed into bars, discussing indecent subjects and insulting and beating each other.[80] There was one nation in Poland, however, that formed a significant exception to this picture: Jews, who did not even believe in Christ, were free of the widespread addiction to drink. As everyone knew, "although he supports himself by dealing in drinks, a Jewish drunk is hard to find!" It was a Christian's shame and disgrace that the sober Jew only encountered the Christian as a drunk in his own house (i.e., the tavern). How great a nation the Poles could be, Mikoszewski exclaimed, if they would but learn the restraint and temperance of the Jews, which enabled them to support and enrich themselves![81] The image of sobriety was thus one that Jews would have been eager to sustain, despite all the suspicions it engendered. For not only did it cause nobles to overwhelmingly favor Jews in the relentless competition over tavern leases; it moved certain Christian clergy to extol them as paragons of self-control.

The widespread acceptance of the stereotype is, however, puzzling given the impressive amount of evidence to the contrary. A review of Jewish sources makes it abundantly clear that, notwithstanding the myth, Polish Jews drank, and some drank in excess. In the early eighteenth century, Kaidanover complained that Jews drank even during the earliest hours of the day: "I have noticed that many people in this region are so enslaved to their appetites that immediately upon awakening, hours before dawn, they believe they will die if they do not drink hard liquor." Some drank to the point of intoxication, thinking it "perfectly permissible to indulge their lusts and stubborn hearts," and when the time of morning prayer arrived their prayers were garbled, "a terrible sin . . . which many luminaries have committed."[82] The claims of a moralist like Kaidanover should be treated with caution. But Jewish memoirists confirm that drinking had a place in normative Jewish society. Moses Wassercug celebrated his lottery win by proceeding straight to the local tavern, where he and his colleagues "drank hard liquor" and planned more for Sabbath eve.[83] At Maimon's grandfather's tavern "every Jewish traveler was met at the door with a glass of spirits; one hand making the *salaam* while the other reached the glass."[84]

Then there are the numerous cases of Jewish alcoholism. Maimon himself succumbed to chronic drinking during his stint as a village tutor: "Whiskey had to form my sole comfort; it made me forget all my misery."[85] Several petitions (*kvitlekh*) to the non-Hasidic miracle worker Rabbi Elijah Guttmacher, which will be discussed in greater depth in chapter 5, introduce us firsthand to the Jew who "drinks and is always drunk."[86] Some families were feeling the economic effects. Tzeitel bat Shayna's husband could have made a decent living as an agent, but, she wrote, "he drinks a lot until he is inebriated, and his livelihood has diminished as a result, and also there is always an argument between them."[87] Jonathan ben Feiga Reizel's drunkenness had brought his household to the brink of starvation and forced him to pull his children out of school for lack of tuition money. His wife, Liba bat Zela, beseeched Rabbi Guttmacher to "turn his heart to good, so that he will no longer be a drunkard, for it has been several years since he became a drunkard." She insisted he had been a pious and scholarly man before, and, referring to herself in the third person, as many of the petitioners writing these *kvitlekh* intermittently do, begged Rabbi Guttmacher to "pray for him to turn his heart to good so that she will no longer be deprived of bread."[88]

Chronic drunkenness naturally bred domestic conflicts. Sarah bat Leah wrote that her husband, Moses ben Reizel, is "always drunk, and he comes home and quarrels with his aforementioned wife. And he does damage and causes [material] losses and she has no rest when he comes home. And he also hit his eldest son for no reason." Sarah asked the rabbi to instill a new spirit in his heart so that "he will never again get drunk for the rest of his life, and so that there will be peace between him and his wife and children and all their children."[89] Berish ben Rekhel personally asked the rabbi to "put a fear of heaven into his heart... for he is always engaged in drinking, to turn his heart to good to repent, so that he can support his wife and four children." His wife, Tsirel bat Esther, managed to add that her husband "quarrels with her because he is a bad man (*ish beli'al*) and a drunk."[90] The wife of Abraham Moses ben Hayya Sarah, "grandson of the genius... our teacher Jacob" despaired that her pedigreed husband had "made a lot of money as an agent, but not always in a kosher manner: once in a game of cards and once in drunkenness, God forbid." She asked Guttmacher to "remove this shame from him and let him walk in the right path."[91] Hena bat Yuta had divorced her alcoholic husband ten years earlier, but the rabbi who granted the divorce was "one of the new-style doctors, because of our many sins." To make matters worse, Hena's husband was trying to get her back on a technicality, claiming that the divorce was not according to religious requirements: he had been drunk at the time.[92]

Several Jewish men approached Guttmacher on their own, pleading with the rabbi to save them and their families from the consequences of their drinking. Jacob Simon ben Rebekah took to drinking after he was outbid for a lease: "And he is like a ship in the sea, 'and there was a mighty tempest in the sea so that the ship seemed likely to be wrecked [Jonah 1:4]'... and he is accustomed to cheer himself with cases of liquor, and he became ill with a dangerous weakness of the heart from this."[93] Solomon ben Reizel confessed that "he drinks a lot of liquor to the point that it makes him drunk, and because of this he has no domestic tranquility. And may God have mercy on him and guard him so that he doesn't drink anymore."[94] Isaac Eizik ben Rachel, a widower, admitted that he "drinks more liquor than he needs, and then he beats his children, so he asks to give him a cure for this.[95] These men felt that only divine intervention would cure them of the habit.

Chronic drunkenness occasionally resulted in near-apostasy. Joshua Zelig ben Reizel lost a court case with a fellow Jew who owed him money, "and because of his heaviness of heart he became a drunk, and constantly resorted to drinking." According to his wife, Joshua had nearly converted to Christianity before reconsidering:

> And last year he was with the priests in Krakow for several days and wanted to convert, God forbid. And with the help of God he escaped from them to his house and became a penitent. And he engaged in fasting for several weeks and did good deeds. And now for several weeks the court case was renewed [on appeal], and the afflictions returned and he engages in drunkenness as before. And I come in great hardship—please pray for him that his heart will be turned to good, for he is a student of Torah and from good people.[96]

A less dramatic case involved a kosher butcher, who had to give up his occupation, or at least the kosher part of it, because "an obstacle arose from his own hand, which gave him glasses of wine." He had now "abandoned that path completely and swore that he will never drink any drink of drunkenness. And it's been several years and these drinks never touched his lips. And he wants to return to his craft, and "the eyes of Israel are upon him" [1 Kings 1:20] and upon the Upper Holiness." He planned "to appear before the rabbinical court of this town" to ask to be reinstated as a kosher butcher, and asked that Rabbi Guttmacher ensure that the rabbinical court would be understanding.[97]

Alongside these individual cases of excessive Jewish drinking is the collective reputation of members of the extremely popular Hasidic movement, whose leaders endorsed joy—including alcohol-induced joy—as a means of attracting the divine presence. While it is difficult to gauge the size of the Hasidic movement, and one scholar has attempted to downplay it, certain internal Hasidic and external Polish Christian observers agree that the movement attracted about one-third of the Jewish community in the Kingdom of Poland by 1830 and grew substantially over the next several decades.[98] Traditionalist-oriented *mitnagdim* ("opponents"), who were committed to stemming the movement's growth, attempted to stigmatize Hasidic gatherings as something "seen only on days of drinking and joy, in their imbibing of wine and dancing, and in their dancing like rams, each man grabbing his neighbor's neck, and chanting and singing, 'The Rabbi ordered us to be joyful.'"[99] Hasidic leaders (sing. *tzaddik*; pl. *tzaddikim*) were sometimes the worst drunks: the tzaddik Levi Isaac of Berdichev (Berdyczów), a polemicist wrote, habitually "'drinks up a river' [Job 40:23] . . . and afterwards he lies on his bed and takes his afternoon nap until midnight."[100]

Reports of Hasidic drunkenness by East European maskilim (Jewish proponents of Enlightenment-based reform) are even more numerous, charging that Hasidim, "the drunkards of Ephraim" (Isaiah 28:1), believed that they could achieve ecstatic mystical states through drinking and were even known to discuss privileged, esoteric teachings in an intoxicated state: "And to fill his throat such a one takes a keg of whiskey, and when he is filled to the brim he expounds the lore of the Chariot-Throne".[101] According to Ezekiel Kotik, a maskil from Kamenets (present-day Belarus) who was no picture of sobriety himself,[102] the Hasidim in his town only respected a person who was "always merry, loved the bitter drop, and started dancing all on his own." If an older, wealthy man didn't feel like dancing, he was forced to take a shot of liquor, after which "he'd be already tipsy, dancing for all he was worth."[103] Liquor-induced merriment was for them a permanent condition, for "every day was a holiday and a reason for making merry." Hasidim demanded that even someone who had to commemorate a death anniversary (*yortsayt*), traditionally a day of fasting, must treat them to a drink; if he was wealthy "he had to supply plenty of drinks, and after the service the bottle was passed around and things got lively."[104] Individual Hasidim were full-blown drunks. A Hasid named Yankel was "always drunk as Lot;" while Israel, a Hasid who supported the Polish cause for independence, "started drinking, drowning his melancholy in the bitter drop" after the suppression of the 1863 uprising against the tsar, to the point that it began to affect his health.[105]

Descriptions of Hasidic drinking habits by maskilim in the Kingdom of Poland are similar. Abraham Stern, the Kingdom of Poland's first prominent maskil, informed government officials that during their "clandestine meetings" after the departure of the Sabbath, Hasidim were accustomed to "drink, sing, and jump, which commonly lasts until midnight, and often throughout the entire night."[106] According to Y. Y. Trunk, Jews on pilgrimages to the tzaddik Isaac of Warka (1779–1848), one of the preeminent Hasidic leaders of the mid-nineteenth century, "enacted out and out Hasidic ecstasies. Barrels of liquor were opened and a feeling prevailed of religious ecstatic Hasidic togetherness."[107] One of the crudest maskilic satires to ever come to light blames the fatal fall of the premier Polish Hasidic leader of the early nineteenth century, the Seer of Lublin (d. 1815), on a drunken attempt to urinate out his window: "Before he finished relieving himself, the flesh still in his hand [see Num. 11:33], he staggered like a drunken man [see Ps. 107:27] and fell completely from the high open window down to the ground, upon the excrement." He was discovered lying in a rubbish heap, his genitals exposed.[108] Historian B. Ann Tlusty has suggested that the symbol of the drunkard served not only to discourage social disorder but also to titillate and amuse, giving audiences a kind of vicarious indulgence. In a context where hunger and deprivation were facts of life, she argues, "a body filled to overflowing, spilling its contents into the environment, clearly expressed excess, but this could be understood in a celebratory as well as a critical sense." However, in a Jewish cultural context, invoking grotesque rhetoric usually reserved for anti-Christian polemics was unambiguously negative, impugning the Hasidic leader's very Jewishness.[109]

A more restrained but elaborate satire of Hasidic drinking culture is *Sefer ha-tikun*, most likely written by S. Y. Friedlander.[110] The title derives from the kabbalistic notion that Jews can repair cosmic flaws by means of rituals, good deeds, study, penance, esoteric mindfulness, and, according to Hasidim, the act of drinking a toast. *Sefer ha-tikun* is exclusively about the latter method of cosmic repair, and is best translated as "Book of Toasts" (the word *tikn,* derived from the Hebrew *tikun* [cosmic repair], actually means "toast" in Yiddish). It begins with an imaginary teaching purporting to be from the kabbalistic classic the Zohar: "One who is about to pray must gladden his soul with wine, and this is the secret meaning of the verse 'they served God joyfully [Ps. 100:2].'" As there is no joy without the finest wine and liquor, drinking a toast is the most effective method for lifting up the fallen. Charitable funds must be used to buy liquor for sacred toasts which—like the everlasting light in the synagogue—must never cease. Once, we learn, a non-Hasidic Jew refused to make a toast, so the Hasidim confiscated his *tallit* and *tefillin* and sold them. The authorities were alerted, and the Hasidim were forced to remain in prison, sober, for an entire year. "Who can appreciate the great sorrow endured by our brothers, who had to interrupt their everlasting toasts and sit bareheaded, God forbid, for an entire year?" Upon their release, the Hasidim decreed double toasts to make up for the cosmic interruption.[111]

The satire that follows, entitled "The Laws of Toasts," purports to be a commentary on a section of the preeminent codification of Jewish law, the *Shulḥan Arukh* ("Set Table"). One is required to make a toast when he builds a house, sells a house, and when his house burns down. One must make a toast when he gets married. If the groom is a widow, he must drink for each wife; an elderly man who marries a virgin must drink forty-nine toasts.[112] If the father of the bride refuses to drink a toast the couple must divorce; and the Polish Hasidim are accustomed to beating the recalcitrant father with his own slipper. Toasts are also required for births, circumcisions, bar mitzvahs, a child's first day of school (thirst for liquor is equated with thirst for Torah), a divorce (to celebrate the prospect of a new spouse), the death of a parent (Polish Hasidim drink such toasts at noon and midnight; Lubavitcher Hasidim only drink one large one at noon), the death of a spouse (to comfort the living spouse and celebrate the imminent remarriage), the appearance of a visitor to town (visitors are equated with beggars, who are equated with Hasidim), and the Sanctification of the Moon ceremony (toasts inspire holy vision). These prescriptions would have kept a Hasid drinking all day long. Yet the commentator insists it would be wrong to think that Hasidim are ever actually drunk—their toasts only kept them in a state of holy rapture and communion with God.[113]

In the old days, according to the next section of the satirical code, Hasidim were so holy that the size of one of their small toasts was equal to one of our large ones, and "one of the famous Hasidim," whose soul was a reincarnation of the souls of the biblical drunkards Noah and Lot, drank himself to death in order to rectify their souls. All the tall tales about tzaddikim that slackers recite as they sit pantsless by the stove in prayer house are, in actuality, only for the sake of the toasts that follow each recitation. They must also drink a toast when they put their pants on to recite the afternoon prayer. In our generation, because of our sins, extra toasts are needed; and to ever refuse to drink a toast is a disgrace that strengthens the forces of impurity.[114]

The proper times to drink a toast, according to the satire, are day, night, Sabbaths, festivals—in fact every day except Yom Kippur, when food and drink are forbidden. Some drink the toast in their house, some at the study house, but the great do both. Some drink during the morning prayer, some before, and some as early as sunrise in order to "inflame their prayer." On Sabbaths and festivals, one is to drink toasts only during the several hours between the morning and afternoon prayers, but on Simchat Torah and Purim one is to drink throughout the day while walking in groups with torches and breaking windows (unlike mitnagdim, who vainly study Talmud all night, Hasidim know that joy is the basis of worship, and that there is no joy without wine).[115] A large toast may be drunk in two stages, but S___Hasidim (presumably referring to Stolin Hasidim) drink it in one gulp. Liquor that does not make you flinch and put your hands on your face and cause your legs to tremble is ritually disqualified (*pasul*) because it does not reach the "Upper Mind." The only groups exempt from drinking are the deaf (they might not hear the proper amount and drink too little), fools and children (they might drink improperly), and the elderly (they might take too long or, God forbid, spill). When it comes to drinking toasts one must err on the side of strictness, and the liquor must be as strong as possible.[116]

SACRED DRINKING IN HASIDIC SOURCES

The usefulness of such sources might be dismissed on account of their agenda, which is to stigmatize the Hasidic movement by means of a derogatory motif formerly reserved for gentiles. But inner Hasidic sources confirm the normativity of sacred toasting and further contest all the confident claims about Jewish sobriety. Sometimes, a passage seems to be right out of "Book of Toasts" itself. One Hasidic book of customs explains, for example, that when a guest comes to a Hasidic prayer house (*shtibl*) it is customary to ask him to make a toast because it takes the guest's mind away from his business affairs and reminds him of his holy purpose.[117] Hasidic sources indeed prescribe drinking toasts on the death anniversary of one's parents or teachers, a practice that is particularly controversial because it contradicts earlier rabbinic dicta to fast on those days. How is this acceptable? The Hasidic commentator Yeḥiel Shapiro of Tomaszpol explains that when the tzaddikim of this generation perceived that Jews were too spiritually weak to fast or mortify their flesh, they decided it would be best to replace fasting with feasting. According to Shapiro, feasting is actually preferable to fasting because the presence of God (*shekhinah*) does not dwell within sadness. As a result, "the custom arose that even the poor of Israel, who don't have the means to host a feast on a death anniversary, still distribute drinks of liquor and 'bread offered as dessert'[Talmud Ber. 41b], for by this means they uphold the commandment to give charity." Shapiro relays a tradition in the name of the tzaddik Aryeh Leib, the "Shpoler Zeyde" (1725–1812): "When a man gives a cup of liquor to his friend to drink it is true charity, for it seizes his heart and restores his spirit." He then demonstrates that the Hebrew word for charity, *tsedakah*, is actually an acronym for the Russian phrase meaning "plum brandy (*tslivovits*) is good to buy for a starveling."[118] Another redactor attempts to bolster the association between death anniversaries and merrymaking by quoting classical descriptions of the periodic ascents of the souls of tzaddikim, who would stand on their graves and dance.[119] In doing so, he reveals the Hasidic custom's affinity with the Slavic "Forefathers" ritual on All Souls Day, according to which participants brought food to the cemetery and summoned the souls of the dead to join in feasting and drinking.[120]

Endorsements of drinking, ostensibly for a higher purpose, can be traced back to Hasidism's earliest phases. The founder of Hasidism, the Besht, a one-time tavernkeeper himself, was reputedly able to outdrink gentiles by recalling his awe of God and achieve sublime mystical heights while imbibing liquor on the holiday of Simchat Torah.[121] A later tradition claims that the Besht drank mead in order to "sweeten" (i.e., mitigate) divine justice.[122] The first collection of Hasidic sermons, *Toldot Ya'akov Yosef*, offers a parable of a captive prince who received a letter from the king about his impending rescue, and in order to celebrate his secret joy went "with the inhabitants of the city to the tavern . . . and rejoiced with wine," implying that we, too, should rejoice with wine on the Sabbath.[123]

Even Lubavitcher Hasidism, a purportedly more rationalistic school, endorsed liquor-infused celebrations. An entry in the memorial book of the Liozna burial society from 1826 decrees that someone must provide "good liquor for the joy of the 19th of [the month of] Tevet" to commemorate the release of R. Schneur Zalman of Lyady, the first Lubavitcher tzaddik, from prison (in 1798).[124] A manuscript version of R. Schneur Zalman's *Kitzur likute amarim* contains a Yiddish recipe for lemon liquor in the editor's handwriting. Lubavitcher disciples evidently felt comfortable mingling their master's lofty discourses with a "gallon of Arak spirit of 17 %, a quart of lemon juice, a liter and a half of flour-sugar or a liter and a quarter of good sugar."[125]

Lyrics to Hasidic drinking songs imply the religious leadership's wholehearted approval: "Let us all together, together / Greet the *rebbe* (tzaddik).... Let's all drink wine and pour the whiskey down our gullets / Raise a rumpus till the break of day." According to another song: "The *rebbe* told us to be gay / To drink whiskey, not wine." These endorsements may seem unbecoming of religious leaders, as Hasidism's opponents were quick to point out. But they are consistent with the early Hasidic leaders' embrace of moderately antinomian conceptions like worshipping God by means of feasting, storytelling, singing, dancing, and yes, drinking.[126]

At the same time, Hasidic endorsements of liquor sometimes carry stern warning labels against over-consumption. A fascinating example is an imagined history of the Jewish liquor trade relayed to the Polish tzaddik Solomon of Radomsko:

> The drink called liquor [*yayin saraf*, lit. "burning wine"] has medicinal benefits because this drink did not used to exist at all, and it is not mentioned in the Talmud or Midrash. And only at the time of the expulsions from Spain and Portugal etc., when Jews were driven into these [Polish] lands, did they inquire in Heaven what will be their source of livelihood there. And they answered, "A new drink will be created in the world, liquor, and the gentiles will love to drink that drink. And the Children of Israel will sell it to them, and from this will be the foundation of their livelihood." And since it is something that descended from above, of course it is a good, healing thing. However, one should only drink a little, and also mix it with water.[127]

Liquor, according to this tradition, is to be valued for its health and economic benefits. But it is mainly meant to be drunk by gentiles; Jews should drink only in moderation. Another ambivalent tradition explains that by toasting "To life!" we ensure that the drink will only be for the sake of life

Figure 1.5: "The Hasid and His Wife" (Le Chasside et sa femme), Leon Hollanderski: *Les Israelites de Pologne* (1846). Note the bottle of liquor in the Hasid's hand.

and not damage our well-being."[128] The tzaddik Naḥman of Bratslav warns that "by means of [wine], the blood boils and all kinds of sins are committed, God forbid. It also damages one's livelihood and makes him impoverished." Only those who have completed the recitation of ten psalms known as the *tikun ha-kelali* (general rectification) "are elevated by means of their drinking."[129] A Lubavitcher song laments: "There is eating and there is drinking / The only trouble is that there is no praying."[130]

Hasidim believed that when they did drink it was different from non-Jewish drinking, for alcohol reveals the nature of the soul: "When Children of Israel sit together to drink [the result is] love of God and love of friends," one tradition claims. "But when the gentiles begin to drink, we see quarrels and murder among them."[131] Hasidim preserved this conceit by being careful to always supply a religious rationale for heavy drinking—a Jewish holiday, a lifecycle event, the commemoration of a significant event in their tzaddik's lifetime, and so on.[132] Ethnocentric sentiments aside, it does appear that the encoded tendency to keep liquor-saturated celebrations within a religious framework distinguished Hasidic drinking—from carousing in the tavern, from European Christian carnivals that tended to free one from the strictures of religious dogma and piety, and from drinking bouts that served to test and display one's masculine virility.[133]

Hasidic drinking was also more discreet, to judge by the typical settings of heavier Hasidic consumption—"clandestine meetings" (according to the movement's critics, cited above) held in a prayerhouse or a tzaddik's court rather than in the extremely public tavern. This discretion is reflected in Hasidic drinking songs, which rarely contain a hint of non-Jewish presence. In contrast, Polish drinking songs often seem intended for the ears of the Jewish tavernkeeper and his wife or daughter, the latter two imagined running off with their Christian lovers and the cash box, thus doubly emasculating the Jew.[134]

The cultural consequences of the more public nature of Polish Christian drinking practices are vividly illustrated in a Hasidic tale, according to which a village tavernkeeper once complained to his tzaddik about his difficulty praying on account of his gentile customers' drunken, lewd conversations. The tzaddik, according to the tale, responded with the following story:

> During my travels on the road it so happened that I arrived at a tavern in a village and it was prayer time. And there was no separate room, rather only one large room filled with drunken gentile men and women, for it was one of their religious holidays. And one of them was playing the violin, and the gentile men danced with the gentile women. And there was no place for me to pray other than in this room. And I prayed in one corner of the dwelling. And I recall that I prayed there deliciously precisely *because* I heard and saw with my own eyes their profane words and deeds.[135]

The tzaddik concluded with the wise pronouncement that "if there is such enjoyment from carnal things, then how much more so from spiritual things."[136] Undoubtedly, the same tzaddik drank copiously with his Hasidim at his court or inside their raucous prayer houses on the slightest spiritual pretext. But what a difference! The tavern functioned like a one-way mirror through which Jews observed members of the dominant culture at their drunken worst. Thanks to the encoded discretion, the dual myth of Jewish sobriety and gentile drunkenness was able to live on.

Only occasionally do we find non-Jewish witnesses to Hasidic drinking. Police responding to noise complaints reported that Hasidim played riotous drinking games in their prayer houses before spilling out onto the Jewish street in joyous song.[137] British missionaries observed, more sympathetically, that "before their devotions [Hasidim] indulge freely in the use of mead, and even of ardent spirits, to promote cheerfulness, as they regard sorrow and anxiety as particular hindrances to the enjoyment of union with God," and that Hasidim drank mead on Friday afternoons "after the warm-bath (which is customary in Poland), with a view to their being in a cheerful frame of mind during evening prayers."[138] Such outsider reports are rare.

Jewish drinking was not, of course, limited to Hasidim. Both Hasidic and non-Hasidic Jews drank liquor before, during, and after their everyday meals. A nineteenth-century commentary on blessings over food, attributed to both the tzaddik Isaac of Warka and the non-Hasidic Solomon Zalman Lipschitz, chief rabbi of Warsaw, freely acknowledges that "in these lands" Jews were accustomed to drink liquor during their meals. The point of contention is whether one should recite a separate blessing over liquor. The commentary rules that there is no need to make a blessing over liquor drunk during one's meal "in order to arouse one's appetite," for it is considered subordinate to the meal itself. But as a precaution, one should try to "make a blessing on a little liquor before the meal." In addition, there is no need to make a blessing over liquor drunk during the meal when the purpose is to "warm [the] stomach to digest the meal." But the commentary recommends that, "as all the authorities wrote unmistakably that one should bless it when one drinks it to help digest, one should therefore take care not to drink it for digestion until after the blessing after the meal."[139] Another code from the period confirms that "most people enjoy liquor before their meals," for which reason "it is for us the wine of the land (*hemer medinah*)."[140] And if someone ate something exclusively for the purpose of "mitigating the harshness" of liquor, i.e., as a chaser, he need not make a blessing over that food.[141]

Jewish religious leaders thus may have tolerated drinking, but they also sought to regulate it. The pre-Hasidic ethicist R. Isaiah Horowitz attempted to draw a sharp distinction between the improper state of "great drunkenness" (*mevusam*) and the more proper state "mildly intoxicated" (*besomi*).[142] Hasidic commentator Hayyim Eleazar Shapira went further in his toleration of drinking, deeming wine crucial for attaining the required degree of joy on the Sabbath—it was actually a substitute for Temple sacrifices.[143] But he, too, cautioned that there are "two kinds of drunkenness," being drunk and being what today we would call "buzzed" (*be-medumdam*). One was only permitted to recite blessings in the latter state.[144]

Extensive discussion developed around the practice of substituting wine for the Sabbath morning blessing with liquor, which had a much more intoxicating effect. R. David ha-Levi Segal ("The TaZ," ca. 1586–1667) deemed hard liquor the "wine of the land" and thus an acceptable substitute, reasoning that real wine was too expensive in Poland-Lithuania and noting that "the majority of the masses in those countries drink liquor on a daily basis" instead. On this logic, R. Abraham Abele Gombiner ("The Magen Avraham," ca. 1633–ca. 1683) forbade Sabbath morning blessings over liquor in neighboring Hungary, where "wine grows and is easily found." Even when Hungary and Galicia (the name given to Austrian Poland) were united under Habsburg rule, the fact that they were separated by the Carpathian Mountains, which are extremely difficult to traverse in wintertime with barrels of wine on account of the snow, meant that liquor remained the "wine of the land" in Galicia but not in Hungary.[145]

Similarly, the Hasidic leader Schneur Zalman of Lyady declared liquor to be the "wine of the land" based on his sense that, while "disgusting drinks like that which they call *kvas* or *barszcz* [i.e., borscht] in these lands are not considered any more important than water," mead and liquor were, in contrast, more valued, and thus similar to actual wine.[146] Numerous tzaddikim agreed, and are known to have recited the Sabbath morning blessing over hard liquor.[147] The contemporaneous Hasidic commentator Shapira recalls a circumcision ceremony from his childhood in Białobrzegi, Poland, during which liquor was substituted because people were too poor to afford wine. He also relays that R. Ḥayim Halberstam of Sanz, a Galician tzaddik who spent several Sabbaths in Hungary, honored the Magen Avraham's distinction. After the blessing was made over the wine, because liquor was not the "wine of the land" in Hungary, he then made it over liquor in line with the Galician custom.[148] Opinions were only divided over whether one was required to drink the required measure, a *rivi'it*, of hard liquor, which would surely make one drunk.[149]

Certain tzaddikim did abstain from liquor and warn against excessive drinking. Yet they could never proscribe it entirely, out of respect for earlier masters.[150] A tradition about the Seer of Lublin and his disciple Shalom Rokeaḥ of Belz (1779–1855) captures what may have been the movement's first public division over drinking:

> The holy rabbi, the rabbi Shalom of Belz, of blessed memory, was once spending the Sabbath with the holy master of Lublin, of blessed memory. And on the eve of the holy Sabbath, he handed him a glass of wine to drink. But as [R. Shalom's] custom was to never drink any intoxicating drink, he did not want to drink it this day, either. But he also did not want to refuse the command of his master, of blessed memory. As a result, when his master, of blessed memory, set the glass on the table before him, he hesitated so intensely that the glass split! And he filled it again, and told him to drink, and then a third time, and finally said to him, "Did you come here to break all of my glasses?" And Rabbi Shalom answered him, "I don't drink wine." So he ceased to give him any more.[151]

Neither tzaddik was entirely in the right, or perhaps both were right. A message of ambivalence encouraged the kind of judicious, regulated drinking that the movement's leaders could accept.[152]

Removed from the East European context, Hasidic redactors in America and Israel today sometimes appear scandalized by the enshrinement of East European Hasidic drinking practices. As great tzaddikim were known to have made the Sabbath morning blessing over liquor, no one should "dare to second-guess them, God forbid," writes one commentator, with obvious discomfort. Yet it is really only appropriate for "one who is accustomed to drinking hard liquor every morning, and a small cup of hard liquor is pleasing and delicious for him before his breakfast." The commentator himself confesses that he personally does not enjoy hard liquor at all, nor even the effects of wine. He prefers to make his blessings over grape juice (*grayp jus*).[153]

CONCLUSION

The stark formulation in the famous Yiddish song *Shiker iz der goy* (The gentile [*goy*] is drunk) appears grossly simplistic in light of the evidence we have reviewed here: "The goy goes to the tavern / He drinks a glass of wine / Oy, the goy is drunk, drunk is he / Drink he must, because a goy is he./The Jew goes to the study house / He looks at a book / Oy, the Jew is sober, sober is he / Learn he must, because a Jew is he."[154] In fact, Polish Jews— particularly Hasidim—indulged in liquor, and sometimes excessively. Their tendency to do so under regulated religious auspices and within Jewish spaces meant that their drinking was less free and visible to outsiders.

This is not to dismiss Polish Jewish sobriety as completely illusory, a creation of successful image management. If the true rate of Jewish alcoholism had approached its Christian corollary, one would expect rebukes against drunkenness to have appeared in rabbinic sermons as frequently as they did in Christian ones. In fact, such rebukes appear but rarely. Equally telling is the fact that Jewish clergy never felt the need to found temperance societies as did Christian clergy all over Eastern Europe. But levels of Jewish alcohol consumption, while remaining low relative to the Polish societal norm, rose in tandem with it over the course of the nineteenth century. Perceptions of Jewish sobriety were greatly exaggerated, as were totalizing claims about Polish Christian drunkenness.

Polish reformers cultivated an equally distorted image, predatory Jewish sobriety. The peasants only drank excessively, they argued, because sober Jews enticed them into drunkenness in order to more easily dupe them. Even Mickiewicz felt the need to stress that Yankel "kept his accounts strictly and without any trickery," a backhanded compliment that implies that Yankel's honesty was exceptional. These attitudes drew upon a wellspring of peasant folklore, which warned listeners about the snares of the Jew alongside the snares of drink. They, too, likely contained a kernel of truth: some Jewish tavernkeepers probably did overcharge and over-serve members of a rival and sometimes hostile community. But reformers were never justified in insisting, as they continually did, that the sober Jewish tavernkeeper was solely to blame for peasant drunkenness and debt.

Such constructions of the "other" do not, of course, fully capture the relationship between the Christian customer and his Jewish tavernkeeper, who, as we have seen, played such an important role in Christian weddings and religious feast days and was such a vital resource for customers in need of advice, loans, and so on. In the next chapter, moreover, we will witness how local Christians enabled their Jewish tavernkeepers to observe, or more accurately circumvent, Jewish Sabbath and festival restrictions. Given that high level of mutual dependency, the grotesque polemics reviewed in the current chapter seem to have mainly served to repel each group socially in order to help guard against taboos like out-marriage and conversion.

Nevertheless, the relationship was volatile. Social commentators, believing their mission was to protect the peasant from the Jewish tavernkeeper, fanned the flames of mistrust, while the Polish government, for reasons of its own, stepped up its efforts to tax and ban Jewish tavernkeeping out of existence. With the failure of one uprising against the tsar (1830) after another (1863), the image of the Jewish tavernkeeper-as-exploiter would come to be accompanied by the image of the Jewish tavernkeeper-as-traitor. Who else, Polish rebels wondered out loud, could have been tipping off Russian troops and foiling their attempts to achieve sovereignty? Whatever hopes Mickiewicz placed in his honest and patriotic tavernkeeper were soon dashed along with hopes for an independent Poland. Only the conservative landowners and those under their authority seemed willing to protect and conceal the Jewish tavernkeeper. Each of these countervailing processes proved particularly intense and focused in the semi-independent Kingdom of Poland, which emerged as a kind of laboratory for tsarist social engineers, social reformers, and Polish patriots alike, yet repeatedly succumbed to the weight of tradition.

CHAPTER 2

Rural Jewish Prohibition in the Kingdom of Poland

In the opening scene of *Żyd polski, czyli Każdy ma swoje przebiegi* (Polish Jews, or Everyone Has His Ploy; 1820), by Polish playwright Adam Kłodzinski, Ryfka and her mother are seated in their tavern working themselves into ecstasies over the new lifestyle they will attain once Ryfka marries the clever, ambitious Icyk. In a clamorous Polish-Yiddish pidgin, Ryfka's mother cries, "Afterwards we'll be able to go live with you and abandon this tavern. . . . Oy, vey! Oy vey! We're going to be rich!" Young Icyk is currently away at a trade fair selling goods he received from Ryfka's father, Hersz False (Falsz), who is appropriately named: the goods turn out to be stolen, and Icyk is hauled before the local clerk. In an attempt to save himself Icyk turns informer, revealing to his interrogator that Hersz False not only gave him the stolen goods to sell but also surreptitiously runs a tavern, despite a governmental prohibition against Jews selling liquor. When interrogated, Hersz False admits that he lives in a tavern with his family, but insists that only a Christian sells the liquor there. The clerk is unconvinced. However, during a recess several Jews bribe Icyk to withdraw his denunciation, and then proceed to steal the interrogation transcripts from the clerk's pocket. Without his records, the petty official is paralyzed and has no choice but to drop the charges. Icyk resumes his dishonest trade and Hersz False continues to run his tavern by means of a Christian front. The provincial bureaucracy once again proves impotent in the face of Jewish solidarity and cunning, Kłodzinski seems to say.[1]

Hersz False cuts a rather poor figure next to Mickiewicz's honest and patriotic Yankel. But there remains a glimmer of humorous appreciation for False's resourcefulness that also sets him apart from the more sinister tavernkeepers who appear in later Polish Romantic literature. Józef Dzierzkowski's *Śliska do przepaści droga* (Sliding Toward the Precipice; 1858), for example, is a study in Manichean contrasts: a vigorous, honest peasant who dutifully works the nobleman's sun-drenched fields and attends services in the village's wooden green-domed church is contrasted with a pale, degenerate peasant who abandons the nobleman's fields to frequent the dark, seedy tavern on the village outskirts, where the Jewish tavernkeeper "smiles like a devil must smile," drugs him with vodka, and lures him into a nocturnal smuggling venture along dark, craggy mountain paths, destroying his life.[2] Kłodzinski's farce is not only more lighthearted than this tragic tale, it is more realistic—so realistic in fact that a similar scenario later appears in the archives, albeit with a very different resolution.

THE BLUMROZEN AFFAIR

As the historian leafs through the archival files of the Interior Ministry of the Kingdom of Poland to gain a sense of life there, the words "Jews," "taverns," and "villages" pop up incessantly. The immediate impression is of a preoccupation, if not obsession, with rural Jewish tavernkeeping among Polish bureaucrats. First come the memos bemoaning the evil effects of Jews and taverns on villages; then the proposals for how to put an end to the lethal three-way combination; then the decreed fees, restrictions and bans; and finally the triumphant statistics charting its demise. At first glance, the end of the rural Jewish liquor trade seems a fait accompli, just as many postwar historians have assumed.

But on second glance, we begin to detect a vibrant counternarrative weaving its way through the series of decrees. First, there are the relentless complaints—by officials, social commentators, local priests, and occasionally even a Jew—that Jews are continuing to sell liquor in one village, in several villages, and in villages all over the kingdom despite the restrictions and bans. The complaints are followed by investigations, in which officials discover that a local Jew has simply hired a Christian to serve the liquor while remaining, for all intents and purposes, the village's tavernkeeper. Most disturbingly, it all seems to be occurring with the full knowledge and participation of the noble who owns the village, not to mention the Christians who frequent the tavern. A genuine local conspiracy. The officials order the Jew's immediate expulsion from the village, reprimand the noble, and retreat in a huff to the provincial capital. Local life usually returns to normal, albeit with a different Jewish tavernkeeper for caution's sake.

The most elaborate such case preserved in the Interior Ministry archives, the so-called Blumrozen Affair, reads almost like a play, if not a farce. In 1840, Lord Franciszek Kisielnicki (henceforth Lord K.) and Solomon Wolfowicz Blumrozen of Stawiski signed a lease contract for a tavern in the village of Kisielnice. The contract stipulated unabashedly that, apart from the maintenance of a restaurant, alcoholic drinks were to be sold by a "Catholic bartender," i.e., not by Solomon himself. By this means, Solomon would probably evade the prohibitive liquor concession fee required of all Jews since 1812, as well as impending legislation against Jews serving liquor along main rural roads. The price of the lease was high: two thousand zlotys, with an additional four hundred zlotys to be paid as compensation to a Jew named Mejer Dawidowicz, who ran a tavern in nearby Kobylin and had enjoyed monopolistic privileges. Solomon promised never to sell vodka meant for the lord's court, falsify sales, nor shortchange the court in any other way. He assumed responsibility for the safety of travelers, and promised to hire only orderly peasants and "guard the honesty of the tavern as a woman guards her honest reputation." Solomon was to begin operations on April 23 to avoid any delay caused by the approaching Passover holiday.[3]

But something went wrong. On August 5 of the next year, the central government in Warsaw received a complaint from Solomon that Lord K. had allowed another Jew, Zelka Wigdorowicz, to bilk him out of his lease for an additional four hundred zlotys. Solomon reminded officials that Zelka, as a Jew, was forbidden by a new decree to live in and run a tavern by a main village road. (Solomon's own tenure had commenced before the decree was announced.) Zelka's so-called restaurant was really a tavern in disguise that offered many varieties of liquor and yielded Lord K. two thousand zlotys per year. In fact, Lord K. was also allowing Jews to sell liquor by main roads in Kobylin and Poryte, his other villages. Like young Icyk in the Kłodzinski farce, Solomon had turned informer.

As the Łomża district commissioner commenced his investigation, both the informer and his main target were nowhere to be found. Solomon had fled, and Zelka just happened to be away at a trade fair in the town of Jedwabne. The investigators therefore began with Lord K., who immediately invoked the traditional lord-Jew symbiosis:

> As an owner of a roadside village who must always consider the convenience of travelers, I could not neglect to hire Jews who would continually provide for the

needs of [traveling] Jews. What is more, people of this faith show themselves to be orderly, and this work requires orderly and suitable people, and for this reason as well I hired Jews. I tried with all my might to fulfill the will of the regime by not having him live there or sell liquor. If someone has accused me of allowing liquor to be sold there by this people, it occurred without my knowledge, and those responsible deserve prosecution.[4]

Lord K.'s deposition provides rare explanations for the nobility's continued insistence on having Jews run taverns during this period of crippling Jewish-specific concessions and bans. Jews, he reminded his interrogators, were still best suited to meet the traveling Jewish merchants' needs, presumably their dietary and Sabbath requirements. Jews, moreover, were "orderly," a code word for abstemious.

Lord K. then entered into the details of the case. Zelka had not encroached on Solomon's lease by outbidding him; Solomon's ouster was his own doing. Residents of surrounding villages could attest to how many times Solomon had "disturbed the peace." Investigators could see for themselves how peaceful, clean, and orderly the tavern had become and how thoroughly travelers' needs were satisfied since Zelka took it over. The enterprise generated little money, but the satisfaction of travelers was Lord K.'s main reward. Zelka ran neither a tavern nor a bar—Lord K. employed Christians for that purpose. Zelka had been expelled as a result of a false accusation, and should be restored and compensated. The Jews in Kisielnice and Kobylin, who had always been law-abiding and had always operated legal businesses, were being unjustly interrogated, tried, and expelled.[5]

But the Łomża commissioner knew that neither Zelka nor Solomon had acquired a liquor concession for their "restaurant" and that there were more cases of illegal Jewish tavernkeeping in Lord K.'s holdings.[6] As Zelka was still being located, the commissioner expanded his investigation into the other villages mentioned by Solomon, setting his sites on Mejer Dawidowicz of Kobylin. Interestingly enough, every local Christian who was interrogated vouched for Mejer, denying repeatedly that he was selling any liquor. Mejer lived near the tavern, they explained, but only ran a cheap restaurant where he also sold hay, oats, and straw. They added that he raised winter corn on a patch of land, and that his son, Bendyt, worked the half *włok* (around 110 square feet) of land Mejer had entrusted to him.

Alas, Jan Smiarkowski, a twenty-two-year-old Christian bartender in Poryte, let it slip to that he was effectively serving as a front for Mejer's tavern. He admitted that Mejer either put up the money for Jan to purchase his vodka and beer supply from the village of Kisielnice or purchased the liquor supply himself. Mejer also regularly approached Jan on Lord

K.'s behalf for an "assignation" (funds drawn upon outstanding portions of quarterly lease payments to pay workers, make purchases, and so on). As compensation for his bartending duties, Jan received 20 percent of the liquor profits from Mejer, in addition to the small plot on which the tavern itself stood and two *morgs* of land (about 2.7 acres) for cultivating his own crops, all of which was technically leased by Mejer's son Bendyt.[7] Then Józef Pomikowski, a forty-five-year-old Christian bartender in Kobylin, admitted that Mejer also occasionally collected the proceeds from liquor sales in his tavern, and that he brought the money to Lord K. so that he could pay his workers. In other words, Mejer was doing everything short of directly selling the liquor.[8]

Mejer's own testimony further lays bare the mechanics of the thriving underground rural Jewish liquor trade. He was forty-four years old with five children, had been born in the village of Dobrochy, and had been leasing land and a cheap restaurant, formerly a tavern, in Kobylin for two years. As his lord's trusted administrator, involvement in the liquor trade was unavoidable:

> I made an agreement with Jan Smiarkowski to receive 20 percent of the liquor profits in Poryte. I also received a vegetable garden and a piece of land with a tavern on it. I also admit that frequently, when in Kisielnice, Lord Kisielnicki, as my lord, ordered me to bring vodka to Poryte twice a month for Smiarkowski. I also admit that during my trips to Kisielnice village Lord Kisielnicki gave me his assignation for the Poryte tavern, and that I gave the lord the money. Under no circumstance may I be judged as having sold liquor in the Poryte tavern.... I only went to Poryte on Lord Kisielnicki's business upon his express command.[9]

Mejer sought refuge under the old system of feudal patronage. His lord had ordered him to transport liquor and carry out other related tasks, and he had dutifully complied. District officials were not impressed. Mejer, his son Bendyt, and the rest of his family were summarily expelled.

The focus of the investigation then shifted back to Zelka, who had finally been located and brought back. Szymon Rutków, a forty-year-old Christian tavernkeeper in Kisielnice, testified that Zelka never sold alcohol; he only ran a cheap restaurant for Jews. Szymon obtained his vodka and beer directly from Lord K. and brought the proceeds of liquor sales to him to pay his workers, including Zelka. Finally, Zelka himself testified, asserting that he made his living from the cheap restaurant, farming, and a dairy lease.[10] But as he lived too close to a major road, officials expelled him as well.

Local Christians mobilized to fight Zelka's expulsion. In their petition to the authorities, all ten Christian interrogation subjects swore that Zelka only leased a dry restaurant. They even promised to donate money to the police court of Łomża in a demonstration of their fidelity to their oath about Zelka's innocence.[11] We do not know Zelka's fate, but we do know that on July 17, 1842, Solomon Blumrozen dropped his complaint and promised not to pursue it further, only to recant a month later. He complained that Lord K. had "exhausted and ruined" him in retaliation for the investigation he had instigated, and protested that he had not been given the opportunity to present his case or hear the accusations against him. But state officials refused to come to his aid, dismissing him as a "born troublemaker, who is himself guilty." He was on his own now.[12]

The transcripts of the Blumrozen Affair expose a whole array of occupations pursued by rural Jewish tavernkeepers in this period. Mejer dealt with liquor suppliers, processed payments, collected liquor proceeds for the nobleman, and leased land on behalf of his son, which he used to compensate his Christian bartender. In addition, he leased land for raising winter corn and leased cheap restaurants that provided accommodation and supplies for travelers. Zelka's dealings with liquor were just as extensive, if his rival Solomon is to be believed. In addition, Zelka raised cattle; ran his cheap restaurant; sold straw, oats, and hay; and farmed a plot of land. With the cooperation and support of local landowners and peasants, rural Jews somehow managed.

STATE ATTEMPTS TO LEGISLATE TAVERNKEEPING

How did this complex situation of what, in the eyes of the state, amounted to local collusion, evasion, and subterfuge, come about? The criminalization of Jewish tavernkeeping had roots in the prepartition era. During the first decades of the eighteenth century, a legislative tug of war ensued between clergy and reform-minded nobility on the one hand and more conservative nobility on the other. After several unsuccessful attempts by the former to abolish Jewish tavernkeeping in various districts, the 1768 Sejm (Polish diet) finally forbade Jews to run taverns in any towns without the agreement of municipal authorities.[13] Many landowners simply ignored the ban. But many Jewish liquor traders seem to have been pushed out of the towns of the eastern regions and into villages—according to one historian, as many as one-fifth of Polish-Lithuanian towns were virtually emptied of Jews, many of whom resumed tavernkeeping in villages. According to another estimate, more than half of the taverns in the Kiev and Bratslav Palatinates passed into Christian hands over the next twenty years.[14] The Hasidic leader (tzaddik) Menaḥem Mendel of Vitebsk (1730–88) did not consider the measures disastrous, since most Jews whose livelihoods had depended on tavernkeeping simply found new occupations, he claimed.[15] Nevertheless, the enduring perception of pervasive Jewish tavernkeeping set off a high-level debate during the four-year Sejm. A special deputation to the Sejm reiterated past resolutions forbidding Jews from leasing local liquor monopolies and actually proposed extending citizenship to any Jew involved in "useful industry," which included agriculture and crafts but expressly excluded "alcohol retail."[16] Yet certain noblemen insisted that it was their right to staff their taverns with whomever they chose, and saw to it that a proposed ban on rural liquor sales by Jews never even made it to the floor. There was simply no coherence to landowner demands. Some instigated bans on tavernkeeping; others blocked, repealed, or ignored them.[17]

Following the partitions of Poland, liquor policies varied according to each regime and appeared inconsistent. But the common driving principle was cameralism—the attempt to maximize state revenue by dissolving ethnic economic niches and "productivizing" the populace. Applied to Jews, this meant their abandonment of leaseholding and petty trade and transition into "useful" pursuits like agriculture or crafts, though this was to be encouraged only insofar as state revenues were enhanced and order and stability were maintained.[18] These caveats are crucial, for while state imperatives could overlap with those of reformist and entrepreneurial nobles, state officials were more motivated by a drive to homogenize, control, and exploit the country's human capital. They accordingly recoiled at the disorder caused by their own bans and expulsions, and often repealed or stopped enforcing them.

The first decisive assault on Polish Jewish tavernkeeping occurred as part of Joseph II's reforms in Galicia (Austrian Poland). Joseph forbade the awarding of new liquor leases to Jews on February 9, 1784, over the protests of prominent Polish landowners.[19] Decrees issued the following year abolished Jewish leaseholding in general.[20] The combined effect was the displacement of around fifteen thousand Jewish families, many of whom gravitated to larger towns. However, Joseph relented somewhat five years later in response to numerous complaints, and the process of involuntary urbanization began to reverse itself. A 1789 patent reinstated the right of Jews to contract leases for markets, stalls, pastures, and roads in towns and permitted Jews to return to the countryside as farmers and manufacturers, while those who currently possessed licenses were allowed to resume selling alcohol in their own homes. Though the patent still expressly forbade Jews to lease taverns, the restriction was only enforced—unevenly, at that—until Joseph's brother Leopold's ascension to the throne in 1790. The new emperor prudently heeded the protests of Polish landowners, who blamed their revenue losses on the Jewish tavernkeeping ban, and allowed enforcement to lapse almost completely.[21]

The first major state-sponsored assault on the Jewish liquor trade thus failed, like Joseph's other ambitious agrarian schemes, because of landowner pressure.[22] A policy of nonenforcement endured for much of the next century, and there was little new legislation apart from a prohibition against selling drinks to peasants on credit in 1796 that was so ineffective as to require reiteration in 1804. Soon, it was as if nothing had happened at all. Nineteenth-century memoirists attested to a flourishing and uncontested rural Jewish liquor trade throughout Galicia.[23] Prominent novelists and playwrights like Stanisław Wyspiański (1869–1907) often set their Jewish-run taverns in Galician towns and villages.[24] Beginning in 1879, a new genre of Galician anti-Semitic tracts reveled painfully in the pervasiveness of Jewish-run taverns, tracing all drunkenness, usury, corruption, theft, contraband, cheating, speculation, national division, foreign influence, and generational decline back to them. One gains the impression that Jewish tavernkeepers retained their prominence longer in Galicia than in any other area of the partitions.[25]

Events transpired in a similar way, albeit on a smaller scale, in the Polish lands absorbed into Prussia. Here, the Jewish liquor trade was banned in villages in 1793 but Prussian officials, fearing an influx of unemployed rural Jewish tavernkeepers into towns, could not bring themselves to fully implement it.[26] The regime also made little headway during its decade-long occupation of parts of central Poland. In 1805, King Frederick Wilhelm directly notified a nobleman of his "discontent" about the latter's continued employment of Jewish lessees in his taverns, breweries and distilleries in the town of Mogielnica, and demanded their immediate removal. The nobleman retorted that Mogielnica was his inherited town and denied that any law had been broken. "From the moment Mogielnica was acquired by my honored father," he argued, "the local liquor monopoly [*propinacja*] was given to no one but Jews, and similarly after the third year that I received Mogielnica none other [than a Jew] was given the local liquor monopoly." Considering that long tradition, how could it be that "this year it is suddenly against your kingdom's laws"? The noble had, moreover, received no notification whatsoever about a prohibition against granting Jews liquor leases. He at least required some warning before he could remove Jews, and insisted that the king absolve him since he was unable to install anyone else at the moment. The matter seemed to rest there, indicative of a wider sense of resignation among officials in the Prussian partition, who complained in 1844 that the Jews' "economic and occupational habits, especially those created by petty trading and the sale of alcohol, are still damaging the lower classes of the people, among whom the traditional religious viewpoint still dominates."[27]

The most far-reaching and painful measures occurred in Polish territories incorporated into the Russian Empire, which formed most of the Pale of Settlement. In 1783, the new Byelorussian governor-general P. B. Passek temporarily deprived Jews of the right to distill liquor, but landowners pressured the Senate to reaffirm that right two years later.[28] Then came Tsar Alexander's 1804 statutes. According to the infamous Article 34, "No Jew . . . in any village or in the countryside, is allowed to hold a lease on a tavern, drinking house, or inn, either in his own name or in another's, nor to sell liquor, nor even to live where this is done, except when passing through."[29] Actual expulsions were planned for sixty thousand Jewish families in 1808 and were sporadically carried out, but were halted by imperial decree for fear of arousing Jewish disloyalty during the impending Napoleonic Wars.[30] A remarkably liberal Jewish Committee of 1812 counseled against future expulsions on ethical grounds, adding that, in any case, they would not alleviate the peasants' drinking problem in the least. After all, they reasoned, Christian tavernkeepers would surely seek profits just the same as Jews.[31]

Yet a decade later, after a famine in 1821, as many as twenty thousand Jews in the Chernigov and Poltava provinces were expelled at the instigation of the Malorussian (Ukrainian) military governor, Prince Nicholas Repnin.[32] The trauma of these expulsions was such that Hasidic leader Abraham Joshua Heschel (1748–1825) declared a public fast. Hasidic tradition even interpreted these expulsions in eschatological terms ("Prior to the coming of the Messiah," a Polish tzaddik is said to have reassured R. Abraham, "all Jews will be evicted from the villages").[33] But it was not Jewish observers alone who were horrified by the expulsions. Polemics raged within the tsarist bureaucracy itself until the expulsions were finally halted by Repnin's replacement, Vasili Levashov, in late 1835.[34] Eventually (in 1850), the government instituted a crippling excise tax and limited the right to lease taverns to first guild merchants. But this at least made it possible for Jews like the memoirist Ezekiel Kotik's grandfather to lease the excise tax, accumulate great wealth, and regulate the activities of the still numerous Jewish tavernkeepers in Kamenets.[35] As in Galicia, bans and expulsions could not be sustained.

Liquor policies in the Russian Pale of Settlement were not automatically applied in the Kingdom of Poland, a semiautonomous, constitutional entity that was only half-absorbed into the Tsarist Empire. Instead, the tsar, as "king" of Poland, maintained the lucrative policy inherited from the predecessor state, the Napoleonic Duchy of Warsaw (1807–14): increasingly expensive liquor concessions as a prelude to outright expulsions. The architect of that policy had been Minister of Police Ignacy Sobolewski (1770–1846), who considered the problem of Jewish "control" of the liquor trade a central concern. (According to available data, Jews may have still leased around 85 percent of all taverns and distilleries.) Sobolewski had to move fast, since Napoleon's expected conquest of Lithuania could bring hundreds more Jewish tavernkeepers and their landowner enablers into the picture. He dismissed landowner warnings that outlawing the Jewish liquor trade would provoke mass Jewish emigration, for, he reasoned, what country would take them in? Nor did he take seriously landowner predictions of dire financial losses, as he was sure they would easily find Christian replacements.[36]

On October 30, 1812, an all-out ban on Jewish tavernkeeping was decreed for the Duchy of Warsaw. From July 1, 1814, on, "no Jews, whether in a town or a village, [would] be allowed to sell, produce, or serve any liquor, not under their own name, nor under an assumed name, nor on someone else's account as a colleague, agent, assistant, servant, worker, or under any other title." Any Christian who facilitated a Jew's sale of liquor was to be punished. In the two-year interim, Jewish tavernkeepers were required to purchase a liquor concession (*konsens*). The probable function of Jewish-specific concessions—though never articulated—was to incentivize honesty and loyalty among a mistrusted segment of the population, for any short-term gains from cheating, abetting criminals and enemies of the state, and so on would be overwhelmingly offset by the permanent loss of a concession for which the Jew had already paid dearly. Concessions also enabled officials to keep tabs on their bearers, for each one noted its bearer's age, height, hair and eye color, distinguishing marks, facial and body type, and even nose shape.[37]

But Napoleon had already begun his long retreat from Moscow. His defeat, and the creation of the tsarist Kingdom of Poland in 1815, reopened the question of Jewish tavernkeeping. A flurry of pamphlets by Polish publicists urged the complete removal of Jews from the liquor trade in the countryside in order to rehabilitate society in general and the peasant in particular. All of society's ills were attributed to rural Jewish tavernkeepers. They "draw farmers, their wives, and even their children into alcohol addiction," one publicist claimed, "to such an extent that the poor farmer has drinks in his head half the time and despair the other half, probably surrendering the last of his yearly harvest to the Jew and his drinks."[38] In autumn, another claimed, Jews collect their debts in the form of grain and livestock, sometimes with the assistance of the landowner or gendarmes. Peasants often had to borrow animals and implements from the landowner for the preharvest.[39] According to another, rural Jewish tavernkeepers falsified measures, illegally sold peasants alcohol on credit, and destroyed both them and their lords.[40] One landowner at least admitted the culpability of his own group: "We skinned the peasant using the Jew's nails." (After all, it was the nobles who owned the taverns.) But his was an isolated voice.[41]

Yet there is little support for the common assumption that the accusations of publicists profoundly shaped the regime's Jewish policy.[42] Liquor concessions were just too lucrative. If any nongovernmental group in the kingdom affected the legislation process at this stage it was the Jewish lay leadership, whose lobbying efforts and 120,000-zloty bribe to the powerful Nicholas Novosiltsev (ca. 1768–1838), in addition to dramatic petitions and delegations to the tsar himself, achieved an indefinite postponement of the 1812 ban. Novosiltsev's proposed bill regulating the status of the new kingdom's Jewish population actually permitted rural Jews to continue running taverns, though his bill was rejected with horror by the Council of State: "As long as the liquor connection between Jewry and the populace is not broken," the council's spokesman, Kajetan Koźmian, proclaimed in response to that suggestion, "Polish towns will not emerge from decay, villages from poverty, agriculture from infancy, and the common people from ignorance."[43] Polish policy makers were also willing to consider the Jewish policies of other like-minded rulers at that stage. Interior Minister Tadeusz Mostowski (1776–1842) made inquiries into policies in Galicia, and in 1816 resolved to emulate their prohibition against Jewish liquor sales to peasants on credit, which proved as ineffective in the Kingdom of Poland as it had in Galicia.[44]

For the most part, Polish officials sustained the concessions policy introduced during the Duchy of Warsaw era. The only significant departure was the price: concessions rose from an average of fifty zlotys (1815) to four hundred zlotys (1824) to 650 zlotys (1828).[45] Memos to Viceroy Józef Zajączek (1752–1826) reveal that the steady escalation of liquor concessions in the kingdom was intended to gradually squeeze Jews out of the liquor trade: "were the Jewish payments for permission to sell liquor in taverns to gradually increase," Sobolewski confided, "the number of those making a living from this pursuit would continually diminish and they would be forced to support themselves from other kinds of occupations."[46] This vice-like method also had the convenient effect of squeezing out handsome revenue for the state, to such a degree that it was pursued consistently throughout the first half of the century despite a chorus of dissenting voices from reform-minded landowners, who would be satisfied with nothing less than outright expulsion, and conservative landowners who complained, in contrast, that Jewish attrition from the liquor trade was hurting their profits.[47]

There was, of course, a human cost to this strategy. In 1825, right before the convocation of the first Jewish Committee, which consulted with an Advisory Committee composed of Jews, leaseholders from the Podlasie district delivered a rare Hebrew petition to "our Jewish lords on the Advisory Committee," whom they were sure were concerned about "the common good [tovat ha-klal]." Jewish villagers and urban merchants alike, they claimed, had no way to support themselves because all Jews leasing plots from the nobility, even those with no tavern on them, were saddled with such exorbitant concession fees that "it would be impossible to support oneself even if 'the land yields crops' [var. on Deut. 11] and 'the wine presses are filled' [var. on Joel 2]." Even Leipzig merchants who leased land in the countryside were forced to pay concessions on nonexistent taverns. (According to Privy Minister Turkul, this was occurring because "Jews, under the pretext of leasing lands, in actuality engage in the sale of drinks on these lands, without paying the tax to which the rest of their coreligionists are subject.")[48] "How many thousands of souls of Israel cry out for bread when there is none, and what is there to do?" the petitioners intoned. "And the merciful tsar, may he be exalted, is far away and we cannot reach him, and whom can we call on for help?"[49]

Viceroy Zajączek himself was concerned about destitution among erstwhile tavernkeepers. Three years earlier, he had asked the Interior Ministry to examine whether the escalation of liquor concessions and the removal of Jews selling liquor on state land might in fact be the cause of "current Jewish misery," which included a recent epidemic among former rural Jewish tavernkeepers.[50] On November 15, 1822, the Interior Ministry reassured him that this was not the case. There were no former tavernkeepers among the dead and their plight had been exaggerated. According to the Treasury's figures, 649 Jews had dropped out of the liquor trade on state land, and 5,215 Jews had been evicted unilaterally from land owned by the Polish nobility. Among these Jews, sixty-seven had resumed the sale of liquor in Warsaw. Therefore, the total number of Jewish families that were driven out of the liquor trade amounted to only 5,797. (In actuality, the number of Jewish families that dropped off official registers had reached 13,565 that year.)[51] As the typical Jewish family consisted of four to five members, the Interior Ministry calculated, only a total of 28,985 Jews, or one-tenth of the Jewish population of the country, were driven out of tavernkeeping, most by landowners of their own accord.[52]

The report offered different reasons for Jewish destitution than costly liquor concessions and expulsions. First was excessive Jewish reproduction (notwithstanding its own estimate of only two to three children per family), for as the Jewish population increased, so did its misery. Another culprit was assuredly Jewish culture: "The misery of our Jews derives from their superstitions and customs, which set this people apart from other classes of inhabitants." The Jews of the kingdom were, finally, impoverished because "instead of competing in only good, natural trades" they avoided real work. The report observed that "it would be of great benefit to the state were Jews to conquer their disgust for those branches of industry in which people of other faiths engage, which are equally open to [Jews], and from which it is suitable for them to benefit."[53] The report added, surprisingly enough, that "*no* industry in our country is forbidden to them. And even the commendable right of citizenship in this country is guaranteed by the royal decree of October, 1808, to those who worthily renounce their distinguishing [Jewish] symbols." Zajączek was reminded that the "main harm and persecutory force for Jews was the kahal [Jewish communal self-government]," and that as all kahals had been formally dissolved earlier that year, Jews were now free to enter agriculture, purchase land, enter domestic servitude, build roads, or work in factories. The Jewish-owned factory in the Marymont district of Warsaw was offered as an example.[54]

The report's callousness is hard to deny. If one-tenth of the entire Jewish population had indeed lost its main source of livelihood (a more accurate estimate was one-fifth, although many went underground), then the effects of liquor concessions were hardly negligible.[55] While it was easier to blame landowner evictions for Jewish departures on private lands, they were more likely due to the fact that many Jews were too financially stretched by concession fees to meet their lease payments. Even less just were the charges of Jewish contempt for "honest" work. The training of Jews as craftsmen had met considerable resistance owing to guild prerogatives.[56] As for land ownership and the establishment of factories, only a few of the most wealthy and influential Jews in the Kingdom of Poland managed to obtain the right.[57] How ironic that the report should mention the factory in Marymont, which was established by Józef Bereksohn for the production of calico: the government had actually denied Bereksohn's petition for permanent residence in Warsaw on behalf of his six Jewish dyers, who came from various villages, despite his insistence that they had mastered the craft better than his English workers.[58] Nor did the 1821 abolition of the kahals, the "main harm and persecutory force for Jews," provide any real improvement for Jewish economic prospects. Kahals were, in any case, replaced by new Jewish representative bodies known as "Synagogue Councils." The Interior Ministry thus completely denied the government's role in creating a minor human catastrophe, preferring blame the Jews themselves.[59]

The report would thus appear to justify older explanations of Jewish policy based on official anti-Semitism. Yet the Interior Ministry's recommendations for how to alleviate Jewish destitution reveal a powerful counter pressure to anti-Jewish animus: the government should allow Jews to acquire land, which—it is important to note—remained the primary source of wealth and status. The Treasury should designate substantial tracts of state land for agriculture for all Jews, allowing them to make use of Treasury forests and fields and to purchase or lease village land; and the Treasury should exempt the new farmers from special Jewish taxes, the author insisted. The agricultural proposal is strange given the authors' suspicions about the Jewish work ethic and Mostowski's own prior warnings that Jewish farmers would surely exert a negative influence on peasants. But taken together the recommendations betray a genuine cameralist optimism about diverting rural Jewish energies into "positive" pursuits.[60] A law permitting Jews to lease land under certain conditions was passed the very next year.[61]

The Interior Ministry's was not the only report to merge anti-Jewish sentiment with cameralist optimism. Another went much further, warning that "a secret Jewish society has come to light only now which is doubtlessly expanding throughout our entire land and will undoubtedly expand into neighboring lands and anywhere that Jews live."[62] This Jewish cabal was currently accumulating members and planning an insurrection, the anonymous author claimed. An investigation that very day had revealed that a society in Sokołów was collecting contributions for Jews in Jerusalem for the purpose of funding a "Jewish revolution." He therefore proposed twenty-eight tough restrictions on Jewish life, including, of course, the demand that "Jews must be completely expelled from taverns." And yet, if Jews were willing to go into crafts and farming and "eradicate every difference between them and Christians," they should be awarded citizenship and relieved of all special taxes, he advised.

In 1826, the new government-appointed Jewish Committee proposed a tough-love policy of swift, total expulsion from the liquor trade in accordance with the intentions of the original 1812 decree. "Taverns and bars are a favorite vocation for [Jews] and a most harmful one for the country," the committee report argued. "The more they enter onto a different, nobler path, the more our country will benefit. But this path has not yet been cleared for them. Only when they are deprived of the first means of supporting themselves will the second path open up." Jews had lost a great deal of profit as a result of costly liquor concessions, but were trapped in a kind of stupor, self-destructively clinging to their taverns. Wrenching them from the liquor trade would benefit not only Christians but Jews themselves.[63]

It is remarkable how different the attitudes of these Jewish Committee members were from those of their earlier Russian counterparts. In 1807, the Russian Jewish Committee had urged the tsar to desist from his policy of "resettling" Jewish tavernkeepers from the countryside on the grounds that it would inevitably "bring complete destruction" upon as many as 60,000 families and result in widespread social disorder and disloyalty at a time when war with France was becoming a real possibility.[64] The Russian Jewish Committee of 1812 explained that the difficulty in removing Jews from the liquor trade lay not in the Jews' stubbornness, nor in local political authorities' ineptitude, but rather in historical circumstances. When the ancient kingdom of Israel was overthrown, Jews had been scattered throughout the world and forced to engage in whatever economic opportunities were left to them by native residents. They found tolerance and freedom in Poland-Lithuania, where the nobility took full advantage of their arrival. As distilling and leaseholding were the main sources of the nobility's profits, and as Jews were forbidden to purchase land themselves, Jews had been "forced at the pleasure of the landlords, on whose lands they were settled, to give themselves over exclusively to the sale of vodka." Expulsions of Jewish tavernkeepers might actually succeed in turning Jews into farmers and farmers into tavernkeepers; but this would merely deprive landowners of their best workers in both areas! Nor would expulsions actually temper the peasants' drinking habits, the ultimate goal.[65]

In a similar spirit, key Polish officials spoke out against the 1826 Jewish Committee's recommendations. Ignacy Badeni (1786–1859), director of the Administrative Council of the Interior Ministry, doubted that Jewish tavernkeepers could easily be forced onto agricultural settlements, since many Jews (2,314 by his count) preferred to pay the liquor concessions even if it meant destitution. He also seized upon cameralism's main contradiction: If we acknowledge the idleness and dishonesty of Jews, he argued, then how does it make sense to place land in their hands? Would they not further demoralize the peasantry in the countryside? Badeni also dared to question the logic of curtailing the Jewish liquor trade, or any other trade for that matter. "In my opinion," he boldly concluded, "no type of industry can be considered inappropriate for classes who, for lack of land, do not engage in farming."[66]

Matteusz Muszyński, a clerk in the Consumption Tax Office, spoke out against the Jewish Committee's expulsion proposal on a combination of pragmatic and humanitarian grounds. Outright expulsion of Jewish tavernkeepers in 1812, when it was originally decreed, would have deprived the Treasury of substantial liquor concession revenue. Moreover, "suddenly cutting off 17,561 families from their livelihood without opening up for them other means for making a living would have been like setting their houses ablaze" and would only have succeeded in increasing the number of vagrants and criminals in the kingdom. Muszyński included a table to demonstrate how the rising liquor concession policy had satisfied the intent of the 1812 decree without such collateral damage. Fifteen thousand Jewish families had been squeezed out of the liquor trade, and the number of officially registered Jewish tavernkeepers had plunged from 17,561 in 1814 to a mere 2,329 in 1828, a sevenfold decline. As for the agricultural solution, Muszyński argued that it was far better to start with a few Jewish farmers, whose success would entice other Jews, than to drive Jews into farming en masse.[67] The recommendations of the 1826 Jewish Committee received little further consideration.[68]

Many studies of the decline of Jewish tavernkeeping in the Kingdom of Poland end with Muszyński's figures, creating the impression that Jewish tavernkeeping continued to dwindle to nothing.[69] Such logic places an unwarranted trust in official data gathered for a polemical purpose. It moreover leaves us without an explanation for the continued polemics against rural Jewish tavernkeepers over the next decades and, no less problematically, overlooks the widespread practice of using Christian fronts for taverns.

But even if we were guided solely by official legislation and data, this impression would be false. The only way that officials of the increasingly desperate Polish Revolutionary regime could think to win Jews over to their cause during the 1830 uprising was to grant them liquor concessions. In early 1831, a Płock county commissioner proposed free liquor concessions as a way to "interest the Jewish people in wider national matters." Such an initiative would demonstrate the "vast good will of the regime, and [Jews] would become advantageous in wartime."[70] Another county administrator agreed that "in consideration of the powerful feeling among distillers amid residents that they are suffering losses," and in view of the fact that "Jews are free to engage in other industries without [concession] payments," the central government should permit Jews to run concession-free taverns. Such benevolence would "favorably incline them to our good cause."[71]

The proposal faced stiff opposition. The Treasury argued that the "present threatening moment of war" necessitated Jewish liquor concession revenue.[72] The presiding minister also opposed the measure, calling attention to the 1812 decree and reiterating the government's goal to "gradually free the production and sale of liquor from the Jewish people, which was achieved by raising the costs of concessions each year." Like Muszyński, he was satisfied that "over the past sixteen years we may say that the first praiseworthy aim of freeing the village residents from the immoral influence of Jewish-sold drinks was almost completely achieved. Landowners were not only ensured profits from local liquor monopolies without harm, but new branches of liquor production had been opened to them . . . along with new branches of the grain trade." What the Płock delegation was proposing would not only allow Jews to "temporarily sell liquor and demoralize the peasants, but also bring about their collapse by means of establishing numerous distilleries in the country; . . . and without achieving the intended goal of inclining Jews to the national cause, we would lose the country in several years." Finally, he pointed out, the Treasury would lose 961,300 zlotys from the concession, which it could ill afford.[73]

If a policy of free liquor concessions was deemed unaffordable, however, few could argue against expanding the number of Jews eligible to purchase liquor concessions on fiscal grounds. That summer, as the Polish revolutionary army began to suffer serious reversals, the Treasury decided to allow Jews who had possessed concessions prior to 1821 to purchase them again in Stanisława County "in consideration of the present calamities." This would roughly triple the number of qualifying Jews, which would both allow "a large number of Jewish residents of Stanisława to support themselves" and, at the same time, "allow public revenues to satisfy the needs of the nation."[74] Soon, in view of a need for "relief from the enormous catastrophe caused by the current military losses in the Mazovia district and damages to a significant part of Stanowica estate," the Polish revolutionary regime extended the eligibility policy throughout the kingdom. Openly Jewish-run taverns sprang up all over the place.[75]

At the same time, many Jews were already running taverns illicitly. And to judge by those cases preserved in the archives of the revolutionary regime, their punishments were light when they were discovered. For example, the regime looked into a complaint by the mayor of Biały that a Jew named Józef Weinthal was producing and selling liquor without a concession.[76] During the ensuing investigation, Chaim Joselowicz Berier testified that Józef, along with several residents, had engaged continually in the sale of vodka and beer without a concession, and that he had sold about ten gallons of vodka and beer purchased from the Granowski tavern. Esther, who ran the Granowski tavern, testified that she had indeed sold Józef liquor because he had claimed to have a concession but swore that Rabbi Dawidsohn had intervened and anulled the sale. Józef Tyski testified that when the Christian tavernkeeper Mackiewicz was living in the accused's house (presumably as Józef Weinthal's front), he had never seen him produce or sell liquor, but he had seen the accused give vodka and beer to various travelers upon request. Mackiewicz corroborated this testimony, adding that Józef often lent him vodka. But others admitted that Józef had either sold or given them liquor.

Józef denied the accusations, maintaining that when someone came into his guesthouse and needed beer or vodka, he "took the travelers' money, supplied them with drinks, and brought the money to the lessee of the local liquor monopoly. He never enjoyed any advantage from it."[77] The commission settled on an awkward compromise. While he was liable for double the concession fee, six hundred zlotys plus the costs of the criminal proceedings, Józef's fee was reduced to one-sixth of the amount and he was absolved of responsibility for the costs of the proceedings. Józef asked to be forgiven the entire amount since his innocence had been acknowledged (either he was innocent or guilty, he reasoned), but was denied. Still, his sentence was light in comparison to similar proceedings in other periods.[78]

Openly Jewish-run taverns continued to spring up. In the wake of the uprising, the tsarist regime sometimes compensated Jewish families whose members had been killed by Polish troops, and compensation nearly always took the form of a liquor concession. Berek Kolinski, a tavernkeeper's son, reported that his father had been murdered by Polish insurrectionists in 1831 and that his widowed mother had received a liquor concession for the town of Kolno as compensation. Now his mother was eighty years old and ill and could neither work as a tavernkeeper nor afford the concession. Berek asked officials to let her have the concession for free or to at least allow him to purchase the concession in his own name as a reward for his father's "loyalty to the true regime." The last phrase suggests that his father may have indeed been aiding the Russians, although there was an obvious motivation for saying so.[79]

The postuprising period saw both new residential privileges for wealthy Jewish liquor traders and new liquor concessions for less wealthy Jews thanks to the grim pragmatism of the kingdom's new viceroy, Ivan Paskevich (1782–1856). As long as political conditions in the kingdom felt unstable, Paskevich valued Jewish loyalty and Jewish entrepreneurship more than Jewish social or economic normalization. A major Jewish liquor manufacturer named Abraham Winawer obtained special residential rights in Warsaw in exchange for an annual contribution of thirty-four thousand gulden to the treasury. And over one-quarter of the Jewish liquor concessions in state-owned Mazovian towns by 1837 were doled out during the six years following the uprising.[80] Surreptitious Jewish tavernkeeping seems to have been just as widespread. "For a certain amount of time since the Revolution," complained one reformist landowner in 1831, "many lessees and possessors of liquor monopolies have, without consideration of the law, installed Jews in breweries and taverns, some of which are in villages and on Catholic roads, where in practically every case Jews engage in the enterprise without concessions." The anonymous writer considered this an abuse of the Treasury and "enormously inconsiderate of the law," and recommended that owners of liquor monopolies who engaged in such deception, that is, nobles, be denounced to the regime and fined accordingly.[81] A few years later, another reform-minded nobleman corroborated the open secret of underground, concession-free Jewish tavernkeeping.[82]

It proved almost impossible to stamp out. Part of the reason was a lack of will: tsarist officials, stung by the yearlong success of the Polish insurrectionists, had bigger fish to fry, while landowners considered Jewish tavernkeepers crucial to the restoration of their war-ravaged estates. But an even more important reason was the favored tactic, the employment of Christian fronts. This tactic, seen already in the Blumrozen Affair, was readily and widely adopted by Jews because it was merely a natural extension of the well-entrenched practice of using Christian fronts to evade economically debilitating Sabbath and festival restrictions. Jewish tavernkeepers had already been employing Christians to evade their own laws for centuries.

RABBINIC ATTEMPTS TO LEGISLATE TAVERNKEEPING

To the extent that historians have considered the Jewish perspective on official liquor policy at all, they have taken the occasional protests by Jewish lay leaders to indicate universal Jewish distress.[83] But internal Jewish sources betray a deep ambivalence about tavernkeeping on the part of rabbis. Some rabbis expressed discomfort over the violence and sinful behavior associated with the occupation.[84] However, the principal objection was not tavernkeeping per se but rather the tendency among tavernkeepers to violate or circumvent prohibitions against liquor production and sales on Sabbaths and festivals in order to keep their taverns profitable.[85] An examination of rabbinical sources shows that Jewish tavernkeepers were actually engaged in a two-front struggle, against both the state and their own religious leaders. The latter struggle had been raging for centuries.

In 1590, Rabbi Meshullam Phoebus of Krakow authored what would become the basis for future rabbinic decrees (*takanot*): a lengthy condemnation of the widespread practice of selling beer, mead, and liquor on the Sabbath by means of non-Jews. Owners of taverns (*brey-hoyz*) were leasing their establishments to gentiles on Sabbaths and festivals and completing unfinished work after sundown. Many were serving Jewish and Christian customers on the Sabbath and collecting payment later in the week. (Meshullam Phoebus actually permitted this practice in the case of Jewish customers, who at least knew not to bring the bottles outside the permissible domain.) They were even raising pigs, which could be fed from the byproducts of brewing and distilling. Each kahal in the Krakow District was instructed to appoint enforcers armed with the power to fine and excommunicate.[86] Rabbis in the Lithuanian provinces tried repeatedly to combat similar practices.[87] Two later rabbinic decrees, one from Ludmir (Włodzimierz/Volodymyr-Volyn'skyi), dated 1612, and one from an unidentified locale, dated after 1648, accused tavernkeepers of continuing to employ questionable methods on Sabbaths and festivals. Some were leasing their taverns to their gentile servants on those days. Others were having gentiles come in to repair machinery on the Sabbath, when it was not in use.[88]

More than one rabbinic authority went so far as to blame the Chmielnicki massacres of 1648 on village tavernkeepers. According to R. Bezalel Darshan of Przemyśl, "The blood of fathers and sons, the blood of pious men and women, the blood of saintly men and women, and the blood of baby boys and girls still suckling at their mothers' breasts who had never sinned or committed any crime (many were trampled by horses and did not even receive a partial burial), and the blood of rabbis and their disciples was spilled like water" in 1648. Why had God displayed such wrath toward a land so filled with Torah, wisdom, and good deeds? "God is righteous; it is *we* who are wicked because of our repeated desecrations of the Sabbath." More specifically, "a select group, the majority of village dwellers who undertake businesses called leaseholding [*arendas*]" was responsible. Although some were righteous and pious, regularly gave charitable donations to the poor, and provided livelihood for Torah scholars (an allusion to wealthier, large-scale lessees), "most of them do not observe the Sabbath, because of our many sins. For all their livelihood is with the villagers, and they mingle with them and learn their ways." Those tavernkeepers were accustomed to "buy and sell on the Sabbath through the agency of the villagers, all in a deceitful manner" and would order their gentile servants to "do this and that work, and sit with them and instruct them how to repair whatever has spoiled the job." Darshan had felt powerless to stop them: "Oy for my eyes, which saw this many times! And I had no way of protesting it." But now that so much blood had been spilled, so many Torah scrolls had been reduced to ashes, so many synagogues and study houses stood neglected, and so many orphans wandered helplessly throughout the land and abroad, perhaps they would listen.[89]

Apparently, they did not. An extant post-1648 rabbinic decree actually contains breathtaking leniency. The fact that village taverns were typically leased by Jews but owned by noblemen by this period provided an opening for more pragmatic rabbinic authorities. As in the countryside the lessee alone was responsible for providing beer for the entire local population, and as monopolistic restrictions prevented residents from buying beer from a different nobleman's domain, some rabbis deemed the tavernkeeper's position to be similar to that of a toll collector, who may continue to collect tolls on the Sabbath. A tavernkeeper could sublease his tavern to a gentile and even lend the gentile the sublease payment, provided it was lent on interest (which functioned as a service fee).[90]

The rabbis also permitted sales on Sabbaths and festivals when there was mock compulsion. Upon a tacit prearrangement, a nobleman or nobleman's servant could enter the tavern and "demand," with a threat of force, a quota of malt. His servant could then bring it outside the permitted domain and sell it or use it to produce beer or liquor. Any ordinary gentile could "demand" a quota of beer to bring outside the domain to sell as long as the original "demand" occurred on Friday afternoon. Finally, although a tavernkeeper was expressly forbidden to sell to his lodgers on the Sabbath, if a member of the lord's entourage or an upper clergyman demanded a drink while threatening violence, the sale was permissible. Such "threats" became pro forma, and help explain perceived rudeness.[91] This long experience in circumventing Jewish law by means of Christian collusion would prove invaluable when it became necessary to circumvent state law.

By the nineteenth century, legal fictions had become the norm. Rabbinical authorities sought only to curb the worst abuses and regulate fictitious sales. A Galician rabbi, Solomon Drimer of Skole (near Lemberg/Lviv, now in Ukraine), wrote of his inner struggle over the practice. "Selling" one's tavern to a gentile partner on Friday afternoon violated rabbinic law, he reasoned, yet there were extenuating circumstances: a recent change in the excise tax in Galicia made it impractical to cease operation entirely on the Sabbath. He felt less uncomfortable if the "transfer" occurred before Friday, which looked less suspicious. But in the end, he refused to commit to a decision. During the 1830s, he recalled, members of his community had approached him requesting contracts for fictitious sales. Drimer had consulted with his teacher, the rabbi of Buczacz, who proved reluctant to render any decision. So Drimer informed his community that, like his teacher, he would not render a decision either. However, if they could manage to procure a contract from another rabbi, he would not stand in their way. And thus they did: a rabbi from a nearby town proved willing to write up contracts for them. Drimer admitted, "Even had I ordered my community to be more strict, they would not have listened to me," because losses from ceasing operations were too great and the practice of fictitious sales was too rooted.[92] This episode illustrates a rabbi's impotence in enforcing his own standards of piety at the expense of his community members' livelihood, a subject already explored at length by historians.[93] But it also reveals a certain kind of piety among the community's tavernkeepers, who insisted on procuring *some* sort of legal fiction rather than simply ignoring Jewish law.

Nor was Drimer himself always so unyielding. Elsewhere in his collected responsa we find his own instructions for drawing up contracts for fictitious sales, preceded by a strange caveat: "I have a version of a fictitious sale contract somewhere, but it is difficult for me to look for it because I am extremely weak and receiving medical treatment, and it is even difficult for me to write. So I will write Your Eminence an abstract of this procedure, and Your Eminence will read between the lines."[94] Notwithstanding these protestations, Drimer proceeded to offer a lengthy and intricate description of a proper legal fiction. The main principle was to avoid having the gentile resemble an agent or a worker, both of whom were considered legal extensions of the owner himself. Instead, as the *Shulḥan arukh* commentary *Magen Avraham* explains, the gentile must resemble a junior partner. This was accomplished by lending the gentile his share of the lease payment on a small amount of interest and by allotting him one and a half days' worth of the tavern's profit, that is, an amount equivalent to a Sabbath day plus a buffer period, on a random weekday. One also had to be sure that all utensils were "leased" to the gentile on the Sabbath, while all products (malt, hops, etc.) were "sold" to him.[95]

Rabbis in the Kingdom of Poland must have felt a similar ambivalence. But in 1804, the future chief rabbi of Warsaw and preeminent legal authority in the region, Solomon Lipschitz (1765–1839), put his foot down. In what reads like a throwback to the 1590 decree, he announced that "the tavernkeepers must act according to Torah and not profane the Sabbath. And it is appropriate to appoint enforcers for this purpose, for it would be difficult for me to enforce all of this by myself. And it is also too onerous for the lay leadership [*parnasim*]."[96] Lipschitz's very acceptance of a rabbinical position, he proclaimed, was an act of self-sacrifice motivated by exactly those kinds of Sabbath desecrations. "It was difficult for me to accept the yoke of public office," he confessed, "and all my life I would have preferred to avoid it." But the high incidence of Sabbath violations among tavernkeepers had persuaded him that it was "the will of heaven." It is difficult to know what exactly Lipschitz meant by "Sabbath violations"—were rural tavernkeepers in his domain not even bothering with legal fictions, or did he consider their legal fictions invalid? Either way, it does not appear that Jewish tavernkeepers had an ally in the man who was soon to be appointed chief rabbi of the kingdom's capital.[97]

Leaders of the burgeoning Hasidic movement are known to have intervened on behalf of tavernkeepers to prevent the usurpation of their leases. But others strongly condemned tavernkeeping. The tzaddik Menaḥem Mendel of Vitebsk dismissed the Byelorussian bans on Jewish liquor leases as "a joke" and advised Jews to simply learn a new trade, since it was in any case a business "of ill repute and impervious to all blessings."[98] The tzaddik Menaḥem Mendel of Rymanów (Galicia; d. 1815) went furthest, publicly linking rural tavernkeeping with assimilation. Lessees of village taverns, he argued, could neither pray in quorums nor immerse themselves in ritual baths. Worse, they were violating the Sabbath, and their children were mingling with gentiles and "slipping into coarseness [*gashmiyut*]." R. Menaḥem Mendel actually supported the Galician bans of 1784–85 and, according to one tradition, went so far as to issue his own ban. But he soon had to relent. His star disciple, R. Naftali Tzevi of Ropczyce, allegedly made a dramatic pilgrimage to his court in the middle of winter and, nearly frozen to death, reminded his master that before his ban "we stopped to rest in each and every village, and we drank liquor and tea, and warmed ourselves until the next village, and then the next one." Now, on account of his master's ban on rural Jewish tavernkeeping, a Jewish merchant nearly froze to death during the winter months as he himself had for lack of Jewish hospitality. R. Menaḥem Mendel, according to this tale, was moved to rescind his decree.[99]

R.Menaḥem Mendel's fears about assimilation among rural tavernkeepers and their children were not unfounded. Assimilation is typically associated with urbanized elites who gain exposure to new ideas and fashions through their non-Jewish neighbors. But the pervasiveness of more passive forms of assimilation among rural Jews, in particular tavernkeepers, is corroborated by the memoirist Jan Slomka, who explains that in the old days, when there was a good deal more contact between Jews and Christians in villages, Jewish tavernkeepers' children "grew up so much with Catholic ones that they were converted." The baptisms had to take place in secret and the neophytes were forced to "keep out of sight for a while." Usually it was tavernkeepers' daughters who converted, marrying hired farmhands or sons of farmers.[100] Rural tavernkeepers gained a reputation for assimilation and conversion in the Kingdom of Poland, as well. The memoirist Y. Y. Trunk's maternal grandfather came from a family of "coarse Polish village Jews" and spent his childhood "among the peasants and gentile girls.... We swept that whole past under the carpet."[101] On Yom Kippur, one of the only times during the year when village Jews streamed into the towns to worship in synagogues and prayer houses, the tzaddik Moses Elyakim Beriyah of Kozienice fulminated against government officials who "taxed the village dwellers who leased *arendas* until they could no longer bear it," a reference to prohibitive liquor concession fees. "And because of our many sins, several of the villagers were forced to apostatize because of their need to make a living."[102]

Widespread conversion among rural Jewish tavernkeepers in the Kingdom of Poland is confirmed in an official investigation into complaints that Jewish customers were refusing to purchase liquor from apostate tavernkeepers. The latter were still technically Jewish according to Jewish law, but were assumed to be no longer complying with the legal requirement to sell off their leavened products to gentiles during the entirety of Passover.[103] Some rural Jewish tavernkeepers followed the self-proclaimed messiah Jacob Frank into Catholicism in 1759. Five years later, officials identified between seventy and eighty Frankists running taverns in nine villages in the Lublin District whose new Christian status immunized them from concessions and bans.[104] These cases of apostasy by rural tavernkeepers taught Jewish religious leaders to fear villages even more than cities, where at least there was a robust, segregated Jewish community. A Hasidic poet compared living in a village to courting a diseased gentile woman wearing a gold crown—one could profit handsomely from rural tavernkeeping, he implied, but only at the cost of lethal contamination.[105]

CRIMINALIZATION

Most rural tavernkeepers in the Kingdom of Poland did not convert to Christianity, choosing instead to either move to towns or conceal themselves behind Christian fronts. But in 1840, when the kingdom's political situation seemed to be stabilizing, the latter practice came under scrutiny. On November 18 of that year the State Council raised the alarm: on nearly every main road linking villages there were taverns where Jews simply "hire Christians to sell liquor."[106] The viceroy, Ivan Paskevich, responded with a kingdom-wide expulsion decree for Jews who resided in or near taverns along main roads in the countryside.[107] There was even talk of expelling all rural Jews, who were "commonly engaged in defrauding and ruining the villages through the greatest swindles" even when they were not running taverns.[108] But for now, local officials were instructed that "without exception, every Jew who under some pretext lives in a tavern by a main [rural] road is to be expelled."[109] This was the law that Solomon Blumrozen invoked when he informed on Zelka, Mejer, and Lord K.

Among the expulsion decrees and special appeals preserved in the Interior Ministry archives from that year, several stand out. Israel (Srul) Isaac Erlichman's home in Piaski (Lublin District) had been destroyed during a series of night fires and, though the lives of his family were spared, they were bereft of their property save a few articles of clothing. In a demonstration of noble paternalism, a certain Lord Prażmowski had taken them in, allowing them to settle in one of his villages and run a tavern. But the state would not leave them in peace to pursue even this "miserable living" and had expelled them. Israel protested that his cottage lay about three hundred feet from the tavern and that he did not harm the Treasury in any way (i.e., by evading concession payments). He begged the Interior Ministry to consider his sad condition as well as his "good morals and enlightenment," and enclosed testimony by the Piask Municipality confirming the night fire and loss of all his property. But the Lublin District governor reported that Israel's cottage was actually only eighteen feet from the tavern and that the inspector had caught him selling liquor there.[110]

Hirsz Goldszmidt, a watchmaker, claimed that he had been improperly expelled from his town by local Polish officials in retaliation for his pro-Russian activities during the 1830 uprising, and enclosed signed testimony by a Russian infantry captain citing his "services and operations" on behalf of the Russians. Vindictive local officials who supported the Polish cause had used the new ban on Jewish residence in taverns on main roads to expel him from the town, he claimed, though he did not even reside in a tavern. Hirsz requested that officials explicitly acknowledge his right to reside in his town and (as long as he was being accused of being a tavern-keeper anyhow) grant him a concession for running a tavern.[111]

Landowners sometimes personally intervened on behalf of "their" Jews, providing powerful evidence of the enduring lord-Jew relationship. When Mordecai Rozenblum was expelled from the village of Gudel (Augustów District), the owner of the village, Jan Rakussa, submitted an indignant appeal. Upon receiving word of the ban on Jewish liquor sales along major village roads, Lord Rakussa claimed, he had waited until the expiration of Mordecai's contract and then duly removed him from the tavern in deference to the law. But he had allowed Mordecai to continue to sell oats, straw, and hay and to run a cheap restaurant (*garkuchnia*) and tea shop for travelers on Petersburg Road. Lord Rakussa was adamant that Mordecai was not furtively selling liquor and maintained that he had warned him to do business in a separate building from the tavern, now run by a Christian named Michał Neth. Mordecai should therefore be allowed to stay and run his restaurant. After all, another Jew, named Dawidowicz, ran a cheap roadside restaurant in the village of Godlewo, and in any case the law only forbade Jews to reside in taverns by main roads.¹¹²

At this point Lord Rakussa laid bare his practical motivations: the unwarranted expulsion of the Jew Mordecai had caused him annual losses of one thousand zlotys. This expulsion was therefore a violation of his right to the full use of goods on his lands. In addition, the area was a trade hub for the county, and the loss of a cheap Jewish restaurant/hotel would inconvenience Jewish merchants by depriving them of a place to sojourn on the Sabbath. By eliminating the village's sole hospitality enterprise for Jews and its sole Jewish proprietor, the government had greatly impeded local trade, another infringement on Lord Rakussa's rights.¹¹³ Officials felt inclined to agree. But the police division upheld the expulsion on the grounds that Petersburg Road, where the restaurant lay, was used often by Viceroy Paskevich's family during their travels. It would not do to rouse his suspicions.¹¹⁴

The 1840 ban on Jewish roadside taverns was certainly discriminatory, but it should be understood against the backdrop of growing alarm over epidemic drunkenness in the kingdom. Liquor was becoming at once cheaper to produce and more profitable. Some taverns offered all-you-can-drink tickets for one and a half kopeks.¹¹⁵ It was by now customary for noblemen to pay their peasants for extra work with drinking vouchers (*kwitki*) instead of money. Taverns seemed to loom everywhere: "Whether by a main or side road, muddy, sandy, clay, filled with holes or ditches, taverns and bars hover like enchanted castles, and in one after the next there is cheaper and cheaper vodka."¹¹⁶ Villages had taken on a plundered and abandoned look. Children roamed around half-naked, their parents spending their days and nights in the tavern where "a great hubbub, screams, songs, or quarrels and brawls of the half-drunk and drunk resounded everywhere."¹¹⁷ One social critic had witnessed tipsy mothers "soothing their crying children by pouring liquor into their mouths instead of food." Peasants were forgoing meat for vodka, as only the latter could be had on credit. Outside the tavern, draped across fences, lying in gutters or almost anywhere else, drunken peasants were as common as mushrooms and stones.¹¹⁸ Early alcohol-related deaths were on the rise, with one hospital in the town of Rawa reporting thirty-three such fatalities in 1841 alone.¹¹⁹ In 1844, annual liquor consumption amounted to more than three gallons of 100-proof liquor per head, about six times that of mid-twentieth century Poland.¹²⁰ Lower clergy founded a temperance movement with a sharp anti-Jewish edge, and had some success extracting sobriety oaths from newlyweds.¹²¹

This last development smacked of subversion—only the state was supposed to be administering oaths in secular matters—and the tsar was finally moved to act.¹²² As of July 23, 1844, Christian-run taverns and distilleries were required to pay concession fees and other taxes.¹²³ Vodka could now be sold only during the seven months of winter, it was to be taxed, it could not be more than 47 percent alcohol, and it could not be overly cheap. Liquor voucher payments to peasants were outlawed. Music, understood as stimulating the urge to drink, was prohibited in taverns on all days except Sundays. The number of taverns was to be restricted according to town size, and there could only be one per village. Only middle- to large-scale landowners retained the right to distill vodka. It was now illegal to leave a drunk person unconscious in the street—tavernkeepers were required to bring them to the authorities—and in many cases guards were posted outside taverns, either permanently or on Sundays, Christian holidays, and market days. Not surprisingly, these regulations were rarely enforced, and the tavern police (*stupajków*) became objects of jokes and satires. But the state's ramped-up efforts to control alcohol production and sales would endure down to the 1848 revolutions, at which point the tsar thought it best to relax his grip.¹²⁴

On July 5, 1844, Jewish tavernkeeping in the countryside was finally outlawed altogether in the Kingdom of Poland.¹²⁵ A decree four years later forbade rural Jews from selling beer, mead, and wine. The result was a precipitous decline in officially registered Jewish tavernkeepers. In 1844, only 149 rural Jewish families (compared with 1,917 urban Jewish families) were registered in the liquor trade.¹²⁶ By 1858, there were officially none. Revenues from Jewish liquor concessions declined from 1,509,000 zlotys in 1820 to 107,000 zlotys in 1844, to 63,000 zlotys in 1858.¹²⁷ But this was more than compensated for by new taxes and concessions on Christian liquor establishments.¹²⁸

One might have expected a mass rural Jewish migration into towns and cities. Remarkably, however, the rural Jewish population held steady at around 15 percent of the total Jewish population throughout the entire legislative onslaught. In real terms, the Jewish population in villages approached seventy-five thousand at this point and would grow to eighty-nine thousand by 1858. Defying the current historiography's urbanization narrative, which assumes a rapid Jewish exodus from the villages, a hardened core of rural Jews who had survived the skyrocketing liquor concessions of the 1820s actually found ways to survive in the countryside, thanks in great part to local landowners' willingness to abet their continued involvement in the liquor trade.¹²⁹ Only outsiders were fooled: the poet-reformer Władysław Anczyc (1823–83), for example, criticized the growing number of Christian tavernkeepers in rural areas in comparison to all those "restless Jewboys," who were no longer running taverns but still managed to trade and engage in other useful occupations.[130] In fact, in 1858—the very year that rural Jewish tavernkeepers ceased to exist statistically—officials were once again noticing that Jews, under the guise of merely residing in taverns, were "secretly" continuing to engage in the sale of liquor.[131] The main effect of the 1844 ban on rural Jewish tavernkeeping had been to enlarge an already substantial underground Jewish liquor trade.

ABOVE-GROUND TAVERNKEEPING IN THE COUNTRYSIDE

As far as we can tell, the most common means of Jewish survival in the countryside after the 1844 ban was surreptitious involvement in the liquor trade. Bootlegging flourished as well.[132] Usually, local bureaucrats and police on meager salaries could be bribed with liquor, the region's "liquid currency," to look the other way.[133] But some Jews found legal ways to sell liquor in the countryside during the crackdown period. Jews could still lease state-owned land containing over ten peasant households and legally distill and sell liquor there, provided they used a Christian front, a curious endorsement of the very practice the authorities were trying to eradicate everywhere else.[134] Jewish merchants of the First Guild were sometimes permitted short-term leases on taverns.[135] Rural Jews continued to lease liquor excise taxes.[136] Those with urban liquor concessions or general leases (which usually included taverns) sometimes indirectly ran, legally or not so legally, taverns in villages.[137] In addition, since 1823 it had been legal for Christian tavernkeepers to hire Jewish employees to "serve other Jews according to Jewish requirements," which ensured a continued Jewish presence in rural taverns.[138] Finally, thanks to special privileges obtained in the wake of the 1830 uprising, several Jews were able to openly engage in the liquor trade in the countryside on a large scale during this period, the most brazen example being that of a Warsaw Jew named Matthias Cohn. His case reveals itself in the hitherto untapped files of the Treasury archives.

It began in 1854, when a Christian lessee named Franciszek Golębiowski decided not to renew his three-year liquor monopoly lease for the Samsonów network of twenty-six villages. His annual payment for the holdings had been 3,103 rubles, but he had lost about 4,500 rubles so far. No one was going to bid on the disastrous lease because it was "not worth half of what [he] paid." Franciszek declared that he was prepared to let the next three-year term go for half of what he had paid. His only desire was "to see that this liquor monopoly, for lack of any competition, did not fall into Jewish hands." He was all too aware that Jews in the nearby town of

Kielce "contented themselves with a small profit margin on vodka, which they sell cheaply to peasants." They would probably do the same with his liquor monopoly if given the chance.[139]

Franciszek finally managed to find a non-Jew to take the lease off his hands, Jan Milanowski. But the very next year, Jan himself was making inquiries with officials in Warsaw. He proclaimed that he had only assumed the lease himself as a "sacrificial offering to avoid a Jewish takeover." But at the end of his first year, Matthias Cohn and Raphael Glucksohn had approached him with an irresistible offer of 2,130 rubles annually for the next twelve years. Jan wanted to know whether he could pass the lease on to those Jews even though his contract expressly stated that he could not. Failure to do this, he insisted, would mean his ruin.

The Administrative Council confirmed that Matthias and Raphael had possessed special privileges for leasing rural liquor monopolies since the early 1830s, suggesting that their privileges were a reward for pro-Russian activities during the uprising. Matthias was eventually exempted from paying concession fees altogether. The Administrative Council approved the transfer of the lease to Matthias and Raphael with the stipulation that they not employ Jews to sell the liquor and that their privileges only be bequeathed to a direct line of descendants. In 1855, at the height of rural Jewish prohibition, Matthias and Raphael became the legal lessees of a twenty-six-village, twelve-year liquor monopoly.[140]

In contrast to the prior, non-Jewish, lessees, Matthias and Raphael did not wait for the unprofitable lease to somehow begin generating income. They began to build, constructing new taverns and staffing them with workers. At the same time, local authorities did everything they could to frustrate their plans. The county assessor first tried to claim that the term of the contract was only for one year. After this claim was refuted by authorities, the district commissioner refused to transfer the holdings to Matthias and Raphael because of outstanding lease payments: Franciszek and Jan had failed to take care of nine months' worth of expenses (according to Matthias and Raphael), or Matthias and Raphael had failed to fulfill certain obligations to Franciszek (according to Franciszek). In response to Matthias's relentless petitions, officials in the central government determined that, despite the probability that Matthias did have outstanding obligations to Franciszek, the district commissioner must confirm the Jews' lease. But the assessor continued to stall. He was busy with other tasks; then, he needed to be reassured that one lease could have two Jewish managers, particularly considering that Jews had been banned from selling liquor in villages. Four years would pass before Matthias and Raphael were able to take full control of the lease.[141]

Part of the reason for the holdup was a large-scale investigation. In 1859, privileged Jews like Matthias and Raphael came under scrutiny when Treasury officials discovered that a number of Jews were running taverns in towns and villages without concessions, "residing everywhere and litigating frequently against Christians" while ignoring Jewish restrictions on rural liquor sales. Some had purchased land and were hiring Christians to work it. Were certain exceptional Jews really allowed to do this, the Treasury inquired?[142] The Interior Ministry explained that certain Jews had indeed been granted special liquor concessions, transferable to their descendants, in the wake of the 1830 uprising, including Matthias Cohn, Rafael Glucksohn, Abraham Cohen, Lejzor Margulies, Enoch Henigsztejn, Chaim Rosenthal, and Solomon Glass. Their numerous progeny—sons, sons-in-law, grandsons, even nephews—were now utilizing those privileges. Such privileged Jews had increased through reproduction to the point that the regime's program to dissolve the rural Jewish liquor trade was being seriously undermined. The worst offenders were members of the Cohn clan. Jews held liquor monopoly leases under the name "Cohn" in about forty villages in the Międzyrzecz environs belonging to Lord Radzynski, in additional villages around Słowacinek, in the Radzyn environs, and now, as we have seen, in twenty-six villages in the Samsonów environs. The Treasury recommended introducing expiration dates for their contracts, while the Interior Ministry recommended limiting the privilege to sons in a direct, patrilineal line of descent. Ultimately, this would all prove extremely difficult to enforce.[143]

In the meantime, Matthias fired off petition after petition to regional and Treasury officials, arguing that he was being unlawfully deprived of the profits promised in his Samsonów contract and demanding permission to complete the transfer of the lease to his name. When he and Raphael did finally assume full possession in late 1859, Matthias demanded restitution. He had, after all, been paying taxes on the land for the past four years! How could the Treasury justify collecting taxes from him on land that was not truly in his possession? And if it was in his possession and he had been taxed lawfully, why had the Treasury not helped him take full possession of it so that he could derive profits from it? As the rightful possessor, he deserved compensation.[144]

The Treasury felt compelled to agree, though its offer of restitution was far less than what Matthias expected. He let them know it. Not only was the promised amount less than half of what he deserved, Matthias argued, the figures were inconsistent: seventy-three rubles one year, 135 rubles another, all for the exact same holdings. Such disparities did not make sense. Matthias himself calculated that he had lost 264.445 rubles annually in liquor profits from fields and meadows that had not passed into his possession; another two hundred rubles per year in lost profits from land that was not fit for liquor production, another 33.54 rubles per year for compensating his peasant workers, and another 9.825 rubles per year for peasant taxes to which he had been entitled.[145] Later, he revised the figure to 297.985 rubles per year (omitting the two hundred rubles of lost profit and the 9.825 rubles for taxes), explaining that without land and meadows during these years he had been unable to compensate his bartenders and distillery workers by allowing them to work that land. He had also been improperly fined, he claimed.[146]

The county assessor proved persistent, too. As soon as the Samsonów holdings were transferred to Matthias and Raphael in 1859, the assessor halted their construction of a large distillery on the grounds that it would "threaten age-old uses of water, which will be diverted to the production of vodka," and that the passing carts of sand would harm existing structures."[147] At the same time, he employed a reverse strategy, ordering Matthias and Raphael to build or renovate a total of twenty-five taverns at their own cost. This was intended to break them, at once depriving them of a large distillery and forcing them to make huge expenditures on unprofitable taverns.

Matthias and Raphael fought to continue construction on the distillery and attempted to reduce the number of tavern projects to eighteen, arguing that several of the taverns were located in abandoned areas and would prevent the Treasury from maximizing its revenue. One tavern was too far from the local church, which meant that worshippers would not have a place to rest or find shelter during bad weather after services. Another was too close, an affront to the worshippers' religious sensibilities. An existing distillery had been built on an estate that had since collapsed and did not have enough land for cultivating potatoes, while the cultivation of grain would be difficult because of nearby mining. At the same time, they sought permission to construct new taverns in more strategic locations. A new tavern should be built in Cminski near the roads rather than renovated on its present site in the middle of the wilderness, they argued, and not at their own cost. (It was supposed to have been rebuilt by the prior lessee.) Matthias requested an investigation into these cases, and made so bold as to insist that it be "impartial."[148]

As entrepreneurs, Matthias and Raphael did not oppose the construction of new taverns per se. In fact, they complained that they had lost profits because there were no taverns near certain peasant communities, demanded permission to complete construction projects that had been unjustly halted, and asked to be allowed to remove a dilapidated tavern that was in danger of collapse—drinks were now being sold in local peasants' houses instead—and erect one in a better location. What they opposed was irrational renovations or new constructions that would serve no one and "harm the Treasury." Treasury officials were moved by this logic, and several cases were resolved in their favor.[149]

Beginning in 1861, Matthias and Raphael had to contend with the process of peasant emancipation. Tsar Alexander II's representative in Poland, Margrave Wielopolski, spurred on by Polish patriotic street demonstrations and a desire to steal the insurrectionists' thunder, sought to abolish compulsory labor and switch over completely to rent payments. A tsarist decree of May 16, 1861, allowed peasants possessing at least three *morgs* of land to "ransom" their labor, thus putting an end to compulsory labor in the kingdom. Over the next three years, the tsar would come increasingly to realize that many peasants were supporting the Polish revolutionary government because it promised them full title to land. In February, 1864, he would accordingly declare peasants full owners of their holdings. Landowners would be indemnified for lost land with state bonds, while patches of land around taverns and mills would remain part of their manors. But the peasants would, in theory, be fully emancipated.[150]

Matthias did not oppose these measures in principle. But he did protest the fact that they were being carried out without consulting leaseholders. He demanded that land redistribution be done in a just, moral way, and asked to see the precise calculations, because "people are not perfect and can err in their calculations." He also complained that he had been deprived of free peasant labor for his taverns and distilleries and that certain meadows that belonged to his lease had been redistributed, all without compensation. Nor had he and his partner been compensated for peasants who had vacated the estate thanks to their newfound freedom.[151]

In April 1863, four months after the outbreak of the uprising, Matthias began sending more alarmist petitions. The insurrectionary disturbances had caused a two-year stagnation in business throughout his network of taverns; armies passing through had drunk up his liquor for free; and peasants had violated his monopoly. The worst catastrophe occurred in Występa Tavern, located on the Warsaw-Krakow highway, where Russian soldiers had drunk and eaten their fill without paying and then burned the tavern down (perhaps they suspected the tavernkeeper of espionage). Matthias estimated the cost of a new tavern at 2,500 rubles and estimated his total damages at twelve thousand rubles. The following February, he appealed to the government for relief from the next installment on his lease, which he was in no state to pay. This time, however, his requests were denied.[152]

CONCLUSION

Matthias and Raphael represent the outer limits of the rural Jewish liquor trade during rural Jewish prohibition. Their special privileges allowed them to openly run village taverns, and they seized the opportunity. In comparison to the prior, non-Jewish, lessees of the Samsonów liquor monopoly, they proved extremely industrious, building a large distillery as well as tavern after tavern in strategic locations. They also proved more litigious, fighting what they saw as unjust behavior by the prior lessee, the county assessor, the district commissioner, and the Treasury, demanding compensation for lost profits and damages, advocating for more efficient renovation and construction projects, and avoiding unprofitable projects in the name of protecting the Treasury.

Their assertiveness was a rational response to discrimination. In attempting to succeed in a market that had been declared off-limits to Jews, Matthias and Raphael had little choice but to be more resourceful, demanding, and persistent than their Christian predecessors. New forms of discrimination against a group with a long history of involvement in the liquor trade and few viable alternatives thus encouraged adaptation rather than the desired exclusion. This adaptability was no less characteristic of more typical rural Jewish tavernkeepers, whose surreptitious liquor sales provide an unexpected picture of interethnic coexistence. Instead of the Jewish solidarity and cunning depicted in much Polish Romantic literature, we find pragmatic interethnic solidarity against a meddling absolutist state, an outgrowth of earlier attempts by tavernkeepers to circumvent Jewish legal and ritual constraints. Christians therefore proved absolutely integral to both the religious observance and economic survival of Jewish tavernkeepers.

The fact that much of the region's liquor trade was underground was not, in itself, unusual. Historians estimate that as many as half of the drinking houses in Western and Central Europe were unlicensed.[153] But in the Polish case unlicensed tavernkeeping entailed members of the dominant culture helping members of an out-group evade discriminatory state legislation to pursue the region's most lucrative trade. This underground interethnic symbiosis also prevailed in other parts of tsarist Russia, where the liquor trade was no less vital: Prince Nicholas Repnin complained, for example, that "some landowners, tempted by the money they received from Jews, thoughtlessly protected them. . . . Being indifferent to the welfare of the peasants who belong to them, for their own selfish temporary advantage [they] want to have Jews present in the country in order to make money through them."[154] The socioeconomic coalition was simply too profitable for the state to dismantle.

As we have seen, the state did occasionally undermine the coalition. Solomon Blumrozen appealed to the state when he felt the nobleman unjustly breached his contract. But everyone else in the case followed the familiar pattern: Lord K. protested expulsions of Jews who proved adept managers of his enterprises; Mejer argued that he was simply doing his lord's bidding; Zelka denied all involvement in tavernkeeping. As for the local Christians, there is nothing to suggest that their defense of Zelka exceeded the bounds of practicality. They, too, were most likely doing their lord's bidding. In the countryside, feudal obligations died hard.

Historians have understood the legislative assault on the rural Jewish liquor trade in the Kingdom of Poland as a product of nefarious landowner influence, a casualty of the collapse of the noble-Jewish symbiosis. Indeed, a small coterie of aristocratic publicists had been urging the removal of rural Jews from the liquor trade since the first partitions, and certain entrepreneurial landowners were resolved to cut out the Jewish middleman. But such landowners were in the minority. Most noblemen considered Jews useful as tavernkeepers, not as farmers or craftsmen. If it were otherwise, one would expect unilateral expulsions of Jews on a mass scale, since the lords never needed state legislation to rid themselves of Jews on their estates. Even the state's comparatively moderate experiments in Jewish productivization placed it at odds with landowners accustomed to enjoying full autonomy on their own estates.[155]

The anti-Jewish liquor legislation was fundamentally shaped by Polish officials who, though Polish landowners themselves, were committed to sustaining the lucrative status quo inherited from the prior regime and satisfying the tsar's dictates.[156] The few changes they did implement during the early nineteenth century were inspired by cameralist goals like revenue enhancement and social consolidation. A gradual elimination of Jews from the liquor trade through rising liquor concessions cleverly satisfied both imperatives. But the policy was less successful than many were willing to admit. Rural Jews, well practiced in circumventing Jewish law by "selling" and "leasing" their enterprises to Christians on Sabbaths and festivals, now simply hired Christian fronts to elude the concessions with the landowners' full knowledge and complicity. The Polish writer E. T. Massalski considered their position unassailable. When the Jewish tavernkeepers in his novel learned that "already in Petersburg they are thinking of expelling us from villages to towns," an older Jew shrugged, "Nu, let them think." The lords needed them too much, he knew.[157]

But it was never easy. During his ethnographic expedition, I. L. Peretz contemplated the inability of statistical science to measure the personal toll of such illicit trades: "Does it know how long their hearts continued to bleed afterward? Can it count the sleepless nights that preceded the first illegal act, or the times when children writhed with hunger cramps and limbs tossed with fever before the first glass of unlicensed liquor was poured?"[158] Rural Jewish tavernkeepers now led doubly illegal lives—circumventing Jewish Sabbath observance laws in order to keep their taverns running on those days while circumventing state concession fees and bans in order to keep their taverns running at all. Most rabbis appreciated the extenuating circumstances and proved willing to draw up legal fictions. And when the state stepped up its efforts against rural Jewish tavernkeepers in the 1840s, most landowners proved willing to circumvent new laws that would deprive them of the right to economically exploit their Jews. But criminalization exacted a heavy psychological toll (see chapter 5).

The 1844 ban on Jewish tavernkeeping in the countryside was enforced for almost two decades, after which there was a relaxation. Although the 1862 decree for enhanced Jewish rights still specifically prohibited the sale and production of alcohol by Jews in the countryside unless all the village's inhabitants were Jewish (that is, Jewish agricultural colonies), an attitude of benign neglect can be seen setting in. When asked for his opinion on how to modify the partial emancipation decrees of 1862, the governor of Suwałki replied bluntly that the lingering restriction on rural Jewish tavernkeeping ought to be discarded, since, in any event, Jews now simply ignored it.[159] This meant that local Christians ignored it as well.

As we will see in the next chapter, only in certain larger towns and cities could one begin to see a social realignment, with age-old feudal relations giving way to unmediated contact between Jews and the state. In the wake of the 1830–31 uprising, urban Jewish petitioners seeking exemption from economically debilitating legislation increasingly began circumventing noblemen and Jewish communal leaders alike, appealing directly to government officials and bringing their reasoning into alignment with cameralist and enlightenment imperatives. In the case of cities, historians are thus more justified in declaring an end to the noble-Jewish symbiosis. But in the kingdom's vast expanses of smaller towns and villages the lords continued, as always, to manage local economic life and entrust their enterprises to Jews.

CHAPTER 3

The Urban Jewish Liquor Trade in the Kingdom of Poland

When the memoirist Moses Wassercug learned of plans to build a new road outside the Płock city walls in 1803, he immediately purchased a plot of land there and obtained the bishop's permission to construct a luxurious stone tavern. The results were spectacular—a fifty-one-by-forty-one-foot multistory stone tavern and adjacent house consisting of a total of twenty-three units subdivided into rooms and kitchens, a *mikveh* (ritual bath), a copper boiler, an enormous stable, a carriage garage, ample storage space, wells with "sweet, good water," a liquor distillery, brewery, and the finest sukkah in town.[1] When the stable and garage burned down in 1808, Wassercug began to replace them with an even more magnificent structure.[2] But his renovation attracted too much attention: before he could finish, Napoleonic officers requisitioned his stable and confiscated his distillery equipment. Wassercug repeatedly petitioned the "ministers in Warsaw" for their return, and finally found success some six years later.[3]

Wassercug's account illustrates how grandiose Jewish-run taverns in big urban centers could be. Inventories of rural roadside taverns provide a good occasion for comparison. The "Female Archer" tavern, on the road from Garwolin to Osieck, was built of wood and covered with a thatched roof with a protruding brick chimney. It had a front porch with three pillars supporting the overhanging roof, and an adjacent stable containing four stalls. The main barroom had four windows with small panes and shutters, a brick oven, one "ordinary table," a floor of clay tiles, and a ceiling of wooden planks. The inner chamber had wooden stairs leading down

Figure 3.1: *Tavern on Łęczyński Street in Lublin.* Photograph by T. Chrzanowski (1867).

to a cellar.⁴ The Puznowiecka tavern, on the road from Parysów to Osieck, was built of wood and covered with a thatched roof with a protruding clay chimney. Its front porch and four-stall stable were also made of wood. The barroom had three windows with small panes, a stove in the center made partly of brick, a single table of pinewood, two benches by the wall, two by the stove, a floor of clay tiles, and a ceiling of wood planks. There was an inner chamber with a single, pane-less window.⁵ Urban taverns not only tended to be more grandiose, they were also usually more sanitary. Harro Harring found that near Warsaw "in some of the public houses kept by the Jews, the traveler often meets with accommodation which he might look for in vain among Polish Christians." Harring followed his observation with some unkind words about Polish Christians on the topic of sanitation.⁶ It is quite telling that Christian observers who invoked rural Jewish taverns to reinforce notions of Jewish filth, discussed in the first chapter, remained silent on the subject of Jewish taverns in cities.

Wassercug's ordeal with the Napoleonic officers is also instructive in that it illustrates a momentous reconfiguration occurring in urban centers throughout postpartition Poland. Before starting construction on his tavern in 1803, Wassercug had approached the regional bishop; five years later, when attempting to reclaim it, he went straight to ministers in the capital city, Warsaw. This shift is reflective of a larger trend toward a more centralized, bureaucratized rule in the cities of central Poland. The first to feel its effects were Christian townspeople, who saw their liquor monopoly prerogatives eroded during the last days of the Polish-Lithuanian

Commonwealth. At the turn of the nineteenth century, the nobility's city jurisdictions (*jurydyki*) were decisively and rapidly eliminated by the new absolutist regimes.[7] For Jews, who lacked many basic rights, the experience of centralization was often even more traumatic.

At the same time, Wassercug's case illustrates that, even if enlightened absolutist rule could be arbitrary and oppressive, particularly during wartime, it did provide a more central address for complaints. Some Jews, moreover, discovered that officials in the new, constitutional-based regimes predicated their rule on legalistic, cameralist, and rationalist notions that one could deploy in one's defense. As a result, the new urban petition, in contrast to the traditional *supliki* brought before noble town owners, espoused many of those same principles.[8] The early nineteenth century thus witnessed the emergence of a new Jewish discourse that pivoted on notions of the common good, individual rights, and civilized mores.

Petitions by individual Jews—usually working women who did not have as much of a distinctively Jewish appearance as their husbands—flowed in steadily throughout the century. These petitions tested the contours of enlightened absolutism in the Kingdom of Poland, pressuring officials to live up to their own professed ideals and challenging their sense of priorities, as we shall see. Authoring an effective petition within the new reality required moving beyond personal afflictions and speaking to broader societal concerns while avoiding any radical conceptions of tolerance and enlightenment that state bureaucrats might find threatening. This careful formulation was then delivered directly to Polish officials without the mediation of a nobleman or Jewish communal body. The very act of petitioning thus created a sense of enhanced agency. And in the act of assembling the necessary rationalist, enlightenment-based arguments, however pragmatic their original motivation, we begin to witness the glimmerings of a less parochial consciousness. Scholarly discussion about a Polish Jewish "modernization process" must, without a doubt, address the self-advocacy of these urban Jews in constitutional Central Poland.

As discussed in the last chapter, rural Jewish tavernkeeping was first burdened with escalating concession fees and then banned in two stages, on major village roads in 1840 and then completely in 1844. While many rural Jewish tavernkeepers, as we saw, merely installed Christian fronts and proceeded with business as usual, some were deterred by the potential fines and expulsions or forced out by law-abiding nobles, and were left with little choice but to migrate to towns and cities. There, at least, they could potentially resume tavernkeeping legally. Policy makers believed that Christian townspeople were less easily manipulated by predatory Jewish tavernkeepers; that enough Christian townspeople possessed the requisite literacy and business acumen to run taverns themselves, thus presenting virtuous alternatives to Jewish-run taverns; and that the greater police presence in towns forced Jewish tavernkeepers to behave themselves. These attitudes were in evidence throughout Eastern Europe. For example, the notorious Malorussian (Ukrainian) military governor Nicholas Repnin, architect of the largest wave of Jewish expulsions from the countryside (in 1821), considered village residents "a poorly educated, simple-hearted, and gullible population that does not know how to protect themselves from [Jewish] pushiness and temptation," but believed that "town dwellers are more educated, more alert, and more cautious." In towns, as a result, "Jewish crimes" were rare.[9]

Those rural Jewish tavernkeepers who moved to towns and cities in the Kingdom of Poland and attempted to resume their profession had to contend with a whole new set of obstacles. Urban liquor concessions were more costly than rural ones; police surveillance was indeed more rigorous; and competition from other taverns was fiercer. Worst of all, one had to contend with mounting residential restrictions that were in great part intended to discourage Jewish tavernkeeping. Jews who lived in Warsaw had it particularly rough, since new residential restrictions in 1824 were accompanied by immediate, large-scale expulsions from the finest streets and thoroughfares. Those who were spared expulsion labored under a constant feeling of dread that their own street was next on the list. To live as a Jew in Warsaw was to live as if suspended between past legality and future illegality.

At the same time, Jews who had become sufficiently acculturated, disavowed tawdry occupations like tavernkeeping, and possessed a requisite amount of wealth could hope to receive special permission to remain on the finest streets and thoroughfares. Such exemptions followed the logic of social engineering: rewarding rich, acculturated Jews while marginalizing the poor and less acculturated would, it was assumed, enlarge the former category and serve the greater good. And some Jews who petitioned for exemptions really fit the bill. It is they who have enjoyed the spotlight in modern Jewish historiography—maskilim (proponents of Enlightenment-based reform), integrationists, and assimilationists who emerged around this time not only in Warsaw but in other large cities like Odessa, Kiev, Vilna, and St. Petersburg.[10]

But as soon as urban Jews learned that decrees could in principle be evaded, many a poor, less acculturated Jew facing expulsion from a newly restricted street decided to try his or her luck, too. After the failed uprising of 1830–31, officials received a veritable flood of petitions from urban Jews all over the kingdom who felt they deserved to be compensated for damages incurred during the fighting or rewarded for their loyalty or neutrality, usually in the form of a liquor concession on a restricted street. In light of the more pressing need for loyal subjects who could help rejuvenate the economy, officials found they had a difficult time sticking to their original goals. The archives of the Interior Ministry preserve hundreds of such petitions and records of the debates that they sparked within the Polish bureaucracy.

RESIDENTIAL RESTRICTIONS AND THE JEWISH LIQUOR TRADE IN WARSAW

In 1812, Ignacy Sobolewski (1770–1846), the new minister of police and architect of Jewish liquor policy in the Napoleonic Duchy of Warsaw, had reached the point of exasperation. Despite the formal exclusion of certain Warsaw streets from Jewish settlement, decreed in 1809, Jews had continued to pour unrestricted into the capital, clogging up and defacing the most beautiful streets and depriving Christian residents of their share of profits. Some Christians had fled the city to escape the rush of these vexatious neighbors. In contrast to the situation in Krakow, where a separate district restricted the influx of Jews and afforded good police surveillance, Jews had practically laid siege to Warsaw. They had fanned out along routes leading to the city center and established their notorious taverns, luring in unwary villagers who were approaching the city with produce for sale, plying them with liquor, and, after the villagers had become drunk and disorderly, buying up their produce cheaply for resale to city residents at a markup.

There was one part of Warsaw where Jewish settlement was less noisome: the northwesternmost section. Sobolewski noticed that this section was practically uninhabited—it was hardly even known to locals—and contained just a single church that no longer held regular services. It was large enough to resettle almost the entire Jewish population of Warsaw, which he estimated at eleven thousand. It had healthy, dry air and possessed ample space for market stalls, a synagogue, and other religious institutions, and was even located near the Jewish cemetery (presently, Jews had to traverse the whole city to reach their cemetery). Best of all, it could be surrounded by sturdy walls. If Jews were relocated there en masse, they would no longer bother residents and visitors with their untidiness and intrusiveness, and they would no longer blemish the city's principal streets. Warsaw's pleasant cityscape, beautiful homes, and hefty profits—currently held captive by Jews—would be restored. A sizeable minority of

Jews, about 2,800, would be allowed to remain in the nicer sections of the city provided they were indistinguishable from Christian residents and did not continue to run taverns (at present, Sobolewski noted, there were 654 Jewish-run taverns in Warsaw alone). The rest, however, would be confined to what looks a lot like a ghetto.[11]

Sobolewski was not regarded as petty or mean-spirited by his fellow officials; in fact, he was praised by colleagues for his talent, education, modesty, and restraint.[12] Frederick August, the Duke of Warsaw, was receptive to his grandiloquent appeal. His decree the following year (1813) claimed to be a mere fulfillment of the 1809 decree, but it was more in line with the Sobolewski proposal. The 1809 decree had labeled a handful of Warsaw streets, portions of streets, and areas like the Old City "restricted" (*exymowany*), meaning off limits to Jewish residences and businesses, citing the "indecent state of affairs" resulting from so many Jews living on principal or narrow streets; accompanying dangers like conflagrations, epidemics, lack of cleanliness, lawlessness, and disorder; and, finally, the nature of the economic activities in which Jews typically engaged.[13] At the time, it had seemed expedient to only rule out a few neighborhoods. But now, the majority of Jews were to be confined to the northwestern section of the city, albeit without the sturdy walls envisioned by Sobolewski, an area which Frederick August designated a "Jewish city." The rest of Warsaw was to be off limits. Those Jews with the means to do so could purchase empty lots or knock down wooden structures and build stone houses, but only within the newly designated Jewish quarter (the 1809 decree had allowed such practices even on restricted streets).[14] As one historian has already noted, this clever, if draconian, policy effectively enlisted Jewish wealth and initiative to build up a desolate section of the city while at the same time arresting unwanted Jewish expansion.[15]

Frederick August's 1809 and 1813 decrees may have looked like ghettoization. But there was something novel about both: Jewish families who possessed at least sixty thousand zlotys, eliminated their beards and other distinguishing marks, enrolled their children in Polish schools, and fit a desired professional profile (factory owners, large-scale merchants, doctors, artists, etc.) were eligible for exemption. The policy thus rewarded acculturation and penalized fidelity to traditional sartorial and educational norms. But the wealth requirement also suggests a strong fiscal concern that, true to the dictates of cameralism, often trumped all other considerations. There were twenty-two exempted Jewish families in Warsaw by the time the duchy was dissolved in 1815.[16] The residential policy was adopted, and its restrictions and exemptions were expanded, when much of the duchy came under tsarist control, proving to be one of Napoleon's most enduring legacies in the region.

When the tsarist Kingdom of Poland was formed in 1815, the interethnic jostling began almost immediately. Christian residents approached the tsar's new Polish viceroy, Józef Zajączek, with a demand to reimplement the segregation policy in Warsaw. Jewish mercantile elites, for their part, approached the tsar's chief Russian representative in Poland, Imperial Commissioner Nicholas Novosiltsev.[17] The Jewish representatives had chosen wisely: Novosiltsev proved to be the decisive power in the new kingdom. Inspired by their proclamation that "religion does not determine the measure of a man," and perhaps even more by their sizeable financial gift, Novosiltsev brushed aside Zajączek's protest that violating prior residence decrees would arouse Christian ill will and increase the threat of epidemics. He saw to it that the residential decree was suspended for the next six years.[18]

Six years later the Christian townspeople, helped by recommendations made by the Committee on Towns (1815–16) and Interior Minister Mostowski (1816–18), finally prevailed.[19] In 1821, Tsar Alexander decided to revert back to the 1809 "restricted streets" policy, which, it is important to point out, had never been rigorously enforced.[20] Apparently unaware of the 1813 "Jewish city" decree, Alexander prohibited Jews from living or working on the streets and areas mentioned in 1809 and added new restricted streets to the list. The result was not a ghetto, but an inverse ghetto: a horseshoe shaped zone of streets open to Jewish settlement and businesses in the remainder of the city called a *rewir*.[21] In addition, the tsar required nonresident Jews who wished to do business in Warsaw to pay a sojourner's tax (*billet*) and an escort fee (*geleitzoll*), both in force since the Duchy of Warsaw period.[22]

Unlike his predecessors, however, Tsar Alexander rigorously enforced the residential decree. Expulsions from homes and businesses on Warsaw's restricted streets proceeded apace in 1824, causing a ripple of panic throughout Jewish Warsaw. At the same time, however, the exemption policy (on the basis of the 1809 decree) was honored. By 1836, 124 Warsaw Jewish families possessed exemptions, joined by an additional seven families by 1842.[23] Nevertheless, if the policy was intended to entice Jews to integrate with Warsaw's general population, it actually had the effect of compounding Jewish difference. Exemptions effectively sifted the most prominent acculturated Jews out of Jewish neighborhoods, leaving behind a more tradition-oriented and traditionalist-led mass. Jewish neighborhoods only became more distinctly Jewish.

Another prime motivation behind residential restrictions was a reduction of Jewish economic overrepresentation. The commissioner of Mazovia explained that Jewish quarters functioned "not only to cleanse the main streets of Jewish slovenliness, but to give Christians an opportunity to make profits and become more industrious."[24] Restricting areas where Jews were able to live and work would give Christian townspeople a fighting chance and, paradoxical as it may seem, help unify the kingdom by reducing anomalous Jewish economic behavior.[25] Most importantly, residential restrictions would lure desirable Jews away from the liquor trade and into preferred types of trade on the more attractive restricted streets. The Mazovian commissioner believed that the exemption policy had almost achieved the goal of drawing Jews away from tavernkeeping. Many Jews had, as a result of the policy, established factories on restricted streets that would have continued to flourish were it not for the 1830 uprising. Unfortunately, during the uprising those same Jews had exploited the general disorder and obtained concessions for taverns on restricted urban streets from the Polish revolutionary regime, making a mockery of all prior efforts to exclude them from the liquor trade.[26]

While it is doubtful that many Jews would have traded their factories for taverns, the commissioner's impression was not entirely false. As mentioned earlier, the rate of awarding liquor concessions to urban Jews did accelerate during and after the uprising.[27] By 1858, at the height of "rural Jewish prohibition," slightly over 37 percent of the kingdom's urban taverns were legally run by some 1,675 Jewish families, an average of almost four Jewish-run taverns per town. This was an increase of 290 taverns from just two years earlier.[28] In addition, Jews legally ran other kinds of urban establishments that sold liquor.[29] The economic goal of residential restrictions remained as unfulfilled as the social goal.

A glance at the annual incomes of urban tavernkeepers illustrates why Jews should have continued to gravitate toward the trade in spite of steep concessions, residential restrictions, and explicit government disapproval. In Lodz in the 1820s, several decades before the town developed its famous textile industry and was transformed into a large city, Jewish tavernkeepers earned between one and six thousand zlotys per year and formed the majority of "elders" on the Jewish self-governing council. Few Jews working in other occupations were able to even break the thousand-zloty mark.[30] The prices of tavern leases in other towns also reflect their profitability. On Stanisław Potocki's Wilanowski estate, Levy Szymkowicz leased a tavern in the small town of Dąbrowiecka for 2,400 zlotys per year; Zelka Herszkowicz leased the Zawislanska liquor monopoly (including a tavern) and taverns in Zastowski and Zbytki for a total of seven thousand zlotys per year; and Peltza Aronowicz leased a tavern in Powsinski and a smaller tavern in Lisy for a total of five thousand zlotys per year. Although in the latter case something went wrong—Potocki's clerk attempted to annul Peltza's lease on the grounds that he had done "obvious harm" to the taverns—these lessees had reason to expect that they would earn more than their sizeable lease payments. The same was true in the case of town liquor monopolies (*propinacja*), which according to late-eighteenth-century figures from Opatów cost between twenty-eight and thirty-eight thousand zlotys. The profitability of these enterprises illustrates the importance of the liquor trade to the story of urban Jewish economic history.[31]

Jewish tavernkeepers in Warsaw were, on the whole, more affluent than their counterparts in other towns and cities. Their requests for exemption from residential restrictions therefore posed a dilemma for officials, who had to weigh the undesirability of their profession against fiscal considerations. A well-reasoned petition could help them overcome their ambivalence. Dwoyra Rozengartów, threatened with expulsion from her liquor import business on Nowy Świat Street, portrayed herself as an acculturated Jew who wished only to support her children and raise them morally, not to get rich; who had paid her taxes and concessions punctually; who had lived almost exclusively among respectable Christians; and who was not capable of living among Jews (she had "almost never had a Jewish guest" in her home). Dwoyra appealed to her family's sad state owing to losses suffered during the 1830 uprising, and claimed that her husband was too old and ill to engage in trade.[32] She appended a petition on her behalf by Matthias Cohn, whom we met in the last chapter. But they did not get their stories straight: Matthias let it slip that Dwoyra's husband, the supposed invalid, was away at a trade fair in Leipzig.[33] In addition, officials discovered that he did not shave his beard. Nevertheless, Dwoyra was permitted to continue selling liquor on Nowy Swiat Street, probably because of her family's affluence.[34]

Dwoyra's case may be contrasted with that of Zalisz Rosengold, who likewise invoked the loss of all his property during the revolution, during which he "endured persecution and the threat of death without any reward from the regime to this day." Unlike Dwoyra, however, Zalisz did not pretend to be acculturated or desirous of integration with his Christian neighbors. Nor did he seem to have much money. His ambitious request for a free concession for a tavern on a restricted street as compensation was consequently denied.[35]

Other Jewish tavernkeepers demanded legal consistency and respect for their rights. Esther Hedrychowa argued that her liquor concession, originally for a house on the restricted Mokotowska Street, should be applicable to all restricted streets. After all, she had already moved her tavern several times without ever having been bothered by officials.[36] Sarah Bock, a widow, possessed a tavern concession for restricted streets but had been arbitrarily evicted and thus deprived of her lawful right to sell liquor there. She demanded that her right to sell on restricted streets be honored.[37] Numerous other widows insisted on their right to inherit their late husbands' liquor concessions, arguing that if their husbands had qualified, so should they. The regime often agreed.[38]

Perla Mirla Lewin, who had permission to live on the restricted Królewska Street herself, exhibited rare courage by challenging the very justice of residential restrictions. Jews of various occupations had approached her for permission to live in her home and set up businesses there, and she considered their requests reasonable. Jews had previously lived and traded on Królewska Street and today, as a result of residential restrictions, the street was practically empty. A revival could be easily accomplished, as remnants of wooden stores and showcases still existed. The abandoned thoroughfares between Twarda and Nowy Świat Streets would cease to be so terrifyingly gloomy if they were repopulated. Perla then raised a larger objection: "In this enlightened time it is unconscionable to so forcibly restrict the use of such a significant portion of the city." She pointed officials to article 5 in the 1832 Organic Statute, which stated that "difference in religious instruction cannot be a reason for excluding someone from laws that apply to all inhabitants." Restricted streets surely failed to live up to this principle. The Israelite people had never been traitors and were never for a moment shaken from their ties to the throne, she fiercely reminded officials. Was it not fitting that this unfairly debased people be rewarded and that this "dishonorable humiliation" cease? Officials considered Perla's reasoning too radical and rejected her request, telling each other that, after all, Jews had plenty of other places to live and work in Warsaw.[39]

Among other things, these petitions provide fascinating insight into the workings of gender in the Polish Jewish economy, a subject that has only begun to be examined in scholarship. The salient literary image of the working Jewish woman as enabler of her husband's Torah studies has been shown in recent studies to have been more an abstract ideal than a reality. More often, it is now believed, a Polish Jewish wife was a kind of junior partner in a couple's joint economic venture—she would often serve the customers while he would deal with suppliers, production, and the noble who owned the leased enterprise.[40] This scenario is sometimes borne out in evidence at our disposal. According to the social reformer and essayist Jan Glucksberg, for example, Jewish tavernkeepers managed to compete honestly with their Christian counterparts as the cost of liquor concessions began to skyrocket by having their wives and children serve their customers while they became carriage drivers on the side.[41]

However, the situation in a large city like Warsaw seems to have been a bit different. The urban women who authored petitions on their husbands' and families' behalf were more than junior partners. In the effort to evade expulsions and restrictive legislation, their lack of beards, sidelocks, and other outwardly Jewish markers that officials found so odious elevated their importance for the family venture. They, rather than their husbands, had to become the public faces of their businesses, meaning that they, rather than their husbands, had to be the ones to approach officials with exemption requests. In such cases, the concessions and exemption privileges were granted to them rather than to their husbands. Among the unintended consequences of Polish urban residential policy was an enhancement of status for some Jewish women.

Not that all Jewish men took the discriminatory policy lying down. Some, like Dwoyra's husband, simply grew their beards back once they had obtained their privileges, achieving a symbolic victory. Others, upon learning of an 1848 ban on taverns that lay within fifty feet of a church, actually attempted to have their Christian competitors expelled. Michał Celigowski, a Christian tavernkeeper in Warsaw, had received permission to open a tavern "with beer and vodka and music on a grand scale" but was now informed that his tavern lay only thirty feet from a hospital that contained a chapel, and that the loud music and "loose women passing by" were disturbing the patients. Celigowski attacked his denouncer's credibility: he was a Jew named Joel Weinkrantz who was a known criminal and convicted smuggler whose own tavern concession had been suspended for one year.[42] Officials were apparently swayed, and determined that the hospital's chapel was not a chapel.[43] The chief of police himself protested the planned expulsion of a Christian tavernkeeper named Stanisław Kaminski, whose tavern lay 32 ½ feet from a church. Kaminski lived under constant threat of expulsion and had consequently suffered a decline in profits, credit, and property value.[44] But in at least one case, a Jew's denunciation of a Christian tavernkeeper worked: Józef Rybinski's tavern was shut down for being too close to a monastery after Szaye Izymierski complained to officials.[45]

Inevitably, certain Jewish tavernkeepers were tempted to use residential restrictions against their Jewish competitors, too. Sometimes it was out of sheer vindictiveness. Moses Kornblum had been accused of selling excessive quantities of liquor on credit to lower-rank soldiers, causing them to become drunk and disorderly and to fall deeply into debt. Army officials proceeded to shut his tavern down on the grounds that it lay too close to the Mirowski army barracks. Moses protested that his neighbor, Gitl Wolberg, tolerated all kinds of shenanigans in her tavern on a nightly basis, including indecent women and brawls, while he ran a clean and orderly establishment. Why should he, an upstanding tavernkeeper, be the one to suffer?[46]

Jewish tavernkeepers who had followed the messianic pretender Jacob Frank into Catholicism were, of course, shielded from the drama of expulsions, informing, and counterinforming. Ekaterina Emeliantseva's meticulous research has uncovered more than ten Frankist families running one or more lucrative taverns in Warsaw, some of which were located in the palatial residences of nobility. In the 1790s, the Christian municipality had complained bitterly about these numerous "unaffiliated people," neither truly Christian nor truly Jewish, who continued to engage in typically Jewish occupations like selling liquor while "driving regular townsmen from these sources of prosperity." Particularly infuriating was the tendency among Frankists to lease their taverns—in typical Jewish fashion—instead of purchasing them as Christians did, since recent tax increases applied only to owners of taverns. But the complaints went unheeded. A significant number of tavernkeepers thus availed themselves of Frankism's many material inducements.[47]

URBAN JEWISH TAVERNKEEPING OUTSIDE OF WARSAW

After the reintroduction of residential restrictions in Warsaw in 1821, Jewish quarters were established or reinstated in thirty additional towns and cities in the kingdom at a rate of about three per year.[48] In addition, Jewish quarters identified by the term "compass" (*obręb*) were established or reinstated in twenty-four towns possessing *de non tolerandis Judaeis* privileges.[49] Other Jewish quarters were planned but never enforced: a map of Zakroczym, for example, reveals that the town's Sabbath/festival boundary (*eruv*) lay well outside the designated Jewish quarter.[50] In all, there were fifty-five operative Jewish quarters among the kingdom's 456 towns.[51] This might not seem like a lot, but it is important to note that most towns in the kingdom resembled villages from an economic viewpoint.[52] Those fifty-five towns tended to be the largest and most economically vital, which may explain why roughly half of the kingdom's Jewish population resided in Jewish quarters by 1833, the year in which the creation of further Jewish quarters was halted.[53] The very next year those towns received an additional Jewish influx when, in an effort to curtail smuggling (most smugglers were believed to be Jews), Jewish settlement was banned in 111 towns along the Prussian and Austrian borders, bringing the total number of restricted towns to 166. Jews were also expelled from state mining towns in an attempt to undercut the black market in base and precious metals. Most refugees had little choice but to gravitate toward one of kingdom's fifty-five Jewish quarters. Some restrictions were soon repealed, but on the eve of the 1862 liberalization decree Jewish settlement was still restricted or banned in a total of 121 towns in the kingdom.[54] One scholar has suggested that it was those towns possessing Jewish quarters (presumably excluding Warsaw) that came to be associated with the term "shtetl," a semimythical construct that evokes a disproportionately large and highly segregated small-town Jewish community.[55]

As in Warsaw, exemptions for wealthy and acculturated Jewish elites in these towns sometimes served to further intensify the traditionalist atmosphere in Jewish quarters by sifting influential detractors out and pushing wealthy traditionalists in. According to Privy Councilor Turkul, even Jews who owned the finest houses around the market squares of certain towns but did not respond to the policy's cultural dictates were expelled to Jewish quarters before local officials could find Christian buyers for their homes.[56] Yet expulsions probably occurred less frequently in smaller towns, for the economic effects were too acute. During a failed attempt to establish a Jewish quarter in the town of Chorzele, for example, it became clear that four houses around the perimeter of the market square (*rynek*) and two houses on other principal streets were owned by Jews, and that thirty-seven additional houses had Jewish occupants. How would it be possible to find Christians with the financial means to occupy these houses, local officials wondered? Faced with the prospect of empty houses all over town, they concluded that the wealthiest Jews would have to be exempted.[57]

In the case of private, noble-owned towns, Polish officials also had to contend with noble prerogatives. Foremost was the nobleman's control over liquor, his most profitable commodity. Tsar Alexander I's very first assurance to landowners after the formation of the Kingdom of Poland was that "the liquor monopoly is a freedom and a right for landowners, as is the production and sale of every kind of drink, without any fee, on the entire estate, in every village, inn, and tavern."[58] If a noble town owner concluded that the removal of Jewish tavernkeepers from his town's principal streets would harm his liquor revenues, he was likely to make a fuss.

Jewish residents of privately owned towns usually appealed to the state through the mediation of their noble town owners.[59] Of course, the town owner and state official were sometimes the same person, and this could be quite advantageous. In 1820, Moses Sylberberg, who leased the local liquor monopoly and flour mills in the large town of Opatów, petitioned Stanisław Potocki, town owner and chair of the Council of Ministers and the Senate, to use his influence to induce the military to settle soldiers in Opatów and purchase liquor for them at the prior, higher price. Moses described the universal economic distress that year as being the result of low grain prices: farmers could barely obtain one week's worth of salt from the sale of a bushel of grain and could barely meet their basic needs, and merchants of every variety were facing collapse, for who was buying merchandise in such times? Moses maintained that setting liquor prices according to the current low price of grain had made the sale of liquor so unprofitable that a lessee could barely recover half of the cost of his lease. Having the military as a client would alleviate the situation and also benefit the military, which would have access to liquor of different varieties and be happily quartered by local residents. Moses asked Potocki to "quickly persuade the Military Consistory in Opatów to brighten the fate of the town's residents by increasing profits from distilleries and mills" so that they would be able to make their annual payments to Potocki and avoid ruin. By tying his own interests to those of other town residents, the military, and Potocki himself, Moses convinced Potocki to wield his influence.[60]

When disputes arose between Jews and noble town owners, state officials were usually reluctant to interfere. In an especially egregious case, the widow of a tavernkeeper in Biłgoraj had to fight for her late husband's liquor concession against her own son, who had the town owner's backing. State officials ruled that the liquor concession had expired during the course of the proceedings, which effectively allowed the nobleman to award the new lease to whomever he wished.[61] Sometimes the state appeared rather powerless to enforce its will against a town owner. In a drawn-out suit about control over liquor production rights between the successive noble town owners of Pińczów and Jewish tavernkeepers in rare coalition with the municipality, the state decided repeatedly against the noble town owners. But the latter were able to ignore the verdicts and wear down their Jewish and Christian opponents until they were finally willing to settle.[62]

In cases where the town owner had been exiled in the wake of the 1830 uprising, however, local Jews were emboldened to appeal directly to the state. After the Napoleonic Wars, according to Leib Elowicz Kerschenbladt, Adam Czartoryski had granted tavern concessions to Jews in Puławy as part of an effort to rebuild the town. In 1832, with Czartoryski safely in exile in Paris, Leib complained that his tavern in Puławy had been completely destroyed by the Russian army during the uprising, and that the steward of the Puławy estate was subjecting him to "intolerable harassment" for failing to repay his debts. Leib requested a free liquor concession, financial aid, annulment of his debt to the exiled Czartoryski, and an end to the harassment. In addition, Józef Theblum complained on behalf of Jews in the nearby Czartoryski-owned town of Końskowola that Czartoryski's son and successor had "closed off all branches of speculation to Jews" and that thirty tavernkeepers were now deprived of a means of making a living. Józef asked for debt relief, free tavern concessions for twelve Końskowola Jews, and compensation for flour taken by Russian troops. These petitions, though directed through the new centralized channels, made no appeal to broader civic or legal concerns, and consequently failed.[63]

Several years later, Jewish tavernkeepers in Końskowola were themselves objects of complaints by the local parish priest, Father Biescki, who demanded an end to their "tricky, illegal taverns." Jews, he claimed, had illegally established taverns in Końskowola's surrounding villages and, by selling farmers and townspeople drinks on credit, had brought them to immorality, ruin, and debt. They had even employed gendarmes to collect their drinking debts rather than going through the courts.[64] After Father Biescki's initial complaint, the Jews had conspired with the mayor of Końskowola to launch a false accusation against him, which had gotten him fined and proved the Jews' domination of the district. Father Biescki swore that he had nothing to gain personally from his complaint and that he acted only in the "interest of the common good," and he reminded the regime of its duty to prevent legal offenses so as not to encourage future abuses. An official investigation was launched.[65]

Jews in towns and cities that were not privately owned usually appealed to the state directly. In Chelm, one of several royal towns where Jews had enjoyed privileges equating them with burghers, including similar liquor monopoly rights, three tavernkeepers delivered an unusually bold petition. They demanded that their liquor concession fees be waived on the grounds that King Stanisław August of the now-defunct Polish-Lithuanian Commonwealth had granted Chelm Jews "economic rights on par with local Christians" and given them the right to establish taverns, breweries, and distilleries in order to help rebuild and repopulate the town following a destructive enemy incursion in 1777. The tavernkeepers argued that this "promise of equality" exempted them from current liquor concession payments, which were not required of Christian residents. They had, moreover, "striven to improve the general state of the town with as much zeal as citizenship itself would demand." If the regime refused to honor the privilege, depriving them of their "age-old rights," they should be able to have legal recourse. If the law pertaining to the Jews of Chelm had "retreated along with the prior regime's army," they quipped, so too must all the other laws of the kingdom. But the regime had little trouble ignoring their appeal to a decree that had been awarded by a deposed king.[66]

Jewish residents of smaller towns soon had more to worry about than residential segregation and high liquor concessions. After the 1844 ban on Jewish liquor sales in villages was implemented, some officials began to set their sites on small towns, which often were indistinguishable from villages. They attempted to apply a similar reasoning—the need to protect innocent peasants from predatory Jewish liquor sellers—on the logic that, if peasants did not actually live in small towns, they did come in regularly during annual or seasonal trade fairs. According to some officials, the number of trade fairs was "increasing and causing the spread of drunkenness among the farming class."[67] Creating Jewish quarters in small towns was no longer an option, as the formation of new Jewish quarters had been suspended since 1833, but a small town could be redesignated a village with a stroke of the pen. As it was illegal to hold trade fairs or set up market stalls in villages, and as Jews were prohibited since 1844 from producing and selling liquor in villages, reverting a small town to village status would ingeniously deprive local Jews of their livelihood and force them to leave. Where would they go? Most likely, to Jewish quarters in larger towns.[68]

To this end, officials devised a plan to re-categorize some 225 smaller towns as villages. One dissenting official, wary of the plan's destabilizing effects, was reassured that "the trade and industry in these [small] towns is of little value, and is mostly limited to liquor, significantly less to markets and fairs, and only takes place between Jews and peasants."[69] But local Christians and Jews alike vocally opposed the scheme, and sometimes joined forces to resist it. In the small town of Chodel, for example, thirty-eight Christians and three Jews signed a joint petition in which they protested that they were "very poor and cannot bear the burden" of a reversion to village status.[70]

Residents of towns, whether Jewish or Christian, were most of all concerned with retaining their right to hold trade fairs, whose importance is vividly illustrated in E. T. Massalski's programmatic novel *Pan Podstolic* (Lord Podstolic). A trade fair, Massalski's protagonist observes, brings merchants together from far-flung places, increases the production of handmade goods, acquaints locals with new conveniences, and "stimulates in them a desire to afford, through work and industry, to buy such products." Witnessing one town's revival during a trade fair, Lord Podstolic exclaims: "Such movement, such life, revived from a cloudy yesterday and a lifeless valley, gives us a sense of the difference between a country of trade and one that is exclusively agricultural. In one moment, industry arrived here, and everything came to life." True, trade fairs were still plagued by Jews, who sold the peasants food they had just purchased themselves at a markup, bought up their carts of hay at rock-bottom prices with money and vodka, and lured them into their taverns to drink watered-down liquor and relieve them of any profits they might have acquired. Nevertheless, after the trade fair ends, "silence will once again cloud the town with its gloomy tint, and life will be numbed by the lazy plow." The local economy would once again rest exclusively on Jewish-run taverns, which exercised a purely negative influence.[71]

In the end officials reconsidered, but not out of any feeling of benevolence. They voiced fears that the resulting migration out of small towns would cause Jewish populations in the remaining, larger towns to swell to unacceptable proportions, and that this would effect a complete Jewish conquest of local trade and the creation of "a veritable state within a state" in towns with Jewish quarters.[72] The total number of towns was only slightly reduced.

Officials then attempted to at least cut down on the number of urban Jewish-run taverns, which in their estimation had mushroomed to unacceptable proportions. According to one estimate, 2,322 Christians and 1,385 Jews ran a total of 3,707 urban taverns by 1856. The larger the city, the more Jewish-run taverns: in Warsaw alone, 317 of the city's 570 taverns were Jewish-run. Officials tried to place caps on the total number of taverns according to population size, with uneven success. In the Lublin District the target number was 676 taverns, and the official number of taverns was reduced from 808 (1844) to 703 (1852) to 637 (1856).[73] The number of taverns in Zamość, which had a target number of sixteen, dropped from thirty-seven (1844) to thirty-five (1852) to eighteen (1856). But other towns refused to budge, and some even showed an increase. In Opatów, the number of taverns almost doubled between 1848 and 1856.[74] Moreover, radical discrepancies suggest that officials did not really have a handle on the situation. In Warsaw, there was a discrepancy of eleven taverns between two different surveys for the year 1848.[75] In Kock, one survey identified only one tavern in 1844 and one tavern in 1852, while another identified nine taverns in 1848 and seven taverns in 1856.[76] Even the basic task of rendering tavernkeeping what scholars call "legible" seemed beyond their capacity.[77] The only thing the attempted reduction invariably did provide was another handy excuse for rejecting Jewish requests for liquor concessions. In 1848–49, there were nineteen such rejections in the Lublin District on the grounds that the tavern limit had already been reached in the towns in question.[78]

COLLECTIVE PROTEST: THE JEWISH COMMUNAL LEADERSHIP

What were Jewish communal and supracommunal leaders doing throughout all the rising concession fees, bans, expulsions, and restrictions? One would expect such leaders to vocally oppose policies that threatened to destroy their constituencies' economic mainstay. But they protested liquor policies infrequently, usually only before or after a major political shift. This reticence is worthy of emphasis, since historians have tended to focus almost exclusively on them.[79] When Jewish leaders did intervene, their protests seem to have had some impact, since they, too, had mastered the new civic-minded discourse. The most effective intervention occurred after the demise of the Duchy of Warsaw, when several delegations of Jewish communal leaders approached Novosiltsev for help staving off planned expulsions of Jewish tavernkeepers from the countryside.[80]

In 1832, in the wake of the uprising, a Jewish delegation composed of Warsaw and regional representatives approached Viceroy Ivan Paskevich with the argument that one could remove all Jews from the countryside and the peasants would remain oppressed and impoverished so long as landowners refused to switch to monied rents, and that concession payments for urban taverns, which were "but infrequently visited by the peasants," served no other purpose than to enhance state revenue at the price of Jewish ruin. It is possible that their memo played a role in the awarding of many new liquor concessions to Jews during this period.[81]

In 1856, following the death of Nicholas I and the Russian defeat in the Crimean war (a period known as the post-Sevastopol détente), the Warsaw Synagogue Council and the chief rabbi of Warsaw, R. Dov Ber Meisels, an avid supporter of the Polish cause for independence, decried the liquor policy in a joint petition. Expulsions from village taverns, they insisted, had neither improved the lot of the peasantry nor curtailed their "addictions." All they had done was impoverish Jews (one had only to look at the state of their clothing) and force them to cram into the Jewish quarters of various towns, all of which compromised public hygiene; stunted the kingdom's industrialization; fomented hypercompetitiveness, poverty, and misery; and suppressed the physical development of Jewish adolescents. The latter spent their entire youth developing only intellectually, and only through religious books. Freedom of residence would encourage Jews to develop a civic sense and an awareness of industry and other new developments, and to finally branch out into a greater variety of trades than liquor.[82] In 1857, a petition by the Warsaw Synagogue Council members to Tsar Alexander II likewise protested that the expulsions of Jews from rural taverns had achieved nothing more than the Jewish population's economic collapse.[83] Neither petition moved Polish officials to reconsider their ban on rural Jewish taverns, but they may have influenced the debates leading up to the equalizing measures decreed in 1862.

The Warsaw Synagogue Council achieved modest success in 1861, when the General Military Governor of Warsaw attempted to ban the sale of food and beer in taverns in Warsaw and Praga. Back in 1844, probably as part of the general crackdown, officials had determined that combined vodka-food and vodka-beer establishments "eased the development of addiction to drunkenness among workers," but tavernkeepers had managed to forestall a ban on such establishments. Now, officials wanted to implement it. The Warsaw Synagogue Council argued that during such a critical economic time, around five hundred families currently fighting for survival in the Warsaw liquor trade would be completely ruined. They would be unable either to support themselves or to pay their concessions, fees, and "extremely steep" rents. The privy government councilor acknowledged this consideration, but weighed it against the "goal of achieving the common good" by preventing the working population from addicting itself to alcohol as easily, spending its "last, hard-earned penny" on drinking debts, and becoming demoralized. Nevertheless, the measure was forestalled yet again.[84]

COURAGEOUS CHRISTIANS

It was unusual for urban Christians to overcome their historical competitiveness with Jews and question conventional wisdom about the need to restrain the Jewish liquor trade. But it occasionally happened. In the critical year of 1844, B. Alexandrowicz, a Polish contributor to a mercantile periodical, made so bold as to dispute "all the noise and commotion about Jewish lessees getting our people drunk and demoralizing them." He asked his readers, rhetorically, "Who settled [Jews] in taverns, who lowered the price of drinks to the point of worthlessness in order to facilitate horrible drunkenness?" (Answer: the nobility).[85] That same year, a contributor with the initials "O. O." broadened the challenge to conventional wisdom. First, he argued that drunkenness was actually *less* of a problem in the countryside, because peasants and landowners who became drunks were forced to abandon their fields and thus paid a much higher price for their addiction. It was urban workers, housekeepers, and artisan guild masters who had less to lose and were therefore "with rare exceptions" drunks. Their children grew up to be drunks, too, because landlords preferred not to bear the cost of raising their servants' children, while master craftsmen did not take responsibility for apprentices beyond their initial training. Left to their own devices, urban youth wandered from town to town and fell in with bad company. It really did not matter who ran the taverns. "Whether it is a Jew with a liquor concession or a Christian," O. O. argued, "they are all the same. They try to persuade everyone to drink, induce them to drunkenness, pay for everything with vodka, bring vodka to the houses of those who want it and those who don't want it, and in most towns illegally receive help from the nobleman's court collecting their drinking debts."[86] He proposed that limits be placed on the sale of vodka and that the practice of leasing taverns be banned, whether the lessee be a Christian or a Jew.[87] In response, another contributor reminded O. O. that this was the nineteenth century, not the Middle Ages. Freedom of settlement meant that servants and artisans could move anywhere they chose. And wherever there is a "righteous, fair, and authoritative lord, people are prosperous, goodhearted, peaceful, and sober." But O. O.'s rejection of anti-Jewish clichés had been anything but medieval.[88]

Occasionally, individual government ministers spoke out against anti-Jewish liquor policies, too. As we have seen, Minister Badeni wondered aloud how any type of industry, including liquor, could be considered inappropriate for Jews or anyone else who, "for lack of land, do not engage in farming" (see chapter 2, above). More official doubts were voiced after the famous intercession by British Jewish philanthropist Sir Moses Montefiore in 1846.[89] Privy Minister Turkul was moved by Montefiore's argument that Jewish urban liquor concessions were unreasonably high and should be inheritable. He also had to admit that their rationale did not make sense, because "experience does not show the situation of the peasants to have improved since Jews were prohibited from selling drinks in [rural] settlements." He wondered if it might not be better to allow Jews to return to tavernkeeping in the countryside, since "they have less aptitude for other kinds of work," and since rural Christian tavernkeepers "distract themselves from other, incomparably more useful pursuits" like farming and crafts. Turkul also disliked the glaring inconsistencies in the urban tavernkeeping policy. Jewish tavernkeeping should either be completely banned or concessions should be equalized for all inhabitants, provided the tavernkeepers demonstrated "certain moral qualities."[90]

Such protests may have had a long-term effect. While the Jewish Committee of 1858 still clung to the official line, interpreting urban Jewish liquor concessions as a benevolent alternative to outright expulsion, the 1862 decree for partial emancipation of the Jews was a marked improvement.[91] Although it still prohibited the sale and production of alcohol by Jews in the countryside unless all the village's inhabitants were Jewish, that is, in Jewish agricultural colonies, it finally equalized urban Jewish liquor concessions with those of Christian inhabitants. At least every urban tavernkeeper had to shoulder the same burden now.[92]

CONCLUSION

Most urban Jewish tavernkeepers on the verge of expulsion or ruin could ill afford to wait around for Jewish communal leaders to intervene or for sweeping governmental reforms to be enacted. They had to learn to deploy the new civic-minded reasoning themselves, or at least with the help of professional petition writers. The whole exercise was, of course, primarily an attempt to gauge what members of the state apparatus wanted to hear in order to salvage their families' livelihood. But novel ideas are not so easily shed once they have been put to good use. In such petitions we may be witnessing the emergence of a new Jewish cast of mind and an enhanced sense of agency. Individual Jews not only mastered a discourse based on notions of the common good, they deployed that discourse without the mediation of Jewish communal leaders or members of the nobility, and occasionally to good effect. Some, like Perla Lewin, had absorbed the Enlightenment message more fully than the government bureaucrats themselves.

It was no accident that the new individual assertiveness appeared in urban centers, where noble autonomy had receded, where degrees of integration and secular education had been attained by select Jews, and where novel ideas were more easily exchanged. Official urban policies encouraged this individual assertiveness by awarding select Jews the right to live and work on restricted streets. But official policies were never ideologically consistent enough to effect more than that. As tavernkeepers on the verge of expulsion from choice streets were quick to learn, wealth nearly always trumped acculturation. And as we will see in the next chapter, loyalty to the tsarist regime during uprisings trumped even wealth. These inconsistencies have perplexed many historians, but are understandable within the logic of imperial cameralism. When it came down to it, ensuring the state's fiscal and political survival took priority over any experiments in social engineering.

CHAPTER 4

Soldiers, Smugglers, and Spies

Jewish Tavernkeepers during the Polish Uprisings of 1830 and 1863

In 1831, Jews from a town in the Samogitia District, in historical Lithuania, gathered in the local study house to discuss the current Polish insurrection against the tsar. Chaim Aronson, an acculturated Jew who was present at the meeting, emerged with the feeling that he finally had begun to understand the general Jewish attitude toward the Polish cause: "Each and every one of them dissembled in saying that he sought only love and brotherhood for those who took up arms on behalf of their flag: they spoke thus out of fear alone, for their feelings for all Governments were colder than ice. This was not due to any religious hatred, or to any differences in customs, but solely because of their continual cruelty towards the Jews throughout the whole of every year."[1] Persecution had simply rendered Jews apolitical: "It was the opinion of these oppressed people that the very occasional benefit which the Government bestowed upon them came from considerations of policy and economics, and could be likened to the care which a farmer showed his pig, or a shepherd his flock." Aronson concluded that the Jews of Samogitia did not care whether it was a "Pole or a Russian or a Chinese emperor who ruled over them." All governments treated Jews the same; none, in any event, was the royal House of David.[2]

This attitude toward political sovereignty, enshrined in the Talmudic dictum *dina de'malkhuta dina*—the law of the current kingdom is law, no matter which kingdom it may be—is what we have come to expect from the majority of Polish Jewry. But oddly enough, the passage follows right on the heels of a description of a fervently pro-Polish Lubavitcher Hasid named Moses ben David. So long as Moses lived among the Jews of Samogitia, Aronson tells us, the Poles would never harm them, for "his loyalty to the Poles and his love for the [Polish] people was well known to the Polish leaders, who did not conceal their plans and strategies from him."[3] Sure enough, on Passover eve, as terrified Jews fled the approaching Polish troops, Moses urged them to return to their homes and was able to ensure their safety.[4] It is quite difficult to square this Hasid's patriotism with the prior, more familiar model of cold pragmatism.

The complex issue of Jewish political alliances is crucial to our understanding of Jewish tavernkeepers, for it was they who became lightning rods for Polish recriminations in the wake of failed uprisings and other conflicts. According to an anonymous memo written during the War of 1812, for example, "Jews residing in villages transported messages from tavern to tavern like a relay race, with unbelievable rapidity; and Moscow, because of their uninterrupted communication, knew about the tiniest details, movements, and strategies of the [pro-Polish Napoleonic] army."[5] After the 1830 uprising, a periodical produced by a cadre of exiled Polish political elites known collectively as the "Great Emigration" complained that Jews had been allowed to resume tavernkeeping in the countryside as "a reward for the Muscovite patriotism of the Jews and a punishment for the Polish patriotism of the Poles," while another denounced new Jewish liquor concessions as "a further installment in the rewarding of Muscovite spies."[6] Admittedly, many Jews were awarded liquor concessions in the wake of uprisings (see chapter 3, above). And it seems plausible enough that tavernkeepers should have been favored as informants by Russians troops, considering their location, their traditional function as news sources, and their continual contact with large groups of strangers. But the presumed link between Jews, espionage, and the liquor trade has never been properly examined. The Polish archives hold some real surprises.[7]

JEWISH ATTITUDES DURING THE 1830 UPRISING

The 1830 uprising occurred mainly in the Kingdom of Poland, where constitutional guarantees had been scaled back and violated, where the army under the command of the Russian Grand Duke Constantine had stood demobilized and humiliated, and where expressions of Polish nationalist sentiment had been increasingly muffled by a network of secret police and informants. On November 29, 1830, Polish cadets staged an attack on Constantine's residence at Belweder Palace. Armed rioters filled the streets of Warsaw, massacring Jews in the poorhouse for allegedly spying for the Russians, until order was finally restored by a Polish revolutionary dictatorship.[8] Eventually, Jews were given a role in the revolutionary regime, albeit somewhat reluctantly, as national and civic guardsmen. Although the Tsarist army would suppress the uprising a year later, the brief experience of independence and the crushing disappointment that followed inspired works of great poignancy and genius by Polish exiles like Chopin, Mickiewicz, and Słowacki.

Historians like R. F. Leslie are less enthusiastic about the 1830 uprising, dismissing it as a rash venture that would not have improved the lot of the common people even if it had succeeded.[9] The inability of the rather conservative revolutionary leadership to project a coherent vision for social change may explain why some peasants expressed remarkably similar sentiments to those of the Samogitia Jews cited in the introduction to this chapter. "We do not like the Russians," one peasant conceded, "but will it be better for us peasants if we drive them out or destroy them? . . . Indeed, it will be better for the *lords* when they defeat the Russians. So let *them* fight them." Some peasant soldiers feigned death on the battlefield rather than risk their lives for what seemed to them an alien cause.[10]

Prewar Polish historians were nevertheless more critical about perceived Jewish disloyalty. Jewish historians strove mightily to combat such notions, compiling extensive information on the 137 acculturated Jews known to have volunteered for the Polish army and National Guard during the conflict.[11] To their list we might add more Jewish patriots, such as the four Jews mentioned on a list of forty-six "suspicious persons" who were interrogated and imprisoned on the eve of the uprising and another Jew among eighteen Polish prisoners of war.[12] But the whole exercise begins to feel rather apologetic, a point to which we will soon return.

Contemporary Polish historians have opted for a compromise of sorts. While dutifully noting support for the 1830 uprising among acculturated Jews, who served as volunteer soldiers, guards, medics, and financial contributors, they often maintain that the majority of Jews brazenly overcharged insurgents for army supplies, did brisk business with Russian soldiers, engaged in espionage on their behalf, and remained generally indifferent to the Polish cause. One recent study invokes an assessment made back in the more anti-Jewish context of 1936: "Closed within their business interests and the concerns of their separate existence, divided from the world by a wall of Hasidism, they did not feel love for those who lived and fought before their eyes around their houses."[13] Jewish behavior during the uprising is thus understood as a function of membership in one of two groups: a vanguard of wealthy, acculturated polonophiles, and an undifferentiated mass of fanatical, aloof Hasidim.[14]

This diachronic picture has admitted advantages for the contemporary discourse on Polish-Jewish relations since it provides some common ground—both groups can point to the acculturated cadre as evidence of a splendid Polish-Jewish coexistence. And if we restrict ourselves to sources on acculturated participants in the 1830 uprising on the one hand and members of the official Jewish leadership on the other, the picture even appears valid. Among the acculturated group, Józef Berkowicz formed a voluntary Jewish unit of the National Guard composed of Jews who were willing to shave their beards, against traditional Jewish proscriptions. The leading Jewish integrationist Jacob Tugendhold praised the volunteers' loyalty to "the soil upon which your forebears found refuge centuries ago, where the dusts of generations of your forefathers lie ... that should be, and is, your *homeland*."[15] A graduate of the modern Warsaw Rabbinical School recalls learning patriotic songs, wearing paper hats with the Polish colors, reading Mickiewicz and Polish history, and building ramparts by the Praga bridge. Much as he regarded the uprising as an affair strictly for the gentry and intelligentsia, in contrast to the next one (1863), he nevertheless felt an exalted patriotic feeling awakening in him and his fellow students.[16]

But petitions by acculturated Jews to tsarist officials *after* the suppression of the uprising, preserved in the archives of the Interior Ministry, begin to spoil the picture. Abraham Kinderfrajnd was a liquor importer and lessee of the liquor monopoly in Zamość who supplied the army with vodka. He professed to know how to read and write Polish and German perfectly, be "moral," and enjoy good relations with Christians. Not only had he not left Zamość during the uprising, he had maintained "proper ties with the true [i.e., Russian] regime," a fact attested to by eight Christian municipality members.[17] Local Christians also vouched for a Jewish doctor named Brauman during his bid for citizenship, describing his selfless ministrations to Christians during a cholera epidemic and emphasizing that he was "peaceful" during the uprising.[18] Józef Weilano, who wore "civilized clothes" and claimed not to distinguish himself from Christians in any way, boasted of having been appointed manager of a store in Lodz by the Russian Imperial Army during the uprising as a result of his fidelity.[19] Mojzesz Amszewicz, who had earned a silver medal from the Russian army during the 1812 campaign and had served in Grand Duke Constantine's court, narrowly escaped murder at the hands of the Warsaw mobs during the first days of the uprising and was financially ruined because of his loyalty to the tsarist regime.[20] Fiszel Handelman, who ran a tavern and a tobacco store and engaged in international trade, informed officials that he knew Polish perfectly, had had "nothing at all to do with the uprising, and at the same time demonstrated sympathy toward the legal regime by serving the Russian Imperial Army and serving as a deputy of the Lublin Synagogue Council during the revolutionary period." The regime awarded Fiszel citizenship and a gold medal.[21] In other words, one can compile information on acculturated Jews who supported the Russians just as historians have done for those who supported the Polish cause.

The other side of the assumed equation—the allegedly quietist or purely pragmatic Jewish majority—also finds support in certain sources. Markus Wohl, a Hasidic tavernkeeper from Krakow, fit the stereotype of political opportunism to a tee. He requested citizenship in the Kingdom of Poland as a reward for having helped ransom a Russian officer held prisoner in Galicia during the uprising, and claimed to have greatly improved on land that had come into his possession through foreclosure. He now wished to settle on it and assume full ownership. But Polish officials determined that Markus was nothing more than a scoundrel who had done little but build a tavern and brewery on his land and had fallen deeply into debt. They indignantly rejected the requests of this "Jew whose politics are confined to considerations of financial gain" and forbade him to live in the kingdom.[22]

The attitudes of Synagogue Council representatives could appear to confirm the image of political apathy among the less acculturated Jewish mainstream as well. Synagogue Council members—who, it must be remembered, derived their authority from the state and stood to suffer most from tsarist retribution—evinced only pragmatic support for the Polish revolutionary regime, as reflected in their cautious endorsements of the proposed Jewish unit. The hefty increases in the "recruitment tax" paid by Jews in lieu of military service, which have been criticized by several historians, were partly their idea. During the first weeks of the uprising, requests for such increases began to stream in from regional Synagogue Council representatives eager to prevent their constituencies from being drafted. A Polish district commissioner, in an interesting reversal, argued indignantly *against* any increase in the Jewish recruitment tax, believing it unfair that military service should fall only on "the Good Christian Citizenry, while less useful Israelites are only liable for a fee of a few zlotys." He was rebuffed, however, in view of the "pressing needs of the Treasury."[23]

Yet attitudes among the less acculturated varied as much as those among the more acculturated. Some traditionalists appeared passionately pro-Russian, particularly those who resided in the Russian Empire proper and had witnessed excesses by Polish troops. Jacob Lipschitz, having witnessed the hanging of an accused Jewish spy, evinced sheer contempt toward the Polish rebels: "In truth they had no weapons, no artillery, and no soldiers apart from serfs who knew neither discipline nor the difference between right and left." Many had been foolish enough to go up against the Russian army with scythes and sickles.[24] In the Kingdom of Poland, Jacob ha-Levi Levin, who was falsely accused of espionage by Polish rebels and taken captive along with his famous brother-in-law Solomon Marcus Posner, rebuked the rebels for their ingratitude toward the tsar, who had helped Poles develop their economy and "out of his great love for them helped them out of all their difficulties, more than any other people under his rule."[25] In contrast, Posner himself declared that he and his son were "patriotic" and "burning with love of the native land," Poland.[26]

Volunteers of the Polish insurrectionist regime's more traditionalist Jewish Civic Guard, consisting of Jewish volunteers who insisted on keeping their beards, actually outnumbered the acculturated Jews of the National Guard by a ratio of more than four to one. A Jewish memoirist named Pinḥas Schweitzer describes thirty of such volunteers on the streets of his native town, Będzin, carrying swords and wearing caps emblazoned with the words "Security Guard." "This was an unforgettable picture," Pinḥas recalls with continued amazement. "Pious Jews in long capotes abandoned their trade and their study houses and patrolled the town markets."[27] A Polish revolutionary soldier recalls being amused at the sight of ragged adolescent Jews in uniform shooing street urchins away from the entrance of the Saxon Gardens in Warsaw. One of the Jews announced proudly, "Don't laugh, sir; I also belong to the armed forces, for I am a member of the Civic Guard."[28] Jewish tavernkeepers, for their part, were known to harbor Polish rebels from time to time. Oral traditions recall cases of Polish noblemen hidden by Jewish tavernkeepers who would "crawl out from behind the oven once the Russians had departed, twirl their mustaches, and shout at their protectors 'Jews, off with your hats!'"[29]

When we peer behind the "wall of Hasidism," there are more surprises. According to Hasidic sources, Menaḥem Mendel of Kotzk (Kock) and Isaac Meir Alter of Ger (Góra Kalwaria) circulated a decree urging their devotees to raise money for the Polish National Guard.[30] A Hasidic servant who volunteered for the Polish army was allegedly saved from a bullet by R. Isaac Meir's blessing.[31] After the suppression of the revolt these tzaddikim had to flee to Brody, then under Habsburg rule, to avoid police scrutiny. R. Menaḥem Mendel changed his surname from Halpern to Morgenstern, while R. Isaac Meir changed his from Rothenberg to Alter. The latter's later bid for the post of assistant rabbi of Warsaw was unsuccessful after he was denounced for having supported the Polish rebels.[32]

Hasidic polonophilia endured throughout the lands of partitioned Poland, especially in the Kingdom of Poland, during the period between the 1830 and 1863 uprisings. The tzaddik Ḥayim Me'ir Yeḥi'el Shapira of Mogielnica confessed to feeling depressed and guilt-ridden after the angelic representative of Poland appeared to him in a dream and chastised him for not having prayed for the uprising's success.[33] Gecl Salcstein, a Kotzker Hasid and antiquarian Polish book dealer whom the Polish press deemed "a promoter of knowledge and discoverer of Polish cultural treasures," was kept under strict police surveillance as a result of his pro-Polish activities.[34] Memoirist Ezekiel Kotik describes "Israel, the Polish Patriot Hasid," a Kotzker from the town of Siedlce who trumpeted his pro-Polish sentiments in Kotik's grandfather's tavern and then slid into alcoholism and despair after the suppression of the 1863 uprising. That so many pro-Polish Hasidim were Kotzkers suggests that the political attitudes of tzaddikim determined those of their thousands of devotees. This sense is reinforced by the insurrectionist General Samuel Rozycki's report that "although in many other cases the Jews were also unfriendly towards us, however, that morning, the Jewish inhabitants of Kotzk made all efforts, not sparing their furniture and household goods for barricading the streets."[35]

A most extraordinary Hasidic tradition relates that the tzaddik Samuel Abba of Żychlin (Lodz District) "used to always pray that the government and kingdom of Poland would be raised up and restored," and preached sermons in favor of Polish independence:

> And the mouth of our rabbi of blessed memory used to constantly utter that the bringing of the righteous Messiah depended on this [Polish restoration]. Because first, the Polish state had to have its autonomy restored as a reward for granting permission to exiled Israel to come and settle in its land, and for receiving [Israel] with open arms . . . after its expulsion from Germany and other lands, . . . and allowing it to raise the banner of Torah and Hasidism, to the extent that all of our rabbinic authorities of the *Shulḥan arukh* and all of our masters of Hasidism emerged from the innards of the Polish state.[36]

R. Samuel Abba preached these ideas despite the presence of tsarist spies in his audiences. It was a particularly dangerous time to be spreading such a message—the Russians had just uncovered a conspiracy led by Father Piotr Ściegienny in autumn of the prior year.[37] R. Samuel Abba was accused of espousing a "new creed in order to draw the people of Israel to him so that they will band together and rebel against the Russian Kingdom that rules over the Polish state," and was condemned as "one of the emissaries of the insurrectionists, who sent him to turn the hearts of the children of

Israel and co-opt them in order to win over their minds and return the state of Poland to their own hands."[38] On a Sabbath eve in 1845, Russian soldiers surrounded R. Samuel Abba's study house, arrested everyone inside, confiscated all the books, and imprisoned the tzaddik in Kutno for three weeks. Only the intervention of the most influential Warsaw Jewish lobbyists (shtadlanim) secured his release.[39]

Of course, acculturated Jews suffered for their support of the Polish cause as well. Józef Berkowicz, organizer of the Jewish unit of the National Guard, spent his remaining days in exile in Paris. Berkowicz was an unlikely exilic patriot—the son of the first Jewish colonel, Berek Joselewicz, who had fought in the Napoleonic legions and died a heroic death, he had been accused of acquiring an illegal stipend upon his mother's death, and several witnesses had attested to his bad character during the ensuing trial. His efforts to form a Jewish legion during the uprising were seen as an attempt to clear his name. But Berkowicz continued to display a yearning for Poland's resurrection long after he had been exiled, composing a gushing paean to Polish valor and resistance to tsarist despotism in a novella entitled *Stanislaus the Polish Lancer* (London, 1846). His fidelity to the Polish cause forms a stark contrast to the behavior of Jacob Tugendhold, who, ever the careerist, swiftly renounced his support of the insurrection in order to recover his governmental post. Such behavior was typical of many bureaucrats—Polish and Jewish—in the wake of the uprising. The tsarist regime, lacking sufficient numbers of skilled and literate clerks, had little alternative but to forgive them.[40]

It is difficult to explain Jewish motivations for supporting a Polish cause that seemed to promise them so little. Acculturated Jews may have been betting on emancipation. Less acculturated Jews may have feared that the notorious recruitment and cantonist decrees that had been tearing apart poorer segments of Jewish communities in the Russian Pale of Settlement since 1827 would be extended to the kingdom next. But certain Hasidic Jews, similar to Berkowicz, carried their Polish patriotism into exile. One Polish author experienced this as an epiphany while conversing with a Jew named Srul of Lubartów during his Siberian exile. "I no longer doubted that this old Jew, this fanatic Hasid, was pining for [Poland] just as much as I was," he wrote, "and that we were both sick with the same sickness. This unexpected discovery moved me deeply."[41]

This is not to say that there was not also a good deal of apathy and double-dealing among the kingdom's Jews. Historian Leon Hollaenderski, writing some fifteen years after the event, summed up the Jewish dilemma: "the Poles beat the Jews suspected of serving Russia; the Russians gave the knout to the Jews because they thought that they assisted the

Polish insurrection."[42] In such a situation, many must have simply hoped to survive the conflict with their lives and livelihoods intact. The archives only occasionally preserve evidence of a Jew managing to play to both sides successfully. According to one case, tsarist officials decided to reward a tavernkeeper named Elias Berko Chwat, who had fought in the 8th Infantry during the Napoleonic Wars and had had his tavern destroyed during the uprising, with citizenship and a special privilege for producing and selling liquor on a restricted street. Unbeknownst to them, Elias's two sons had volunteered for the Polish army during the uprising.[43]

JEWISH ESPIONAGE DURING THE 1830 UPRISING

In the absence of popular support for the 1830 uprising, espionage remained a constant problem for insurgents, and few were ready to suspect their fellow Poles. According to one former rebel, "most spies were Jews and German colonists, and occasionally foreign residents and craftsmen."[44] Another veteran lamented, "In our own country Moscow had, through Jews, better spies than we did."[45] Exiled Prince Adam Jerzy Czartoryski concluded that "the enemy almost always received in a curious way news about the movements of our troops, which proves that Jews served them."[46] The literary critic and former rebel Maurice Mochnacki explained, "Spying aroused reaction on our side. We hung the Jews, we were forced to hang them." In addition to spying, according to Mochnacki, Jews supplied Russia like a "giant artery that spread across the country in every direction, from the tavernkeeper and factor in Berdichev all the way to the throne of the autocrats!"[47] Only Antoni Ostrowski, a commander of the Polish National Guard who had been favorably impressed by his Jewish volunteers, publicly and vigorously denied the oft-repeated claim among his colleagues "Jews, rascals, spies aid Moscow."[48]

The archives of the Polish revolutionary regime happen to preserve extensive lists of accused spies from 1830 to 1831. Surprisingly, such lists contain a sizeable majority of Polish Christian names. There were only three Jews among forty-three arrestees on one list; three Jews among fourteen arrestees on a second; six Jews among nineteen arrestees on a third; two Jews among eight arrestees on a fourth; eleven Jews among seventy arrestees on a fifth; and on the sixth and largest list, fifty-eight Jews among 134 arrestees.[49] The suspected Polish Christian spies have been effaced from Polish national history and memory, leaving only a residual memory of accused Jews. If Poland was the "Christ among the nations," Jews were supposedly its Judas.

It should be emphasized that those on the lists were only accused, and that accusations did not always prove true. A Polish commander in Warka reported that seven Jews had been caught and were presumed to be spying for the enemy because they did not register with the local police, but upon examining them he was "convinced that there is no evidence of the guilt of these Jews."[50] But having one's innocence determined was not always enough. A Polish general listed twenty-two accused Jews as possibly including "several who should be considered innocent." Yet he preferred to err on the side of caution, since "setting them free could be harmful to our cause." Perhaps a few guilty ones had been caught in the net.[51]

The experience of arrest could be traumatic for Jews and Christians alike. A Jewish prisoner was plundered and had his life threatened with a razor. A Polish Christian prisoner was beaten until his head bled.[52] The experience sometimes encouraged altruistic gestures between Jews and Christians. A Polish Christian imprisoned on spying charges, left to nearly starve to death, was rescued by a Jewish merchant named Abraham Goldman. According to a Christian mayor, Abraham had passed food to the prisoner via his daughter at no cost and eventually helped him escape from the fortress by passing him a key. As a result, Abraham had suffered "intolerable curses and harassment from the Polish Revolutionary army, in particular at the hands of the 17th infantry under the command of Colonel Sierakowski." Soon Abraham himself was arrested for spying, placed under police surveillance, and forced to suffer "great losses." He nearly lost his life when a Polish revolutionary officer entered his house and attempted to shoot him as a suspected spy.[53]

Maltreatment by the revolutionaries caused some to question their legitimacy. The wife of an accused Polish Christian spy who had been languishing in prison for months scolded police, "'Free Poland' is not just a hollow phrase; it must be realized in actuality."[54] But maltreatment also bore fruit, as many accused spies agreed to become Polish agents in exchange for their freedom. Bernard Goldring, arrested for spying, is later listed as a member of the secret police and described as of the "Mosaic persuasion, forty-four, round face, dark hair, tall body, black eyes, long nose with whiskers, resident of 335 Nowe Miasto, Warsaw, married, merchant with merchandise from Nuremberg and collector for the lottery, signed on as an Agent for 126 zlotys per month under the label 'award for contributing to a regiment in 1823.'" Bernard's main duty was to report on "every step" made by new arrivals to Warsaw. The number of agents serving the Polish revolutionary regime rose to seven hundred.[55]

False accusations could prove fatal, particularly for Jews. The insurrectionist leader Ostrowski recalls a tragic incident that occurred as his cavalry was passing through a certain village and a Jew was spotted peering out from a hole under his rooftop. "Halt! We have a spy! Bring him down." The man was hanged on the spot. Ostrowski still felt pangs of conscience several years after the affair: "It turned out that this Jew, hiding in fear of ill treatment, had taken refuge and was looking out from above to see whether the danger had passed. He was totally innocent, and a father of six children." Thanks to Ostrowski's sense of decency, the officer responsible for the execution was demoted and imprisoned, but "the Jew who was hanged remained hanged, and his children, it was reported to me, remained orphans in the direst poverty. Can we really demand that they sincerely love Poland?" Ostrowski rejected the notion that the proportion of Jewish spies was any higher. But one should not be surprised if "some Jews should be found cowardly enough to become spies" after witnessing such treatment.[56]

The case of the entrepreneur Solomon Marcus Posner, mentioned earlier, illustrates how easily a Jewish proprietor could be arrested on false pretences. On March 4, 1831, a contingent of twelve Cossacks in the Russian army appeared at Posner's agricultural colony in Kuchary and forced him to provide them with bread and vodka. After they departed, Posner's son immediately reported their presence to Polish rebels in the area, at great personal risk. The next day, another band of Cossacks appeared asking for bread and vodka, and this time Posner claimed he didn't have any. That evening, yet another small Cossack contingent appeared, took hay, and confiscated a horse that belonged to Posner's caretaker. Toward the end of March, a merchant came with the intention of purchasing six hundred gallons of liquor from Posner, who patriotically refused to sell it when he learned it would be resold to Russian troops. All might have been well, but Posner had enemies: he had helped convict the mayor of a neighboring village of theft and perjury several months earlier. In retaliation, the mayor denounced Posner to the rebels for having aided the enemy troops with bread and vodka. Posner, his son, and five friends and relatives were arrested, and remained in fear of their lives for months until an investigation cleared them. His estate and factory in ruins, and having endured the loss of six hundred gallons of unspecified liquor, two hundred gallons of vodka, silver items, and other possessions, Posner requested compensation from the revolutionary regime and might have eventually received it had the uprising not been quashed.[57]

Surprisingly enough, the few tavernkeepers on lists of accused spies were non-Jews. Andrzej Michalski, listed as a Catholic tavernkeeper in Warsaw, was arrested for signing a receipt for one hundred zlotys that came from a Jewish tavernkeeper, but the transaction turned out to be legal. Jakub

Weinman, a Protestant tavernkeeper in Warsaw (possibly a convert), was released from prison when the Secret Police found the denunciation of him to be groundless. Another Polish tavernkeeper, Vincent Makowski, was arrested for spying as well. If we rely on the insurrectionist archives we come up empty-handed.[58]

SMUGGLERS

While Jewish criminality looms large in the anti-Semitic imagination, archival sources reveal that the black-market system throughout the formerly Polish lands was neither absolutely criminal nor disproportionately Jewish. The ambiguity was especially noticeable during periods of military conflict. After the suppression of the 1830 uprising, for example, Russian Major General Glutan felt compelled to intervene on behalf of Pesach Herszkowicz, Abram Ickowicz, and Zelig Gilbertowicz, three Jews who were imprisoned for smuggling during the fighting. The general explained that the three Jews had served the Russian army by "supplying them with various things." They had traveled with his division to the town of Kielce and, unable to procure any tobacco there for the troops, had acquired it illegally. The general conceded that the tobacco office was correct to arrest the Jews and confiscate (in addition to forty-one boxes of tobacco) some soap, a half pack of candles, seven gems, 652 zlotys, and two horses with carts. But the culprits had been sitting in prison for the last few months. The general believed that "these Jews have suffered enough by not being able to sell their merchandise," and asked that they be freed and compensated for their confiscated goods.[59] In a similar incident, General Witt, the governor of Warsaw, requested the return of 470 pounds of coffee, three horses with carts, fifteen quarts of fruit, and five hundred zlotys, all confiscated from the Jew Mojzesz Boruchowicz, since he had been attempting to supply those goods to the Russian army as it had approached Warsaw. The army had needed all the supplies and information it could get.[60] The lesson in these cases seems to be that smuggling was not a crime if it benefitted one's own army, particularly during wartime.

When it benefitted the other side, of course, it was a different story. A Polish spy report complained of Jews energetically selling "numerous, varied foreign products" like tobacco, tea, leather, and horses to Russian soldiers in territory that had come under their control. Worse, the spy accused Jews of informing Russian soldiers about which homes were sheltering Polish rebels and which ones offered the best opportunities for pillage.[61] In another case, the Polish Revolutionary regime arrested two Jews for "supplying vodka to the enemies," i.e., the Russian army.[62] In a third case, Manas Lichstain, a fourteen-year-old boy, was caught selling liquor to the Russians. Manas's mother explained to the revolutionary authorities that in February her son had gone with certain people from Warsaw to the village of Gluchowce with vodka and had bought 127 gallons of vodka in Siekierek. But she maintained that none of her son's vodka was given to the Russians. Moreover, she argued, everyone else who was involved had been freed, and only her young son remained in the Chęciny prison with arrested spies. Nevertheless, Polish revolutionary officials had testimony claiming that her son had loaded bottles of vodka onto the frozen Vistula River and transported them to the enemy army, and that he had intended to transport another 105 gallons to Warsaw "with Mojzesz Milszteyn and others." Her son would have to remain in prison in Chęciny until the Treasury completed its investigation.[63]

Smuggling was always a crime during peacetime. It did not matter that inventories of seized contraband reveal the most innocuous goods, including sugar, coffee, linen, silk, woolens, cotton stockings, and so on.[64] In the aftermath of the uprising, replenishing Treasury coffers required strict enforcement of duties and tolls. The cost of these sought-after commodities was especially prohibitive because the tsarist regime, in the wake of the 1830 uprising, had erected a punitive customs barrier with Russia that would remain in effect for twenty years.

As in the case of espionage, the evidence of disproportionate smuggling among Jewish tavernkeepers is largely anecdotal. And as in the case of espionage, lists of arrestees for smuggling are quite ethnically and religiously mixed. During the 1830–31 uprising, a list of twenty-two convicted smugglers included fourteen Jews; a list of twelve convicted smugglers from the town of Płock included four Jews; but a list of twelve convicted smugglers from Lublin District did not contain any Jews at all.[65] Whatever the actual proportion, however, the stereotype of the Jewish smuggler held such power as to cause Polish lawmakers to ignore the findings of their own investigations.

In early 1834, official investigations revealed involvement by Poles, Germans, and Jews alike in smuggling schemes. The first such investigation occurred in Sokołów, where a customs chief had observed "several shady Jews involved in defrauding the Treasury." He arrested two Jews, Abraham Rosenbaum of Sokołów and Mejer Grun of Warsaw, but Abraham and Mejer insisted on their innocence, requested the return of their legal merchandise, and agreed, in turn, to denounce some "actual" smugglers. The customs official agreed, but was disappointed to find that most of their leads only disclosed the activities of non-Jewish culprits. He learned, for example, that a Polish border guard named Lipowski, presently on vacation, was in on smuggling schemes. Thanks to Lipowski, a merchant pretending to sell food was able to get his contraband through Gródek, the main point of entry for contraband on the Russian side of the border. He also learned that in Konstantyn, there was a Christian tavernkeeper who "does an effective imitation of Jews" by engaging in smuggling. This was the only language the investigator could find to describe a Pole who was engaging in a presumably Jewish endeavor.[66]

Another Christian tavernkeeper, Jakub Kurlag, told the investigator more of what he wanted to hear, namely, that there were indeed Jewish smugglers in the area. But the investigator probably did not appreciate Kurlag's explanation: because of the miserable economic condition of Jewish tailors, tanners, tavernkeepers, salt traders, and other petty traders, Kurlag argued, such Jews were "obliged by circumstances" to abet foreign Jews passing through their towns.[67] The investigator also learned that two years earlier, on the night of March 4, 1832, a transport of goods had been passed illegally to Captain Sianozecki, who used military carts to bring them to the town of Wincenta and was assisted by an officer named Kazacki. Jewish merchants distributed the goods. In addition, two Jewish merchants from the town of Międzyrzecz obtained merchandise from over the border three weeks earlier and were now awaiting the return of a Polish customs clerk named Chrzanowski, presently on vacation, who would expedite their venture. Other investigators were carrying out surveillance on the Jew Gedalia Markusfeld, who was bringing suspicious goods, including thirty-nine scarves and some silk, from Łomża. Officials had seized six hundred pounds of coffee and some arak, but no one had come forward to claim it. A significant amount of sugar, coffee, arak, and textiles were also found stashed in a field by Kielcze village. Investigators learned that the contraband had been conveyed by some ten to twenty soldiers under the command of two Prussian officers, with the help of two border guards who had been injured during the crossing.[68]

Further investigations produced an equally rich religio-ethnic mix. Several Jews were caught with contraband upon their return to Russia from the Leipzig trade fair.[69] But a list of five people who were considered "likely to attempt to smuggle across the Russian border" contained only Christians: a wool merchant, a textile merchant, a tailor, a coppersmith, and a soap maker.[70] Officials also discovered that the memoirist Harro Harring, mentioned earlier, had slipped illegally over the border with a false English passport under the name Edward Benett, along with other Christians.[71] These investigations did little to support beliefs about the Jewish profile of smuggling.

Figure 4.1: Alexander Rizzoni, *Jewish Smugglers*, 1860.

It mattered little in the end. So entrenched was the stereotype that the only solution to smuggling that officials could muster was to ban Jewish residence in border towns. A decree from May 1834 outlawed most Jewish settlement in 111 towns along the Prussian and Austrian borders. Only Jews who engaged in occupations like farming, domestic servitude, crafts, or factory work were allowed to remain, for such occupations did not "lend themselves to fraud." Numerous Jewish families were thus made to suffer dislocation for the crimes of a few coreligionists and their Christian collaborators.[72]

There were also local versions of "smuggling," such as bootlegging or the theft and resale of an employer's liquor. Such cases entailed the same strong Jewish-Christian symbiosis as transnational smuggling, and seemed to defy assumptions about ethnic solidarity just as frequently. A Jew named Samuel Ryngler, for example, was caught selling five barrels of mead, thereby defrauding Markus Goldman, a Jewish lessee of the local liquor monopoly. Samuel had cost Markus a total of nine hundred zlotys, yet was only fined six hundred zlotys and the cost of the proceedings. Perhaps authorities were less concerned when an operation only involved one Jew defrauding another.[73]

An investigation in May 1831 uncovered the most extensive transcendence of ethnic allegiances. A Jewish tavern worker named Hirsz Rozenthal, it appears, had been stealing liquor from his Jewish boss, Jakub Freudenreych, and stealthily selling it to Christian tavernkeepers throughout the area for months. A Polish landowner (Woyciech Sierociński) testified that Hirsz had arrangements with certain tavern workers to provide him with food in exchange for the illegal vodka "because the tavernkeeper [Jakub] did not give him enough food, probably only enough for a decent meal when he had a flask of vodka to give him [to use as currency]." Hirsz was evidently selling his boss's liquor to Christian tavernkeepers because he was hungry.[74]

During the continuation of the investigation, the mayor of Mogielnica questioned three Christian wagon drivers (Ignacy Czarnecki, Józef Zawiski, and Antony Zawistak), three Christian tavernkeepers (Antony Chajecki; his wife, Maria; and Jan Przedozynski), two Christian tavern workers (Tadeusz Paszkowicz and Karol Hanneke), and another landowner who supplied liquor (Antony Ciempiniak), in addition to Hirsz and Jakub themselves. Hirsz was running quite an operation. He transported liquor by wagon, by boat, and by rolling barrels through fields. He compensated his drivers by letting them drink from the barrels he was transporting, and paid them a little extra for promising not to tell the buyers. He sold yeast, beer, mead, and vodka to at least ten taverns in the vicinity, storing and combining barrels in various cellars and barns. Karol Hanneke, a tavern worker in Starowiejski detailed six transactions amounting to twenty-seven gallons for a total of 112 zlotys. The landowner Sierocinski testified that he knew of at least one incident in which Hirsz had transported three barrels holding about 7.5 gallons of liquor to Antony Zawistak's house on Otakeski Street.[75]

When it was finally his turn to testify, Hirsz came out swinging:

> I completely deny the charge of Woyciech Sierocinski, who claims that when going to Stary village . . . the tavern worker gave me a certain amount of liquor, for I never took any vodka from this worker nor took any home; he only sometimes gave me a couple of little bottles of vodka in the tavern. And I also do not admit that I transferred three barrels to Otakeski [street]. I only sometimes mixed vodka in Owczarz tavern in Stary village. And finally, although this vodka belonged to the Jew Jakub Freudenreych, I did not take it from the tavern worker; rather, Jakub himself always allowed me to take this liquor. In addition, I do not admit to the charges of other people and the tavern worker Karol Hanneke, and declare that their testimony is false and that I never took liquor from that tavern worker, only from the lessee Freudenreych.[76]

Hirsz's denial was impressive for its forcefulness, but it relied entirely on the corroboration of his boss, whom he had defrauded. Predictably enough, Jakub Freudenreych declared that it was "a falsehood down to the last detail that the Jew Hirsz Rozenthal was permitted to take the liquor, all the more so to mix it." Maybe he was at Owczarza tavern and at Formal tavern in Stary village of his own accord, but Jakub had certainly not agreed to the journey, "for when I did give him liquor it was only sometimes a single quart for the Sabbath, at most two quarts, and never several gallons."[77] Hirsz's fate is left to the imagination. But it is probable that his new home was the local prison, where he was hopefully better fed.

A related issue was the use of Jewish-run taverns and former taverns, now cheap restaurants (*garkuchnie*), as storage depots and places to fence contraband and stolen goods. It seems reasonable to assume that the experience of running technically illegal taverns had blurred the boundaries of criminality for some tavernkeepers to such an extent that they were rather easily drawn into such ventures. No one, of course, admitted their involvement. A Jewish tavernkeeper named David Berger was fined and deprived of his liquor concession in 1852 on the charge that in his tavern "there occurred nightly flirtations," and that he was a "conduit for stolen goods that a certain woman stored with me, for which I was wrongly arrested, and which I know nothing about." David sought a cancellation of the fine and the return of his liquor concession on the grounds that he had been loyal to the Russian monarchy and had provided the Russian army with horses during the 1830–31 uprising. Significantly, he did not take credit for any acts of espionage.[78]

The most extensive investigation into such practices occurred in the Lublin District. Once again, the operation defied ethnoreligious allegiances. In August of 1850, two Jewish merchants were attacked by bandits and robbed of 304 zlotys. In response to the incident, the district governor made a personal inspection of every legal tavern on the road to Warsaw within his jurisdiction, but "did not find fault with any tavernkeepers, all of whom are known to be upstanding and beyond suspicion." He felt it more prudent to focus on "Jews who run cheap restaurants, whose coreligionists roam about at night without purpose and give shelter to some individuals who have engaged in theft and help them to hide their stolen items." The governor believed that the attack on the Jewish merchants was connected to a cheap restaurant in Ryki, called Pod Bocianami (Under the Storks). A Jewish land lessee named Eli Rozenberg was the proprietor of the restaurant, where "a number of Jews [would] come to him carrying primarily stolen goods." Many stolen items had already been found with Eli.[79]

The road from Ryki comprised a veritable theft zone, the governor explained. It extended ten miles toward the Vistula River, was covered by trees and foliage, and had many buildings and settlements inhabited by Jews, including "limitless" numbers of cheap restaurants, about one every two miles. The Jews there assisted and provided shelter to coreligionists who committed thefts and assaults. Police in the area were too understaffed to be effective. The Ryki landowner had been called upon to expel thieves not only from Pod Bocianami but from all of his land. Other landowners had been likewise warned about Jewish roadside restaurants. For the sake of order in this area and the safety of residents and travelers, the governor recommended that Jewish-run restaurants be limited to points along the road where there were post offices. Gendarmes and Cossacks should be brought in to patrol the area and clean it up. And Jewish proprietors of such restaurants should be made to purchase a concession for their cheap restaurants, just as Christians running taverns had been required to do since 1848.[80]

The central government's response to the report was measured. There was no sense in expelling Jews from roadside establishments, officials in Warsaw argued, for they sold hay, straw, bread, and vinegar to travelers in addition to running restaurants for traveling Jewish merchants. Expulsions would only hurt local economies. On the other hand, the Warsaw officials liked the concession proposal, so long as it was limited to 7.5 kopeks. Sure enough, in 1853, rural Jews who had made the transition from running taverns to running roadside restaurants since the 1844 ban on rural Jewish tavernkeeping were once again made to purchase concessions.[81]

In the meantime, investigators learned of a band of horse thieves who worked the road from Bełżyce (Lublin District) to Miklos village (Radzyn District). By arresting and interrogating all known thieves in the area they learned that Eli continually provided refuge for thieves. The Jew Hillel Hoffman would also attest to this. Moreover, a tavernkeeper told them that a train conductor had told him that he saw Eli with the thieves Abraham Szajnglas and Hirsz Kaczka, drawing horses and oxen toward a band of highwaymen in the dead of night. Finally, additional thefts had occurred within three miles of Eli's house, which could not be mere coincidence. The district court therefore ordered Eli's expulsion, forbidding him, in addition, to live near any main road.[82]

The sentence was not carried out. A higher court ruled that "hearsay against a Jew is never just, for only evidence can establish guilt." No matter how strong one's moral conviction and how widespread the rumors may be, the verdict continued, there can be no sentencing without proof. The court acknowledged the mayor of Ryki's opinion that Eli must be expelled, but also considered the opinion of the landowner, who had stepped in to protect his Jewish lessee. The landowner testified that the previous mayor of Ryki and former residents, who "wish[ed] to possess the [Pod] Bocian[ami] properties" and had lost a prior case against Eli, had falsely denounced him, caused him enormous losses, and succeeding in getting him expelled.

A new investigation would undoubtedly show that the accusations against Eli were "false and groundless," the landowner promised. The court consequently acquitted Eli, but issued a veiled warning: the Ryki landowner was surely not so stubborn about wanting his lease money as to overlook Eli's guilt and allow him to ruin his property. If he was willing to vouch for Eli, he must agree to take responsibility for all theft and abuses on his lands.[83]

It is quite possible that the nobleman was covering for Eli because he was in on the theft ring. It seems unlikely that he would go to such lengths to protect Eli for a mere lease payment. While we have noted landowner complicity in the case of the underground Jewish liquor trade, we have yet to consider a similar phenomenon in the black market. It is also quite possible that Jews were indeed found among the bandits who roamed the region, to judge by prior investigations. In the Ukraine in 1825, for example, officials had arrested nine members of the Kinskaia gang, including their leader, the Jew Iosel Liubarskii, for the robbery and murder of a retired colonel and five Mennonites. A three-year investigation resulted in their conviction.[84] Closer to the time and place of the current discussion is a case in Łomża from 1840. According to police, a twelve-year-old Polish Christian boy was going through the forest in search of his father when he was allegedly attacked and beaten by five bandits whose physiognomy and dress revealed them to be Jews. Officials pondered whether the incident was an attempted ritual murder, since the boy claimed that he had nearly been killed by the bandits; but they rejected that interpretation in the end.[85]

JEWISH ESPIONAGE DURING THE 1863 UPRISING

Ignacy Kraszewski's *Para czerwona* (The Red Couple, 1905), a novel about the 1863 uprising, introduces the reader to two distinct types of Polish Jews. First, we meet the young Dr. Hensch, a restless Jewish Renaissance man who plays the piano, sings, draws caricatures, studies chemistry and biology, knows several languages, writes verse, "falls in love every three days," and cares for wounded Polish partisans. Next, for a brief moment, we come upon his mirror opposite, a Jewish tavernkeeper dangling from a pine tree, hung as a traitor. Although Kraszewski's story centers on Dr. Hensch, both characters embodied prominent images of Jews during the 1863 uprising.[86]

The former image of positive Jewish participation in the 1863 uprising has achieved iconic stature. Polish artists and poets, in addition to prose writers like Kraszewski, have reveled in this moment of Polish and Jewish brotherhood, however brief it may have been. Alexander Lesser painted the iconic scene of Rabbi Dov Ber Meisels accompanying the archbishop of Warsaw at the funeral of the first victims of the demonstrations in 1861 that led up to the insurrection. The death of the Jewish student Michał Landy, who took up a cross from a wounded fellow protester before being shot down himself, inspired a dramatic painting by Tony Robert-Fleury and a poem by Cyprian Kamil Norwid. Jewish historians have, of course, compiled meticulous information on the estimated two thousand Jews, mainly Warsaw polonophiles, who fought in Polish units.[87]

Writers, artists, poets, and historians have been more reluctant to delve into the second type, the traitorous Jewish tavernkeeper. But as Kraszewski's novel shows, this second type was also emblazoned onto the Polish national imagination; and much as it may endanger the image of Polish Jewish cooperation, it is our task here to reflect as accurately as possible what the sources say about Jews' political loyalties and alliances, particularly when they concern the liquor trade. Surprisingly enough, given the tendency to celebrate it as a moment of Polish-Jewish brotherhood, the evidence for Jewish spying is actually more abundant in the case of the 1863, or "January," uprising. It turns out that certain Jews did, indeed, work decisively and energetically against this uprising, and the archives contain stark revelations by tavernkeepers and aspiring tavernkeepers.

They are rather easily identified. After the uprising's suppression, Jewish loyalists once again came forward to claim their prize from the tsarist regime, which nearly always took the form of a liquor concession. Knowing they no longer had anything to fear from the Polish rebels, they were quite candid about their services, and their harrowing tales are preserved in the kingdom's police archives. Among the most forthcoming is a petition by Lejb Kroszynski, a tavernkeeper's son. "At the time that the commotion began in the country," he reported, "I did not avoid any cost or effort to be useful to the True Regime, and I was even willing to endanger my life to provide reports about every secret guard on the side of the insurrectionists that was threatening from over the border, and they were not able to escape or retreat, as witnessed by Col. Troktfetter." Lejb's activities had paid off handsomely for the Russian troops, for "several defense parties of the insurrectionists were discovered and caught because of my reports, and every aspiration was achieved because of my other important services." Lejb was even candid about his motivations: he did all this, he wrote, "so that at any time of need, I may expect the grace and care of the regime."[88] Army officials had promised Lejb seventy-five rubles "as compensation for crucial discoveries and important news," which he had not yet received. But he would be content with a liquor concession for a tavern in the town of Słupiec, where his father ran a tavern on a nontransferrable concession.

According to Lejb, the town was permitted a total of seven taverns, and there were at present only four.[89]

Abram Lubelski, an aspiring tavernkeeper, took credit for a significant Russian victory, claiming, "Because of my positive inclination, I was the first in the kingdom, in the year 1863 on January 11–12, to take a risk and reveal the secret position of the insurrectionists. And I thereby protected two installments from night attacks, and they slaughtered the [rebels'] 3rd and 4th Magolewski Infantry."[90] Abram had been promised a liquor concession for his troubles. Since then, however, his property and health had been ruined because he had been "persecuted by the insurrectionists." The Jewish residents of Szydłowiec had been ordered to contribute four thousand rubles to the rebels if they did not hand Abram over to them. The rebels had even taken the rabbi of Szydłowiec into the forest as collateral, and the rabbi had been saved only thanks to the appearance of the Russian army. Abram was presently living, he wrote, on "funds that I have long possessed from serving gendarmes in the town of Radom, for Paskevich's gendarmes in the Radom District can testify in detail that I was useful to him, and can even testify to the sum that I was paid for various useful things I uncovered for the regime." As his reward, Abram requested a free concession for running a tavern, "for I am in no state now to pay the concession fee." In spite of all his troubles, however, the regime denied his request for a liquor concession on the grounds that he had never possessed one before.[91]

Izrael Ejzenberg's account is even more suspenseful. During his second week in the town of Opatów, the insurrectionists had entered and engaged the Russians for several hours. Shortly after the battle, Israel was recruited as a spy and sent out on his first mission:

> The high commander of the [Russian] army entrusted me with a secret expedition, the task of transporting a message with the strictest caution on the road to the town of Kielce and passing it into the hand of the High Commander Czengier and [he] most solemnly ensured me that the True Regime will give me the greatest reward. Having left Opatów at eleven at night, having sewn up the aforementioned message for my expedition in my bag, I delivered it to the address in Kielce the following morning at nine. However, my life was most dangerously threatened on the way, for in the village Olszowni insurrectionist gendarmes held me for two hours, and then nearly forced me to stay in Opatów. On the way back armed insurrectionists also harshly seized me in the village of Napęków, and everyone debated what to do with me. And only by divine grace was my life saved. I carried out the entire journey myself, renting a wagoner and paying him well.[92]

Izrael, too, assumed that the promised "greatest reward" would take the form of a liquor concession.[93]

Gerszon Szyldyner spied on the Russians' behalf out of a genuine feeling of loyalty. Before the 1863 uprising, he wrote, "[I had] always served officers of the army, and was on familiar terms with them. And from this I was inclined to be loyal to the true Russian Regime." He therefore elected to spy for tsarist troops stationed in his native town of Tomaszów. "In the beginning of 1863, when the insurrection made an attempt on this community, I notified the high commander of the army, Major Colonel Kozakin Dunski, who was at that time in Tomaszów, that he needed to be extremely careful at the time of the attack." Gerszon's warning had "saved their lives, for on January 23 the insurrection attacked Kozakin's army in Tomaszów." Gershon had remained with the army until its retreat, after which he "passed messages over great distances for Colonel Enochin."[94] Gerszon had suffered enormous material losses and, convinced that his life was in danger, had gone with Kozakin to the Zamość fortress on the Sabbath with his wife and three remaining children, "having had five children, two of whom had died from afflictions and lack of funds." In view of these personal catastrophes, Gerszon had been awarded a liquor concession for Tomaszów. But he could not afford the fee. So he requested "rights equal with Christians for selling state drinks without payment for the Treasury concession, and not only in Tomaszów but in other towns where the normal number of taverns function." He apparently did not realize that Christians were now required to purchase concessions too.[95]

Some tavernkeepers merely supplied one side or another with provisions and horses, and not always voluntarily. Lejb Lewkowicz had been "deprived of horses and funds by the Russian army during the 1863 uprising, which he gave freely." He now requested reimbursement, including a liquor concession.[96] Izrael Sonnenberg requested a liquor concession because, in fear of his life, he had supplied wagons to the Polish rebels that were crucial to his livelihood.[97] Others had had their taverns destroyed by rowdy troops. Szlomo Goldberg had suffered 4,700 rubles of damage from both the Polish and Russian armies during the insurrection.[98] Florjan Golewski, a Christian tavernkeeper in Milosny village, suffered losses when Russian troops drank up all the liquor in his tavern. He requested a liquor concession for Warsaw as compensation.[99]

As in the prior uprising, the tsarist government sometimes compensated the families of those hanged by the Polish rebels. Towa Goldsmith's husband, son, daughter, and two grandsons had been "hanged by the rebels near the town of Bełżyce in April 1863, and their money was discovered and stolen during their arrest." Several witnesses, including the mayor of Bełżyce and the brother of the rabbi of Bełżyce, witnessed the affair; and "the priest of Medzowiec village, who ordered the hangings so that many were widowed and orphaned, even stole our pillow." Towa requested a concession for selling vodka and beer in Kurów and compensation for the stolen valuables, amounting to three hundred rubles.[100] Antonina Kostecka, the Polish Christian widow of the mayor of Konary, "who had been faithful to the True Regime and was murdered in November 1863 by the insurrectionists," requested a liquor concession in Warsaw as compensation.[101]

Of course, no Jews who spied for the Polish side came forward. But certain Jews were deprived of their liquor concessions for allegedly having provided support to Polish rebels, which does undermine the Polish stereotype of the traitorous Jewish tavernkeeper. Izak Rozenblatt, an elderly tavernkeeper, claimed that he had been falsely denounced and cruelly deprived of his concession:

> I am eighty-eight years old. I lived like an elderly person, led a life without any complaints, and never sent a complaint to the government when I worked as a tavernkeeper selling state liquor in the city of Warsaw. And then, at the peak of my life, when my days were already numbered, my concession for selling state liquor was revoked, and, at a time when my old age deprived me of physical strength and when I was no longer able to start any new enterprise, I lost my means of making a living.[102]

Izak proclaimed that the loss of his concession came as a complete surprise to him. When he went before the chief of the tsarist police to inquire, he learned that he had been "denounced by another who wanted to take over [his] concession" for aiding the Polish rebels.[103]

One also has to wonder about those who claimed to have been held by Polish rebels against their will. Józef Nowotny, a Christian tavernkeeper deprived of his liquor concession for joining the Polish rebels, protested that he had been forced to join the rebels, claiming, "Two people whom I did not know came to my residence at night and threatened my life if I did not go with them, and they violently took me with them from my residence; and, taking me with them through an unknown wilderness and forests, they brought me at last to a band of insurrectionists in the forest." Józef had begged the rebels to return him to his family, to no avail. Finally, he wrote, "after several weeks I saw an opportune moment and managed to escape and return to my family."[104] The story of a Jewish tailor named Fajwel Wejntraub sounds more convincing:

> At that time [1863] there existed a band of rebels, and, for some unknown reason, a man named Jan Górnicki, who had been mayor of the village Rozniszew in the Radom District and had joined up with these insurrectionists, violently and forcibly took me to the camp of Polish rebels. And I, unwilling, resisted his command, but this Jan Gornicki came to my apartment with seven insurrectionists during the month of April and took me forcibly with him anyhow, and brought me to the village Wola Magnuszeska. Jan Dyj, of this village, intended to make me his driver, and took me to this camp and treated me like he was my owner ... tying my hands together at the recommendation and command of Jan Gornicki.[105]

When the Russian army attacked, the rebels forced Fajwel and others to flee with them, and "like prisoners [they] were transported for four miles, to the village of Chinów; and during the three-day journey Jan Dyj murdered peasants by hanging them."[106] Fajwel saw it was time to beg for his own life:

> As I had a wife and three children, I made a desperate request, and several strangers begged them as well, and my life was spared, but at the price of misery and want and continual bondage in the village Chinów, for day and night I remained like a prisoner, naked and with tears flowing, all the more so when I thought of my wife and children, as well as my innocence. And thus went my imprisonment for five days. But during the battle with the Russian army, I was barely freed by the cannon regiment.[107]

Fajwel stumbled home to his wife and children "in misery and loss," including the loss of much of his vision. Because of the insurrectionists' continued attacks, he hid himself for about thirteen weeks, during which time his wife "had to sell everything down to the last bedclothes." As he could no longer support himself as a tailor, owing to his loss of vision, Fajwel requested a concession for running a tavern in the Radom District.[108]

As moving as Fajwel's story is, we cannot rule out the possibility that he had joined the rebels willingly and concocted the story to protect himself. However, it did sometimes occur that Jews were held by rebels for lengthy periods of time, as the Posner episode illustrates. Hasidic oral tradition likewise records an incident in which a wealthy Jew suspected of supporting the Russians was seized by the Polish rebels, fined by the revolutionary court for thirty thousand zlotys, and then set free. In accordance with the tzaddik's prophesy, the tsarist government returned the money to him after the suppression of the uprising.[109]

One final case is particularly indicative of the confused nature of loyalties during this period. When Józek Budzin, a Polish Christian resident of Warsaw, was in Siedlce, he spotted two young men running from a burning wooden building. After helping to put out the fire, Józek helped round up the youths and discovered matches on them. He immediately formed a search party and proceeded to the youths' apartment, where their mother and sister were discovered, he wrote, "holding a secret meeting with eight soldiers and one Jew whom I don't know, with tracts containing [Polish] insurrection songs and a chest filled with different materials that should be burned." Thanks to Józek's efforts, the Christian and Jewish conspirators were arrested, and the mother was eventually executed. Józek asked to be rewarded with a liquor concession for Warsaw, or at least some money.[110]

It is particularly fascinating and instructive to find a Jew among the conspirators betrayed by Budzin, a Polish Christian. And taken together, the above cases prove how difficult it is to generalize about political loyalties. Poles and Jews alike supported the uprisings, supported the imperial regime, or just preferred to be left alone. But it seems likely that most representative of the Jewish population was the weaker type of support for the Polish cause expressed so candidly by the Hasidic leader Abraham Isaac Kahana of Ciechanów in a letter to Rabbi Dov Ber Meisels from April of 1861. Several days earlier, R. Abraham writes, a Polish nobleman had asked him to enjoin his followers to sign a pro-Polish petition to the tsar. R. Abraham felt torn: the regime had warned him against supporting such manifestos; at the same time, the local nobility lived peacefully with the Jews, and "their generosity of heart awakens love among Jews... so that a people who a short time ago was scorned by every nation can now be counted on to gather together with them for the sake of the common good." The nobility in Abraham's region had even "miraculously" allowed Jews to join merchant guilds, own land, and engage in agriculture (these were most likely promises made to undercut the recent liberalization of Jewish policy). R. Abraham added wistfully that most Jews "would like to fulfill the wishes of the nobility and not vex them," but were reluctant to oppose the "actual regime." The centuries-old relationship between Jews and Poles, which we have defined as Jewish-Christian interaction within heavily prescribed roles, thus generated sympathy for the Polish insurrectionists, especially those who were nobles, but not a willingness to risk life and livelihood for them.[111]

Whatever the specific Jewish attitudes might have been, it should be acknowledged that a defenseless diaspora community can ill afford to openly oppose either side of a military conflict. The Jewish predicament is articulated beautifully in a memoir by Cecilia Stueckgold, daughter of

R. Joseph Hayim Karo, the rabbi of Włocławek. When a tsarist official demanded that R. Karo explain why certain Jews had contributed to the Polish national fund during the 1863 uprising, Cecilia writes that her father replied that the Jews of Włocławek had neither armed guards nor firearms. "When therefore armed men appeared at midnight demanding a contribution, how could they avoid compliance?" The tsarist official answered, "Through heroism." R. Karo flattered the official by pointing out that *he* might have heroically refused, "but the rest of us were not of the stuff that heroes were made of and preferred to sacrifice the purse rather than their life." R. Karo reiterated that argument when the same official discovered a poor Jewish tailor sewing uniforms for Polish insurgents: "Entirely at the mercy of the insurgents, who make short shrift of recalcitrants," the rabbi reminded him, "what else could the poor Jew do?" The most prudent course was to try, as best as one could, to appease everyone.[112]

Polish landowners who felt ambivalent about declaring war on the tsarist empire found themselves in a similar predicament. One nobleman who was discovered offering aid to rebels and summoned before a Russian general explained, "If . . . the insurgents come to my place and ask for horses, carts and corn, I must give them what they want, or they will hang me. If, however, I let them have anything more than I am actually forced to give, you will hang me." At best, the nobleman could determine the shape of his legacy: "If *they* hang me my son will never find a wife in Poland nor my daughter a husband, and fifty years after my death people will turn their backs upon my grandchildren. If *you* hang me monuments will be erected in my memory." The nobleman concluded, "As a matter of prudence I cannot refuse to assist the insurgents," and the Russian general tacitly agreed.[113]

CONCLUSION

When it comes to accusations of disproportionate Jewish spying, smuggling, and banditry, one is tempted to credit the very resilience of the belief. Alternatively, one could write off the charges as anti-Jewish slander that possessed no more validity than, say, legends about Jewish ritual murder. A truer generalization probably falls somewhere in between. But what the sources explored here disclose beyond a doubt is the complex ethnic makeup of all such ventures. For every Jew accused of spying for the Russians there were several Poles accused as well. For every suspected Jewish smuggler there were Polish border guards and non-Jewish merchants involved too. And for every Jewish restaurateur or tavernkeeper who provided support and refuge to Jewish and Christian bandits there was probably a Polish landowner on the take. Smugglers, spies, and thieves, it turns out, were much less prone to discrimination than the enlightened government bureaucrats who pursued them. Antisocial activities may provide the period's most advanced model of interethnic symbiosis.

The failure of two successive uprisings was a devastating blow for those Poles who aspired to nationhood. It is unsurprising that some began casting about for enemies within, and that they would be loath to accuse their fellow Christian Poles. The lack of Polish Christian support for the uprisings has also been a painful realization for Polish nationalist historians. The rise of Polish nationalism was a slow and uneven process, and certain Christian Poles prudently chose short-term financial gain or discreet neutrality over an uncertain national resurrection. The tsarist government was, moreover, able to complicate and undercut the spread of Polish nationalist sentiment by decreeing emancipation for the peasantry, who composed around 80 percent of the population.

Rather than continue to grapple with the question of whether an unemancipated segment of the population like the Jews was sufficiently supportive of the Polish cause, a question which seems increasingly absurd the more it is pondered, we would do better to invert the question: Why did members of that unemancipated segment participate in Polish insurrections at all? It is one thing to sympathize with the aspirations of Polish rebels, many of whom were nobles with whom Jews had cooperated economically for centuries. It is quite another thing to take up arms on their behalf, as about two thousand Jews did in 1863. This novel behavior contributes to our understanding of Jewish modernization, which, in addition to the new level of individual assertiveness in the public sphere charted in the last chapter, seems to have involved a new willingness to resort to violence for political aims. Yet for most Jews in the kingdom, internal cultural movements like Hasidism or the Haskalah remained much more profound and formative than either Polish nationalism or imperial loyalties. Even Moses the Hasid, the Polish patriot described in the introduction to this chapter, was more Hasid than Polish patriot.

Closer to our direct purpose is the question of the effects of the uprisings on the region's economic mainstay, liquor. Here, too, the picture is mixed. The uprisings did help some Jewish tavernkeepers and aspiring Jewish tavernkeepers, reflected in the number of liquor concessions awarded to those who had remained "faithful to the True Regime" and in the general relaxation of enforcement during the decade following each conflict. On the other hand, those Jews who were suspected by Polish rebels of aiding the Russians sometimes lost their lives, while those caught backing the Polish rebels were deprived of their concessions, expelled, and sometimes exiled. Given such alternatives, Jewish tavernkeepers could be forgiven for just hoping that the storm would pass with minimal destruction of life and livelihood.

The question of Jewish loyalties did not, in any event, matter very much to those members of the Polish nobility who retained their estates after the uprisings. They continued to install Jews in their taverns regardless of their real or perceived support of one side or the other during the conflict. One might ascribe this rather extraordinary forgiveness to a fear of tsarist reprisals should a Jewish tavernkeeper complain that he had lost his lease in retaliation for having supported the "True Regime." But most landowners were probably driven less by fear than by inertia. Among those who had been spared expulsion and land confiscation, and who were thus probably more accommodationist toward tsarist rule to begin with, the momentum of traditional practices and beliefs overcame any lingering nationalist indignation. They preferred to deal with Jews, just as before.

CHAPTER 5

The Tavernkeepers Speak

Polish Jewish Tavernkeeping in the Wake of Peasant Emancipation

Mordecai ben Esther, a father of five, had run a profitable tavern for seven years. But one day "a certain man from our camp"—a Jew—took over the local liquor monopoly lease and refused, for whatever reason, to allow Mordecai to renew his concession. Mordecai was now forced to open a store instead, and enjoyed little success. To add to his woes, "all his wealth and possessions are scattered among the lords. He lent Lord Sokolowski six hundred rubles, and it has been very, very hard for him to collect it from him, for he is not in a good financial state. And also with Lord Chelchocka, three hundred rubles, and with Captain Anikel in the amount of five hundred rubles, and with Lord Opowski in the amount of one hundred rubles."[1] Mordecai needed some divine intervention. So like thousands of other Jews in the Kingdom of Poland and beyond during the early 1870s, he set off on a journey to the court of Rabbi Elijah Guttmacher (1796–1874), the "Tzaddik of Grätz." The journey entailed crossing the border, for Grätz (Grodzisk Wielkopolski) was located in the Prussian partition of Poland, but Mordecai believed it was worth it. Once there, he dictated a long petition to R. Guttmacher's court scribe, imploring the tzaddik to "pray for him that the Holy one blessed be he will have mercy on him and send salvation quickly to rescue him from the hands of the goyim," that is, his recalcitrant debtors. Mordecai also asked the tzaddik to advise him about whether to attempt to open another tavern, for "he really, really wants to establish a tavern as well."[2]

R. Elijah Guttmacher was not the kind of Jewish miracle worker we usually read about. Not only was he not Hasidic; he was a star disciple of the rigorous, non-Hasidic talmudic authority R. Akiva Eiger of Poznań, whom he continued to consult throughout his career. Guttmacher moreover evinced support for the relatively progressive seminary of R. Esriel Hildesheimer (founded in Berlin, 1873).[3] And he actively supported Jewish settlement in Palestine, dismissing the conventional notion that "suddenly the gates of mercy will open . . . and all will be called from their dwelling places" to the Land of Israel.[4] Yet Jews like Mordecai streamed toward him during times of crisis as they would toward the most renowned Hasidic tzaddik.

In an undated letter, Guttmacher complained that he felt overburdened by "the broken-hearted who sometimes come here asking [him] to arouse God, blessed be He, to heal them . . . and give them advice." For about a year now, he wrote, "men, women, and children have been coming from adjacent countries to this place, the land of Prussia, . . . and remain many days until I agree to speak with each and every one of them."[5] During the last year of his life, 1874, Guttmacher took the extraordinary measure of posting a lengthy appeal in the Hebrew periodical *Ha-Magid*, in which he complained of poor health and lack of sleep, protested that he lacked kabbalistic learning, and denied that his blessings were any more potent than those of a simple man. He had beseeched other rabbis to relieve him of his burden, but was advised not to discourage a generation so weak in faith. Guttmacher had made sure that all the petitions (*kvitlekh*) "remained with him, and were bound together after a certain amount of time and kept in a special place." But from now on, he would only accept brief requests for blessings for the ill by telegraph.[6]

Around 1932, a group of amateur ethnographic collectors (*zamlers*) discovered a trove of over six thousand petitions to R. Guttmacher in an attic in Grätz and delivered their haul to the YIVO Institute for Jewish Research, at that time located in Vilna.[7] In 1942, the Nazi taskforce Einsatzstab Rosenberg[8] transferred the collection to the NSDAP Institut zur Erforschung der Judenfrage (Institute for Investigating the Jewish Question) in Frankfurt-am-Main, minus a small selection of letters that remained hidden inside the Vilna Ghetto. In 1945, the collection was recovered by the US army and returned to YIVO, now located in New York, along with the hidden portion. From that point on the Guttmacher petitions have sat in New York City virtually untapped.[9]

These thousands of requests, scrawled on scraps of paper of varying sizes, illuminate many facets of daily life in Eastern Europe. Petitioners requested the tzaddik's heavenly intervention for the healing of disease, demonic possession, infertility, and sexual dysfunction; they sought his advice in matchmaking, domestic disputes, and, most frequently of all, business. Their petitions imbue our image of East European Jewry with light and shadow, revealing the shtetl as a shifting scene of familial solidarity and breakdown, piety and apostasy, and economic competition and cooperation across ethnic lines. They suggest a need to modify the reigning secularization narrative, which posits a rapid, unidirectional weakening of traditional mores, rabbinic authority, and magical belief and an allegedly rapid urbanization and industrialization process. The petitions force us to slow down, revealing how during the 1870s even a non-Hasidic rabbi could possess a long supracommunal reach owing to his miracle-working reputation; how traditional social mores retained their hold over matchmaking, marriage, and divorce; and how old economic arrangements between Jews and nobles like tavern leaseholding and moneylending continued to predominate. They afford us a precious last glimpse of a world still relatively unaltered by the industrialization, economic crisis, and mass migration that characterized the next decade.

The Guttmacher petitions also complicate the images of tavernkeepers found in celebrated classics of Polish and Yiddish literature from the same period. The tavernkeepers who visited Guttmacher rarely resemble the coolly deceptive characters portrayed in works by Boleslaw Prus (e.g., *The Outpost*) or Henryk Sienkiewicz (e.g., *Charcoal Sketches*).[10] Nor do they conform to the image of promiscuous affability in S. Y. Abramovitsh's *The Wishing Ring*, which assures us that "anyone who travels knows that most innkeepers have shining faces and sweetly smiling lips; that they're mild, gentle souls who rejoice and are as glad to encounter newly arrived guests as they would be to meet members of their immediate family."[11] Even Abramovitsh seemed to miss the gut-wrenching worry that lay just under the surface. Theirs was a harried life, thrown repeatedly off balance by recalcitrant noblemen, jealous competitors, unscrupulous informers, and vindictive government officials. When catastrophe struck, many had little choice but to appeal to a miracle worker, who might be persuaded to move the heavenly and earthly powers to compassion on their behalf.

Petitioners were not the least put off by Guttmacher's protestations of magical impotence, nor should they have been. Shortly before the publication of his appeal in *Ha-Magid*, the periodical's editor, Eliezer Lipman Zilberman, had urged Guttmacher to renounce his miracle-working abilities altogether, warning him that if he did not do so everyone would "say that he had become a Hasidic rebbe and *ba'al shem*, God forbid." But Guttmacher had refused to go that far.[12] In fact, he was currently devoting a whole section of his book *Tsofnat pa'neaḥ* to the subject of miracles, in which he detailed his exorcisms and healing triumphs. He merely cautioned his readers:

> All these miracles were done out of necessity, and were imposed on me by force. And they were only accomplished by means of prayers and entreaties and sometimes also common cures like fumigating the ill and immersing them in the river in summertime, for one should rely on nature as much as possible, and also the recitation of the eighteen benedictions for several days. Often I have thought, "Now who will tolerate the heretics and the progressives who say that nothing exists beyond nature?"[13]

Guttmacher thus believed that miracle working helped combat modern skepticism—signaling his active involvement in a new kind of project, one we might term "traditionalism".

In a certain sense, Guttmacher's career was merely representative of a common tendency among earlier non-Hasidic rabbinic celebrities to perform miracles alongside their principal duties as legal experts and preachers. His famous teacher R. Akiva Eiger of Poznań is known to have ordered amulets and recipes for healing remedies from the folk healer R. Israel Yona Landau.[14] R. Solomon Zalman Lipschitz, the chief rabbi of Warsaw, was said to have healed the ill, cured mutes, and indirectly caused the death of an informer against the Jewish community.[15] R. Jacob Krantz, the famed "Dubno Maggid," who lived in Zamość during the last eighteen years of his life, reportedly asked the Zamość synagogue sexton to inform him every day "who was ill, and so on" so that he could intercede in heaven on their behalf."[16] Rabbi Tzvi Hirsch Paltrowitz of Nowogród, a regional legal authority in the Kingdom of Poland, reportedly saved his town from a fire by waving his handkerchief.[17]

What was different in Guttmacher's case, however, was the scale of his miracle-working enterprise, attested by the frenzy of petitions to him from locales throughout the Kingdom of Poland, from the far reaches of Eastern Europe, and occasionally even from Western Europe and America. The promises of modernity seemed to only bolster Guttmacher's enterprise, for such promises yielded much disappointment (e.g., a petitioner who had consulted many "expert doctors" now realized that "all the doctors are frauds and liars, so he has decided to abandon the promises of the human doctors and seize faith in the strength of God, who is the best of the doctors, and after that, faith in the prayers of tzaddikim"). Guttmacher's outsized stature eventually caught the attention of one of the devotees of the Hasidic tzaddik Aharon of Chernobyl, who reported to his dumbfounded master at length about this "German" rabbi dressed in Hasidic garb who had "hundreds of thousands" of petitioners seeking blessings, remedies, and amulets.[18]

The attraction of a Prussian Polish, non-Hasidic court for Jews living in the Kingdom of Poland in particular may have had to do with timing. Guttmacher's court flourished during the interregnum between the death of the preeminent Polish tzaddik Isaac Meir Alter of Ger (d. 1866) and the maturation of his grandson Judah Aryeh Alter (1847–1905), who would come to be known as the "Sefat Emet" ("Language of Truth") after his acclaimed book of that title. The court in Ger would become the main address for the kingdom's ill, infertile, possessed, and dispossessed again after Alter had reached a more mature age. But in the early 1870s, it was Guttmacher's court in the western town of Grätz.

THE POST-EMANCIPATION ECONOMIC REALITY

It is important to emphasize that the Jews of the Kingdom of Poland were by no means fully emancipated by the law on Jewish rights of June 5, 1862. Restrictions on Jewish purchases of real estate remained in effect, especially in the many areas where labor duties had not yet been converted into rents. Jews could not hold local government offices such as *wójt* (chief officer of a group of villages), *sołtys* (village head), or *ławnik* (councilman). In 1866, Jewish college graduates were theoretically permitted to hold positions in the administration, but this did not occur in practice. Jews still could not employ Christians as domestics. And they still could not lease taverns and distilleries legally in the countryside, save on Jewish agricultural colonies.[19]

Historians stress, instead, the effects of peasant emancipation on Jews, a process which began in the Kingdom of Poland in 1861 and culminated in full peasant emancipation in 1864. The post-emancipation period is regarded as a time of rapidly disintegrating traditional Jewish economic mainstays that relied on the Polish nobility, itself in rapid decline as a result of the loss of free labor and land. The result for Jews, we are told, was mass pauperization. One study claims that "the emancipation of the serfs in 1863 dealt the medieval division into economic spheres a blow that devitalized the functions of moneylender, factor, petty merchant, and steward."[20] According to another study, the post-emancipation generation of Jews was forced out of trade and into less lucrative areas like crafts and factory work.[21] A more recent study pushes the decline back even further, claiming that "the social crisis in East European Jewry was the result of a protracted process, going back at least to the 1850s."[22]

A thoroughgoing revision of East European Jewish economic history lies outside the scope of this volume. But it should be noted at the outset that the above studies rely quite heavily on data derived from the 1897 census. To project these data backward onto the economic situation a generation earlier, as many studies seem to do, is to flatten the nineteenth-century shtetl experience and lend an air of inevitability to the first large-scale emigration wave in the 1880s. In the Kingdom of Poland, at least, the situation in 1897 did not resemble that of prior decades, particularly those preceding the cataclysmic 1880s. For one thing, a comparison to earlier data reveals significant changes in the Jewish occupational structure over time.[23] It turns out that, while the proportion of Jewish artisans in the kingdom did indeed increase, so did the proportion of Jews involved in trade, most likely petty trade—from around 11 percent in 1843 to 39 percent of the Jewish population in 1897. The younger generation was not driven out of trade and into crafts, but rather driven into *both* crafts and trade from leaseholding, mainly tavernkeeping. This flight from leaseholding was, as historians suspected, a result of the decline of nobility-dependent pursuits. But the crucial question is when, precisely, such pursuits began their steep decline.

To determine that, we need to determine when the nobility's own steep decline began. As studies by Polish historians during the 1960s demonstrate, the nobility as a whole did not actually lose much after emancipation in the short term. In fact, during the twenty-five years following

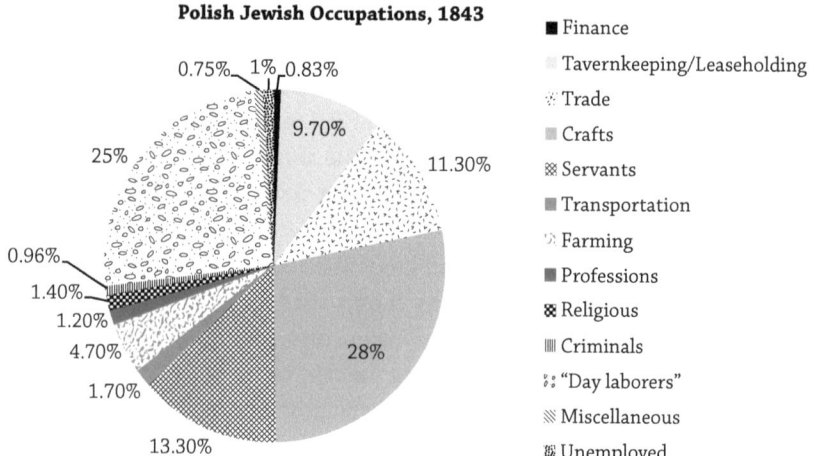

Figure 5.1: Source: A.N. Frenk, "Di tsol yidn un zeyere basheftikungen in di shtet un derfer fun Kenigraykh Poyln in 1843tn yor." *Bleter far Yidishe Demografye, Statistik un Ekonomik 3* (1923), Table 2 (from the Warsaw Finance Archives). Sample size 106, 514.

Jewish Occupations, early 1870s in Guttmacher Collections (actual figures)

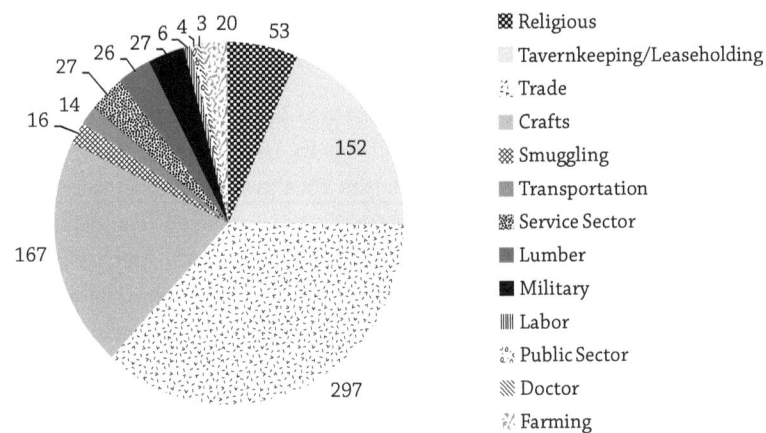

Figure 5.2: Source: YIVO, Elijah Guttmacher Collection, RG 27; 816 petitions reporting occupations, not including moneylending, a side occupation.

Polish Jewish Occupations, 1897

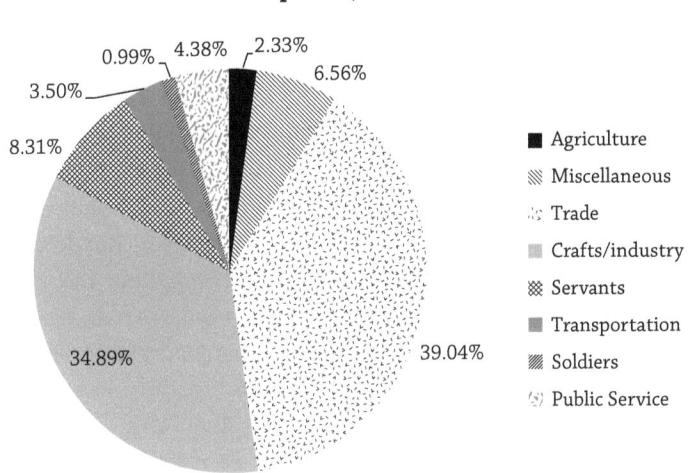

Figure 5.3: Source: The 1897 Census, in Ettinger, *Ben Polin le-Rusyah* (Jerusalem: Zalman Shazar, 1994), p. 268, and Bohdan Wasiutyński, Rola ekonomiczna żydów w królestwie Polskiem, p. 384.

emancipation, the small-scale nobility made a net gain in land of almost 24 percent, in many cases by buying up land which peasants could not afford to pay taxes on or redeem. The gains of the peasantry as a whole, in contrast, amounted to a little over 12 percent during the generation following emancipation.[24] The only group to suffer a net loss was the large-scale nobility, whose land possession declined by 16.5 percent during this period, hardly a rapid and wholesale collapse. Most managed to stall land redistribution for decades and retain full possession of their forests, pastures, and tavern plots, which meant they could deny any recalcitrant peasants access to them.[25]

The impact of peasant emancipation was further blunted by a soaring grain trade. Notwithstanding a brief dip in 1873, the 1870s were boom times according to many measures: the total area of land under cultivation grew considerably; grain stocks increased; improved crop rotation and other methods began to spread; advanced agricultural machinery made its appearance; and the value of grain exports rose dramatically. In addition, peasants continued to imbibe the most popular byproduct of grain, liquor, and as the nobility's liquor monopolies were kept in place in the kingdom until 1898, the peasants could still only buy it at their local lord's tavern.[26] Troubled landowners were kept afloat by loans from the Land Credit Society and from Jews, and cushioned by a good lumber market that allowed them to sell off their forests. In fact, about 11 percent of the kingdom's forests were cut down in the 1870s.[27] As depicted by Yiddish author Joseph Opatoshu, "the dense forests of Poland moaned, thinned out, and fell into Jewish hands. The logs were bound into rafts. And during the summer season the Jews sent the logs floating down the Vistula and the Zholdevka to Germany."[28]

It was only in the early 1880s, when improvements in steamship and rail transport permitted a large influx of cheaper American and Russian grain into western and central Europe, that Polish grain prices plummeted and the devastation of the larger part of the nobility began. The drop in grain prices precipitated a full-blown agrarian crisis throughout the 1880s and 1890s, during which grain production nearly ground to a halt, land sell-offs and landowner bailouts escalated, and middling gentry experienced rapid degradation. At this point, noble-dependent occupations like moneylending and leaseholding really did become less viable. "You think we live on moneylending?" asked a respondent to I. L. Peretz's 1890 ethnographic survey. "It lives on us. Debtors don't pay, so their debt grows. The more it grows, the less it's worth, and the more of a pauper I become. It's the truth!" The respondent went so far as to offer all his deeds and notes to Peretz for 25 percent of their face value. "I'll throw in the tavern, too!" he added.[29] Jews also became physically vulnerable. In 1881, when the first vodka-fueled mobs began to snake through southeastern Russia along the railroad lines, leaving in their wake thousands of destroyed Jewish properties, hundreds of Jewish rape victims, and forty Jewish fatalities, there were now few noblemen who could stand in their way. Pogrom waves, fear of pogrom waves, and an ever-deepening economic crisis (the era's new factories could not or would not sufficiently absorb the pauperized Jewish populace) sparked off the first major East European Jewish emigration to America and Palestine.[30] According to Peretz, "The nineteenth century in its old age appeared to have caught cold and to be running a slight fever. Nobody could imagine that this marked the onset of a grave illness, a madness."[31]

But the pre-1880 picture is much more mixed. Jewish reports about the first decade or so after emancipation are contradictory, sometimes even self-contradictory. Ezekiel Kotik first tells us what we are accustomed to hear: in the aftermath of peasant emancipation, "what was ruinous for the gentry was no less so for a large section of the Jewish population, who derived their livelihood from the lords.... It seemed at the time that the spring from which Jews had drawn their livelihood for hundreds of years had completely dried up, and the chance of finding new livelihoods was small, perhaps even nonexistent." Ten pages later, however, Kotik provides a very different depiction of the same period. The government had abolished the nobility's monopoly on the production and sale of alcohol, he claims (incorrectly). But there was nevertheless a palpable "feeling of relief" within the Jewish communities, "as if the winds of freedom were blowing." The nobility's loss of status meant that "a new epoch was in the offing for the Jews," some of whom were able to become lords themselves. "This was, undoubtedly, one of the best periods experienced by the Jews in their Russian Diaspora," Kotik now decides.[32]

In contrast to Kotik's erratic impressions of rupture (whether bad for the Jews or good for the Jews), I. L. Peretz's memoirs suggest plodding continuity. Peasants in the Kingdom of Poland who were released from serfdom remained "quiet, submissive folk," because they were "still unsure of what to do with their freedom." The younger peasants continued to submit to their elders, "who slapped them when they failed to fall on their knees before the landowner, cap in hand and face to the ground." Only new peasant recruits who had not yet been called up for army service were willing to flout the old rules of conduct. "Freed from the regimen of the village and not yet subject to the military, they would break loose: cut the sidelocks off a Jew, grab a bagel from a stall, smash a window in the tavern." But after this short reprieve, they, too "deferred once again to the Jew, who had served during the years of serfdom as the intermediary between them and the landowner. In the village they still depended on "Moshke"— their generic term for the Jew. They didn't go to the doctor without first consulting him, or to a lawyer without first asking his advice, and sometimes 'Moshke' himself was their arbitrator." In Peretz's estimation, little changed over the next fifteen years.[33]

TURNING TO RABBI GUTTMACHER

The approximately six thousand Guttmacher petitions at YIVO suggest neither rupture nor absolute continuity during the decade following emancipation, but rather a sense that the triangular relationship between peasant, nobleman, and Jew was being subjected to new stresses and fissures. Those Jews who were not able to benefit directly from new opportunities in lumber and land ownership did face new competition from enterprising peasants and impoverished nobles. But the functions of moneylender, factor, petty merchant, and steward were not devitalized; Jews were not forced out of trade and into crafts and industry; and Jews did not experience a collective, full-blown economic crisis. Usually, it was the same old problem of how to deal with spendthrift nobles, indebted peasants, and competitive fellow Jews (but increasingly, Christians) in traditional realms like trade, moneylending, and leaseholding.

Guttmacher's most frequent request was for "success in collecting debts from the gentiles," often a side endeavor for tavernkeepers and merchants. One petitioner, a widow named Sarah Leah bat Esther, asked Guttmacher (again, in the third person, as these petitioners often did) whether he thought it wise for her "to quit all trade and give her money into the hands of the nobles on interest."[34] But the tzaddik probably advised her against it, for attempting to collect debts from members of the dominant culture could be precarious, even hazardous. Solomon Samuel ben Zelda, a tavernkeeper from Uniejowice, was in despair because, he wrote, "A gentile named Alexander owes me money amounting to over one thousand zlotys [approx. 160 rubles], and he has threatened me over and over again. I worry about this a lot because it is my wealth and rightful possession." To make matters worse, Solomon Samuel was in the process of losing his tavern. He had leased it from a gentile named Bogumił Potoczek with the understanding that he could remain there for years, "and thank God, for I now have a means of making an honorable living." But Potoczek had recently changed his mind and planned to give the dwelling to his son. Solomon now appeared to be without a tavern and without a means to recoup his sizeable loan.[35]

Jewish lenders to the nobility, though tending to be better off economically, also lived in constant worry. Abraham ben Frieda of the village of Osjaków had leased a tavern and distillery from Lord Antoni Sodoski for over eight hundred rubles per year and had also lent him a huge sum of money. Lord Sodoski had put all the lease money into a dowry and was about to lease the village of Ostrowno for two thousand rubles. Abraham now feared that Lord Sodoski would never be able to pay him back.[36] Joseph

Moses ben Roda, who had loaned large sums of money to "difficult goyish lords," provided Guttmacher with a precise accounting:

> the sum of 134 rubles from Lord Altonoski, who lives in the village Biała Góra;
> in the village Domanowo from Lady Kroscinska, 290 rubles;
> in the village Wierszek from Lord Krakanoski, 340 rubles;
> in the village Złoczek from Lord Galczinski, 150 rubles;
> in the village Starzek from Lord Rembonski, 150 rubles;
> in the village Psary from Lord Aszkanoski, 200 rubles;
> in the village Paniszczów from lord Chrzanoski, 200 rubles;
> in the village Polek from the successors of a gentile, 340 rubles;
> in the village Pietrów from Lord Bagotloski, 330 rubles;
> in the village Czarnów from Lord Jamon, 900 rubles.[37]

The same "difficult" lords and ladies wished to enter into business ventures with Joseph, but he was understandably concerned about their financial status.[38]

Moneylending occurred between Jews as well, albeit with a noticeable shift in attitude. Isaac ben Frieda Roda ha-Kohen complained that "he has many loans scattered among people [i.e., Jews] and among the goyim," a distinction that speaks volumes.[39] Leib Michael ha-Kohen ben Tzvetel appealed for "success with the people with whom he trades and with those who owe him money, especially the gentiles, may their hearts turn to deal compassionately with him, and especially one nobleman from whom he derives most of his livelihood who has become angry with him."[40] A Jewish tavernkeeper named Jonah ben Sarah Perl, who owed money to Rabbi David Schwartz, admitted that he felt badly because the rabbi was "presently in great poverty and asks for the debt." But what could he do? He owed prior debts to gentiles that his current tavern profits did not cover, and was simply incapable of paying the rabbi back.[41]

That these petitions portray distress is unsurprising considering the nature of the enterprise: few wrote petitions unless they were in dire need; and petitioners were usually attempting to redress what scholars of religion term "affliction" by asking the tzaddik to intercede with the divine via prayers, blessings, charms, and so on. But the sums lent to nobles that we have seen thus far were quite substantial, and one needed a great deal of capital in the first place to suffer such woes.

Interestingly, the nobility did have an alternate credit source, the Land Credit Society (established in 1825). But many nobles preferred credit from Jews, presumably because it was better to owe money to one's social inferior and economic dependent than to a governmental organization (Jews typically provided credit to local nobles from two months to one year at 5 percent interest).[42] It is not unlikely that Jewish lessees, for their part, felt pressured to extend loans to nobles in order to ensure the continued renewal of their leases. At the same time, the obstacles and restrictions for Jews attempting to purchase land, as well as the kingdom's modest level of industrialization in the 1870s, meant that loans to nobles also remained one of the best ways to invest one's money. Moneylending thus solidified the noble-Jew relationship and created new opportunities for Jewish prosperity, however risky.

The more frequent phrase "debts among the gentiles" probably refers to the numerous small-scale loans scattered among the recently emancipated peasantry. Emancipation was a double-edged sword, for it required that a peasant family come up with cash to redeem and pay tax on land they had worked on for centuries.[43] In addition, many peasant families needed or wanted to extend their holdings. Both efforts required credit, and the Peasant Bank of the Kingdom of Poland was not established until 1890. Until then, they had to turn to local Jews.[44] The question of whether Polish Jewish moneylending—so downplayed by early modern historians—increased in the wake of peasant emancipation cannot be answered definitively at this point for lack of data, but the impression is that it grew explosively.[45]

For their main occupation, most Jews still seemed, like Mordecai ben Esther (cited at the beginning of this chapter), to "really, really" want to lease a tavern. In spite of the impressive rhetorical and legislative assault, formidable concession fees, and the fact that Jewish tavernkeeping was technically illegal in villages, leasing a tavern from a nobleman remained one of the best options for making a living in the early 1870s. Out of the 816 petitioners who reported sources of livelihood in the YIVO collection, 114 leased taverns or liquor monopolies (figure 5.2). There were more taverns among petitioners than stores (ninety-two). And there were many aspiring tavernkeepers, too. Mordecai ben Rebekah provides the most candid explanation: he currently ran a "cigarette business, called *sekartin*, but without much success; and he [wanted] to engage in the tavernkeeping trade." Switching to the first person, he writes, "And please let God help me support myself from this, because I only make one ruble thaler per day, and I can make five ruble thalers from a tavern."[46]

Those who quit tavernkeeping soon regretted it. Tzevi Eliezer ben Ḥaya Beila quit "because of the profanation of the Sabbath it involved" and became a broker instead, but had not enjoyed any success.[47] His act was unusually pious—as discussed earlier, most tavernkeepers felt that they were shielded from divine wrath if they abided by rabbinically endorsed legal fictions. A more casual attitude is reflected in a petition by Zalman ben Gitel, a "homeowner known as a great host and philanthropist," who boasted to Guttmacher in rough, colloquial Yiddish: "I observe the holy Sabbath . . . and the great merit will stand with me when the Great Sabbath [preceding Passover] comes, and I will prepare for the Sabbath and holiday this Thursday. I have a brandy-house tavern and take care of things with two goyim, who are my right hand. One who lives there has the name Lipinski; the other is named Kwiatkowski." While it was kind of Zalman to mention his gentile workers by name, implying that the tzaddik should bless them, it did not seem to occur to him that employing them to run his tavern on holidays was the least bit controversial. If he did possess the required legal fiction, he did not feel the need to mention it.[48]

Many tavernkeepers simply requested continued success in their prosperous businesses, evincing anxiety about competition and uncollected debts, as well as unrelated problems like illness, matchmaking, fertility, and their sons' Torah studies. A few were well-educated, even sons of town rabbis.[49] Some were involved in several additional enterprises. Jacob ben Gitel requested "success in trade and in all his businesses, and especially in his store that sells liquor and other drinks." His main concern was that his wife suffered from headaches and toothaches.[50] Judah Leibush ben Rebekah Leah requested continued success in "the tavern and in his trade and distribution," as well as "abundance and great wealth." Judah then offered a litany of rich man's woes. "And what to do about the buyers who begin to buy and then after some time go with different merchants? And may he collect the debts. And whether to begin to trade with the nobles. And many arise against him every day and oppress him to the end. And what to do with the fodder business? For they will not allow it to be combined with the trade he has in his tavern. And he is not sure whether to buy a lottery ticket."[51] Between the manifold complaints we glimpse enterprises of diversity and scale.

Every liquor trader worried about increasing numbers of competitors, a consequence of the recent post-emancipation freeing up of peasant labor, capital, and mobility. Ezekiel Tzevi ben Gitel, who leased the local liquor monopoly in Kramsk village, asked the tzaddik "to repel the gentiles, who arise against him to take his livelihood, may they not touch him, so that he can support his household in profit and honor. And especially the gentile Florkowski, for he harms him a lot, and the evil secretary who helps him, called Władysław Kolantkowski, may his name be blotted out."[52] Barukh ben Eve asked the tzaddik to repel those who "stood against him to take his liquor concession" and ensure that he could continue to run the "house in which he lives in abundance."⁵³ Abraham Ḥayyim ben Sarah complained that "the distillery he leased in the village Walencen from Lord Szmindeski has been losing much money, Heaven forfend." But he had hope—he stood to be reimbursed by state officials for an improper inspection fine, and had designs on the local liquor monopoly, if only he could find favor with Lord Kalockowski.⁵⁴ Samuel Issar ben Yuta, a lessee of a local liquor monopoly, was most concerned about the fact that he "has lain with his wife for seventeen years and she has not become pregnant." He requested continued success with his liquor lease and asked the tzaddik for protection against "his enemies who arise to take his livelihood and the informers who inform against him to cause his downfall."⁵⁵ Moses Judah ben Sarah ha-Levi requested continued success in his tavern, his sole business, and asked the tzaddik to cure his daughter of "the shakes."⁵⁶ Ḥayyim ben Miriam lived under "a bad and very violent gentile, and his name is Stanisław ben Słoma, and he wrongs him in various ways," yet his tavern was apparently doing alright.⁵⁷ Tavernkeeping represented a decline in status for Bentzion ben Hadassah, who had once been a contractor for troops stationed in Stawnica until several Jews had "surrounded the regiment [there]," that is, outbid him. But he, too, seemed to be doing alright.⁵⁸

Others were not doing alright. Some complained that the profits from their tavern or liquor monopoly leases were "diminishing little by little," and a few asked if they should perhaps take on partners.⁵⁹ Mordecai ben Hannah's tavern and sugar store were not in a good state despite the fact that "kosher people did good deeds and lent [him] money and merchandise."⁶⁰ David Joseph ben Ḥayya asked the tzaddik to "raise his tavern trade's glory and status" because he was a "man of very precious spirit, and everything suddenly reversed on him and he lost all his wealth and property in a great abyss."⁶¹ Isaac Tzevi ben Frieda, a distiller, approached the tzaddik "with weeping and cries for mercy, for he was at the very top and now he has declined little by little until he has nothing more to support him."⁶² Hannah Reizel bat Miriam and her husband, Dov Ber ben Ḥayya, could not make enough profit "sitting in the tavern selling drinks" and were forced to travel throughout the villages selling bread and buying up eggs. They were frequently robbed by the numerous bandits on the roads, and their very lives were sometimes endangered.⁶³

Some sought to renegotiate the terms of unprofitable leases or get out of them altogether. Ḥayyim ben Esther asked the tzaddik to incline the noblemen's hearts to lower the liquor monopoly lease amount from that of the prior year and, he wrote, "give it to him cheaply according to what I wrote them."⁶⁴ Jacob ben Ḥayya resolved to travel to the nobleman after Passover to renegotiate his tavern lease.⁶⁵ Tzevi ben Feigel tried to get out of his disastrous lease. Lacking a liquor concession himself, he had done the customary thing and installed a Christian front. But he had lost control of the gentile, who proceeded to sell so much liquor on credit to his friends and family that it was impossible to collect all the debt. The lord had refused, under any circumstances, to release Tzevi before the end of the three-year term.[66] Jonathan Leib ben Frumet simply fled, leaving his wife and six children behind in the unprofitable tavern to support themselves. Not surprisingly, the nobleman informed them that they would have to leave. Jonathan asked the tzaddik to "please pray that the nobleman's heart will be moved to keep them there and pray that he be able to pay him for last year."[67]

Certain Jews, because of their pious or scholarly dispositions, were just not cut out for tavern life. Akiva ben Kasha made only a meager living from his tavern but had been "content with his portion" because it had allowed him time to study Torah. Unfortunately, competition from other taverns had begun to take its toll: "Many arise against his enterprise, and if it weren't enough that his livelihood is diminished, they have also caused his Torah study to diminish." In addition, the debts he owed were "as cruel as snakes and ravens."[68] Peretz ben Nokha, from the same town, was in a similar bind. After he left his "father-in-law's table" he had lost all the dowry money in failed business ventures, so his father had set him up in a tavern. But Peretz did "not have the strength to engage in this kind of trade, for he [had] no desire to learn it, and it [involved] many nuisances." He moreover could not turn a profit because he was "a charitable man."[69] Ḥayyim ben Shindel, a tavernkeeper who claimed to have no desire "to get rich, but only have his son learn the Torah of God," was also unable to turn a profit.[70] In Nathan ben Zele's case, it was his wife who was not suited to tavern life. He had run a tavern in his native town of Zgerz, near Lodz, for about five years. But as "the hours were many and the preparations [of drinks] few, and as my spouse, may she live, has a weakness of constitution and wanted to settle in an apartment close to her parents' town," he wrote, Nathan decided to relinquish his tavern and move to Kazimierz Dolny. In addition to help finding a new occupation, he needed help expelling the demon that prevented his wife from bearing children.[71]

In a region like Galicia, where the clergy-led temperance movement enjoyed some success, Christian morality could pose a significant threat to a Jewish tavernkeeper's business. A Galician petitioner complained that "a priest named Kazimierz Asacki wants to deprive and take livelihood from the Jews, and forbade all the gentiles in the area from drinking liquor from the Jews." The petitioner asked the tzaddik to have God "put him in a trance to stop his evil thoughts about Jews, and let him fall by means of the merits of our fathers." There may have been some truth to peasant accusations that Jewish tavernkeepers in Galicia were prone to mock temperance advocates and lure sober customers back into vice, for temperance was bad for business.[72]

But in the Kingdom of Poland, where the temperance movement had been effectively suppressed by the Polish regime (see chapter 2), non-Jews increasingly posed a threat as competitors, not moralists. Contrary to Werner Sombart's claim that Jews were the first to be committed to the "spirit of capitalism" and the principles of free trade, monopolistic practices and ethnic protectionism were as yet unquestioned in Polish Jewish society. Age-old communal ordinances forbade Jews to compete with and outbid fellow Jews (with limited success, as we shall see), while other ordinances attempted to protect the Jewish community from external competition "lest money fall into non-Jewish hands."[73] The latter sentiment is captured in a Jewish dyer's complaint about "a gentile named Tom ben Mariana Lewindowska" who had immigrated from Prussia. It did not matter that Tom was "a good and beautiful dyer, with very beautiful colors," for he was, the dyer wrote, "taking away my livelihood, which I held exclusively in this town until now," and he "always schemes to deride my work."[74] The gentile competitors of David ha-Kohen ben Gitel and his wife had gone so far as to "spread the rumor that they are sorcerers and say that they did sorcery against them." He felt the need to add that his gentile competitor was "a completely evil man and an informer against Israel in general and particular," thus a threat to the Jewish collectivity.[75]

The same ethnic protectionism increasingly prevailed in the liquor trade. Ḥayyim ben Krindel, who had lost the local liquor monopoly lease to "a gentile named Szelkiewicz," informed R. Guttmacher that he was not the only Jew affected. Many local Jewish tavernkeepers depended on the liquor monopoly and had to "suffer losses in everything because of him."[76] Moses ben Lana of Czechowice, who had more children than he could count (nine according to the body of the petition and ten according to his list of requested blessings), was forced to uproot his family and leave his tavern when a "gentile came and encroached on him and seized his livelihood" by outbidding him. Moses asked the tzaddik to obstruct the gentile's designs against him and plant within the nobleman's heart the will to restore his lease.[77] Mordecai ben Udel, a father of four, asked the tzaddik to "topple the gentile Janin ben Jaknicki, who," he wrote, "is a bad neighbor to me and took my livelihood and forced [me] to lease the tavern to another gentile, and left me without a livelihood, for he is a persecutor of Jews."[78] Some resorted to curses:

> Menaḥem Moses ben Feiga, for success in the tavern, and to repel the gentile from there who arose against the Jews and took their livelihood. May the customers

not go to him, and may the scent of his drinks become so putrid that they can no longer stand the taste or tolerate his drinks. And to cause his downfall, which all the Jews and the widows and the orphans need, because he took away their livelihood. And also, may the police harass him so that he does not prosper in what he sells, for he seizes the livelihood of Jews.[79]

While resorting to a curse may seem extreme, the increase in non-Jewish competitiveness was perceived as an act of aggression against the Jewish community, suggesting an economic aspect to the emerging traditionalism.

A tavernkeeper's situation was even more precarious when he or she leased space from a gentile who was a potential competitor. Asher Anshel ben Rebekah had leased a house, tavern, and store from a gentile for the past thirteen years. But now that the gentile had begun selling liquor himself, he had ordered Asher to move out, offering him a different house and store on the condition that he sell only flour there.[80] In Piaker village, where the local liquor monopoly lease was administered by a representative of the state, a local nobleman was a potential bidder. Abraham Jacob ben Sarah had leased the liquor monopoly for the past six years, until "the lord from that village went to the authorities and seized his livelihood."[81] At the same time, Jews were not completely helpless when pitted against nobles, to judge by the number of lawsuits mentioned. One petitioner asked the tzaddik to help him "win the suit he has in court with a count [*graf*]" whose servant had bolted with the 1,300 rubles given to him for purchasing liquor. He had won the case, but the count was appealing the decision.[82]

Yet encroachments by fellow Jews occurred just as often, defying our nostalgic image of East European Jewish solidarity (or its anti-Semitic corollary, Jewish collusion). If one vacated one's tavern because of fire damage or some other calamity, there were throngs of Jewish contenders vying to take it over at a higher price. Tavern leases were vulnerable even under normal circumstances. Nathan Nata of Bielany village had leased the local liquor monopoly for nineteen years until "Isaac Judah ben Reizel and Moses Joseph came to remove his sustenance from him until he was bereft of everything."[83] Meir ben Rachel leased the liquor monopoly in Nechlyn village, but another Jew settled there and, Meir wrote, "encroaches by means of a tavern and a shop, and he sells more than I do, and more cheaply. And there is always an argument."[84] Hertz ben Reizel, who had for the past year been running a tavern in a new, high-rent house on a street where "there are rarely passersby and customers," complained that a Jew named Enoch Zalman currently ran a tavern on the same street and "stands on the road and does not let anyone enter my tavern."[85] Aaron Ḥayyim ben Feigel complained of headaches and a decline in business since Nathan ben Sarah had set up a tavern next to his a half year earlier. Now he had "no livelihood except for the tiny bit that he sells now, and even this leaves him in need, because they do not come to him to buy but rather to drink on credit, to the point that the human soul can barely endure." Aaron was afraid of Nathan because, he wrote, Nathan "always vexes me—may he not, God forbid, perform any sorcery against me." For good measure, he slipped in a request for blessings over lottery ticket numbers 11,766 and 22,763.[86]

Then there were informers, both Christian and Jewish. As we have seen, the situation of Jewish tavernkeepers remained particularly precarious in villages, where the Jewish liquor trade was technically illegal. Yet instances of informing on rural Jewish tavernkeepers to state authorities are rare enough in the Guttmacher collection to suggest that the nobility essentially retained its grip over local populations. In most cases, anyone who informed the state about an illegal Jewish-run tavern would have had to answer to the noble, for it constituted an affront to his authority, caused him embarrassment, and cost him money.

The rare law-abiding noble was, however, receptive to informers. Moses Judah Leib ben Esther had leased a "restaurant" for the past ten years from the town owner for more than one hundred rubles a year, receiving very little profit, and had tried to sell liquor there without a concession. Local Christians continually informed the noble, until he finally fined him for about eight hundred zlotys. Moses then took the extraordinary step of turning to the state. He first appealed to the "governor in Petersburg," who ordered him to pay the fine without delay. But during that time a "great lord of our country" annulled a portion of the fine. So Moses decided to attempt another petition to St. Petersburg, this time not through the governor. His request to Guttmacher was "to have mercy on us and annul the fines and save us now so that we have no fines at all."[87]

Usually, the state was the enemy. David Ber ben Eve, a father of five children, lost his liquor concession because of "the gentile director, who stands on his spirit and informs on him in writing and incites other people to encroach on him." He beseeched the tzaddik to "obstruct him and topple him," and to help him obtain another liquor concession "so that he can make a living and support his household in honor."[88] A more surprising case is that of David Leib ben Rachel, who found himself in court fighting "a fine of one thousand [zlotys] on account," he wrote, "of one of the gentiles having informed on me regarding the tavern that I transferred to a gentile woman on the holy Sabbath day so that I would not profane the Sabbath day." David's informer had violated the centuries-old silent arrangement between tavernkeepers, rabbis, nobles, and local Christians. While it could not have interested state authorities that a Jew had employed the woman to avoid breaking the Sabbath, they would still have been concerned to prevent anyone—even a non-Jew—from selling liquor without a concession in their own name.[89]

Yet informing was not only a Jewish-Christian affair, as seen in a poignant petition by Esther Golda bat Malka, a grass widow (*agunah*). Once again we are witness to the breakdown of Jewish solidarity. Esther's husband, Gabriel, had gone to England for good, it seemed, and left her and their six children to fend for themselves. Among other things, this was a blow to her economic well-being: as spouses were typically business partners, the loss of the ability to remarry meant the permanent loss of a natural business partner. In Esther's case, "God had mercy on her" and enabled her to lease a tavern from the local nobleman, and she was able to support her children profitably and respectfully. But it all came crashing down when "evil Jewish neighbors arose and informed on her to the nobleman," and they were given two weeks to vacate the house.[90] The nature of the tale-bearing is unclear (was she accused of short-changing the nobleman in some way, or engaging in illegal activities?), but the result was disastrous. Esther begged the tzaddik to plant compassion in the heart of the nobleman so that he would allow her to remain in the tavern, and to plant in her husband's heart the will to come back from England and support his family. She did not seek retribution, only survival.[91]

Outright widowed spouses, usually female, constituted a larger proportion of Guttmacher's petitioners. The adjustment for more well-to-do widows could be, paradoxically, more terrifying and disorienting, since some had no experience in the working world. Beina, widow of the former head of the rabbinical court in Stryków, confessed that "she does not know where to turn, for her posture is weak, and her children depend on her, and she is the granddaughter of the *tzaddik ha-manoaḥ* Joseph Perinbach, of blessed memory, . . . and she asks the *admor* to pray for her and advise her what to do." Beina possessed "some hundreds of rubles" but had no idea what to trade in.[92] Once they had their bearings, however, well-to-do widows could wield enormous familial authority and benefit from their husbands' political and economic privileges.[93]

The picture among female widowed tavernkeepers is mixed. Several only asked for continued success, adding reminders that they required suitable marriage matches for themselves and their children or healing of illnesses that threatened their ability to support their "orphans."[94] Feigele bat Rachel requested a speedy recovery, "for it has been about eight days since her health declined . . . and today she spit up blood, God help us." She had to be able to continue to singlehandedly run her profitable tavern and "support her children, the orphans, and marry off her daughter, the betrothed Mirel."⁹⁵ Pesa Sarah bat Eidel, a widow of sixty years, had run her tavern successfully for years but was now "weak and [could not] run it by herself." Should she hand the tavern over to her married daughter, sublease it to another person, or simply get married again?⁹⁶

The widow Pesa bat Hannah's tavern had done well for three years, but then, she wrote, "people [i.e., Jews] saw my success and were envious of me and they also established a tavern." Now, thanks to the new competition, her profits had been cut in half. To make matters worse, she had procured two betrothal offers for her only son, Joshua Falk, but "evil people" had slandered him and scuttled the deals.⁹⁷ Ḥayya bat Hanka's concession for her unprofitable tavern had become prohibitively expensive. She also had "no peace" from her daughter Sarah Hadas, her only child ("for she has not merited a son"), who had been abandoned by her husband without a formal divorce "and she suffered greatly from this and went out of her mind from it. Now, with God's help, she has been restored, but she remains very angry." Sarah Hadas's husband had finally divorced her, but she was in need of a new match "so that she can be normal [*ragil*]." How to procure a dowry out of such meager earnings?⁹⁸

Other widows, too, complained that their taverns were insufficient for providing their daughters with dowries. Reizel bat Sheindel had been left with ten children, and her eldest daughter was ready for marriage.⁹⁹ Sarah bat Feiga, from the same town, had only two daughters but owed a dowry of "one thousand *zuzim*." She needed to come up with the money fast, for the groom was about to go off to the army. Sarah had her own problems, too. After being widowed for a year and a half, she had married another widower, "but he was a drinking man and he loved to play cards and other things." So she divorced him by means of a rabbinical court's decree, but was ordered to pay half of the cost of the proceedings. As she had not yet been able to collect the sum from her debtors, her drunken ex-husband, she wrote, presently "wanders from place to place, and I must provide his meals."¹⁰⁰ Hannah Beila bat Sarah Deborah had little success with her tavern and was afflicted with "the illness called *shliketchen*." But there was hope—she was recently engaged to "the widower, son of the rabbi of the town of Brodnica, named Jacob David ben Eve."¹⁰¹

Whether married, divorced, or widowed, Jewish men and women continued to seek to engage in tavernkeeping because it remained lucrative and accessible for Jews. But it was a life that seemed increasingly fraught with anxiety. Sometimes a person lacked the scrappiness the occupation required. One's luck could be reversed by the appearance of new competitors, both Christians and Jews. And in the worst instances a tavernkeeper could be informed on by jealous or vindictive locals, both Christians and

Jews. An informer could bring about heavy fines and banishment. At that point little helped except the tzaddik's prayers.

CONCLUSION

S. Y. Abramovitsh once had his alter ego, Mendele, confide: "I keep on the side—this is between the two of us—a little tavern that doesn't bring in much; but my goat, knock wood, is a good milker; and I have a rich cousin not far from here who can be milked in a pinch too."[102] Mendele's humorous aside relays important features of Jewish tavernkeeping during the 1870s—surreptitious liquor selling, side occupations, familial assistance, and so on. But his carefree tone also obscures the grating worry that the Guttmacher petitions lay bare. Landowners could be tempted by a better offer; energetic competitors could set up shop down the street; and, most devastatingly of all, powerful state officials could shine their spotlight on a technically illegal venture. Isaac Babel's story "At Grandmother's" better captures the more typical feeling of impotent rage:

> And once more I heard my Grandmother's stories. Long ago, many, many years ago, there was a Jew who ran a tavern. He was poor, married, burdened with children, and traded in bootleg vodka. The commissar came and tormented him. Life became difficult. He went to the *tzaddik* and said "Rabbi, the commissar is vexing me to death! Speak to God on my behalf!" "Go in peace," the *tzaddik* said to him. "The commissar will calm down." The Jew left. At the threshold of his tavern he found the commissar. He was lying there dead, with a purple, swollen face.[103]

Such crude revenge fantasies emerged out of a helpless awareness that the whole enterprise could disintegrate on the whim of one zealous official.

Competition, informing, and state interference may be seen as increasingly numerous cracks in the old edifice. New kinds of pressures were beginning to be felt, too. Well-meaning polemics in the new positivist press advocated transforming taverns into "folk houses," where political meetings and discussions could take place for the empowerment of the peasant, and where less intoxicating beverages would be served.[104] In 1876, a polemic against Jewish tavernkeeping appeared in the guise of a historical monograph by a respected Polish historian, arguing that the eighteenth-century Jewish tavernkeeper had "successfully exploited" the Polish people because he "possessed a lure for enticing them: vodka."[105] Positivist journalists and esteemed historians had joined the fray.

But the foregoing analysis illustrates that the state assault on Jewish tavernkeeping remained largely ineffective, notwithstanding the picture derived from official data and legislation. While larger urban centers may have witnessed an erosion in both noble authority and the traditional lord-Jew relationship, Jews in towns and villages like Baruch Benedict ben Esther were still petitioning R. Guttmacher for help "finding favor in the eyes of the noblemen, so that he can earn a bit of money."[106] And as long as the lord-Jew alliance held, governmental initiatives aimed at normalizing the Jews' economic profile were usually frustrated.

Certain Jews did, however, prove more receptive and adventurous. The next chapter follows those few tavernkeepers and other Jews who complied with the inducements and demands of government officials and reformers by engaging in agriculture, serving in the army, or sending their children to state-sponsored schools. Such officials and reformers were certain that those endeavors would cure Jews of their desire to engage in the kingdom's most lucrative industry.

CHAPTER 6

Farmers, Soldiers, and Students

Reforming Jewish Tavernkeepers

In 1834, the nobleman and exiled insurrectionist Antoni Ostrowski published a lengthy reflection on his hopes for the Jewish future in the Kingdom of Poland. Ostrowski was a different kind of reformer. While he had no great affection for Jewish tavernkeepers, he was sure that without Jewish trade the Polish population would have likely starved, and that the inevitable solution to the kingdom's supposed Jewish problem was nothing less than full emancipation. In the meantime, there was much the state could do to ready Polish Jews for their ultimate freedom, including re-education, military conscription, and providing inducements to take up farming.

The latter two projects were particularly controversial in the kingdom, since it was widely held that Jews were congenitally unsuited to military service and agricultural work. As a commander of a Jewish National Guard unit, however, Ostrowski had seen Jews fight courageously once they were permitted to serve. Some had even been decorated for bravery. And as owner of Tomaszów Mazowiecki, he had witnessed a number of Jewish families in his town found an agricultural colony, and they were now planting orchards and cultivating land, however awkwardly. Despite the Jewish disdain for agriculture, there was good reason to hope that granting land to rural Jews, at least, would be effective. Subjected to military discipline and enticed into agricultural work, Ostrowski proclaimed, Jews would renounce their "deceitful" occupations and become civilized.[1]

This chapter seeks to give such projects a proper hearing, and is thus not limited to their effects on Jewish tavernkeepers alone. Historians are rightly skeptical about the transformative effects of farming, soldiering, and state-sponsored schooling, especially in the absence of opportunities for Jewish educational and professional advancement. But the limited successes of those projects and their more typical failures deserve a re-examination in light of new sources, several of which afford glimpses of real-life cases of tavernkeepers who beat their liquor stills into plowshares and swords or sent their children to state-sponsored schools. If the projects rarely had the expected transformative effect, it was more due to a misunderstanding of basic human motivations and needs than ill intentions on the part of the state. An analysis of this misunderstanding forms a fitting conclusion to our tragicomic imperial story.

FARMERS

The agricultural solution to the Jewish question excited both the deepest skepticism and the wildest optimism. Popular folk idioms ridiculed the very notion ("As suitable as a Jew for farming" went one insult; "He has as much success as a Jewish farmer" went another).[2] There was also real anxiety about the prospect of Jews owing land, for reasons we will explore. Yet Jewish farming captivated the imaginations of Polish reformers, and nothing could dissuade them. Even the most vocal Judeophobes were willing to concede that agriculture would solve the problem of Jewish tavernkeeping. The first attempt to make this case in the newly formed kingdom appeared in an 1816 letter from Adam Czartoryski to the viceroy on behalf of the Commission for the Peasants that advocated evicting Jews from tavernkeeping and settling them on the land as farmers, rendering them healthier and more useful.[3] Crafts were sometimes proposed as an alternative to tavernkeeping, too, and were sometimes even acknowledged as the more realistic alternative for such an urbanized population. But no one seemed prepared to take on age-old Christian guild restrictions. So land cultivation remained the favored means to lure Polish Jews out of the liquor trade.[4]

To a certain extent, optimism about the possibility of diverting rural Jewish energies into agriculture was not misplaced. Brewery lease contracts, of all things, provide evidence of a centuries-old Jewish engagement in the direct cultivation of land, since Jewish lessees of breweries tended to raise their own grain and hops while feeding their cattle, poultry, and pigs on brewery byproducts. Certain rural Jews engaged in farming exclusively during the early modern period.[5] In the late eighteenth century,

Jewish families established agricultural colonies in the Bracław and Łomża districts, and additional Jewish agricultural colonies appeared over the next several decades and formed a basis of modern Socialist and Zionist projects.[6]

But Polish officials seemed to waver once it came time to implement an agricultural option. In 1823, in response to Zajączek's inquiries about the "current causes of Jewish misery" discussed earlier (see chapter 2), the tsar had endorsed efforts to entice the kingdom's Jews into farming, declaring that Jews were now free to settle on state land and on empty or uncultivated areas provided that they "work the land they lease and not engage in the production and sale of liquor."[7] But not all Jews, and not all land. Only those Jews with proof of sufficient finances could lease a small amount of state- or church-owned land that was not already spoken for, and only for a limited period, unless it was fallow. Settlers were granted materials for erecting buildings, but these buildings would pass into the landowners' hands at the expiration of their lease. Jewish farmers were temporarily exempted from certain taxes, but were still responsible for both agricultural and kosher meat taxes.[8]

The 1826 Jewish Committee in Warsaw concluded that farming was the cure for Jewish tavernkeeping. In response, Ignacy Badeni posed a set of hard questions. How much empty land was really available for the numerous Jews who were to be driven out of taverns? Should non-tavernkeepers be encouraged to settle the land too? And was it not possible that few Jewish tavernkeepers would actually take the bait? Or did the committee plan to violently force them to become farmers? Badeni, for his part, had serious doubts that there would be either enough land or enough takers. Perhaps poor, young, and healthy Jews would take up farming, on the example of several rich Jews. But this modest contingent would have little impact. The kingdom's Jewish population would remain as large as ever, he predicted, while opportunities of the present class of farmers (he must have meant minor gentry) to improve the sizes of their own lots would only be diminished. Finally, Badeni evinced grave doubts about the committee's fundamental assumption that "a Jew devoted to honest agricultural work will have neither the time nor the opportunity for harming others." Swindlers, he reasoned, would remain swindlers, whether or not they worked the land.[9]

But the dream remained alive. In 1843, Viceroy Paskevich convened a committee to formalize the process of attracting Jews to agricultural work. He offered Jewish farmers what he thought were irresistible inducements: exemptions for twenty-five to fifty years, depending on the size of their agricultural colony, from the newly decreed military conscription and the notorious kosher meat tax. That same year, he unilaterally allowed nine wealthy Jewish merchants and industrialists to buy land on freehold for the purpose of settling twenty-five Jewish families, provided they saw to their accommodation, implements, and livestock.[10] In 1845, he awarded medals to several Jewish business leaders for their contributions to the agricultural initiative. But he stopped short of investing government funds or permitting unfettered land purchases.[11]

Jewish leaders of all kinds urged the process on. More radical integrationists like Jacob Tugendhold might have been expected to embrace an agricultural project.[12] But more traditionalist Jewish business and religious leaders voiced their support as well. In 1841, in a grand display of unity, the rabbi of Warsaw, Ḥayyim Davidsohn; the tzaddik Isaac of Warka; the rabbi of Praga, J. M. Muszkat; the future tzaddik Isaac Meir Alter; the entrepreneurs Solomon Posner, Jacob Epstein, and Isaac Rosen; and all members of the Warsaw Synagogue Council signed a lengthy decree in Hebrew and Polish, shot through with biblical and Talmudic quotations, that represented agriculture as an age-old, traditional Jewish pursuit. The current Jewish estrangement from agriculture, the dignitaries argued, was unnatural and mainly the fault of Israel's enemies, who had deprived Jews of the ability to purchase land. Now that Jews lived under a caring regime, they should participate in its agricultural program. Rabbis and assistant rabbis were admonished to encourage their respective communities in this vein.[13]

Fifteen years later, a total of fifty-six Jewish agricultural colonies had been established by noble and Jewish entrepreneurs, with an estimated 4,405 members. In addition, a handful of Warsaw mercantile elites obtained the right to own land outright, so long as the management of the property was "entrusted to People of the Christian Faith." Judyta Jakubowicz, Józef Redlich, Jakub Epstein, and Temerel Sonnenberg-Bergson had won the right by 1827.[14] Theodore Toeplitz received the right in 1833; and Mattias Cohn and Raphael Glucksohn received it in 1855, without, as we have seen, relinquishing their extensive networks of taverns. By 1861, thirty-two sons of well-to-do parents possessing special privileges were able to purchase land upon graduating from the agricultural school in Marymont.[15] Of course, the vast majority of Jews were not granted the right. But the overall number of Jewish farmers and their families at the mid-century, including colonists, is estimated at thirty thousand. In all, they composed about 5 percent of the Jewish population. Considering the inertia inherent in estate-based societies, and that there was no real government investment beyond tax exemptions, these results were impressive. [16]

On the other hand, 95 percent of the Jewish population was still not farming, and many were still running taverns legally and illegally. Frustrated officials in the Interior Ministry blamed Jewish stubbornness. The obvious Jewish disgust for agriculture, they reasoned, could not be the fault of the regime, which had not only permitted agricultural colonies but offered inducements. Jews had simply ignored their overtures and continued to crowd into towns and cities and engage in trade, speculation, and excessive breeding. How, then, to save the towns and their vulnerable Christian enterprises? Expelling Jews from certain towns had merely intensified the Jewish population in the others, creating a veritable Jewish "state within a state" in each remaining town. Even village Jews resisted real farming, preferring "speculation" like dairy leases and cattle ranching.[17] Agricultural colonies, the report concluded, had been a benevolent solution to the problem that Jewish enserfment was "forbidden by God according to Mosaic law." But agricultural colonies could not be forcibly imposed on the Jewish population, and they required capital. The only recourse was to push on by means of Jewish money: granting wealthy Jews the right to acquire real estate, parcel out that land to Jewish colonists, and fund these enterprises by means of an annual fee collected from the Jewish community. In other words, the government should not have to bear the costs.[18]

Three years later, in response to concerns raised by the philanthropist Moses Montefiore, more sympathetic voices began to be heard in government circles. The minister state secretary admitted that experience shows that few inhabitants return to farming once they are diverted from it. "Can we be surprised, then, that the Jew, who has never before engaged in land cultivation and is more accustomed to commerce and craftsmanship, does not willingly think of the plough?" As for agricultural colonies, despite tax breaks and military exemptions, "no one has yet thought seriously about this subject; on the contrary, in 1823 the Government Commission on Finance resisted it by every means." The main problem, he concluded, was that there was no budgetary allocation in the kingdom for establishing Jewish colonies, as in the Tsarist Empire. The kingdom should therefore divert a percentage of those taxes levied exclusively on the Jews to agricultural colonies, while Jewish founders of agricultural colonies should be granted honorary citizenship, as they were in the Russian Empire proper.[19]

Not surprisingly, Jewish supporters of the idea also held the government accountable for the modest pace of the transition. In 1831, Jan Glucksberg noted the government's inadequate financial commitment and suspected officials' motives. It looked to Glucksberg like they were merely trying to settle Jews on "wastelands" far away from Christian settlements in an effort to isolate them from Christians, and the likelihood of a Jew "leaving tavernkeeping and cultivating a wasteland" was slim.[20] In 1856, the Warsaw Synagogue Council pointed to the "praiseworthy results and good neighborly relations with Christians" in places where Jews did possess and cultivate land. The real problem, council members argued, was the many restrictions on rural residence and land ownership. Remove those unreasonable impediments and more Jews would take up the plow.[21]

Most historians concur with these latter arguments, condemning the agriculture project as a series of half measures hampered by prejudice, stinginess, and mistrust. But Jews played a role in undermining the project, too, wittingly or unwittingly. Some failed to grasp that the whole point of the agricultural initiative was to wean them off the liquor trade despite fairly explicit reminders. A Jewish land entrepreneur named Mojzesz Wejsman requested, on behalf of five Jewish families who had settled on his land, permission to produce and sell liquor without paying for a concession. Officials looked into the matter and found that Jews who owned land *could* sell liquor without a concession, so long as it was done through a Christian intermediary. Notified of this loophole, Mojzesz then protested that it was unfair that a "stranger" should profit from his liquor sales, and reiterated his request to run a concession-free tavern. After all, he pressed on, where produce from the land was insufficient for colonists' support, they were entitled to set up stores for agricultural implements without purchasing a concession. The exasperated officials concluded that settling these incorrigible Jewish families on the land "did not restrain them from the usually harmful industry [i.e., tavernkeeping] among peasants."[22] Officials were likewise indignant that Eliasz Rogorinski, as soon as he acquired land, strove "to establish not only a distillery but even a tavern," which surely was counter to the regime's intention to wean Jews from their "addiction to selling liquor."[23] Abraham Simon Cohn, who had received special real estate privileges in the wake of the 1830 uprising, was deprived of them in 1841 as punishment for leasing the liquor monopolies in his villages to fellow Jews.[24]

Jewish colonists unwittingly thwarted the regime's intent in other ways. A Kalisz county commissioner discovered that many Jews were having their Christian servants do the actual farm labor.[25] In addition, some were attempting to engage in "speculation" on their land. Before he was deprived of his privilege, Abraham Simon Cohn's request to lease a different tract of land was denied because "restrictions on Jews are meant to prevent hypercompetition over land leases; exception is only made for Jews who are sincere in their desire to become farmers, not speculators.[26] Officials predicted that Isaac Blawat and Isaac Birenszwajg's proposed construction of a factory on farmland they were leasing near Lodz would not lead to "virtuous agriculture" but rather create a "speculative trade settlement and harmful factory district that would continue to expand."[27] Lewi Kozmirek's request to purchase land in Pawlikowice (Łomża district) seemed innocent enough.

He was considered "completely progressive in the eyes of the regime, which desires to civilize the Jewish people, the surest way being to direct them toward agriculture." He even vowed not to engage in the liquor trade, nor any other activity that would prove harmful for neighboring peasants. But then it came out that Lewi was owed over 1,500 rubles by the current landowner of Pawlikowice, who had only been able to come up with half of the amount. Officials realized that the land purchase was going to function as a foreclosure for a Jewish moneylender, not exactly what they had had in mind when they conceived the agricultural project. His request was denied.[28]

Undoubtedly, a contradiction lay at the heart of the agricultural project: on the one hand, farming was to magically provide a solution to the Jewish problem of tavernkeeping; on the other hand, Jewish land ownership and leasing—the only real way to lure Jews away from lucrative tavern leases—was to be heavily restricted. But officials were jittery. What if Jews, with their legendary wealth, began buying up Poland and destroying in the process a glorious agrarian way of life? Julian Ursyn Niemcewicz's conspiratorial, masochistic *Rok 3333, czyli Sen niesłychany* ("The Year 3333, or an Incredible Dream," written in 1817 and published in 1858) imagines a scenario in which Jews acquired the right to purchase real estate and very soon, as a result of their "gold and perseverance . . . the loveliest estates were in Jewish hands." The once beautiful Wilanów estate was now owned by "Prince Palatine Itsek Szumlowicz," and now contained a "huge distillery, a brewery, and a slaughterhouse on the premises."[29] Bolesław Prus's novel *Placówka* paints a nightmarish picture of a noble manor that had fallen into Jewish hands, part of a larger process of hasty post-emancipation land sell-offs. When the protagonist visits the manor, he is "terrified at the vision of destruction" wrought by its Jewish owners:

> In the windows there were no panes, in the open doors there were not even doorknobs, the walls were tattered, the floors pulled up. The salon resembled a manure pit; in the boudoir Yosel the tavernkeeper's wife had set up chicken coops, and in the lord's office lived several Jewboys, and saws, axes, and shovels lay in a giant heap. The farm's domestic staff, which by agreement had a room there for venerating Saint John, loafed about from corner to corner idly. A coachman of a team of horses sawed unceasingly; a housekeeper lay ill with fever, and one of the carters, once a reputable guy, was under arrest, accused of stealing knobs and doors from stoves.[30]

The new owners, in their single-minded quest for profit, had ravished the preeminent symbol of noble refinement, the manor.

In reality, Jews did not buy up Poland, and the beautiful old order did not rapidly disintegrate. Although the decree of 1862 removed many restrictions on Jewish land ownership, which had been outlawed since 1808, the process of Jewish land acquisition was slowed by prohibitions against Jews purchasing estates that had not yet fixed rents for the peasantry, a process that could drag on for many years. To an even greater degree, it was slowed by the real, rather than imagined, financial state of most of the kingdom's Jews. By 1887, one year after the publication of *Placówka*, non-nobles still owned merely 15.2 percent of the kingdom's private estates. It is not known how many of this modest percentage were Jews.[31]

The several petitions in the Guttmacher collection that do reflect a gradual influx of Jews into land ownership, leasing, and farming during the post-emancipation era tend to defy these authors' expectations of Jewish collusion and conspiracy. Dov ben Beila requested the tzaddik's "blessing on the harvest" for the "field business" he currently leased in Chrusty village from two Jews, "the lords Reb Getzel and Reb Yonah." Several of his livestock and horses had died; he was losing money on the lease, had fallen into serious debt, and was unable to meet this year's installment. He was considering suing the Jewish landowners for having refused to inform him of certain tax obligations at the time of the lease signing and for cutting down a forest and depriving him of a pasture for his animals. Dov had made up his mind to leave the Jewish-owned village for another "field business." Perhaps he would build his own farm with his father, who owned several fields, or perhaps he would move in with his father in the town of Piotrków and go into trade. The problem was that Dov was, he wrote, "not an expert in trade, and my father and teacher, may he live, treats me like a gentile and does not want to rescue me or have mercy on me and my household." The feared Jewish solidarity, a constant theme in non-Jewish social commentaries, did not often materialize in reality—either among Jewish landowners and their Jewish lessees or even among some Jewish family members.[32]

At the same time, having a coreligionist as one's lord did provide the Jewish leaseholder with a new court of appeal. Aspiring or disgruntled lessees could turn to a revered religious authority like Guttmacher. Ephraim Nehemiah ben Rebekah ha-Levi, a desperately poor father of six children, took the unusual step of prefacing his petition with a request on behalf of "the rich man [*gevir*] Jacob from Glodnow village, who also owns Przymja village" for the speedy recovery of the latter's ill daughter, also present at Guttmacher's court. The reason for his unusual request-by-proxy soon becomes clear: Ephraim and his wife had "asked this wealthy man if he would lease them a tavern or other enterprise in Przymja village," but Ephraim was afraid, he wrote, that "he will retract it if he learns about me and my sorrowful condition, for the times are desperate for me. And as is known, the rich only want to do business with rich people." A marginal Jew like Ephraim might prevail, however, with the tzaddik's letter of recommendation and blessing for success:

> However, if I attain the aid of the written recommendation of the holy *admor shelita*, and his holy majesty will agree to this and give me a blessing that I succeed in trade in a lease or tavern in the village Przymja, then the rich man will of course heed the approbation of his great holiness. And he will listen, and satisfy the needs of [my] household and of course give him a tavern or [other] lease in the village of Przymja. And he will be able to support his household, who are wrapped in hunger and need.[33]

With the tzaddik's approbation and blessing, Ephraim was certain that Jacob would consider him a safe prospect.

There were, in addition to Jewish landowners, increasing numbers of Jewish farmers. But they refused to merely raise crops. As Mejer Dawidowicz of the Blumrozen Affair demonstrates (see chapter 2, above), erstwhile tavernkeepers had no problem at all cultivating land, but they also insisted on secretly engaging in the liquor trade, running cheap restaurants and stores, maintaining dairy leases, and so on. Jews were quite willing to become farmers, just not in the restricted manner envisioned by social reformers and government officials. The most typical side-venture for Jewish farmers was lending money to local Christians. David Tuvel ha-Kohen requested Guttmacher's blessing not only for success in his field but also "for collecting the debt from the nobleman Modzroski easily and quickly."[34] Some farmer-moneylenders even attempted to foreclose on noble landowners. Ḥayyim Israel ben Nokha leased a farm from a nobleman and "received much fruit from it." He had also lent money to the nobleman, who, unable to pay off his debt, had offered Ḥayyim the deed instead. But now the nobleman was reneging and planned to sell off the village instead, "for he also owes money to others and they want him to sell the village for the debts he owes them."[35] Pesel bat Mirel had owned an orchard with her husband, but she had "left her husband because he does not walk the straight path." She currently lived in her mother's house with their son and had no means of sustenance. Meanwhile, her husband had sold the orchard to a nobleman, who was using the land for mining. Should she return to her impious husband's house or wait until he comes after her? Pesel asked the tzaddik to "reverse her husband's heart to good so that he will walk in the ways of our fathers, for he is from a good family." She also asked the tzaddik to help her find favor with the nobleman so that he would sell her his barn.[36]

Even failed Jewish farmers seemed to behave differently from their non-Jewish peers, displaying more ability to invest capital in their land leases, fight perceived injustices in court, and take up nonagricultural enterprises when farming did not work out. Moses Eliezer ben Shindel, who leased an unprofitable farm in a village "under the lord named Zarocki," had invested four hundred rubles of his own money in it.[37] Tzevi ben Ḥayya had paid six consecutive years of his lease in advance, and was fighting the gentile leaseholder's efforts to evict him after only three years.[38] Zelig ben Tzirel was being evicted after having leased a field for ten years because, he wrote, "there are people who curse me and influence the lord not to keep me anymore," but he was not completely stranded—he currently supported himself by leasing a wagon with horses, and the nobleman in question still owed him money.[39] The competitive nature of land leases to Jews (in contrast to the land grants to emancipated peasants), as well as a long tradition of nonagricultural pursuits, virtually ensured that Jews would never develop into typical farmers.

Certain rural Jewish agricultural endeavors did not fit the government's restrictive definition of agriculture. An 1844 report charged that the majority of Jews living in rural areas preferred "speculation," by which they meant dairy farming (9,697); crafts (12,976); and, until the enforcement of the ban that year, tavernkeeping (2,106). Only 9,110 Jews were engaged in proper agriculture, the authors of the report estimated, and only 5,382 actually worked the land themselves.[40]

Dairy farming remained one of the more popular Jewish rural pursuits by Guttmacher's day. Similar to tavernkeeping and land leasing, however, competition over leases could be cut-throat. Joseph ben Beila had leased a dairy farm for nineteen years until he had been outbid, he wrote, by "an evil man named Solomon ben Rebekah from my neighborhood, who had been with me on the holy Sabbath at a circumcision ceremony [bris]." Having learned that Joseph paid eighteen rubles per cow each year, Joseph had approached the noble that Monday and offered him twenty-five rubles per cow, which came to an additional 350 rubles annually. The noble immediately called Joseph to him and, "because of his sense of compassion and because [Joseph and his family] had lived under him for such a long time," offered to let Joseph keep the lease for 125 rubles per year less than the price offered by his usurper, which still, however, amounted to a sizeable increase.[41] Sarah Baltna, a widow with four children, was even less lucky. She was outbid for her dairy lease, and had no idea what to do next.[42]

Like other Jewish farmers, dairy lessees took up all kinds of side ventures. Some engaged in wagon driving or shoemaking on the side.[43] Others lent money to local peasants and landowners, with all the attendant risks and heartache. A dairy lessee named Judah Leibush David ben Sarah ha-Kohen had, he wrote, "lent thousands of zlotys to Lady Kwiatkowski, and she does not want to pay. And he owes half of it to other people and cannot pay, and the trees are falling on me." Judah had repeatedly asked for his money and now demanded that she either pay him back or grant him full ownership of the dairy farm.[44] An unsuccessful dairy farmer named Abraham ben Tolda Leah strayed into smuggling. After failing in a finished leather business and accumulating a debt of four hundred rubles, he had become a dairy farmer. But it was not profitable, so Abraham asked the tzaddik whether he thought it a good idea to smuggle leather into the country in order to avoid the prohibitive duties on leather. "And the *admor shelita* advised me that if I had a gentile bring [the leather] in, then if there were, God forbid, any seizure, *he* would have to pay; and he said to do this." Abraham proceeded to do just that, and "bless God I made a profit of several hundreds of rubles from this business. And I also profited in my dairy business," probably as a result of his increased capital. But several Jewish leather importers had discovered his gambit and threatened to inform on him. Abraham demanded the tzaddik's protection, since he had only followed his advice.[45]

Abraham's petition suggests that Guttmacher sometimes condoned smuggling, a sense that is strengthened by the candor of petitions by smugglers (sixteen in all). Many evinced little regret beyond the dangers inherent in spiriting goods across the border. Naphtali Hertz ha-Kohen ben Esther complained that "the border guards [*strażniks*] lie in wait for him and he has no time for serving God and studying Torah." He informed the tzaddik that the border guards names were Nachalski and Nozak (a signal to curse them), adding that both were "converts who apostatized from Judaism."[46] Siva Adele bat Esther, a smuggler's wife, was "very scared and anxious that [her husband] not be seized, God forbid, by the evil goyim, God forbid," for he was an "old and very weak man."[47] Joseph Tzevi ben Bluma was less afraid of the Russian border guards, whom he and his partner supplied with meat, than informers "who constantly scheme and desire to do evil to them."[48] But some did seem to regret their involvement in illicit trade, lamenting that this was the only way they could support their households.[49] One smuggler asked if the tzaddik knew of any legitimate way he could "work within Poland and not have to be in danger."[50] Another, who owed a hundred-ruble fine for smuggling, asked the tzaddik to pray that he receive a "document of legitimacy."[51]

Another popular rural Jewish pursuit was lumber, particularly as nobles began to sell off their forests in an attempt to save their debt-laden estates. Dov ben Breindel dealt in lumber on the side, claiming to be principally engaged in proper farming. This, along with his certified poor health, enabled him to free his only son from military duty. But Dov's son's army discharge had angered the mayor, who denounced them to the military office. An official arrived and began questioning the locals, and was told that Dov "never worked the land and does not work the land now, but only hires other people to work the land, and the father and son only work in business."[52] Having been exposed as a pseudo-farmer, Dov was forced to return his son to the army. In addition, "the wicked mayor, may his name be blotted out, also wants to fine him and add two years [of army service]."[53]

SOLDIERS

Why did Dov consider his son's recruitment to be such a disaster? He probably feared that two decades of military service would destroy his son's economic prospects and, even worse, estrange him from the traditional Jewish way of life. These fears were shared by Jews throughout the kingdom, who often referred to military recruitment as a "plague." According to the Polish memoirist Cyprynus, who was learning kabbalah from Rabbi Mordecai Lejbowicz of Grodno, initial plans to recruit Jews in the Kingdom of Poland were formulated in 1815 but canceled thanks to bribes to Novosiltsev. Cyprynus once teased his kabbalah instructor that the conscription of the Jews had already been decided, and was shocked at the rabbi's reaction: "His whole body began to shake with convulsions; his eyes darkened, and he practically fainted. I gave him water. He finally collapsed and began sobbing and weeping." When the rabbi finally got a hold of himself, he began to pace the room and curse.

"At whom are you hurling such insults, Reb Mordke?" Cyprynus asked.

"Nu, our fine senator!" the rabbi replied.

"What for? What does he have to do with anything?"

"What for? For our twenty thousand ducats . . . oy vey, he tricked, cheated, and destroyed us. . . . He promised us that nothing will happen. We rabbis called upon Jews, poor devils, to fast over the past two weeks, collected twenty-thousand ducats . . . *oy gevalt*! Banditry! . . . even if he returns the money."[54] Yet in the end, Novosiltsev did not disappoint. He first managed to forestall Jewish recruitment and then persuade the Grand Duke Constantine to drop it altogether. There was no Jewish draft decreed in the kingdom until December 24, 1843.[55]

Certain Jews nevertheless volunteered for military service, and some retained the desired changes in their lifestyle and appearance upon their discharge. Petitions from Jewish veterans evince pride in having defied stereotypes by displaying honor and sacrifice for their country, and the veterans demanded a concrete acknowledgement. In August of 1830, just months before the uprising, a Warsaw native named Marek Moszkowicz applied for permission to live on a restricted street in Warsaw on the grounds that he had volunteered for the 10th Infantry Division in 1809 during the Napoleonic Wars, marched on Galicia and Russia [!], and had fought in battles at Raszyn, Sandomierz, Zamość, Dyneburg, and Labiau, where he had been taken prisoner. He had been discharged because of weak health and had returned home to Warsaw to take care of his familial responsibilities. The tsarist regime actually shared Marek's belief that Jewish military service should be rewarded regardless of which side he had fought on, and permitted him to reside on the restricted street.[56]

Officials in the Polish revolutionary regime were not as responsive. On May 7, 1831, in the heat of the November Uprising, Henryk Finkelsztajn appealed to the regime to waive the wealth requirement in his case because he had risen above the superstitions of his coreligionists and had served for eleven years. The high commissioner had broken his heart by rejecting his petition to live on a restricted street in Warsaw. Those Jews who did meet the wealth requirement had directed their whole lives toward unscrupulously attaining money while he, in contrast, had sacrificed both his prospects for attaining wealth and his very health, and now had to work extremely hard for a piece of bread. Henryk implored officials to measure the thousands of annoyances he had suffered during his lengthy military service against mere money, gained through cunning rather than through noble service. Surely "suffering for the good of the fatherland out of a sense of obligation" was worth more than sixty thousand zlotys, the required limit for residence on Warsaw's restricted streets. Besides, Henryk had become accustomed to cleanliness, and "to live among superstitious Jews would be quite disagreeable." His appeal was unsuccessful.[57]

Marek and Henryk were volunteers, and thus more likely to have been predisposed to the kind of acculturation and integration championed by social reformers. In 1843, however, a kingdom-wide Jewish military conscription forced many unwilling young Jewish men into the military grind. Although the conscription law was not identical to the 1827 military conscription law in the Tsarist Empire proper, which included an infamous cantonist decree that forced Russian Jewish youths of twelve years age and younger into military colonies until they were old enough to serve, Polish Jewish parents felt a similar sense of dread at the potential loss of their young men to the Jewish tradition.[58]

As Dov ben Breindel's son's case demonstrates, farming could provide a way out—the children of Jews who undertook agriculture were exempt from the draft. But the agricultural option does not appear to have been exploited all that frequently by those hoping to evade the draft. Moses Jerozolimski, an eighty-year-old petitioner, provided one explanation for the hesitation: the wealthy members of the Warsaw Synagogue Council, who were "superficially civilized and really lacking in character, conscience, and morals," were discouraging and even preventing Jews from availing themselves of the agricultural loophole for fear that if "Jews who dressed Jewishly" took up farming, then they, the wealthy and assimilated, would have to supply recruits from among their own sons.[59]

Whatever the actual reason for the reluctance, the fact that more Jewish recruits did not simply join agricultural colonies seems regrettable considering the amount of anguish that recruitment engendered. The Guttmacher collection includes hundreds of requests to the tzaddik to use his divine connections to "rescue" petitioners from the "hands of the men of war" or the "soldier's lottery," including petitions by Jews who had fled abroad to avoid service.[60] Parents made desperate appeals to save their sons from the military fate, fearing, "God forbid, that [they] will mix with the goyim and learn their ways."[61] But the tzaddik's blessing did not always work. When Samuel Jacob's son David's time came he sent him to Guttmacher's court, and the tzaddik "blessed him and promised that he will be saved from the hands of the gentiles. And he did not become a soldier." But David was forced to stand in the army lottery again, drew a low number (38), and was imprisoned for trying to evade service. Samuel Jacob continued to believe that "the blessing of the tzaddik will stand and that God will help so that he is not taken to the army and will quickly go free according to the promise of the revered Rabbi."[62]

Some parents financially ruined themselves in "ransoming" their sons from the military by paying off lower officials.[63] And bribery did not always work. Menaḥem ben Zisel had "stood twice before the army commission, and," he wrote, "thank God I left without harm from them." The third time, however, Menaḥem did as he had done before and "gave money to the clerk and bribed him so that [he] would not have to stand again before the commission." He added, "I also gave the monetary bribe to the army scribes." However, one clerk neglected to write that he had already stood before the commission, and as a result, "the decree went out from the government to the gendarmes to seek [him] out." Menaḥem was now forced to serve.[64]

There were legal ways to buy exemption, such as in cases in which the recruit was an only son. But not everyone could afford to pay the exemption fee. Moses ben Golda, a youth on the verge of being drafted, explained poignantly that "he has always been with his father and is not used to being with anyone else, and especially in another country. And his father is a teacher of young children and is poor and deprived and has practically nothing to eat and takes care of children, and cannot afford to redeem his son and pay eight hundred rubles." Moses begged the tzaddik "to rescue him from the hands of the goyim by means of the merit of his Torah and ancestors."[65] A widow named Feiga bat Tirzah begged the tzaddik to intervene with God because, she wrote, "My only son David is twenty years old and next year he must assume the soldier's fate, even though only sons are exempt from this bitter fate." Feiga had petitioned officials and was told that she needed to pay only thirty rubles in lieu of her son's service. "But I am a poor widow and I have no savings," she explained to the tzaddik, adding pessimistically "and it is very bitter for me that my only son, may he live, whose soul is immersed in mine, will depart from my people."[66] In one case, the entire community collected funds to ransom a learned recruit named Moses ben Roza, a father of two children and "a great Torah scholar from a pedigreed family of Israel, a nephew of the rabbi the tzaddik of Chust, of blessed memory" who had stood eight times in the draft and finally faced sixteen years of service. The community collected about two hundred rubles on his behalf, but the impoverished scholar needed at least eight hundred rubles to buy his way out.[67]

Jewish recruits, parents, and entire communities were only slightly overreacting. While recent studies call into question the more alarmist assessments of Jewish army service and forced conversions of Jewish soldiers, there are still clear indications that Jewish recruits were singled out for harsh treatment. Joseph ben Leah beseeched R. Guttmacher, "Pray for me to God, that I find favor in the eyes of the army officers so they will not torment me so much." He was grateful to be stationed in the Kingdom of Poland and not "exiled to the depths of Russia, where there are no Jews." However, he remained miserable because, he wrote, "The officers torment me a lot during my army service."[68]

In addition, Jews who served out their decades-long military terms were often left high and dry by the regime upon their discharge. Some even lacked the necessary funds to travel home to their families.[69] When Moses ben Reiza ha-Kohen came home he was so bereft of funds as to consider leaving his wife again and going east to find work. He entreated R. Guttmacher to at least "work on his behalf so that he can support himself in his own city."[70] Some veterans noticed that gentile veterans were faring much better. Mark ben Tova, who had served a full twenty years, complained that "while all the soldiers who were officers received fields and vineyards on moratoria, they did not want to give anything to him. And he made several requests about this but his voice was not heard."[71] Aaron Isaac ben Judith had "served the tsar" for twenty years, and subsequently found work assisting Jewish merchants for the next six years. But he could barely support himself on account of his physical pains, acquired during his military service. Aaron, too, felt cheated because he had heard that "everyone who serves the tsar is to be given fields," and, he wrote, "They have not given me anything so far."[72] Only in one case among the Guttmacher petitions did a Jewish veteran obtain assistance finding work upon his discharge, "painting a building that they call 'arsenal' for the government."[73]

Nor did the experience of military discipline seem to make Jews more civilized, as officials had assumed. Some veterans returned home changed for the worse. Feigel bat Hadassah's husband, Tzevi, who had been "taken by the soldiers," was, she wrote, now "living with me in my house, not according to the proper way but in great strife, and he goes on the improper path and constantly plays cards and engages in other profane things that are not pious." Feigel had let him know that she would not suffer such behavior, and, she wrote, "Because of this he beat me." It was probably too late for him, for "since he has mingled with the gentiles, he has learned their ways and does not want to live with me when he returns from his work." She asked the tzaddik to "pray to our fathers in heaven to turn his heart to good, or to arrange a proper *get* [divorce]."[74] Yuta bat Mindel's husband did not come home at all. After a little more than four years of military service, he had simply "married another woman," she reported.[75] Tzevi Dov ben Hannah, who had served in the army outside the kingdom for six years, "could not be with his wife as is fitting, God forbid, and because of this she had no children, so she divorced him with the agreement of tzaddikim." He still had not found a wife, a place to settle or a livelihood.[76] These scenarios were exactly what parents of new recruits must have instinctively feared.

Other scenarios were exactly what government officials themselves evidently failed to predict: Jewish veterans fell back on traditionally Jewish occupations. Zelig Witenberg represented a worst-case scenario in the eyes of officials. He explained, "In 1845, I was taken for army service from the town of Augustów. After serving in the army in Battalion/Division 23, Orenburski Corps, I was discharged. . . . I came back to Augustów to my wife, Deborah, and my fifteen-year-old daughter, Hannah, deprived of physical strength and not fit to work for bread, and, what is worse, I lost some vision in my eyes." Zelig could only think of one solution to his predicament: "the freedom to deal in tavernkeeping, either in towns or in villages in the Kingdom of Poland." The presumed effects of military recruitment on Jewish involvement in the liquor trade were all but guaranteed to be minimal if Jewish veterans were left to their own devices upon their discharge. Like Zelig, they gravitated back to tavernkeeping because it remained accessible and lucrative.[77]

STUDENTS

In 1881, the positivist periodical *Prawda* printed an essay titled "The Jew in the Tavern and the Jew in School." Its author, Aleksander Świętochowski, charged, not unreasonably, that when Jews had lost the legal right to establish taverns in villages, they had simply established them under the names of peasants, since "stricter decrees merely teach them to better conceal their operations." The main culprit was the Talmud, he concluded less reasonably, which somehow (he did not specify) encouraged Jews to continue to engage in the sale of vodka. The only real way to reform this nation of tavernkeepers was to draw them away from *ḥeders* and Talmudic education and into proper schools.[78] Another prominent social critic, Klemens Junosza, put forth a similar argument eight years later. "Despite restrictions and edicts," he despaired, "Jews have trafficked in and still traffic in vodka secretly, and even openly." Again, the culprit was Talmudic education. "Neither in Jerusalem, nor in Babylon, nor even during the greatest development of rabbinical studies in Spain, nowhere has the Talmud had so many researchers and commentators as in the dirty one-horse towns scattered about the fields and forests of our fatherland."[79]

Until the recruitment law of 1843, re-education had assumed an importance for social reformers that exceeded even that of Jewish military conscription, for up to that point the kingdom's Jews could still buy their way out by means of a collective recruitment tax.[80] In 1818, Jacob Tugendhold was commissioned to establish the first elementary schools for Jewish boys and girls, and similar schools continued to be established over the next decades. Yet state-sponsored schools did not prove much of a draw. Jewish enrollment in public schools, including elementary and secondary schools, only amounted to 1,672 by 1842.[81] In the modern Rabbinic School, whose language of instruction was Polish and which was established to train modern-oriented rabbis, enrollment rose from twenty-six students at its founding in Warsaw in 1826 to 305 students by 1843. Instead of creating a cadre of enlightened rabbis who would lead their brethren into the light of civilization, however, the school was closed down by the government in 1863 having failed to produce a single rabbi who was acceptable to a Jewish community.[82] The government's lukewarm support for the very educational institutions it initially advocated may seem hypocritical, but such schools were increasingly feared as incubators of Polish nationalism at a time when the regime could ill afford to allow such sentiments to be inflamed.

Another reason for the disappointing results was surely curricular. The prominent maskil Abraham Stern, one of the founders of the Rabbinical School, refused in the end to become its director because he could not abide the marginalization of the Talmud and other canonical Jewish texts in the curriculum. To understand his opposition, it is necessary to recognize the crucial distinction between maskilim like Stern and more extreme Polish Jewish integrationists like Tugendhold and Antoni Eisenbaum. Maskilim envisioned a cultural synthesis between Judaism and European culture along rationalist lines through a modification, not an abandonment, of the traditional Jewish canon.[83] According to the historian Michael Stanislawski, "The excess baggage that had been yoked to the shoulders of the Jewish people by medieval prejudice and superstition would, of course, be discarded, but without the loss—indeed, with the rejuvenation—of a vibrant Hebrew culture and authentic Jewish faith."[84] In contrast, leading Jewish integrationists like Tugendhold and Eisenbaum tended to be government employees who represented the interests of their Christian superiors. Like other enlightened bureaucrats, they sought to Polonize the Jewish population at the expense of the traditional Jewish canon, especially the Talmud. Tugendhold's elementary school curriculum omitted the study of the Bible and Talmud and even Hebrew instruction, the latter a top priority for maskilim.[85]

The more radical Jewish integrationists may have attained political leadership roles in the Jewish community thanks to their government connections, but they were repaid with deep mistrust within the Jewish population, even among maskilim. El'azar Tahlgrin, a maskil, characterized the integrationist leadership as "audacious" and accused them of straying from the "straight path."[86] Moses Jerozolimski, a maskil who himself favored drawing Jews away from "destructive pursuits" and toward agriculture and crafts, offered a more scathing assessment. The integrationists, he charged in his memo to the Interior Ministry, had discarded, along with their traditional Jewish garb, the very principles of religion and morality. Neither Jewish nor Christian anymore, they merely spouted "blasphemy in a virtuous tone." They had donned masks of good character and inveigled their way into the highest offices available to Jews, including the administration of the Rabbinical School. But what did students of the Rabbinical School have to show throughout its twenty-eight (as Jerozolimski has it) years of operation? "Nothing, because although they sought to become rabbis, not a single one of them has attained that honor thus far, for their education is bereft of morality and religious principles and they are therefore completely untrustworthy." Its students were taught to forget about responsibility to "God, the monarchy, and their neighbors." They absorbed, instead, a "perfidious science" without obtaining any skills for honest work.[87]

Moses then took aim at Antoni Eisenbaum, the seminary's director. Eisenbaum, he claimed, was a "freemason" and "freethinker," who was "filled with a spirit that is harmful to the regime." During the outbreak of the 1830 uprising, Eisenbaum had incited his students to join the Polish rebels. Later, Eisenbaum had gotten his students and sons exempted from the draft. Moses concluded with an appeal to the regime to reform the Rabbinical School along Haskalah lines by appointing lecturers of Hebrew and the Jewish religion who had been vetted by rabbis, in addition to a new director and Christian teachers for other language classes. He also requested a new Synagogue Council, one that was purged of radical integrationists. Moses ended with a flourish, insisting that Jews who do not dress in the German style can nevertheless be enlightened and fulfill their obligations to the monarchy, for, he quipped, "it is not fabric but moral fiber that makes a man."[88]

This is obviously only one perspective, and it is in some ways unfair. In fact, Eisenbaum founded a synagogue next to the Rabbinical School in 1839 that only introduced cosmetic innovations to the traditional religious service. But if maskilim like Tahlgrin and Jerozolimski, who desired Jewish occupational and linguistic reform themselves, rejected the legitimacy of the integrationists, one can only imagine how the less acculturated Jewish masses must have felt about them. Nor did integrationists do much to win the masses over. Tugendhold, in an attempt to shore up his credibility among Polish Christians, boasted in print that "anyone who really knows me knows very well that, apart from some basic principles of faith, practically nothing binds me to my coreligionists. I am rarely even with them, for I am always associating with important Christians."[89] A Jew writing under the pseudonym "Elyakim son of the Truth" was probably correct when he informed officials that "the majority of the community is not favorably inclined" toward Jacob Tugendhold and fellow integrationist Abraham Winawer (d. 1857), chairman of the Warsaw Synagogue Council and, ironically, one of the largest liquor distillers in Warsaw. Most Jews in the Kingdom of Poland and throughout Eastern Europe came to regard secularization as just another form of Christianization. Among the main beneficiaries of the educational reform initiatives were, paradoxically, traditionalists, who capitalized on the general alienation and castigated the program as heretical.[90]

Notwithstanding this popular mistrust, the cadre of secularly educated Polonized Jews did continue to grow in size during the second half of the nineteenth century. Integrationists were especially prominent in Warsaw, where, in addition to supporting state-sponsored educational institutions and participating in Polish insurrectionist activities, they established the majestic Great Synagogue at Tłomackie Street, a Jewish hospital and orphanage, and periodicals like *Jutrzenka: Tygodnik dla*

Izraelitów polskich ("The Dawn: A Weekly for Polish Israelites," 1861–63) and *Izraelita* ("The Israelite," 1866–1913), which optimistically gauged the progress of Polonization in Jewish communities beyond Warsaw, including Częstochowa, Lublin, and Włocławek.[91] These periodicals may have only had a readership of a few thousand, but their geographic reach was wide, to judge by the like-minded contributors who began to come out of the woodwork, and together they constituted an important platform for Polonization, integration, and secularization.

One contributor provides a moving account of his first day at a Polish school in Wieluń thirty-five years earlier. As he and two fellow Jews had taken their seats, some students had called out: "Honored Professor, we have Jewboys in class!" But those students had been reprimanded: "We do not care about his religion; treat him like a colleague, like a brother, or else."[92] However, another resident of Wieluń responded to this nostalgic account with the wry observation that the current attendance of Wieluń Jews in public school remained "very thin." Most local Jewish residents, he reminded optimistic *Jutrzenka* readers, continued to "raise their children in complete ignorance of the language of the land." Additional authors of letters to the editors in the early 1860s who had embraced Enlightenment themselves complained of isolation and rejection by their communities.[93]

Guttmacher petitions, which reflect a much more widespread perspective than the integrationist press, only occasionally reflect the penetration of secular education into the kingdom's Jewish communities, notwithstanding Guttmacher's own openness to Hildesheimer's progressive seminary. There was the occasional traditional school teacher (*melamed*) who complained that "the children want to go to the gentile to learn from him."[94] And there was the occasional petitioner who confessed to having acquired secular knowledge. But it was only with ambivalence and regret. Joshua ben Basha, a renowned musician and instrument maker, identified his secular education as the principal cause of his depression:

> For healing and relief from melancholy. And this illness fell upon him in his youth, and God in his great mercy sent him help and he was healed. And now for two years the insanity has fallen upon him anew, after he had been cured of it for twenty-five years. And he is now fifty years old and has grandchildren. And they took him to a hospital in Warsaw. And since he is a good musician, and knows books and several languages, *this* is the cause of his illness: that he dealt a lot in external knowledge, as is known. When the doctors saw his wisdom, for he spoke with them in French, they decreed that he is not crazy and they discharged him from the hospital. And in truth he had a respite, but a sorrow afflicted him, God forbid. For his son of seven years was run over by a carriage and horses and died

from this, and his pain and sorrow were great. However, the illness came upon him, so now they took him to the Jewish hospital, and it has been very difficult for him, for they torture and afflict him a lot.[95]

By ignoring the more obvious causes of his depression—he had a long history of depression and had recently lost his seven-year-old son—and blaming his secular learning instead, Joshua may have been merely telling the tzaddik what he thought he wanted to hear. It is also possible that in that moment Joshua felt genuine remorse for having acquired forbidden knowledge. Either way, such ambivalence toward secular education reflects widespread social disapproval. His account differs markedly from the more familiar testimonials of maskilim, who experienced the acquisition of secular education as revelatory and life-changing.[96]

And what of the occupational transformation that officials and reformers were so certain would result from the reeducation of the Jews? Even when Jews did send their children to state-sponsored schools or obtain a secular education themselves in this period, it did not necessarily follow that they changed their occupational choices. One cautionary case is that of Dwoyra Rozengartów, the Warsaw liquor trader (see chapter 3). Among her main justifications for having earned the right to continue to sell liquor on a restricted street was that her "children go to public school."[97] Another cautionary case is that of Abraham Kinderfraind, the liquor importer and lessee of the liquor monopoly in Zamość (see chapter 4) who had learned to read and write Polish and German "perfectly".[98] Those Jews who sent their children to state-sponsored schools to learn non-Jewish languages or had obtained fluency in those languages themselves felt they deserved to be rewarded, and saw no reason why their reward should not take the form of a liquor concession. Their children, once they graduated from state-sponsored schools, would likely seek the same kind of reward. It was not as if an education in state-sponsored schools opened up new professional routes for them.

CONCLUSION

By "civilizing" the kingdom's Jewish population, officials really meant normalizing them. They were not wrong in identifying Jewish social and economic mores as anomalous. But many Jews could not evidently see why they should renounce a lucrative industry like liquor and enter less lucrative ones like agriculture and army service, nor why they should have their children obtain a state-sponsored education with so little promise of future employment in the professions or civil service upon graduation. Some must have also wondered why, if tavernkeeping was so immoral, anyone should be allowed to engage in it. And some could not have helped but notice the mixed message: the most common reward for Jewish loyalty to the state during insurrections, after all, was a liquor concession.

As a result of this disconnect, we find the tragicomic phenomenon of some of the few Jews who managed to accomplish a transition into farming, serve out a military term, or send their children to state-sponsored schools actually returning to the production and sale of liquor. In the absence of wholesale emancipation, these paths had not helped them or their children significantly better their situation, and in the case of military service their children faced worse prospects owing to decades of lost time. We may well imagine a sequel to Mickiewicz's *Pan Tadeusz* in which Yankel's sons join an agricultural colony, serve in the army, or enroll in a state-sponsored school, only to return eventually to their fathers' occupation.

Nor did the advocates of Jewish normalization ever manage to convincingly explain the value of a Jewish renunciation of tavernkeeping for society at large. Honest officials like Turkul knew that a peasant was not less likely to have a drinking problem if his tavernkeeper was Christian, while Badeni had deep reservations about the supposed transformative power of agriculture. In truth, beyond a tiny group of thinking officials, one detects a shocking degree of wishful thinking. Most merely accepted the assumption that military service, agriculture, and secular education were inimical to selling liquor. Their projects to draw Jews into farming, the army, and state-sponsored schools, had they succeeded, would have probably meant the destruction of the kingdom's surrogate middle class. In the end, Jewish tavernkeeping survived because few of the key players in the liquor trade—nobles, Jews, and peasant customers—could fathom why the state should have been so opposed to it.

Conclusion

With the benefit of hindsight and an array of contemporaneous sources, we have been made aware of a series of illusions that exerted a powerful hold over Polish society's policy makers. The ambitious initiatives aimed at restricting and abolishing the Jewish liquor trade, from concession fees to rural Jewish "prohibition," rested on a set of frail assumptions: that Jewish tavernkeepers were more exploitative than Christian ones; that peasants would be less inclined to drunkenness and material ruin were Christians to take over tavern leases; and that once Jews were pushed out of the liquor trade they would change for the better while Polish society on the whole would become more temperate, healthy, and prosperous. Few officials paused to ask seemingly obvious questions like: Were peasants in areas like the Russian interior, where tavernkeeping was an exclusively non-Jewish affair, any better off? Would Jews really contribute more as farmers? And would the Polish economy really benefit from, or even survive, the loss of its Jewish tavernkeepers? Instead, most officials remained locked in a mental universe of their own making, ignoring the occasional voices of reason that arose from within their own ranks.

Bureaucratic self-delusion about Jews was certainly not unique to the Tsarist Empire, but tsarist officials seemed to excel at it. Perhaps it is the inevitable result of a growing disenchantment with the kingdom's outmoded socioeconomic system, coupled with an inability to make the leap to radical enlightenment experiments like genuine, wholesale emancipation and civil rights. Cameralist-inspired changes like luring Jews into more mainstream but less lucrative pursuits at least provided an illusion of progress while preserving order and enhancing state coffers.

The nobility—the group that originally introduced Jewish tavernkeeping in the Polish-Lithuanian Commonwealth and sustained it long after absolutist officials deemed it socially destructive—were likewise laboring under an illusion. Most noblemen continued to believe that Jews were the only suitable lessees of their taverns. In truth, Jews did tend to be decent enough tavernkeepers. Drinking among Jews was not a pervasive problem, to judge from the sermonic literature; Jewish literacy did tend to greatly exceed that of the peasantry; and Jews could better see to the needs of traveling Jewish merchants. But there was little to suggest that nonnoble Christians were unable to become perfectly competent tavernkeepers as well, especially after they became comfortable with practices like selling liquor on credit. The notion that Christians would be more inclined to drink up the profits was in any case belied by the frequent use of Christians as fronts in the underground Jewish liquor trade. And once Christians were installed as independent tavern leaseholders, they could no more afford to fall into the snares of alcohol addiction than could Jewish tavernkeepers. In this respect, age-old prejudices worked in the Jewish community's favor, ensuring continued economic opportunities even after a series of laws and bans had made installing Jews in one's taverns quite risky.

Jews seem to have clung to certain illusions themselves. For example, Jewish tavernkeepers, surrounded as they were by drunken Christian clientele, indulged in a feeling of cultural superiority that could provide justification for unethical behavior and blind them to the dangers of peasant resentment and social reformers' ire. Even the less ethically problematic practice of allowing customers to drink on credit was precarious, since peasants who owed money to the Jew after a long night of drinking or a poor harvest must have still felt resentful. Such resentment was only kept in check as long as the nobility was willing and able to protect Jews in their domains. Although local Christians continued to cover for technically illegal Jewish-run taverns a full decade after peasant emancipation, this situation could not last forever. As a younger generation who had not known serfdom began to come of age, and as the economic crisis of the 1880s began to throw Polish landowners into disarray, Jewish physical safety became a dangerous illusion. As drunken mobs of semiproletarianized peasants embarked on a series of pogroms, it became painfully clear that liquor, once East European Jewry's economic wellspring, was fuelling its destruction. When the Polish nobility lost its monopoly on liquor—first in Prussian Poland (1845), then in Galicia (1889), and then in the tsarist domains (1898)—the lingering protection afforded by the noble-Jewish leaseholding system was finally lost too.

Perhaps we should not be overly harsh in our judgment. At the time, it may have seemed eminently logical to Polish officials that the experience of tilling the soil, serving in the army, or obtaining a secular education would remake Jews in the image of the kingdom's other inhabitants without requiring too much investment or too radical an experiment like Jewish emancipation. From the landowners' perspective, it may have seemed eminently logical to carry on the centuries-old practice of leasing one's taverns to Jews regardless of what a handful of government officials and social reformers thought, for why take the chance on anyone else? And from the Jewish perspective, efforts to drive them out of the liquor trade must have seemed all too familiar, merely another wave of "evil decrees" that were part and parcel of exilic existence. As long as the lord received his lease payment and the right wheels were greased, many figured, everything would be alright.

One may therefore continue to speak of a nineteenth-century equilibrium between Jews, nobles, and peasants despite state policies like exorbitant liquor concessions, restricted streets in towns and cities, rural Jewish prohibition, agricultural colonies, military recruitment, and projects for secular education that looked to many like another Christianization scheme. The equilibrium endured because Jews were still not taken to be integrable in the Polish lands—they were considered too numerous, wealthy, and culturally distinct. A system composed of mutual dependencies and trust that had worked, more or less, for centuries was difficult to overturn without a broad societal awakening and a new level of trust between Jews and representatives of the state.

The foregoing analysis also suggests a need to let go of some of our own illusions. Impressively arranged governmental data, now accessible in state and regional archives throughout contemporary Poland, can be very deceptive. In the case of Jewish tavernkeepers, whose numbers appeared to dwindle to close to nothing by 1830, one needs to pay close attention to the alternate story told in numerous case studies and petitions. According to this story, Jewish tavernkeepers often went underground, with the full knowledge and complicity of local landowners and peasants. The Jewish liquor trade, although statistically and legislatively invisible, remained as vital as ever.

Another aspect of Polish Jewish history to be reconsidered is the true pace of change during this period. For most of the nineteenth century, Polish Jewry experienced neither mass pauperization nor rapid urbanization and industrialization. While pauperization, urbanization, and industrialization did accelerate during the very last decades of the nineteenth century and were recorded vividly by classic Yiddish writers like S. Y. Abramovitsh, Sholem Aleichem, and I. L. Peretz, the crucial task of historical reconstruction is not helped by projecting those tumultuous decades back upon the rest of the century. For most of the nineteenth century in the majority of the Kingdom of Poland's towns and villages, age-old social relations endured and even strengthened in reaction to state social engineering initiatives. The survival of the centuries-old lord-Jew alliance is observable in the survival the Jewish tavernkeeper, its very embodiment.

A final assumption in need of drastic rethinking is the true extent and significance of Jewish Polonization in the nineteenth-century Kingdom of Poland, manifested in the acquisition or adoption of Polish education, language, and dress, and in support of antitsarist uprisings. This book has argued that modern Jewish historians remain too committed to a secularization narrative that does not do justice to the resilience of tradition, whether conceived in cultural or economic terms. While there did exist a growing cadre of secular-educated, fervent supporters of Polish independence in Warsaw and other urban centers, their size and significance should not be magnified by means of selective emphasis, no matter how much their rationalism and openness might help legitimize East European Judaism for modern readers. By the same token, it is important to resist the urge to minimize traditionalists, e.g. by attempting to downplay the size of a mass movement like Hasidism or assuming the inexorable decline or "erosion" of traditional religious institutions and observance. By magnifying a vanguard of Polonized Jews at the expense of the traditionalist majority, we run the risk of writing ourselves into the Polish Jewish past.

This volume opened with Stefan Garczyński's claim about the seeming preponderance of Jews and Jewish-run taverns in towns throughout eighteenth-century Poland-Lithuania. It is quite telling that one finds the same bitter accusation as late as the eve of World War I. "Our small towns and cities are no longer ours, but belong to foreigners," wrote Father A. Koleński in 1912. "The current municipalities only appear to be in power in small towns and cities; the liquor monopolies hold all the real power. Sober Jews, in a silent economic battle, have foisted intemperance onto us and achieved victory."[1] Koleński could not have known that in just three decades this supposed Jewish problem would be solved once and for all, with little actual benefit to Polish society. A decade after the Holocaust, the Polish poet Marian Piechal (1905–89) penned a stirring tribute to Poland's murdered Jewish population, entitled "Yankel's Last Concert," a reference to Yankel's celebrated dulcimer performances in *Pan Tadeusz*. Once again, the iconic Jewish tavernkeeper was made to embody all of Polish Jewry:

> Yankel stills the strings, unwraps them from the fog of grief,
> And bares all the fires burning in the strings.
> A hand suddenly chokes them, bends the strings down,
> Extinguishes one string after another till they all vanish in smoke.[2]

NOTES

PRELIMS

1. Joseph Roth, *The Radetzky March*, tr. Joachim Neugroschel (Woodstock, NY: Overlook, 2002), 77–78.
2. I have in mind the highly influential book by Yosef Yerushalmi, *Zakhor: Jewish History and Jewish Memory* (Seattle: University of Washington Press, 1982). David Myers perceptively observes that "the very genre of modern historiography which Prof. Yerushalmi and others have seen as the antithesis or bane of collective memory can be and has been the bearer of group memories." See Myers, "Between Diaspora and Zion: History, Memory, and the Jerusalem Scholars," in David Myers and David Ruderman, eds., *The Jewish Past Revisited: Reflections on Modern Jewish Historians* (New Haven, CT: Yale University Press, 1998), 89.
3. Elliot Wolfson, "Lying on the Path: Translation and the Transport of Sacred Texts," *AJS Perspectives* 3 (2001): 8–13.

INTRODUCTION

1. Stefan Garczyński, *Anatomia Rzeczypospolitey-Polskiey* (1754; repr. Whitefish, MT: Kessinger Publishing, 2009), 89.
2. Michel de Certeau, *The Practice of Everyday Life*, tr. Steven Rendall, (Berkeley: University of California Press, 1984), 117.
3. Arno J. Mayer, *The Persistence of the Old Regime: Europe to the Great War* (New York: Pantheon, 1981), 77 and 84.
4. The proportion of Jews in town populations increased as one traveled eastward. See Gershon Hundert, *Jews in Poland-Lithuania: A Genealogy of Modernity* (Berkeley: University of California Press, 2005), chapter 1.
5. S. Y. Abramovitsh, "Of Bygone Days," (1899; 1911–13), tr. Raymond Sheindlin, in Ruth Wisse, ed., *A Shtetl and Other Yiddish Novellas* (Detroit: Wayne State University Press, 1986), 320.
6. It should be noted here that the trajectory of acculturation in Galicia was more complicated, beginning first with Germanization and only gradually moving toward Polonization.
7. For the sake of comparison and simplicity, the Jewish communities of "Western" Europe here include countries like Germany, which are sometimes referred to as part of "Central" Europe.
8. Paula Hyman, *Gender and Assimilation in Modern Jewish History: The Roles and Representation of Women* (Seattle: University of Washington Press, 1995), 8. On the importance of studying emancipation on a state-by-state basis, see Pierre

Birnbaum and Ira Katznelson, eds., *Paths to Emancipation: Jews, States, and Citizenship* (Princeton, NJ: Princeton University Press, 1995), introduction.

9. See, for example, pioneering works like Artur Eisenbach, *The Emancipation of the Jews in Poland, 1780–1870*, ed. Antony Polonsky; tr. Janina Dorosz (London: Blackwell, 1988), and Jonathan Frankel, *Prophecy and Politics: Socialism, Nationalism, and Russia's Jews, 1862–1917* (Cambridge, UK: Cambridge University Press, 1984). On traditionalism, see especially Eliyahu Stern, *The Genius : Elijah of Vilna and the Making of Modern Judaism* (New Haven, CT: Yale University Press, 2013), pp. 3–8.

10. In Antony Polonsky's estimation, "the two groups lived in a hostile but symbiotic relationship, marked both by a degree of social distance, which was lined with mutual disdain, and by strong economic links. See *The Jews in Poland and Russia, Volume II: 1881–1914* (Oxford: Littman Library of Jewish Civilization, 2010), two volumes, 196. See also Ewa Morawska, "Polish-Jewish relations in America, 1880–1940," *Polin* 19 (2006), 71–86.

11. Many minor gentry were too proud to choose anything other than a military career, according to William Jacob's *Report on the Trade in Foreign Corn: And on the Agriculture of the North of Europe* (London, 1826), 78. However, some attempted to compete with Jews for tavern leases. See Dawid Fajnhauz, "Dwór i karczma żydowska na Litwie w połowie 19 w.," in Shmuel Yeivin, ed., *Studies in Jewish History: Presented to Professor Raphael Mahler on His Seventy-Fifth Birthday* (Merḥavia, Israel: Sifriyat Po'alim, 1974), 62–63; Anna Michałowska-Mycielska, *Sejmy i sejmiki koronne wobec Żydów. Wybór tekstów źródłowych* (Warsaw, 2006); and Barbara Stępniewska-Holzer, *Żydzi na Białorusi. Studium z dziejów strefy osiedlenia w pierwszej połowie XIX w.* (Warsaw, 2013), 45–57.

12. Moshe Rosman, *The Lords' Jews: Magnate-Jewish Relations in the Polish Lithuanian Commonwealth during the 18th Century* (Cambridge, MA: Harvard University Press, 1990), 110–113; Jacob Goldberg, "Ha-yehudi ve-ha-pundak ha-ironi ba-ezor Podlasiyah," in *Ha-ḥevrah ha-yehudit be-mamlekhet Polin-Lita* (Jerusalem: Merkaz Zalman Shazar, 1999), 234–35; Goldberg, "Poles and Jews in the 17th and 18th Centuries: Rejection or Acceptance," *Jahrbücher für Geschichte Osteuropas* 22 (1974): 261–68. For a more general picture, see Hillel Levine, *Economic Origins of Antisemitism: Poland and Its Jews in the Early Modern Period* (New Haven, CT: Yale University Press, 1991), 140–45. Locals used more precise terminology, according to an east Ukrainian peasant correspondent from 1884: "All of [the villages] have lessees (*posesory*), who bring with them a whole gang of sublessees (*pakhtiary*), tavern-lessees (*arendari*), mill-lessees (*miroshnyky*), stewards (*factory*), dairy-lessees (*vydiinyky*), familiars (*povyniky*), and whatever else they are called." John-Paul Himka, "Ukrainian-Jewish Antagonism," in Howard Aster and Peter J. Potichnyj, eds., *Jewish-Ukrainian Relations in Historical Perspective* (Edmonton, AB: Canadian Institute of Ukrainian Studies, 1988), 127. By the late eighteenth century, according to Raphael Mahler, "one found Jewish arendas in nearly every town and townlet in Poland." *Yidn in amolikn poyln in likht fun tsifern* (Warsaw: Yidish Bukh, 1958), 107.

13. Solomon Maimon, *Solomon Maimon: An Autobiography*, tr. J. Clark Murray (Urbana: University of Illinois Press, 2001), 10–11.

14. See Moshe Rosman, *The Lords' Jews: Magnate-Jewish Relations in the Polish-Lithuanian Commonwealth during the 18th Century* (Cambridge, MA: Harvard University Press, 1990), 75–105; and Hundert, *Jews in*

Poland-Lithuania, 32–34. According to Hundert, over half (50–60 percent) of all domestic trade was in the hands of Jews during the eighteenth century, and the proportion was significantly higher in the eastern half of the Polish-Lithuanian Commonwealth. On starostas, see most recently Curtis G. Murphy, "Burghers versus Bureaucrats: Enlightened Centralism, the Royal Towns, and the Case of the *Propinacja* Law in Poland-Lithuania, 1776–1793," *Slavic Review* 71, no. 2 (2012): 391. On the patrons of Hasidism in the cities of the Kingdom of Poland, see Glenn Dynner, *Men of Silk: The Hasidic Conquest of Polish Jewish Society* (New York: Oxford University Press, 2006), chapter 3. On Jewish literacy as a determinant of Jewish occupational choices, see Maristella Botticini and Zvi Eckstein, *The Chosen Few: How Education Shaped Jewish History, 70–1492* (Princeton, NJ: Princeton University Press, 2012).

15. Examples on the grain trade include Juliusz Łukasiewicz, *Krzyzys agrarny na ziemiach Polskich w końcu XIX wieku* (Warsaw: PWN, 1968); Łukasiewicz, "O strukturze agrarnej Królestwa Polskiego po uwłaszczeniu," *Przegląd Historyczny* 1 (1971): 296–314; Irena Rychlikowa, "Ziemiaństwo Polskie 1772–1944: dzieje degradacji klasy," *Dzieje Najnowsze, Rocznik* XVII 2 (1985): 3–23; Krzysztof Groniowski, *Kwestia agrarna w Królestwie Polskim, 1871–1914* (Warsaw: PWN, 1966); Andrzej Jezierski, *Problemy rozwoju gospodarczego ziem Polskich w XIX i XX wieku* (Warsaw: Książka i Wiedza, 1984). On a later period, see Mieczysław Mieszczankowski, *Struktura agrarna Polski międzywojennej* (Warsaw: PWN, 1960). On liquor in particular, see Halina Rożenowa, *Produkcja wódki i sprawa pijaństwa w Królestwie Polskim 1815–1863* (Warsaw: PWN, 1961); Józef Burszta, *Wieś i karczma: rola karczmy w życiu wsi pańszczynianej* (Warsaw: Ludowa Spółdzielnia Wydawnicza, 1950); and Burszta, *Społeczeństwo i karczma: Propinacja, karczma, i sprawa alkoholizmu w społeczeństwie polskim XIX wieku* (Warsaw: LSW, 1951).

16. Examples include Artur Eisenbach, "Mobilność terytorialna ludności żydowskiej w Królestwie Polskim," in Witold Kula and Janina Leskiewiczowa, eds., *Społeczeństwo Królestwa Polskiego* (Warsaw: PWN, 1966), 2:179–316; Eisenbach, *Emancipation of the Jews in Poland*; and Raphael Mahler, *Divre yeme Yisra'el: Dorot aḥaronim*, 6 vols. (Merhavia, Israel: Sifriyat Po'alim, 1952–76); see esp. 2:174.

17. Rosman, *Lords' Jews*; Gershon Hundert, *Jews in a Polish Private Town: The Case of Opatów in the Eighteenth Century* (Baltimore: Johns Hopkins University Press, 1992); Hundert, *Jews in Poland-Lithuania*; Adam Teller, *Kesef, koaḥ ve-hashpa'ah* (Jerusalem: Zalman Shazar, 2006); Jacob Goldberg, *Ha-ḥevrah ha-yehudit*; Hanna Węgrzynek, "Zajęcia rolnicze żydów w Rzeczypospolitej w XVI–XVIII wieku," in Anna Michałowska-Mycielska and Marcin Wodziński, eds., *Małżeństwo z rozsądku? Żydzi w społeczeństwie dawnej Rzeczypospolitej* (Wrocław, Poland: Wydawnictwo Uniwersytetu Wrocławskiego, 2007), 87–103.

18. The average Jewish family size was 4.5, according to Raphael Mahler, yielding a total of 79,025 Jews involved in tavernkeeping in 1814. As the total number of Jews in the Kingdom of Poland was 212,944 in 1816, the proportion of officially registered tavernkeepers and their families amounted to 37.1 percent of the Jewish population. For the 1808 figures, see Henryk Grossman, "Struktura społeczna i zawodowa Ks. Warszawskiego," *Kwartalnik Statystyczny* (1924): 35, table 12. For 1814, see AGAD, KRSW 1849, fols. 152–59. For Jewish population figures in 1810, see Bohdan Wasiutyński, *Ludność żydowska w Polsce w wiekach XIX i XX* (Warsaw: Wydawn. Kasy im. Mianowskiego, Inst. Popierania Nauki, 1930), 8. The estimate of Jews running 85 percent of all taverns is derived by comparing the total number of taverns in 1808 (19,749) with the first recorded

number of Jewish tavernkeepers in 1814 (17,561), which is actually closer to 89 percent. I have purposely underestimated to account for border and population fluctuations over those six years (the general population was about 700,000 higher and the Jewish population about 15,000 higher in 1814, but we can assume that new taverns were established to meet new demand).

19. Antoni Ostrowski, *Pomysły o potrzebie reformy towarzyskiéy w ogólności, a mianowiciéy, co do Izraelitów w Polszcze przez założyciela miasta Tomaszowa Mazowieckiego* (Paris, 1834), 102; AGAD, KRSW 6637, fol. 1; WCPL 1830–1831, 339, 26–28. This was also the explanation provided by the St. Petersburg Jewish Committee in 1858. AGAD, KRSW 6632, p. 57. According to the governor of Suwałki Province, the ban on the rural Jewish liquor trade that remained in place after 1862 should be lifted, since Jews everywhere simply ignored it. See Michael Jerry Ochs, "St. Petersburg and the Jews of Russian Poland, 1862-1905" (PhD diss., Harvard University, 1986), 76.

20. Among the 816 Jewish petitions to Rabbi Elijah Guttmacher from the early 1870s that mention the petitioner's occupation, 114 still noted their involvement in the liquor trade. These petitions are notably from the period after the 1862 decree, which opened up new occupations, including land ownership, to Jews. See YIVO, Guttmacher archive, RG 27; and chapter 5, below. On impromptu Jewish taverns see Abramovitsh, "Of Bygone Days": "May our posterity also note that our grandfather's house was suited for a variety of functions. Besides serving as a kitchen, a bedroom, and even a synagogue, on occasion it also served as a tavern" (283); and "In general, Hertzl's way of life was different from that of others in the town. His house never doubled as a tavern, as did the houses of his neighbors" (332).

21. Abramovitsh, "Of Bygone Days," 333–34.

22. See Sholem Aleichem's memoir, *From the Fair: The Autobiography of Sholom Aleichem*, tr. and ed. Curt Leviant (New York: Viking Penguin, 1985), 68.

23. Compare with Yuri Slezkine's neo-Sombartian study, *The Jewish Century* (Princeton, NJ: Princeton University Press, 2004), esp. 41, which asserts that Jews were more economically successful because they were "urban, mobile, literate, mentally nimble, occupationally flexible, and surrounded by aliens."

CHAPTER 1

1. Adam Mickiewicz, *Pan Tadeusz* (1834, repr. London: Polska Fundacja Kulturalna, 1990), Book 4, 161–67. Translations mine.

2. Mickiewicz, *Pan Tadeusz*.

3. Raphael Mahler, for example, concludes that village Jews held 85 percent of *arendas* (leases on immovable property other than real estate) and taverns in the Polish lands by the late eighteenth century, but that this proportion dropped precipitously during the next century. See Raphael Mahler, *Yidn in amolikn Poyln in likht fun tsifern* (Warsaw: Yidish Bukh, 1958), 197. In the Lublin District only about half (712) of the 1,401 rural Jewish heads of families were engaged in the liquor trade in the years 1764–65; however, if we add general *arendars*, whose cluster of leases almost invariably included taverns, the number jumps to 1,236, or 88.2 percent. See Raphael Mahler, "Statistik fun yidn in der Lubliner Voyevodstva," *Yunger Historiker* 2 (1929): table 8.

4. Raphael Mahler, *Hasidism and the Jewish Enlightenment: Their Confrontation in Galicia and Poland in the First Half of the Nineteenth Century*, tr. Eugene Orenstein Eugene Orenstein, Aaron Klein, and Jenny Machlowitz Klein (Philadelphia: Jewish Publication Society of America, 1985), 177–79; Eisenbach,

"Mobilność," 179–207. Data on Jewish urbanization was compiled but partially falsified by Eisenbach, who supplied arbitrary numbers in place of missing data to bring the percentage of Jewish village residence down to 8 percent in 1865. See Eisenbach, "Mobilność," 285. It should also be noted that the Polish term *miasto* refers to both the largest cities and the smallest towns, allowing advocates of the rapid urbanization theory, usually Marxist historians, to give a distorted impression. The government's Jewish population figures for 1844 are 450,027 in small-to-large towns and cities and 74,749 in villages, a total of 524,776, although officials complained about pervasive Jewish census dodging and questioned the merit of continuing to include hundreds of small towns in the *miasto* category. By 1858, around 89,000 Jews were still residing in villages. Archiwum Główne Akt Dawnych (AGAD), Komisja Rządowa Spraw Wewnętrznych (KRSW) 202, pp. 166 and 171; KRSW 6632, fol. 26.

5. Magdalena Opalski, *The Jewish Tavern-Keeper and His Tavern in Nineteenth-Century Polish Literature* (Jerusalem: Zalman Shazar, 1986), 100. I refer to the literary works analyzed there throughout this book. See also Raphael Mahler, *Divre yeme Yisra'el*, 2:174; Eisenbach, "Mobilność,"; and Eisenbach, *Emancipation of the Jews in Poland*, 172: "It was not until forty to fifty years later [probably meaning 1862], when real changes had taken place in the country, that Jews were to be permitted to distil and retail liquor." See also Stefan Kieniewicz, *The Emancipation of the Polish Peasantry* (Chicago: University of Chicago Press, 1969), 92: "In Congress Poland, Jews were forbidden to run inns from 1820 to 1862."

6. This was, for example, the perception of Julian Butrymowicz. See Hundert, *Jews in Poland-Lithuania*, 224.

7. Goldberg, "Ha-yehudi ve-ha-pundak," 234; Jürgen Hensel, "Żydowski arendarz i jego karczma: Uwagi na marginesie usunięcia żydowskich arendarzy ze wsi w Królestwie Polskim w latach 20. XIX wieku," in Ryszard Kołodziejczyk and Regina Renz, eds., *Kultura żydów polskich XIX–XX wieku* (Kielce, Poland: Kieleckie Tow. Nauk., 1992), 88–89; Rosman, *Lords' Jews*, 106–42; Hundert, *Jews in Poland-Lithuania*, 36–38; and Teller, *Kesef, koaḥ ve-hashpa'ah*, 84–85, 128–29, and 164.

8. Jewish tavernkeeping still flourished in other regions. In Galicia (Austrian Poland), e.g., enforcement of imperial bans on rural tavernkeeping was so lax that in 1836 Jewish tavernkeepers were still found in three-quarters of the region's villages. See Mahler, *Hasidism and the Jewish Enlightenment*, 21. According to one Galician memoirist, during the mid-nineteenth century "rural taverns were held by Jews." Jan Słomka, *From Serfdom to Self-Government: Memoirs of a Polish Village Mayor, 1842–1927*, tr. William John Rose (London: Minerva, 1941), 78.

9. Polish-Jewish interaction, according to Rosman, cannot be "glibly characterized as utilitarian. Marriages of convenience are still marriages. They generate a dynamic and entail responsibilities that go beyond the original utilitarian motivations." *Lords' Jews*, 210. The characterization is echoed in such works as Byron Sherwin, *Sparks amid the Ashes: The Spiritual Legacy of Polish Jewry* (New York: Oxford University Press, 1997), 55.

10. Teller, *Kesef, koaḥ ve-hashpa'ah*, esp. 19. The impressions of certain eighteenth-century travelers reflect Teller's more sober view. Friedrich Schulz, e.g., described the condition of the Jews as barely better than that of serfs: both were dependent on the nobleman's goodwill, and whatever greater freedoms Jews might enjoy often proved quite precarious. Schulz, "Podróże Inflanczyka z Rygi do Warszawy i po Polsce w latach 1791–1793," in *Polska Stanisławowska*

1:480, quoted in Adolf Haber, "Ha-pundaka'im ha-yehudiim be-publitsistikah ha-polanit shel 'Ha-sem ha-gadol' (1788–1792)," *Gal-Ed 2* (1975): 7.

11. On Bielsk County, see Anatol Leszczyński, "Karczmarze i szynkarze żydowscy ziemi Bielskiej od drugiej połowy XVII w. do 1795 r.," *Biuletyn ŻIH* 102, no. 2 (1977): 77–85, tables 1, 2, and appendix. In claiming that "94 percent of the tavernkeepers in the Bielsko region were Jews," Rosman misses the distinction between rural and urban taverns in these data. See his *Lords' Jews*, 112 n21. For the Opatów estimates, see Hundert, *Jews in a Polish Private Town*, 65–67. See also a list of around fifty (mainly rural) tavernkeepers registered in Lyakhovichi in 1805, at http://www.jewishgen.org/belarus/lyak_1805.htm (accessed May 4, 2013). This list was published by the Lachowicze Research Group. According to the foreword by Neville Lamdan (2000), "Most of the Jews were born in the Novogrudok 'povet' or in the nearby districts of Slutsk and Slonin. Exceptionally, one had been born in Pinsk, about 65 miles south. Their taverns were located in seven 'parafiya's' (sub-districts) within a radius of about 10 miles from Lyakhivichi. Most of the villages mentioned were tiny and several may have been hamlets at best. The number of Jewish taverns, especially in such isolated places, seems remarkable."

12. On ethnic economies, see Ivan H. Light and Steven J. Gold, *Ethnic Economies* (San Diego, CA: Academic Press, 1999), esp. chapter 1.

13. Rosman, *Lords' Jews*, 110–113; Jacob Goldberg, "Ha-Yehudi ve-ha-pundak ha-kefari," in *Ha-ḥevrah ha-yehudit*, 232 and 238–39. In the case of taverns, the lease included the land itself and often an adjacent field. See Węgrzynek, "Zajęcia rolnicze żydów," 87–103.

14. Eisenbach, *Emancipation of the Jews in Poland*, 188; Eisenbach, "Mobilność," 194–95; N. M. Gelber, "She'elat ha-yehudim be-Polin bi-shnat 1815–30," *Zion* 13–14 (1949): 106–43. Emanuel Ringelblum's claim that small-scale gentry needed to retain Jewish leaseholders while large-scale landowners preferred to get rid of them cannot be sustained. See Ringelblum, *Kapitlen geshikhte fun amolikn yidishn lebn in Poyln* (Buenos Aires: Tsentral-Farband fun Poylishe Yidn in Argentine, 1953), 122–24. For a similar argument regarding Russian Jewry, see John Klier, *Russia Gathers Her Jews: The Origins of the "Jewish Question" in Russia, 1772–1825* (DeKalb: Northern Illinois University Press, 1986), 87–88 (though 69–71 seems to argue the opposite), and Heinz-Dietrich Lowe, *The Tsars and the Jews: Reform, Reaction and Anti-Semitism in Imperial Russia, 1772–1917* (Reading, UK: Harwood Academic, 1993), 28–34.

15. Most Polish officials in the Kingdom of Poland's bureaucracy were Polish landowners themselves but were committed to satisfying the cameralist dictates of the tsar. For the sake of clarity, I refer to them collectively as "Polish officials" or "the state" throughout.

16. Hirsz Abramowicz, *Profiles of a Lost World: Memoirs of East European Jewish Life before World War II*, tr. Eva Zeitlin Dobkin (Detroit: Wayne State Universtiy Press and YIVO, 1999), 60.

17. On the tavern's diverse functions, see Slomka, *From Serfdom to Self-Government*, 78 and 92–94. See also Israel Bartal, *The Jews of Eastern Europe, 1772–1881*, tr. Chaya Naor (Philadelphia: University of Pennsylvania, 2005), 43; Marian Szczepaniak, *Karczma, wieś, dwór: Rola propinacji na wsi wielkopolskiej od połowy XVII do schyłku XVIII wieku* (Warsaw: LSW, 1977), 97–117; and Keely Stauter-Halsted, *The Nation in the Village: The Genesis of Peasant National Identity*

in Austrian Poland, 1848–1914 (Ithaca, NY: Cornell University Press, 2001), 134–141.
18. AGAD, Archiwum Gospodarcze Wilanowe, Administracja Dóbr Opatowskich I/83.
19. Andrei Oisteanu notices a similar church/tavern dichotomy in the Romanian case. See *Inventing the Jew: Antisemitic Stereotypes in Romanian and Other Central-East European Cultures*, tr. Mirela Adascalitei (Lincoln: University of Nebraska Press and the Vidal Sassoon International Center for the Study of Antisemitism, 2009), 175.
20. In one case, a Jew was sentenced to death by burning after a tavern disputation. See Hundert, *Jews in Poland-Lithuania*, 51, and Magda Teter, *Sinners on Trial* (Cambridge, MA: Harvard University Press, 2011), 76–77.
21. Avraham Yaakov Brawer, *Galitsyah vi-yehudeha: Meḥkarim ba-toldot Galitsyah ba-me'ah ha-18* (Jerusalem: Mosad Bialik, 1956), 211. See also Gershon Hundert, "The Introduction to *Divre binah* by Dov Ber of Bolechów: An Unexamined Source for the History of Jews in the Lwów Region in the Second Half of the Eighteenth Century," *AJS Review* 33 (2009): 225–69.
22. W. Ayerst, *The Jews of the Nineteenth Century: A Collection of Essays, Reviews, and Historical Notices* (London, 1847), 130. The account refers to events in 1827.
23. See B. Ann Tlusty, *Bacchus and Civil Order: The Culture of Drink in Early Modern Germany* (Charlottesville: University of Virginia Press, 2001), 162–63; Beat Kumin and B. Ann Tlusty, eds., *The World of the Tavern: Public Houses in Early Modern Europe* (Burlington, VT: Ashgate, 2002), e.g., 14.
24. See Julian Tuwim, ed., *Polski słownik pijacki i antologia bachiczna* (Warsaw: Czytelnik, 1959), 169–333.
25. On the Jewish wine trade and wine culture in medieval France and Germany, see Haym Soloveitchik, *Ha-yayin bi-yeme ha-benayim: Perek be-toldot ha-halakhah be-Ashkenaz* (Jerusalem: Zalman Shazar, 2008), esp. 29–58. See also Soloveitchik, "Can Halakhic Texts Talk History?" *AJS Review* 3 (1978): 153–96.
26. Adam Neale, *Travels through Some Parts of Germany, Poland, Moldavia, and Turkey* (London, 1818), 128–29.
27. Other sources mention herring, bread, and meat as the most common tavern fare. See Szczepaniak, *Karczma, wieś, dwór*, 102.
28. Neale, *Travels through Some Parts of Germany*, 128–29.
29. Neale, *Travels through Some Parts of Germany*, 129 and 146.
30. George Burnett, *View of the Present State of Poland* (London, 1807), 67–72.
31. William Wraxall, *Memoir of the Courts of Berlin, Dresden, Warsaw, and Vienna in the Years 1777, 1778, and 1779*, two volumes (London, 1800), volume 2, 135 and 149.
32. Jeremy Bentham, diary entry, January 6–February 10, 1786, in *The Correspondence of Jeremy Bentham*, ed. Ian R. Christie (London: Athlone, 1971), 3:455. For further descriptions, see 3:597–610. Many thanks to Israel Bartal for bringing Bentham's interest in Jewish-run taverns to my attention.
33. Józef Mączyński, *Włościanie* (Krakow: 1858), 88; printed in Oskar Kolberg, *Lud: Krakowskie* 5 (1871): 167–68.
34. Mączyński, *Włościanie*, 88.
35. The tavernkeeper also occasionally emerged from his tavern. After every Christmas and Easter, he would make personal visits to each household, bestowing drinks and well-wishes in exchange for gifts of grain, eggs, fowl, and other goods. Once again, he never partook of drink himself. See Slomka, *From Serfdom to Self-Government*, 78 and 92–94. And see below.

36. Quoted in Bohdan Barnowski, *Polska karczma, restauracja, kawiarnia* (Wrocław, Poland: Zakład Narodowy im. Ossolinskich, 1979), 56.
37. Józef Ignacy Kraszewski, *Wspomnienia Polesia Wołynia i Litwy* (Vilnius, 1840), 1554–55. It is fascinating to compare the original version to the rewritten one in 1861, in which Kraszewski rather optimistically celebrates the deterioration of the lord-Jew relationship and the movement of Jews out of village taverns and into crafts in Polesia, Volhynia, and historical Lithuania.
38. S. Y. Abramovitsh, *The Tales of Mendele the Bookpeddler: Fishke the Lame and Benjamin the Third*, ed. Dan Miron and Ken Frieden, trans. Ted Gorelick and Hillel Halkin (New York: Schocken, 1996), 96–97.
39. Maimon, *Autobiography*, 145–46.
40. Maimon, *Autobiography*, 82–87.
41. H. N. Bialik, "Avi" (1932). Project Ben Yehudah, http://benyehuda.org/bialik/ (last viewed on July 9, 2013). Translation mine. Interestingly, these polemics tend to single out the male body as a site of revulsion, in contrast to what Alexandra Cuffel finds in her study of medieval polemics. See *Gendering Disgust in Medieval Religious Literature* (IN: Notre Dame University Press, 2007).
42. Zevi Hirsch Kaidanover, *Kav ha-yashar* (Frankfurt, 1705), ch. 24.
43. On other Jewish strategies for achieving a sense of cultural superiority, see Daniel Boyarin, *Unheroic Conduct: The Rise of Heterosexuality and the Invention of the Jewish Man* (Berkeley: University of California Press, 1997), esp. introduction and ch. 1.
44. Goldberg, "Ha-yehudi ve-ha-pundak ha-ironi ba-ezor Podlasiyah," in *Ha-hevrah ha-yehudit be-mamlekhet Polin-Lita* (Jerusalem: Merkaz Zalman Shazar, 1999), 242.
45. Stanisław Staszic, "Jews," in Harold B. Segal, ed., *Stranger in Our Midst: Images of the Jew in Polish Literature* (Ithaca, NY: Cornell, 1996), 40.
46. On liquor specifically, see Haber, "Ha-pundaka'im ha-yehudiim." More generally, see Eisenbach, *Emancipation of the Jews in Poland*, 188, and Gelber, "She'elat ha-yehudim be-Polin," 106–43. However, isolated figures argued that the peasants' lack of education and emancipation was the root cause of their drunkenness. See Józef Pawlikowski, *O poddanych polskich* ([Krakow], 1788), 21–27; and Walerian Łukasiński, "Uwagi nad potrzebą urzadzenią żydów i nad niektórymi pisemkami w tym przedmiocie wydanymi," in *Pamiętnik*, ed. Rafał Gerber (1818, repr. Warsaw, 1860), 201.
47. For the claim about Christians and credit, see Ostrowski, *Pomysły o potrzebie reformy*, 88. On social and familial bonds, see Benjamin of Radzyn, 1858, in AGAD, KRSW 6600, fol. 298.
48. Burszta, *Wieś i karczma*, 145–47.
49. Janina Leskiewicz and Jerzy Michalski, eds., *Supliki chłopskie XVIII wieku* (Warsaw: Książka i Wiedza, 1954), 83, 151, 157, 255, and 283.
50. Rożenowa, *Produkcja wódki*, 112. Some, like the poet-reformer Władysław Anczyc, felt that Christian tavernkeepers were not engaged in "real" work. See his *Pijaństwo: Zguba i nędza włościan* (Warsaw, 1867), 17.
51. Witold Kula, *An Economic Theory of the Feudal System: Towards a Model of the Polish Economy, 1500–1800*, tr. Lawrence Garner (London: Humanities, 1976), 134–41. On the liquor industry in Russia under Catherine in areas largely devoid of Jews, see John LeDonne, "Indirect Taxes in Catherine's Russia, II. The Liquor Monopoly," *Jahrbücher für Geschichte Osteuropas* 24 (1976): 173–207.
52. Hundert, *Jews in Poland-Lithuania*, 37.

53. Maimon, *Autobiography*, 10.
54. Rożenowa, *Produkcja wódki*, 61–67; Kieniewicz, *Emancipation of the Polish Peasantry*, 90.
55. The main innovation of Pistorius was the still head, which was flattened and elongated to prevent the formation of bubbles when the vapor made contact with the liquid. See Sydney Young's *Distillation Principles and Processes* (London: Macmillan, 1922), available athttp://archive.org/details/distillationprin00younrich.
56. Rożenowa, *Produkcja wódki*, 108 and 275. The data cited by Rożenowa appear to derive from different surveys. According to one set (on p. 108), village profits went from 261,546 zlotys to 391,248 zlotys between 1833 and 1839. According to another set (p. 275), village liquor sales in 1838 generated substantially more: 434,758 zlotys. If we add town revenues, liquor revenues reached 555,294 zlotys in 1838.
57. Jerome Blum, *The End of the Old Order in Rural Europe* (Princeton, NJ: Princeton University Press, 1978), 296. The number of distilleries in the Kingdom of Poland reached 2,094 by 1844, with a total output of 13 million gallons of liquor.
58. Maxymilian Chełminski, *Wspomnienia gospodarskie z pięćdziesięciodniowęj podróży po kraju tutejszym, odbytęj w roku 1842* (Warsaw, 1843), 4:31. This reference is to Okalew village.
59. The same change occurred in Galicia and the Russian interior. On Galicia, see Baranowski, *Polska karczma, restauracja, kawiarnia*, 53. On Russia, see R. E. F. Smith and David Christian, *Bread and Salt: A Social and Economic History of Food and Drink in Russia* (Cambridge, UK: Cambridge University Press, 1984), 296. Smith and Christian report a decline in beer consumption of around 65 percent between 1835 and 1858.
60. Haber, "Ha-pundaka'im ha-yehudiim," 3. The assertion also appears in the writings of Józef Pawlikowski (1767–1828), who did not, however, blame Jewish tavernkeepers. See Pawlikowski and Pilchowski, *O poddanych polskich*, 21–27.
61. Kula, *Economic Theory of the Feudal System*, 134–41; Teller, *Kesef, koaḥ ve-hashpa'ah*, 129. On the nature of peasant contact with the market, see Jacek Kochanowicz, *Backwardness and Modernization: Poland and Eastern Europe in the 16th–20th Centuries* (Burlington, VT: Ashgate, 2006), 110.
62. Władysław Smoleński, *Stan i sprawa żydów polskich w XVIII wieku* (Warsaw, 1876), 16; Alina Cala, *The Image of the Jew in Polish Folk Culture* (Jerusalem: Magnes, 1995), 178.
63. Slomka, *From Serfdom to Self-Government*, 95.
64. Slomka, *From Serfdom to Self-Government*, 95–96. According to Hillel Levine, Jewish-run taverns represented "an intrusion of the 'other' into the countryside" whose daily exchanges were always tension-ridden: "Across that barrier of social separation [i.e., the bar] and melded fate, he dispensed drink of uneven quality in exchange for the peasant's coins of uncertain value." Levine, *Economic Origins of Antisemitism*, 9–10.
65. I. L. Peretz, "Impressions of a Journey," tr. Milton Himmelfarb, in Ruth Wisse, ed., *The I. L. Peretz Reader*, tr. Milton Himmelfarb (New York: Schocken, 1990), 75–76. The interview was transcribed in 1904.
66. On relations between Jewish tavernkeepers and peasant customers in Galicia, see Keely Stauter-Halstead, "Jews as Middleman Minorities in Rural Poland: Understanding the Galician Pogroms of 1898," in Robert Blobaum, ed., *Antisemitism and Its Opponents in Modern Poland* (Ithaca, NY: Cornell University

Press, 2005), 49. Ewa Morawska similarly notes that "peasants visited local Jewish store owners or innkeepers to get news and ask for advice (even in matchmaking)." Morawska also notes peasant reliance on Jewish folk musicians and midwives. See "Polish-Jewish relations in America, 1880-1940," *Polin* 19 (2006), 71-86. On the survival of this relationship in the early twentieth century, see Abramowicz, *Profiles of a Lost World*, 61 and 65.

67. See numerous contracts from the late eighteenth and early nineteenth centuries in AGAD, Lubomirsk z Małej Wsi 1348 and 1352. Tavernkeepers also promised not to blaspheme, serve suspicious characters, or collude with members of the noble's court.

68. On watered down liquor, see Abramowicz, *Profiles of a Lost World*, 62. Ironically, "Jewish beer" referred to beer that had not been "baptized," i.e., watered down. See Tuwim, *Polski słownik pijacki*, 59. On the breakdown of such coexistence in Galicia, symbolized by attacks on Jewish tavernkeepers in 1898, see Stauter-Halstead, "Jews as Middleman Minorities," 47.

69. Burszta, *Społeczeństwo i karczma*, 188; Oskar Kolberg, *Dzieła wszystkie*, 67 vols, (Wrocław, Poland: Polskie Towarzystwo Ludoznawcze, 1961–62), esp. vol. 10, W. Ks. Poznańskie pp. 61 and 350. See also the important findings of Szczepaniak, in Burszta, *Społeczeństwo i karczma*, 105–10. On the vital role of ethnography in the formation of Polish nationalism, see Keely Stauter-Halsted, *The Nation and the Village: The Genesis of Peasant National Identity in Austrian Poland, 1848–1914* (Ithaca, NY: Cornell University Press, 2001), 100–103. On Kolberg's attitude toward Jews, including tavernkeepers, see Joanna Tokarska-Bakir, "Żydzi u Kolbergu," in *Rzeczy mgliste: Eseje i studia* (Sejny, Poland: Fundacja Pogranicze, 2004), 49–72, esp. 50–51.

70. See the forthcoming article by Alyssa Quint, "The Culture of Capitalism in Nineteenth-Century Yiddish Song," in *Jewish Quarterly Review*. Courtesy of the author.

71. Maimon, *Autobiography*, 10-17; 145-46.

72. Mark Wischnitzer, ed., *Zikhronot R. Dov mi-Bolihov (1723 – 1805)* (Jerusalem, 1969), 99. My translation. See also idem., ed., *The Memoirs of Ber of Bolechow (1723–1805)* (Oxford: Oxford University Press, 1922), 159–60.

73. Dov-Ber Birkenthal. *The Memoirs of Ber of Bolechow:, 1723–1805*, tr. M. Vishnitzer (Oxford: Oxford University Press, 1922), 167. This translation corresponds to Birkenthal, *Zikhronot R. Dov mi-Bolihov (483–565)*, ed. M. Wischnitzer (Jerusalem: n.p., 1968), 103–4.

74. Ostrowski, *Pomysły o potrzebie reformy*, 101–2.

75. Slomka, *From Serfdom to Self-Government*, 91–94.

76. Jacob, *Report on the Trade in Foreign Corn*, 15 and 65. Whenever peasants sold their produce at market, "a part of the money was first used to purchase salt, and the rest spent in whiskey, in a state of intoxication that commonly endured till the exhaustion of the purse had restored them to sobriety."

77. Tuwim, *Polski słownik pijacki*, 108. Among Jews, in contrast, to drink a lot was to "drink like a gentile." See Bob Rothstein, "Geyt a yid in shenkl arayn: Yiddish Songs of Drunkenness," in The Field of Yiddish: Studies in Language, Folklore, and Literature, Fifth Collection, ed. David Goldberg (Evanston, IL: Northwestern University Press and New York: YIVO Institute for Jewish Research, 1993), 243.

78. Ostrowski, *Pomysły o potrzebie reformy*, 101–2; Slomka, *From Serfdom to Self-Government*, 91–94.

79. On Mikoszewski, see Brian Porter-Szucs, *Faith and Fatherland: Catholicism, Modernity, and Poland* (New York: Oxford University Press, 2011), 166; and R. F. Leslie, *Reform and Insurrection in Russian Poland, 1856–1865* (London: Athlone, 1963), 157–64.
80. Mikoszewski was not asking Poles to forswear alcohol completely. Noblemen could easily replace their distilleries with breweries without suffering a financial loss, and Poles could switch over from vodka to beer. This economic solution, he hoped, would be accompanied by a spiritual one, a move from the taverns back to the churches on Sundays. Karol Mikoszewski, *Kazania o pijaństwie* (Warsaw, 1862), 5, 12, 14–15, 18, 37–38, 43, 47, 54–58, 61–63, 71. For other sermons that mention the problem of drunkenness, see Wiator Piotrowski, *Wybór kazań niedzielnych, świątecznych i przygodnych* (Warsaw, 1840), 55, 201, 262.
81. Mikoszewski, *Kazania o pijaństwie*, 63 and 88–89.
82. Kaidanover, *Kav ha-yashar*, 129, ch. 61.
83. Moshe Wassercug, "Korot Moshe Vasertsug ve-nedivat lev aviv ha-manoaḥ R. Isserel z"l," ed. Heinrich Loewe, *Jahrbuch der Jüdisch-Literarischen Gesellschaft* 8 (1910): 113.
84. Maimon, *Autobiography*, 11–14.
85. Maimon, *Autobiography*, 145–46. Maimon contemplated suicide while "pretty drunk, on the brink of a deep canal" (247).
86. YIVO archives, Guttmacher Collection, RG 27, 198, "Warta 2."
87. Guttmacher, RG 27, 625, "Piotrkow Tribunalski."
88. Guttmacher, RG 27, 435, "Lodz 9."
89. Guttmacher, RG 27, 726, "Kutno (Kutna)."
90. Guttmacher, RG 27, 766, "Chrzanow."
91. Guttmacher, RG 27, 685, "Kalisz 2."
92. Guttmacher, RG 27, 880, no location given.
93. Guttmacher, RG 27, 314, Zawoda.
94. Guttmacher, RG 27, 847, "Sieradz."
95. Guttmacher, RG 27, 824, "Remblielice village n. Dzialoszyn."
96. Guttmacher, RG 27, 774, "Chrzanow 2." Chrzanów was in the Duchy of Warsaw, but became part of the Free City of Krakow in 1815.
97. Guttmacher, RG 27, 877, no location given. On the rabbinical reluctance to accept repentant apostates, see Edward Fram, "Perception and Reception of Repentant Apostates in Medieval Ashkenaz and Premodern Poland," *AJS Review* 21, no. 2 (1996): 299–340.
98. See Polonsky, *Jews in Poland and Russia*, II: 296-7. Glenn Dynner, "How Many *Hasidim* Were There Really in Congress Poland? A Response to Marcin Wodziński," *Gal-Ed* 20 (2005): 91–104; Marcin Wodziński, "How Many *Hasidim* were there in Congress Poland? On the Demographics of the Hasidic Movement in Poland during the First Half of the Nineteenth Century," *Gal-Ed* 19 (2004): 13–49. On Hasidism in the Kingdom of Poland, see Dynner, *Men of Silk*.
99. Ephraim Deinard, *Zikhronot bat ami* (New Orleans, n.p., 1920), 14. See also the first Vilna ban, "Excommunication of the Hasidim," in Paul Mendes-Flohr and Jehuda Reinharz, comps. and eds., *The Jew in the Modern World: A Documentary History*, 3rd ed. (New York: Oxford University Press, 2011), 390.
100. David of Maków, *Zemir aritzim* 3a–4a, in Mordecai Wilensky, *Ḥasidim u-mitnagdim*, 2nd ed. (Jerusalem: Mosad Bialik, 1990), 2:196–97.
101. Joseph Perl, *Revealer of Secrets*, tr. Dov Taylor (Oxford: Westview, 1997), letter 5, p. 29; Israel Zamosc, *Nezed ha-dema*, 28–29, quoted in Israel Zinberg, *A History of*

Jewish Literature, tr. and ed. Bernard Martin, vol. 9, *Hasidism and Enlightenment, 1780–1820* (Cleveland: Press of Case Western Reserve University, 1976), 234.

102. When Kotik decided to debate the local Hasidim, he resolved to "get drunk.... A drunk has more courage." After the debate, he "dropped to the floor dead-drunk—it was quite a disgraceful thing." At a typical circumcision ceremony, Kotik reports, the guests drank tea laced hard liquor and got "good and soused." At a wedding, the Jewish guests "drank and drank without limit." Yekhezkel Kotik, *Journey to a Nineteenth-Century Shtetl: The Memoirs of Yekhezkel Kotik*, ed. David Assaf (Detroit: Wayne State University Press, 2002), 362–63, 128, and 187.
103. Kotik, *Journey to a Nineteenth-Century Shtetl*, 407.
104. Kotik, *Journey to a Nineteenth-Century Shtetl*, 407.
105. Kotik, *Journey to a Nineteenth-Century Shtetl*, 363, 208. For one of the first historical assessments of Hasidic drinking, see Simon Dubnow, *History of the Jews in Russia and Poland: From the Earliest Times Until the Present Day*, tr. Israel Friedlaender, 3 volumes (Philadelphia: The Jewish Publication Society, 1918), vol. 2, 124-25.
106. Abraham Stern, "Information Concerning the Sect of the Hasidim," AGAD, KRSW 6634, pp. 239–43.
107. Yehiel Yeshaia Trunk, *Poyln: My Life within Jewish Life in Poland; Sketches and Images*, tr. Anna Clarke, ed. Piotr Wróbel and Robert M. Shapiro (Toronto: University of Toronto Press, 2007), 23.
108. The satire, by the Galician maskil Samson Halevi Bloch (1784–1845), was probably augmented and edited by Joseph Perl. See David Assaf, "'Ve-ha-mitnagdim hitlozezu she-nishtakher ve-nafal': Nefilat shel ha-Hozeh mi-Lublin be-r'i ha-zikharon ha-ḥasidi ve-ha-satirah ha-maskilit," in Immanuel Etkes, David Assaf, Israel Bartal, and Elchanan Reiner, eds., *Within Hasidic Circles: Studies in Hasidism in Memory of Mordecai Wilensky* (Jerusalem: Bialik Institute, 1999), 161–208. See also Ephraim Fischelsohn, "Teater fun khsidim," in which the Hasidim invite the skeptical maskil to visit their tzaddik and get drunk. In *Historishe Shriftn fun YIVO* 1 (1929): 651.
109. Tlusty, *Bacchus and Civic Order*, 67.
110. There is some question about the true authorship. Israel Davidson writes that, in a private letter from July 23, 1903, David Apotheker took credit for writing the book when in Husiatyn, Galicia. He wrote under a pseudonym because he feared a Hasidic reprisal; he was in the domain of "Reb Motele" of Chernobyl. See Davidson, *Parody in Jewish Literature* (New York: Columbia University Press, 1907), 219 n71. But Barukh Oberlander argues in favor of Friedlander's authorship, based on letters by the latter's student and historian Aaron Marcus. See his "Ha-yerushalmi le-seder kodashim ve-ha-mo"l shelo," *Or Yisra'el* 3, no. 16 (1999): 174–75.
111. S. Y. Friedlander, *Sefer ha-tikun* (Czernowitz, 1881), "Introduction," fols. 3–4.
112. This number suggests repentance, since the reference could be to the fifty gates of *binah* (symbolizing repentance), also the purpose of the forty-nine days of counting the *omer* during the holiday of Shavuot.
113. Friedlander, *Sefer ha-tikun*, fol. 5–12.
114. Friedlander, *Sefer ha-tikun*, fol. 12–17.
115. Friedlander, *Sefer ha-tikun*, fol. 17–18.
116. Friedlander, *Sefer ha-tikun*, fol. 18–20. Women's drinking, it should be noted, is not discussed in the tract.

117. Abraham Isaac Sperling, *Sefer ta'ame ha-minhagim* (Lviv: David Roth, 1928), 2:28. This custom is attributed to the tzaddik Simon of Jarosław. For a fuller exposition of various toasts, see Aaron Wertheim, *Law and Custom in Hasidism*, tr. Shmuel Himelstein (Hoboken, NJ: Ktav, 1992), 335–40.
118. Abraham ben Yeḥiel, *Ḥesed le-Avraham* (Czernowitz, 1884), introduction by Yeḥiel Shapiro of Tomaszpol, the author's grandson. We are reassured that the founder of Hasidism, the Besht, taught that wisdom and methods of worshiping God are hinted at even in non-Jewish languages.
119. Sperling, *Sefer ta'ame ha-minhagim*, 75 (38).
120. Hanna Węgrzynek, "*Shvartze Khasene*: Black Weddings among Polish Jews," in Glenn Dynner, ed., *Holy Dissent: Jewish and Christian Mystics in Eastern Europe* (Detroit: Wayne State University Press, 2011), 55–68.
121. Once, when the Besht drank a large portion of strong wine in the company of non-Jews in the state of Walachia, his "face became red and his hair stood up as though it were on fire," but to the gentiles' great astonishment he was able to recover instantly by remembering his awe of God. The Besht's drinking and dancing with his cohort on the holiday of Simchat Torah threatened to exhaust his entire stock of wine, to his wife's consternation; but the canopy of fire surrounding the company made her reluctant to intervene. Dov Baer ben Samuel, *In Praise of the Baal Shem Tov*, trans. and ed. Dan Ben Amos and Jerome Mintz (Northvale, NJ: Jason Aronson, 1994), 250; 80–81. For an analysis of the first event, see Moshe Idel, "R. Israel Ba'al Shem Tov 'In the State of Walachia': Widening the Besht's Cultural Panorama," in Dynner, *Holy Dissent*, 69–103. On the tzaddik Abraham Joshua Heschel's love of fine wine, see Shlomo Gabriel Rozental, *Hitgalut ha-tsadikim*, ed. Gedalyah Nigal (Jerusalem: Hotsa'at Karmel, 1996), 53. On the Besht's tavernkeeping career, see *In Praise of the Ba'al Shem Tov*, tale nos. 19 and 29.
122. Sperling, *Sefer ta'ame ha-minhagim* 3:112.
123. Jaakov Joseph of Polonoye, *Toldot Ya'akov Yosef* (repr. Jerusalem: Agudat Bet Vialipoli, 1973), 331.
124. YIVO Institute, Simon Dubnow collection, RG 87, 933, I 18.
125. Naftali Loewenthal, "Rabbi Shneur Zalman of Liadi's *Kitzur Likkutei Amarim*: British Library Or. 10456," in Joseph Dan and Klaus Herrmann, eds., *Studies in Jewish Manuscripts* (Tübingen, Germany: Mohr Siebeck, 1999), 128.
126. Ruth Rubin, *Voices of a People: The Story of Yiddish Folksong* (New York: McGraw-Hill, 1979), 170–72; 238. It should be noted that some ethnographers have detected a "Yankee Doodle" phenomenon, wherein songs meant to mock Hasidic drinking excesses were appropriated by Hasidim themselves. See also Rothstein, "Geyt a yid in shenkl arayn," 243-62. On the Hasidic conception of "worship through corporeality" (*avodah be-gashmiyut*), see Seth Brody, "Open Up to Me the Gates of Righteousness," *Jewish Quarterly Review* 89, no. 1/2 (July–October 1998): 3–44. For similar Hasidic attitudes toward food, see Allan Nadler's occasionally hilarious study "Holy Kugel: The Sanctification of Ashkenazic Ethnic Food in Hasidism," in Leonard Greenspoon, ed., *Food and Judaism* (Omaha, NE: Creighton University Press, 2005), 193–211.
127. Yo'ets Kayim Kadish, *Sifte kodesh* (Jerusalem: n.p., 1953), 29. In actuality, most Spanish and Portuguese Jewish exiles emigrated to the Ottoman Empire, Venice, or Amsterdam. Most Polish Jews derived from exiles from German-speaking lands.

128. Kadish, *Sifte kodesh*, 2:3. Our friends should answer "To a good life and to peace!" as added insurance against such damage. "Wine" in these sources appears to represent all alcoholic drinks, including vodka.
129. Naḥman of Bratslav, *Likute etsot* (Lviv, 1858), "Brit," no. 29.
130. Rubin, *Voices of a People*, 238.
131. Yo'ets Kayim Kadish, *Siah sarfe kodesh* (Przytyk, Poland: n.p., 1923), 2:112.
132. For fascinating interpretations of Purim drunkenness in Lubavitcher Hasidism, see Elliot Wolfson, *Open Secret: Postmessianic Messianism and the Mystical Revision of Menaḥem Mendel Schneerson* (New York: Columbia University Press, 2009), 57–58. On non-Jews as a means to benefit Jews, see 230–31.
133. On European carnivals, see Mikhail Bakhtin, *Rabelais and His World*, tr. Helene Iswolsky (Cambridge, MA: MIT Press, 1968), 7. For a comparison to Jewish "carnivals," see Harold Fisch, "Reading and Carnival: On the Semiotics of Purim," *Poetics Today* 15, no. 1 (Spring 1994): 67. Harold Fisch doubts that even Purim is a true carnival, since the reading of the megillah is so central to the holiday. Instead, it is more of a "symbolic Carnival" (69). On the function of European drinking bouts, see Tlusty, *Bacchus and Civil Order*
134. Kolberg, *Dzieła wszystkie*, "Mazowsze" III, pp. 69–71; "Mazowsze" V, pp. 311–14; Olga Goldberg-Mulkiewicz, "The Stereotype of the Jew in Polish Folklore," in Issachar Ben-Ami and Joseph Dan, eds., *Studies in Aggadah and Jewish Folklore* (Jerusalem: Magnes, 1983), 87–88. On the settings of Hasidic drinking bouts, see Abraham Stern, "Information Concerning the Sect of the Hasidim," AGAD, KRSW 6634, pp. 239–43; the report by the entrepreneur Elias Moszkowski from 1845, in AGAD, CWW 1436, pp. 215–33; and Kotik, *Journey to a Nineteenth-Century Shtetl*, 381.
135. Mosheh Ḥayim Klainman, *Or Yesharim* (1924; repr. Jerusalem: n.p., 1967), 155.
136. Klainman, *Or Yesharim*.
137. In 1823, the Parczew Chief reported that twenty local Hasidim were accustomed to celebrate Sabbaths and festivals in rented prayer houses "where sometimes throughout the entire night they make a great noise and celebrate services, with various songs, jumps, dances." They also played drinking games and sang drinking songs in this very place of prayer, after which they would "fly out into the street singing, jumping and producing various shouts." AGAD, Centralne Władze Wyznaniowe (CWW), 1871, pp. 12–13.
138. Alexander McCaul, *Sketches of Judaism and the Jews* (London, 1838; originally published in *British Magazine* in 1834), p. 21; Ayerst, *Jews of the Nineteenth Century*, 102.
139. Solomon Zalman Lipshitz and Isaac of Warka, *Likute shoshanim* (Lublin, 1883), ed. Ḥayim Yesha'yah ha-Kohen, 1:6–7.
140. Jehiel Michael Epstein, *Arukh ha-shulḥan*, 13; quoted in Avraham Ḥayim ben Naftali Tsevi Frankel, *Shabat bet Ropshits* (Jerusalem: A. Ḥ Frankel, 1994), 467. An interesting question is the extent of drinking among women, an issue which I have not been able to examine yet.
141. Lipschitz and Isaac of Warka, *Likute shoshanim*, 1:14–15.
142. Isaiah Horowitz, *Shne luḥot ha-brit* (Amsterdam, 1649; repr. Jerusalem: n.p., n.d.), 2:138.
143. If one has to make the blessing over something else (e.g., tea) for lack of wine, but someone later brings him some, he must drink it even if he has already made the required blessing. Ḥayim El'azar Shapira, *Sefer nimuke oraḥ ḥayim* (1930; repr. Brooklyn, NY: Emes, 2004), 178.

144. See Shapira's gloss on the laws of prayer in the *Shulḥan Arukh*, which forbid one to pray and recite certain blessings after drinking a *revi'it* (roughly three-eighths of a cup) of wine until the effect has worn off: *Sefer nimuke oraḥ ḥayim*, 87–88. For a similar distinction in responsa literature, see Bet Yehudah, *Oraḥ ḥayim*, 85; Divre Yatsiv, *Oraḥ ḥayim*, 244; Yabia Omer, *Oraḥ ḥayim*, 1:11.
145. Shapira, *Sefer nimuke oraḥ ḥayim*, 181.
146. Schneur Zalman of Lyady, *Shulḥan arukh ha-rav*, no. 182, paragraph 2–3; quoted in Shapira, *Sefer nimuke oraḥ ḥayim*, 464–65.
147. A. Frankel, *Shabat bet Ropshits*, "Kidushe raba," 441–43.
148. Shapira, *Sefer nimuke oraḥ ḥayim*, 181–82.
149. The majority said no. Accounts of the customs of earlier tzaddikim were conflicting. One source claimed that the Sanzer tzaddik made the blessing over a small cup of liquor, but an eyewitness claimed that he did so over a large silver cup of liquor. The dispute was resolved by a compromise position that the Sanzer tzaddik must have made the blessing over the large silver cup without drinking a full measure of liquor. Other tzaddikim, in contrast, were recalled making the blessing over a small cup. A. Frankel, *Shabat bet Ropshits*, 459, 467, 470, and 523–25. For the size of a *revi'it*, see note 146..
150. Tzaddikim who allegedly abstained or cautioned against drinking excessively included Solomon Rokeaḥ of Belz, Elimelekh of Leżajsk, Menaḥem Mendel of Vitebsk, and Naḥman of Bratslav.
151. Moshe Menachem Mendel Walden, *Nifla'ot ha-rabi* (Biłgoraj, Poland:, 1911).
152. On Hasidism's conservative form of acculturation, see my chapter "Hasidism and Habitat," in Dynner, *Holy Dissent*, 104–30.
153. A. Frankel, *Shabat bet Ropshits*, 469, quoting Isaac Ze'ev Soloveitchik, the Brisker Rov (1886–1959).
154. Rothstein notes the contradiction between the song and the reality, as well, in "Geyt a yid in shenkl arayn," 258. For the original Yiddish, and an alternate translation, see Mark Slobin, *Tenement Songs: The Popular Music of the Jewish Immigrants* (Urbana, IL: University of Illinois Press, 1996), 193. Alternate lyrics, in a version sung by Cantor Berel Chagy, are available at http://www.youtube.com/watch?v=WX0OKFwLOQU (accessed August 8, 2012). An anti-Hasidic song attempted to stigmatize Kotzker Hasidim in the same manner: "Who is going into shul [synagogue]? / Our holy little Jews / Who is going into the tavern? / Our little Kotsker Chasidim." See the memoirs of Pauline Wengeroff, *Rememberings: The World of a Russian Jewish Woman in the Nineteenth Century*, tr. Henny Wenkart (Bethesda: University Press of Maryland, 2000), 156. On Christian temperance societies in the Kingdom of Poland, see Rożenowa, *Produkcja wódki*, 161–77. On temperance societies in Galicia, see Stauter-Halsted, *Nation in the Village*, 50 and 178.

CHAPTER 2

1. Adam Kłodzinski, *Żyd polski, czyli każdy ma swoje przebiegi* (1820), in "Miscellanea z doby oświecenia," ed. Z. Golinski, special issue, *Archiwum Literackie* 25 (1982): 280–327.
2. Józef Dzierzkowski, *Śliska do przepaści droga* (1858), in A. J. O. Rogosza, ed., *Powieści Józefa Dzierzkowskiego w pierwszem zupełnem wydaniu* (Lviv, 1875), 2:289–330.
3. KRSW 6637, fol. 150.
4. KRSW 6637, fols. 161–62.

5. KRSW 6637, fols. 162–65
6. KRSW 6637, fols. 159–160.
7. KRSW 6637, fols. 166–69; fol. 175a.
8. KRSW 6637, fol. 179. Pomikowski received a tax-free inexpensive restaurant (*garkuchnia*) for Catholics as his sole compensation.
9. KRSW 6637, fols. 189–91.
10. KRSW 6637, fol. 92. On the mid-century emergence of dairy leases to small entrepreneurs, who, "as a rule," were Jews, see Kieniewicz, *Emancipation of the Polish Peasantry*, 95.
11. KRSW 6637, fols. 222–23
12. KRSW 6637, fols. 150–51 and 161.
13. Decrees expelling Jews from leaseholding were issued in the Ciechanowski Palatinate in 1717 and 1718, and in the Warsaw District in 1720 and 1722. The Płock Synod issued a stern warning against installing Jews in taverns in 1733. Complaints and declarations against Jewish tavernkeeping were issued during the sessions of the Sejm in 1738 and 1740. See Smoleński, *Stan i sprawa żydów polskich*, 16. Christian townspeople in royal towns would soon see their own distilling rights encroached upon by the state through the 1776 "*propinacja* law." Now they had to compete with *starostas* and exempted Jewish communities for monopoly rights. See Murphy, "Burghers versus Bureaucrats," 394–95. This conflicts with the undocumented assertions made by Gelber about the 1776 law, which he claims barred Jews from leasing taverns and distilleries in towns, in his "Korot ha-yehudim be-Polin mi-reshit halukatah ve'ad milhemet ha-olam hashniyah," in Israel Halpern, ed., *Bet Yisra'el be-Polin* (Jerusalem: Ha-Mahlakah le-Inyene ha-No'ar shel ha-Histadrut ha-Tsiyonit, 1948), 110.
14. A. N. Frenk," Mehiat mekhirat mashkim," *Ha-Tsefirah*, August 21, 1921; Hundert, *Jews in Poland-Lithuania*, 42; Daniel Stone, *The Polish-Lithuanian State, 1386–1795* (Seattle: University of Washington Press, 2001), 304.
15. Ya'akov Barnai, *Igrot hasidim me-Erets Yisra'el* (Jerusalem: Yad Yitshak Ben-Tsvi, 1980), 119–20. See also Hundert, *Jews in Poland-Lithuania*, 48.
16. Jerzy Lukowski, *Disorderly Liberty: The Political Culture of the Polish-Lithuanian Commonwealth in the Eighteenth Century* (London: Continuum, 2010), 221.
17. For counterarguments by individual publicists who opposed the effort to drive Jews out of the rural liquor trade and seemed to value their contributions, see Haber, "Ha-pundaka'im ha-yehudiim"; Levine, *Economic Origins of Antisemitism*, 214–15; Antony Polonsky, *The Jews in Poland and Russia*, vol. 1, *1350–1881* (Oxford: Littman Library, 2010), 221; and Hundert, *Jews in Poland-Lithuania*, 227–28.
18. On the origins of cameralism (often confused with physiocratic ideals in Jewish historiography), see Jonathan Karp, *The Politics of Jewish Commerce: Economic Thought and Emancipation in Europe, 1638–1848* (New York: Cambridge University Press, 2008), 101–4. On Russian minister of finance Egor Kankrin's version of cameralism, see Walter McKenzie Pintner, *Russian Economic Policy under Nicholas I* (Ithaca, NY: Cornell, 1967), 22–23. On cameralism and Habsburg Jewry, see Lois C. Dubin, *The Port Jews of Habsburg Trieste: Absolutist Politics and Enlightenment Culture* (Stanford, CA: Stanford University Press, 1999), 69. For its later incarnation in the twentieth century, termed "high modernism," see James C. Scott, *Seeing Like a State: How Certain Schemes to Improve the Human Condition Have Failed* (New Haven, CT: Yale University Press, 1998). On the internalization of cameralist ideals by Jewish reformers, particularly maskilim,

see Derek Penslar, *Shylock's Children: Economics and Jewish Identity in Modern Europe* (Berkeley: University of California Press, 2001), 68–84.

19. The proposed expulsion was opposed by five of eighteen *starostów* (elders), four of whom have been identified: Bojakowski, Baum, Tannhauser, and Tschirch. Eight were in favor; the rest abstained. Majer Bałaban, *Dzieje żydów w Galicyi* (Lviv: Nakł. Księgarni Polskiej B. Połonieckiego, 1914), 36.

20. In Hundert, "Introduction to *Divre binah*," 237, the "decrees of 1789 forbidding Jews to hold *arendas* in the villages" seems to actually refer to the 1785 decrees (the 1789 decrees were only a reiteration).

21. Samuel T. Myovich, "Josephism at Its Boundaries: Nobles, Peasants, Priests, and Jews in Galicia, 1772–1790" (Ph.D. diss., Indiana University, 1994), 255–56; 282–84; Josef Karniel, "Das Toleranzpatent Kaiser Josephs II für die Juden Galiziens und Lodomeriens," *Jahrbuch des Instituts für Deutsche Geschichte* 11 (1982): 82, ordinances 32–34. The issue is also discussed, with a lachrymose slant, in Brawer, *Galitsyah vi-yehudeha*, 162–68. According to Jacob Goldberg, during the years 1812–27, there were still 1,378 Jews selling alcoholic beverages in rural areas in Galicia, representing 10 percent of all Jews involved in these activities. This does not include clandestine liquor sales by Jews. See Jacob Goldberg, "Tavernkeeping," in *The YIVO Encyclopedia of Jews in Eastern Europe*, available online at http://www.yivoencyclopedia.org/article.aspx/Tavernkeeping. Accessed February 6, 2011.

22. Blum, *End of the Old Order*, 224–25.

23. The best example available in English is Slomka, *From Serfdom to Self-Government*. See also, in English, Joseph Margoshes, *A World Apart: A Memoir of Jewish Life in Nineteenth Century Galicia* (Boston: Academic Studies Press, 2008), e.g., 163. As late as the turn of the twentieth century, the author and memoirist Stanisław Przybyszewski recalls nights of listening to Jewish music in and around Krakow "till morning in some Jewish tavern". See Larry Wolff, *The Idea of Galicia: History and Fantasy in Habsburg Political Culture* (Stanford, CA: Stanford University Press, 2010), 295–96. The overflow of Galician Jewish tavernkeepers into Hungary was so substantial that Hungarian historians have sometimes used the rising number of tavernkeepers as an index of the entire Galician Jewish influx. See Howard Lupovitch, *Jews at the Crossroads: Tradition and Accommodation during the Golden Age of the Hungarian Nobility, 1729–1878* (Budapest: Central European University Press, 2007), 118–19.

24. The preeminent example is Wyspiański's *Wedding* (*Wesele*, 1901).

25. The first of the new-style Galician anti-Semitic books is probably Teofil Merunowicz, *Żydzi* (Lviv, 1879), 181–82.

26. Jerzy Topolski, citing M. Szcepaniak, estimates the number of Jewish tavernkeepers in Greater Poland as less than 5 percent by the end of the eighteenth century. See "Uwagi o strukturze gospodarczo-społecznej Wielkopolski w XVIII wieku czyli dlaczego na jej terenie nie było żydowskich karczmarzy?" in Topolski and K. Modelski, ed., *Żydzi w Wielkopolsce na przestrzeni dziejów*, 2nd ed. (Poznań, Poland: Wydawn. Poznańskie, 1999), 79. See also Hundert, *Jews in Poland-Lithuania*, 37, and Goldberg, "Tavernkeeping."

27. AGAD, Lubomirsk z Malej Wsi 1405, 10–14. The 1844 report is summarized in Polonsky, *Jews in Poland and Russia*, 1:238.

28. Klier, *Russia Gathers Her Jews*, 69–71. Expulsions continued to be planned, however. In a letter dated July 18, 1800, Count Lubomirski felt compelled to warn the interior minister that expulsions of village Jews in Byelorussia would

injure the region's economy. See Ilyah Luria, *Edah u-medinah: Ha-ḥasidut ḥabad ba-imperyah ha-rusit, 588–643* (Jerusalem: Magnes, 2006), 3–4.
29. Cited in Klier, *Russia Gathers Her Jews*, 141.
30. Klier, *Russia Gathers Her Jews*, 141. Klier notes that the next article threatened recalcitrant landowners with fines, but doubts whether this was actually enforced. Hasidic leader R. Schneur Zalman of Lyady apparently collected funds to assist rural Jews expelled from the countryside in 1810. See Naftali Loewenthal, *Communicating the Infinite: The Emergence of the Habad School* (Chicago: University of Chicago Press, 1990), 109.
31. Mikhail T. Shugarov, ed., "Doklad o Evreiakh imperatoru Aleksandru Pavlovichu," *Russkii Arkhiv* 41 (February 1903): 264. The end of the document contains an explicit admission about the need, in light of the Napoleonic Wars, to avoid alienating Jews. Thanks to Melissa Frazier for deciphering and translating this document.
32. The Chernigov decree was issued on November 29, 1821, and the Poltava decree on May 13, 1822. See Benyamin Lukin, "A Russian Bureaucratic Approach to the Economic Role of Malorossian Jews, 1830," *Jews in Russia and Eastern Europe* 57, no. 2 (2006): 111–31. Compare Klier, *Russia Gathers Her Jews*, 169: when crop failures caused a famine, the local Polish landowners, "who now knew well how to play the game," blamed peasant destitution on the Jews. See also Lowe, *Tsars and the Jews*, 33, 36. The expulsions may have also been part of an attempt to shrink the Pale of Settlement and exclude the Chernigov and Poltava provinces from Jewish settlement as part of a campaign against Sabbatarians (Subbotniki), a Russian Judaizing sect that was active in those provinces. See Eisenbach, *Emancipation of the Jews in Poland*, 151. On the actual relationship between Sabbatarians and Jews, see Nicholas Breyfogle, "The Religious World of Russian Sabbatarians (*Subbotniks*)," in Dynner, *Holy Dissent*, 359-92.
33. The declaration of a public fast on January 14, 1824, is printed and transcribed in Abraham Joshua Heschel of Apta, Isaac Meir Heschel and Meshullam Zusya Heschel, *Igrot ha-"Ohev Yisra'el": Kevutsat igrot, mismakhim ve-haskamot ha-muva'im bi-sefarim ve-kitve yad* (Jerusalem: Mekhon Sifte Tsadikim She'a, 1999), 100–103. Polish Hasidic leader Moses Elyakim Beri'ah of Kozienice (d. 1825), according to one tradition, consoled R. Abraham Joshua Heschel with this eschatological prediction. Relayed through the redactor of Moses Elyakim Beriyah, *Kohelet Mosheh* (Lublin, 1905), 235. Similarly, Mordecai Joseph Leiner of Izbica consoled his audiences with the idea that the gentiles only issue harmful decrees against Israel when they realize that God is bringing salvation to Israel. See Leiner, "Sefer tehilim," on Psalms 99:1, in *Me ha-shiloaḥ* (1860; repr. New York: Lainer, 1984).
34. Lukin, "A Russian Bureaucratic Approach," 116. Repnin claimed that crime had decreased after expulsions of rural Jews, and denied both the destitution of erstwhile tavernkeepers and their importance in the rural economy.
35. See Kotik, *Journey to a Nineteenth-Century Shtetl*, 188 and editor David Assaf's summary on 440, no. 19. The Günzburg family was able to build on their liquor tax farming business to establish a major bank in St. Petersburg. On Jewish leasing of the liquor taxes, see also Benjamin Nathans, *Beyond the Pale: The Jewish Encounter with Late Imperial Russia* (Berkeley: University of California, 2002), 40 and 128, and Polonsky, *Jews in Poland and Russia*, 433. On the prestige of Jewish excise lessees (*aktsizniki*), despite their reputation for religious laxity, see Wengeroff, *Rememberings*, 186; and S. Y. Ambramovitsh, *Wishing Ring*, 229–30.

Wengeroff's husband administered his father's Kovno District liquor monopoly lease (183).
36. The total number of taverns and distilleries in 1808 was 19,749 (the majority, 13,157, in villages). The figure for Jewish-run establishments six years later is 17,561. See Grossman, "Struktura społeczna i zawodowa," 35, table 12, and AGAD, KRSW 1849, fols. 152–59.
37. On tsarist attempts at rendering Jews "legible," see Eugene Avrutin, *Jews and the Imperial State: Identification Politics in Tsarist Russia* (Ithaca: Cornell University Press, 2010). On incentivizing honesty by means of "hostage capital," see Douglas Allen, *The Institutional Revolution: Measurement and the Economic Emergence of the Modern World* (Chicago: University of Chicago Press, 2012), esp. ch. 3. On residential legislation in the Duchy of Warsaw, see Adam Szczypiorski, *Ćwierć wieku Warszawy, 1806–1830* (Wrocław, Poland: Zakład Narodowy im. Ossolińskich, 1964), 39; John Stanley, "The Politics of the Jewish Question in the Duchy of Warsaw, 1807–1813," *Jewish Social Studies* 44 (1982): 57; Hensel, "Żydowski arendarz," 89; and Mark Wischnitzer, "Proekty reformy evreyskago byta," *Perezhytoe* 1 (1908): 170–71. Raphael Mahler speculates that the decree, if enacted, would have "deprived practically half the Jewish population of its income," and was "unique in the history of the modern period." Raphael Mahler, *A History of Modern Jewry, 1780–1815* (London: Vallentine, Mitchell, 1971), 358. These sentiments are exaggerated—as noted earlier, a similar decree was already issued by Joseph II in Galicia, which, thanks to landlord noncompliance, had not ruined "practically half the Jewish population."
38. L. Miller, *Uwagi o żydach*, reprinted in Gelber, "She'elat ha-yehudim be-Polin," Appendix B.
39. Rożenowa, *Produkcja wódki*, 91–95. See also Goldberg, "Ha-yehudi ve-ha-pundak," 246–47.
40. Letter by Andrzej Zamoyski, printed in Jacob Shatzky, *Yidishe bildungs-politik in Poyln fun 1806 biz 1866* (New York: YIVO, 1943), 241, document 8.
41. Quoted in Frenk, "Meḥiat mekhirat mashkim." As Hillel Levine observes in his analysis of Michał Kachovsky's accusations against Jewish tavernkeepers, the Polish nobles who owned the taverns were often presented as "innocent observers who had not fully considered the consequences of the propinacja." See Levine, *Economic Origins of Antisemitism*, 171–72.
42. Eisenbach claims that "press articles and political writings provided an ideological foundation for the government's policy toward the Jews, and were an important factor in the discussion on the political emancipation of the Jewish population." See Eisenbach, *Emancipation of the Jews in Poland*, 181.
43. Quoted in Eisenbach, *Emancipation of the Jews in Poland*, 175. A Jewish delegation first approached Novosiltsev as early as April 15, 1813, while he was still vice president of the Supreme Council of the Duchy of Warsaw. In the Congress Kingdom, Novosiltsev was appointed imperial commissioner—a post designed to reconcile the interests of the kingdom with those of the empire. Subsequent delegations and sizeable bribes ensured further postponements. See Dawid Kandel, "Nowosilców a żydzi," *Biblioteka Warszawska* 2 (1911): 142–43; Frenk, "Meḥiat mekhirat mashkim"; Szymon Askenazy, "Z dziejów żydów polskich w dobie Księstwa Warszawskiego," *Kwartalnik Poświęcony Badaniu Przszłości żydów w Polsce* 1, no. 1 (1912): 8–9; and Ignacy Schiper, *Przyczynki do dziejów chasydyzmu w Polsce*, ed. Zbigniew Targielski (Warsaw: PWN, 1992), 119. A petition to the tsar in 1816 claimed that "200,000 families will starve" if Jews lost

their right to sell liquor." See S. Beilin, "From the Historical Journals: Awaiting the King's Mercy, 1816-1818," *Evreiskaia Starina* V (1912), 340-1. On Kajetan Koźmian's central role in persuading the State Council and Zajączek to restrict the Jewish liquor trade, see Eisenbach, *Emancipation of the Jews in Poland*, 175, and Kajetan Koźmian, *Pamiętniki*, (1858; repr. Wrocław, Poland: Zakład Narodowy im. Ossolińskich, 1972), 3:20–22.

44. AGAD, KRSW 6634, fols. 10–16.
45. The concession amounts depended on the number of households in a given locale. See Jan Rutkowski, *Historia gospodarcza Polski*, vol. 2 (Poznań, Poland: Księgarnia Akademicka, 1950), 213; Rożenowa, *Produkcja wódki*, 60. According to Mahler's calculations, the liquor concession was eight times the initial fee by 1824 and twelve times the initial fee by 1830. See Mahler, *Hasidism and the Jewish Enlightenment*, 178. Additionally, Lubecki reintroduced a state monopoly on alcohol sold in towns and cities. Effectively, this was a new tax on liquor production and sale, since nonlessees of the monopoly paid concession fees (Rutkowski, *Historia gospodarcza Polski*, 211).
46. 1818 memo from Sobolewski to Zajączek, in Gelber, "She'elat ha-yehudim be-Polin," 35. This strategy was reiterated a decade later by Matteusz Muszyński, a clerk in the Consumption Tax Office. See KRSW 1849, 152-9. Hensel regards the concession policy as a result of the regime's realization that it could not force Polish landowners to stop using Jewish lessees, but this probably overemphasizes their influence (after all, the tsarist regime did not feel the need to resort to concessions in the Pale). See Hensel, "Żydowski arendarz," 92 and Hensel, "Polnische Adelsnation und jüdische Vermittler 1814–1830," in Hensel and Heinz-Dietrich Löwe, eds., *Forschungen zur osteuropäischen Geschichte* (Wiesbaden, Germany: Otto Harrassowitz, 1983), 71–93.
47. A historical overview of the liquor legislation by the Jewish Committee in 1826 appears in KRSW 1849, fols. 97–100. On Polish landowner and lessee complaints about Jewish attrition, see Rożenowa, *Produkcja wódki*, 60. Haber assumes incorrectly that anti-Jewish feeling derived primarily from the peasantry, even though his own anti-Jewish sources derive primarily from the urban, educated, and often ennobled Polish publicists. See Haber, "Ha-pundaka'im ha-yehudiim," 9.
48. Montefiore-St. Petersburg Archives (Sergei's collection), Privy Councilor Turkul', Document 14, pp. 226–65, 5c. Translated by Svetlana Rukhelman.
49. YIVO Archives, Simon Dubnow collection, II:7, pp. 1–7. The petitioners concluded with a tribute to the Advisory Committee members, "shepherds leading their flocks to true knowledge, teaching goodness, justice, and uprightness, making every heart joyful and bringing relief to every spirit."
50. AGAD, KRSW 6629, fols. 112–13. This document was first described by Mahler, in *Hasidism and the Jewish Enlightenment*, 179.
51. KRSW 1849, fols. 152–59. Data compiled by the Consumption Tax office.
52. KRSW 6629, fols. 112–19.
53. KRSW 6629, fols. 112–19.
54. KRSW 6629, fol. 119. The Napoleonic regime had briefly granted Jews in the Duchy of Warsaw full citizenship in 1807 but had reinstituted restrictions the following year under what has come to be known as Napoleon's "Infamous Decrees." Those restrictions were to be rescinded in ten years' time if Jews attained an acceptable level of civilization, but the demise of Napoleon rendered

that vague promise moot. See, for example, Stanley, "Politics of the Jewish Question," and Wischnitzer, "Proekty reformy evreyskago byta."
55. KRSW 1849, fols. 152–59.
56. Eisenbach, *Emancipation of the Jews in Poland*, 265–66.
57. AGAD, Protokoły Rady Administracyjnej Królestwa Polskiego (PRAKP) 15, p. 679; Jacob Shatzky, "An Attempt at Jewish Colonization in the Kingdom of Poland," *YIVO Annual of Jewish Social Science* 1 (1946): 49.
58. Eisenbach, "Mobilność," 234.
59. For the latest research on Synagogue Councils, see Eleonora Bergman, "The Synagogue as a House of Elections," in Jurgita Šiaučiunaitė-Verbickiene and Larisa Lempertienė, eds., *Jewish Space in Central and Eastern Europe Day-to-Day History* (Newcastle, UK: Cambridge Scholars, 2007), 67–73. On the continuation of supra-communal institutions, see Artur Eisenbach, "Di tsentrale reprezentants-organen fun di yidn in varshaver firstntum (1807–1815)," *Bleter far Geshikhte* 2 (1938): 33–88. A similar abolition of kahals would occur in the Tsarist Empire proper in 1844.
60. Eisenbach, *Emancipation of the Jews in Poland*, 184. Mostowski had either changed his mind or was uninvolved; by 1822 he was embarking on increasingly lengthy excursions on account of poor health or, more likely, disenchantment with the increasingly obvious limits on Polish autonomy. See J. Skowronek, "Tadeusz Mostowski," *Polski Słownik Biograficzny* 22 (1977) 76.
61. See Marcin Wodziński, "Clerks, Jews, and Farmers: Projects of Jewish Agricultural Settlement in Poland," *Jewish History* 21, no. 3/4 (2007): 290. See also the discussion in chapter 6, below.
62. KRSW/KRPiS 1849, pp. 50–63.
63. KRSW/KRPiS 1849, pp. 97–99. The Jewish Committee in the Kingdom of Poland was composed of four Poles: Ignacy Zaleski (director), Count Walerian Krasinski and Stefan Witwicki (assessors), and Jan Iwaszkiewicz (head of the office). The two secretaries were Stanisław Hoga (Hoge)—a convert—and Józef Kownacki. An advisory chamber, headed by W. Muller, included several wealthy Jewish integrationists.
64. The 1807 Jewish Committee was composed of Czartoryski, Potocki, Novosiltsev, and Czacki. See Shugarov, "Doklad o Evreiakh," 258–59.
65. Shugarov, "Doklad o Evreiakh," 259–62.
66. CWW 1419, p. 39.
67. KRSW 1849, fols. 152–59. See also Eisenbach, "Mobilność," 203–5. Eisenbach fails to note that the figures for 1829 and 1830 are only projections.
68. Eisenbach argues that the landowners who published pamphlets or sat on the Jewish Committee had ceased to view Jewish lessees as economically necessary. See Eisenbach, "Mobilność," 194–95, and Eisenbach, *Emancipation of the Jews in Poland*, 188. For a similar argument regarding Russian Jewry, see Klier, *Russia Gathers Her Jews*, 87–88 (the first such instance being the Senate's 1798 fact-finding commission), and Lowe, *Tsars and the Jews*, 28–34. In contrast, Samuel Ettinger stresses anti-Jewish prejudices among Russian reformers. See Ettinger, "Takanat 1804," in *Ben Polin le-Rusyah* (Jerusalem: Zalman Shazar, 1994), esp. 246–49.
69. Hensel, "Polnische Adelsnation"; Hensel, "Żydowski arendarz"; Mahler, *Hasidism and the Jewish Enlightenment*, 177–79; Eisenbach, *Mobilność*, 179–207.
70. Władze Centralne Powstanie Listopadego 1830-31 (WCPL 1830-31), 339, pp. 7–11.

71. WCPL 1830-31, 339, pp. 1. Another minister, Niemojowski, likewise wrote to the Komisji Rządowej Spraw Wewnętrznych that "in consideration of ways to interest Jews in wider matters . . . freeing every Jewish distiller from concessions would not allow us to expect advantageous results" (p. 4).
72. WCPL 1830-31, 339, p. 2.
73. WCPL 1830-31, 339, pp. 7-12.
74. WCPL 1830-31, 339, pp. 20-22.
75. WCPL 1830-31, 339, pp. 23-24.
76. WCPL 1830-31, 342, pp. 1-7.
77. WCPL 1830-31, 342, pp. 1-7.
78. WCPL 1830-31, 342, p. 8.
79. AGAD, Zarząd Generał Policmajstra w Królestwie Polskim 48, 573-74, 594.
80. On Winawer, see Jacob Shatzky, *Geshikhte fun yidn in Varshe*, vol. 2, *Fun 1831 bizn oyfshtand fun 1863* (New York: YIVO Institute, 1948) 34-35. For Mazovian liquor concessions, see KRSW 187, fols. 182-89.
81. WCPL 1830-31, 339, pp. 26-28.
82. Ostrowski, *Pomysły o potrzebie reformy*, 102.
83. For formal Jewish protests, see Jan Glucksberg (attr.), *Rzut oka na stan izraelitów w Polsce* (Warsaw, 1831), 37-39; Artur Eisenbach, "Memoriał o położeniu ludności żydowskiej w dobie konstytucyjnej Królestwa Kongresowego," *Teki Archiwalne* 21 (1989): 202-3; Raphael Mahler, "A Jewish Memorandum to the Viceroy of the Kingdom of Poland, Paskiewicz," in Saul Lieberman, ed., *Salo Wittmayer Baron Jubilee Volume on the Occasion of his Eightieth Birthday* (Jerusalem: American Academy for Jewish Research, 1974), 2:692-95; KRSW 6600, fol. 236; and Dawid Kandel, "Petycya 1857 r.," *Kwartalnik Poświęcony Badaniu Przeszłości Żydów w Polsce* 3 (1913): 154-55.
84. See Kaidanover, *Kav ha-yashar*, ch. 24, cited in the first chapter. One responsum explicitly prohibits placing a *mezuzah* in an unprotected place in a tavern, in case raucous non-Jewish customers might defile the scroll. See materials cited by Rabbi Menashe Klein in his responsa *Mishnah halakhot* (Brooklyn, 1960), part 12, n222.
85. On the related problem of rabbinic attitudes toward the Jewish wine trade, where the main issue was gentile labor during the early phase of the winemaking process, see Soloveitchik, *Ha-yayin bi-yeme ha-benayim*, 68-70, Soloveitchik, "Can Halakhic Texts Talk History?" 172-73; and Edward Fram, *Ideals Face Reality: Jewish Law and Life in Poland, 1550-1655* (Cincinnati, OH: Hebrew Union College Press, 1997), 96-105. For somewhat similar discussions over the sale and consumption of coffee, see Robert Liberles, *Jews Welcome Coffee: Tradition and Innovation in Early Modern Germany* (Waltham, MA: Brandeis University Press, 2012), esp. chapter 3.
86. Israel Halpern, ed., *Pinkas va'ad arba aratsot: Likute takanot, ketavim u-reshumot* (Jerusalem: Mosad Byalik, 1989), 483-6. On Jewish pig farming, see Węgrzynek, "Zajęcia rolnicze żydów." See also Bezalel ben Solomon, *Korban shabat* (Warsaw, 1873), 121, cited in Jacob Katz, *The "Shabbes Goy": A Study in Halakhic Flexibility*, tr. Yoel Lerner (Philadelphia: Jewish Publication Society of America, 1989), 94-105. One of the very first edicts of supreme institution of Polish Jewish self-government, the Council of Four Lands, warned Jews against leasing the royal tax on alcohol (the *czopowe*), in 1581. See Halpern, *Pinkas*, 1.
87. See Simon Dubnow, ed., *Pinkas ha-medinah, o Pinkas va'ad ha-kehilot ha-rashiyot be-medinat Lita* (Berlin: Ayanot, 1925), nos. 137, 398, 530, 713, 740, 774, and 966.

88. "As people do today"; "an evil custom." Both *takanot* are printed in the appendix to Haim Hillel Ben-Sasson's "Takanot isure shabat shel Polin u-mashma'utan ha-ḥevratit ve-ha-kalkalit," *Zion* 21 (1956): 183–206. See also Teller, *Kesef*, 159–60.
89. Bezalel ben Solomon, *Korban shabat*, 120–21. In addition, R. Berakhia Berekh of Krakow refers to the Ludmir decree in this context. See Ben-Sasson, "Takanot isure shabat," 190.
90. If he did not have an absolute monopoly, as was usually the case in a town or city, he had to sell a discrete amount of liquor outright to a gentile who was not his servant, without enjoying the profit. He could buy back any surplus liquor (but not beer or mead) after the Sabbath. Ben-Sasson, "Takanot isure shabat," 196.
91. Ben-Sasson, "Takanot isure shabat," 197–201. I am grateful to Sol Cohen for this insight. Ben-Sasson missed these cues and took the "threats" literally, interpreting them as a sign of deteriorating Jewish-Christian relations in the wake of 1648!
92. Solomon Drimer of Skole, *Bet Shlomo* (Lviv, 1855), "Oraḥ hayyim," no. 36.
93. See Fram, *Ideals Face Reality*.
94. Solomon Drimer of Skole, *Bet Shelomoh*, no. 50.
95. Solomon Drimer of Skole, *Bet Shelomoh*, no. 50. Drimer refers mainly to a brewery/tavern. In light of the displacement of beer by vodka, this term likely denoted all taverns by this time.
96. Solomon Lipschitz, *Ḥemdat Shelomoh: Drushim ve-ḥidushim* (Warsaw, 1890), 13 (7), no. 3.
97. Lipschitz, *Ḥemdat Shelomoh*, 13 (7), no. 3.
98. "Me'aḥar she-ha-kitrug aleha, en ha-berakhah shorah bah." Barnai, *Igerot ḥasidim*, 118–20. For an alternate translation, see Gershon Hundert, *Jews in Poland-Lithuania*, 48–49. R. Menaḥem Mendel wrote this after his migration to Tiberias in Palestine in 1785.
99. Avraham Ḥayim Simḥah Bunem Mikhalzohn, *Ohel Naftali* (Lviv, 1911), 132–33, no. 373; Gershon Kamelhar, *Mevaser tov* (Podgórze, Poland, 1900), 17–18. See also a truncated version in Mikhalzohn, *Ateret Menaḥem* (Biłgoraj, Poland: n.p., 1910), 34–36, no. 117. A similar account, printed later, is attributed to Tzvi Hirsch of Żydaczów in Mikha'el Braver, *Tsevi le-tsadik*, (Vienna: Toibesh, 1931), 60. According to other accounts, R. Menaḥem Mendel cursed tavernkeepers and forced them to hand their leases over to gentiles. Dob Baer Ehrmann, "Sipurim mehahak maharani mi-ropshits z"l," in *Devarim arevim* (1903; repr. Tel Aviv: n.p., 1963), (two volumes) vol. 2, fols. 40, 45. However, certain Hasidic leaders allegedly helped struggling tavernkeepers hold on to their leases by appealing to wealthy followers,. See Israel Hurwitz, *Ma'asiyot me-ha-gedolim ve-ha-tsadikim* (Warsaw: n.p., 1924), 13–14,.
100. Slomka, *From Serfdom to Self-government*, 91–92. See also Rachel Manekin, "The Lost Generation: Education and Female Conversion in Fin-de- Siècle Kraków," in "Jewish Women in Eastern Europe," ed. ChaeRan Freeze, Paula Hyman, and Antony Polonsky, special issue, *Polin* 18 (2005): 189–219, esp. 192.
101. Trunk, *Poyln*, 5–6.
102. Moses Elyakim Beri'ah, *Be'er Mosheh*, "Yom Kippur" (Józefów, Poland, 1858), appendix. According to a memo by the Censorship Committee in 1823, village Jews prayed in the synagogues of friends or family in towns on the High Holidays. AGAD, CWW 1433, pp. 260–63. On cases of miscegenation in rural Lithuania, see Abramowicz, *Profiles of a Lost World*, 65–66.
103. AGAD, CWW 1409, p. 90. Printed in Zofia Borzymińska, ed., *Dzieje żydów w Polsce: Wybór tekstów źródłowych XIX wiek* (Warsaw: Żydowski Instytut

Historyczny, 1994), 56 n3.3. Converts faced this problem until they produced offspring of "mixed blood," i.e., who were no longer considered Jewish, according to this document.

104. The Frankists were found mainly around the town of Piaski, in Suchodoły, Siedliska Wielkie, Izdebno, Gardzienice, Żukowo, Chmiel, Krępice, Minkowice, Jankowice, and Janowicz. See Mahler, "Statistik fun yidn in der Lubliner Voyevodstva," 107.

105. See the poem by Ze'ev Wolf of Stryków, a disciple of R. Menaḥem Mendel of Kotzk (Kock), in Glenn Dynner, "Hasidism and Habitat: Managing the Jewish-Christian Encounter in the Kingdom of Poland," in Dynner, *Holy Dissent*, 105. See also Manekin, "The Lost Generation," and ChaeRan Freeze, "When Chava Left Home: Gender, Conversion, and the Jewish Family in Tsarist Russia," in "Jewish Women in Eastern Europe," ed. ChaeRan Freeze, Paula Hyman, and Antony Polonsky, special issue, *Polin* 18 (2005), 158.

106. AGAD, KRSW 6637, fol. 1. This was also the explanation provided by the St. Petersburg Jewish Committee in 1858. KRSW 6632, p. 57.

107. KRSW 6637, fol. 26. An additional motivation behind the ban may have been the desire to win peasant loyalty for the tsar at the expense of the Polish lords. On this tsarist scheme, which originated in an 1835 memorandum by Count Kiselev, see Blum, *End of the Old Order*, 234–35. Bans against rural Jewish tavernkeeping were enacted in Lithuania at this time, as well. See Goldberg, "Tavernkeeping."

108. KRSW 6637, fol. 15.

109. KRSW 6637, fols. 5 and 15.

110. KRSW 6637, fol. 29–31.

111. KRSW 6637, fols. 19–22.

112. KRSW 6637, fols. 45–47.

113. KRSW 6637, fols. 45–47. Alyssa Quint argues that Jewish traveling merchants were preferred customers in taverns because they paid in cash rather than eating and drinking on credit like the locals. See Quint, "The Currency of Yiddish: Ettinger's *Serkele* and the Reinvention of Shylock," *Prooftexts* 24, no. 1 (2004): 99–115.

114. KRSW 6637, fols. 43–44, 51–52.

115. Rożenowa, *Produkcja wódki*, 153.

116. K. W. Wójcicki, "Zarysy domowego życia kmiotków naszych," *Biblioteka Warszawska* 2 (1844): 30, cited in Rożenowa, *Produkcja wódki*, 113. On a similar situation in the Tsarist Empire proper, see Smith and Christian, *Bread and Salt*, 309–10. There the crackdown did not occur until 1860 (Smith and Christian, *Bread and Salt*, 312–13).

117. E. Stawiski, "Kronika pewnej wioski," *Biblioteka Warszawska* 4 (1843): 665. Quoted in Rożenowa, *Produkcja wódki*, 153.

118. H. R. z Radzyńskiego, "Uwagi nad artykułem pana S.," *Gazeta Handlowa i Przemysłowa*, 1844, no. 12; F. K. Rutowski, "O Pijaństwie," *Gazeta Handlowa i Przemysłowa*, 1844, nos. 18–20. Quoted in Rożenowa, *Produkcja wódki*, 124. For more sources on widespread drunkenness, see Burszta, *Społeczeństwo i karczma*, 186–88.

119. Rożenowa, *Produkcja wódki*, 126 and 157.

120. Kieniewicz, *Emancipation of the Polish Peasantry*, 91. Jerome Blum seems to arbitrarily increase it to 3.25 gallons. See *The End of the Old Order in Rural Europe* (Princeton, NJ: Princeton University Press, 1978), 48.

121. Rożenowa, *Produkcja wódki*, 161–177. See also Burszta, *Społeczeństwo i karczma*, ch. 4.
122. Liquor sales accounted for approximately 30 percent of state revenue in the tsarist empire proper. See Smith and Christian, *Bread and Salt*, 302, fig. 8.2
123. Establishing a distillery required a liquor concession of 150, 300, or 600 silver rubles (one ruble = 6.67 zlotys), depending on its size.
124. *Dziennik Praw* 34, July 5, 1844, 176–199; Józef Burszta, *Społeczeństwo i karczma*, 25. See also Rożenowa, *Produkcja wódki*, 134–35; 175–76.
125. *Dziennik Praw* 34, July 5, 1844, 189. The law, effective on June 19, 1845, stipulated that Jews could still sell liquor in towns and cities. For a similar process in historical Lithuania, see Fajnhauz, "Dwór i karczma żydowska na Litwie."
126. Statistics of Jewish occupations from the previous year, 1843, suggest a substantially greater Jewish role in the liquor trade: thirty-one liquor distributors, 2,109 liquor distillers, 111 wine makers, 723 taverns, and fifty-four billiard rooms, for a total of 3,028 establishments. See A. N. Frenk, "Di tsol yidn un zeyere basheftikungen in di shtet un derfer fun Kenigraykh Poyln in 1843tn yor," *Bleter far Yidishe Demografye, Statistik un Ekonomik* 3 (1923): 187, table 2.
127. Jan Bloch, *Finanse Kr. Polskiego za cały czas istnienia skarbu Królestwa od d. 1 czerwca 1815 do 31 grudnia 1866 r.* (Warsaw, 1883), table 2.
128. In the early 1850s, liquor yielded about 4,558,540 zlotys per year from private estates alone (including Jewish taxes and concessions). This sum is derived from calculations covering the period from 1850 to 1853, which yielded 18,234,159 zlotys (or 2,733,757 silver rubles) overall and 442,667 zlotys (or 66,367 silver rubles) from Jews. See Rożenowa, *Produkcja wódki*, 231–32. Bloch's figures yield only 287,000 zlotys from Jewish concessions, which suggests that Rożenowa's figures include other types of taxes. On state land, these liquor taxes and concessions yielded only 159,440 silver rubles (1,063,465 zlotys; about 265,866 zlotys per year) during these years, probably owing to the state liquor monopoly, which was leased and generated separate revenue.
129. As noted earlier, this data was compiled but partially falsified by Eisenbach (i.e., arbitrary numbers were supplied in place of missing data to bring the percentage down to 8 percent in 1865). See Eisenbach, "Mobilność," 285. For the official figures, see KRSW 202, pp. 166 and 171, and KRSW 6632, fol. 26.
130. Władysław Anczyc, *Pijaństwo: Zguba i nędza włościan* (Warsaw, 1867), 17. Anczyc, who resided in Warsaw in the mid- to late 1860s, seems to be describing the situation in Mazovia.
131. KRSW 6632, fol. 63.
132. In 1850, a Jew named Icek Markowiecki was discovered in the town of Mierzawa with a large quantity of illegal, watered-down vodka for sale. See Jerzy Piwek, "Rola żydów w gospodarce wielkiej własności ziemskiej między Wisłą a Pilicą w latach 1815–1864, in Feliks Kiryk, ed., *Żydzi w Małopolsce* (Przemyśl, Poland: Południowo-Wschodni Instytut Naukowy w Przemyślu, 1991), 168.
133. LeDonne, "Indirect Taxes in Catherine's Russia," 200; Smith and Christian, *Bread and Salt*, 220.
134. KRSW 6632, fol. 66; KRSW 6600, fol. 190. However, Jewish lessees had to pay a concession according to the number of households (135 rubles for 10–20 households; 225 rubles for 21–40 households; 450 rubles for over forty households).
135. Decreed in 1848. Jewish tavernkeepers were also allowed to complete the terms of their lease contracts (1846). See Fajnhauz, "Dwór i karczma żydowska na Litwie," 71–73. Fajnhauz regards these decrees as concessions by the tsar,

intended to win over Jews during the 1848 revolts. However, this fails to account for other anti-Jewish decrees passed that very year, such as the ban on the sale of other types of liquor.

136. *Listy z zagranicy z powodu kwestii chłopskiéj* (Paris, 1858), 184–85.
137. Rożenowa, *Produkcja wódki*, 199.
138. KRSW 6637, 235.
139. KRPiS 1972, 14–17, 129.
140. KRPiS 1972, 21–38, 73–87, 99.
141. KRPiS 1972, 111–14, 129–87.
142. KRSW 6700, 93–95.
143. KRSW 6700, 95–111.
144. KRPiS 1972, 169–71.
145. KRPiS 1972, 206–12, 234–38
146. KRPiS 1972, 410–12, 612–13.
147. KRPiS 1972, 217.
148. KRPiS 1972, 245–69, 358–63.
149. KRPiS 1972, 311–13, 407–8, 445–47, 479–80. One petition was composed by their steward, Meir Fried.
150. Kieniewicz, *Emancipation of the Polish Peasantry*, 158–72; Leslie, *Reform and Insurrection in Russian Poland*, 53–88, 118–19, 139.
151. KRPiS 1972, 348–51.
152. KRPiS 1972, 568–41, 642–49, 666. In 1866, the end of the twelve-year lease, Adolf Goldfarb took it over.
153. On the high incidence of unlicensed taverns in early modern England and Germany, see Michael Frank, "Satan's Servant or Authorities' Agent? Publicans in Eighteenth-Century Germany," in Kumin and Tlusty, *World of the Tavern*, 21.
154. Lukin, "A Russian Bureaucratic Approach," 122, 131.
155. In Jeremy Bentham's harsh estimation, "these interlopers form the *tiers etat*, standing in the gap between a people of Lords and a people of slaves, in a country not inviting enough to allure better capitalists." See Bentham, diary entry, January 6–February 10, 1786, in *The Correspondence of Jeremy Bentham*, 454.
156. On the bureaucracy of the Kingdom of Poland, which consisted mainly of Polish landowners, see Leonid Gorizontow, "Aparat urzędniczy Królestwa Polskiego w okresie rządów Paskiewicza," *Przegląd Historyczny* 85, nos. 1–2 (1994): 45–58.
157. E. T. Massalski, *Pan Podstolic albo czem jesteśmy czem być mozemy* (St. Petersburg, 1833), 101; Opalski, *The Jewish Tavern-Keeper*, 101. On the peasant loyalty theory, see Blum, *End of the Old Order*, 234–35.
158. Peretz, *Impressions of a Journey*, 60.
159. *Dziennik Praw* 65 (1866), 80–81, art. 252; Ochs, "St. Petersburg and the Jews of Russian Poland," 76.

CHAPTER 3

1. Fifty-by-forty Rhenish feet are the given dimensions. According to Henry Alexander Scammell Dearborn's *A Memoir on the Commerce and Navigation of the Black Sea and the Trade and Maritime Geography of Turkey and Egypt* (Boston, 1819), 2:408, "34 Rhenish feet make 35 English feet."
2. Wassercug, "Korot Moshe, 108–10.
3. Wassercug, "Korot Moshe Vasertsug," 108–10.
4. AGAD, A.G. Wil. Adm. Dóbr Wilanowskich 62, p. 52–53.

5. AGAD, A.G. Wil. Adm. Dóbr Wilanowskich 62, p. 57. Occasionally, stewards recorded tavern proportions. A tavern in Pacznowska village was sixty-six by twenty-four by seven feet; a tavern in Lipciska village was forty-one by twenty-one by eight feet. AGAD, A.G. Wil. Adm. Dóbr Wilanowskich 62, p. 279–80.
6. Harro Harring, *Poland under the Dominion of Russia* (Boston, 1834), 17. See also the comparison between Kamenets taverns and the luxurious tavern in Kobryn, a large district town, in Kotik, *Journey to a Nineteenth-Century Shtetl*, 376.
7. Murphy, "Burghers versus Bureaucrats."
8. For samples of early modern *supliki*, see Adam Kaźmierczyk, ed., *Żydzi polscy: 1648–1772; Źródła* (Krakow: Uniwersytet Jagielloński, Katedra Judaistyki, 2001), 205–27. On the pragmatism of many Duchy of Warsaw officials in these cases, see Aleksandra Oniszczuk, "Jews in the Duchy of Warsaw: The Question of Equality in Administrative Theory and Practice," in Glenn Dynner, Antony Polonsky, and Marcin Wodziński, eds., *Polin 27: Jews in the Kingdom of Poland* (forthcoming, 2014).
9. Lukin, "A Russian Bureaucratic Approach," 118, 123–24.
10. For detailed studies of these groups, see Steven Zipperstein, *The Jews of Odessa: A Cultural History, 1794–1881* (Stanford, CA: Stanford University Press, 1985); Michael Stanislawski, *Tsar Nicholas I and the Jews: The Transformation of Jewish Society in Russia, 1825–1855* (Philadelphia: Jewish Publication Society of America, 1983); Benjamin Nathans, *Beyond the Pale: The Jewish Encounter with Late Imperial Russia* (Berkeley: University of California, 2002); Antony Polonsky's masterful synthesis *Jews in Poland and Russia*, 3 vols. (London: Littman Library, 2010–2012); Władysław T. Bartoszewski and Antony Polonsky, eds., *The Jews in Warsaw: A History* (Oxford: Blackwell, 1991); and the aforementioned works by Raphael Mahler and Artur Eisenbach.
11. AGAD, Rada Ministów Księstwa Warszawskiego 165, pp. 14–24. Part of the confusion over the Warsaw legislation derives from differing definitions of the *rewir*. According to Henryk Bartoszewicz, Frederick August's 1809 decree did not demarcate borders in a specific part of the city and was thus not properly a *rewir*. Eleonora Bergman defines *rewir* more capaciously, considering the restricted streets mentioned there as inversely forming the first *rewir*. See Bartoszewicz, "Projekty rewirów dla ludności żydowskiej w miastach mazowieckich 1807–1830," *Rocznik Mazowiecki 18* (2006): 104–20, and Eleonora Bergman, *"Nie masz bóżnicy powszechnej": Synagogi i domy modlitwy w Warszawie od końca XVIII do początku XIX wieku* (Warsaw: Wydaw. DIG, 2007), 53.
12. Koźmian, *Pamiętniki*, 2:175–80.
13. In issuing that decree, Frederick August had been responding to complaints from the Warsaw municipality about noblemen who allowed Jews to rent apartments in "the most profitable neighborhoods and best houses," often transforming the lower levels of those houses into stores while residing on the upper floors. See Bergman, *Nie masz bóżnicy powszechnej*, 58. The original decree is no longer extant, but it is reprinted in Tsar Alexander's July 10, 1821, decree, published in *Dziennik Praw* 7, 155, note a.
14. Rada Ministów Księstwa Warszawskiego 165, pp. 28–32.
15. Bina Garncarska-Kadary, *Ḥelkam shel ha-yehudim be-hitpatḥut ha-taʻasiyah shel Varshah ba-shanim 1816/20–1914* (Tel Aviv: Tel Aviv University, 1985), 48.
16. Adam Wein, "Żydzi poza rewirem żydowskim w Warszawie (1809–1862)," *Biuletyn ŻIH 41* (1962): 45–70.

17. Akta Kancerlaria Senatora Nowosilcowa 206, pp. 14–18. The same delegation made a similar request of the Grand Duke Constantine, who was military commander of the new kingdom. See Akta Kancerlaria Senatora Nowosilcowa 206, pp. 25.
18. Akta Kancelaria Senatora Nowosilcowa 206, pp. 103–4.
19. Eisenbach, *Emancipation of the Jews in Poland*, 218.
20. Eisenbach (*Emancipation of the Jews in Poland*, 218) dates the decree as May 7, 1822; however, this must be a reiteration of the July 10, 1821, decree.
21. *Dziennik Praw* 7, pp. 155–173. As justification, Alexander cited concerns about the overconcentration of Jews in the capital articulated in the 1809 decree. At the same time, Alexander permitted Jews to purchase empty lots for the construction of stone houses on any street not deemed restricted, departing slightly from the 1809 decree, which permitted such purchases on restricted streets. The tsar's apparent ignorance of the "Jewish city" decree is implied in an investigation into Jewish legal status in Warsaw from around 1816, which only mentions the 1809 restricted streets decree. See Akta Kancelaria Senatora Nowosilcowa 206, p. 90.
22. A somewhat similar policy obtained in Warsaw during the Prussian occupation, initiated in 1799.
23. The policy that Benjamin Nathans terms "selective integration" thus long preceded a similar policy implemented in the Tsarist Empire proper in the late 1850s. See *Beyond the Pale*, 45–79. On exempted families in Warsaw, see Wein, "Żydzi poza rewirem." Only two Jewish families were permitted to live on each restricted street. On 1842, see KRSW 5752. The 131 families mentioned there included a total of 705 people. By 1842, 47 out of Warsaw's 223 streets were "restricted." Over half of those streets—twenty-seven—contained Jewish enterprises.
24. KRSW 187, fol. 175.
25. The "Christian merchants" who appear in the sources seem usually to be Polish, as opposed to ethnic Germans, to judge by their surnames.
26. KRSW 187, fols. 175b–189. Conscious of the fiscal benefits of Jewish liquor concessions, the Mazovian commissioner asked that, at very least, no concessions be granted to Jews in towns formally off limits to Jewish settlement (*de non tolerandis Judaeis*), and that existing concessions be given term limits.
27. KRSW 187, fols. 182–89.
28. KRSW 6704. In 1856, the kingdom had a total of 3,707 urban taverns (1,385 of which were run by Jews) and 18,316 village taverns.
29. Frenk, "Di tsol yidn un zeyere basheftikungen,", 184–93, esp. 187.
30. Aron Alperin, *Żydzi w Łódzi: Początki gminy żydowskiej, 1780–1822* (Lodz, Poland: Wydawnictwo Archiwun Akt Dawnych M. Łódzi, 1928), 28–31.
31. AG Wil. Adm. Dobr. Wilanowski 73, pp. 9, 20, and 25. On Opatów, see Hundert, *Jews in a Polish Private Town*, 64.
32. KRSW 5914, pp. 54–55.
33. KRSW 5914, p. 51.
34. KRSW 5914, pp. 58–61. Note also the case of Samuel Moses Muscat, who asked the prefect of the Warsaw department to approve a license for his purchase of a brick home in Warsaw by appealing to his own utility to the state's treasury and inhabitants, noted in Oniszczuk, "Jews in the Duchy of Warsaw."
35. KRSW 5914, pp. 233–34.
36. KRSW 5914, pp. 161–63.

37. KRSW 5914, pp. 90–93. For other tavernkeepers, see pp. 36–83, 133, 137, 142, 144, 149.
38. A disproportionate number of petitions were from widows, who invoked their desperate familial situation. WCPL 1830–31, 331, pp. 1, 4, 9, 12, 14, 22–26; KRSW 5914, pp. 10–13, 90–91; KRSW 6704, pp. 55, 74, 133, 149, 174, 177.
39. KRSW 5914, pp. 116–20. Cited but misquoted in Wein, "Żydzi poza rewirem," 55.
40. Moshe Rosman, "The History of Jewish Women in Early Modern Poland" *Polin* 18 (2008): 25–56. For the women-as-enablers image, see Iris Parush, *Reading Jewish Women: Marginality and Modernization in Nineteenth-Century Eastern European Jewish Society*, tr. Saadya Sternberg (Waltham, MA: Brandeis University Press, 2004), and Boyarin, *Unheroic Conduct*, ch. 1. It is fascinating how Boyarin, in his otherwise brilliant and pioneering theoretical study, sometimes inadvertently quotes evidence (e.g., the Glukl of Hameln passage) that refutes the "women-as-enablers" image.
41. Glucksberg, *Rzut oka*, 37–38. The earlier, French version is published in full in Eisenbach, "Memoriał o położeniu ludności żydowskiej," 177–215. Glucksberg also pointed out that Jewish tavernkeepers were unusually frugal, and that they retained an advantage, since Jewish merchants and coachmen could not eat in Christian-owned taverns.
42. KRSW 6704, p. 89.
43. KRSW 6704, pp. 152–59.
44. KRSW 6704, pp. 77–80. Kaminski's ultimately successful petition is appended.
45. KRSW 6704, p. 258.
46. KRSW 6704, fols. 29–32. A similar incident occurred among iron traders. Hersz Aleksander Haybuszowicz informed authorities that Szmul Hersz Lantsztain had received permission to live in a house on an excluded street as a result of his separation with his wife, Sura. But he still lived with her there trading in iron products, and "had become uncivilized, walking around with a beard like a typical Jew." Haybuszowicz demanded his coreligionist's expulsion. However, authorities determined that Lantsztain's wife (actually named Szyndel) had received formal permission to trade in iron on the excluded street in 1825, that she in fact lived at a different address, and that her estranged husband lived with his mother on a permitted street. KRSW 5910, fols. 246–47.
47. Ekaterina Emeliantseva, "The House on the Corner: Frankists and Other Warsovians in the Struggle for Spatial Benefits in Late 18th-Century Warsaw (1789–92)," in Šiaučiunaitė-Verbickiene and Lempertienė, *Jewish Space*, 91–114.
48. KRSW 188, fols. 96–97; Protokoły Rady Administracyjnej Królestwa Polskiego, vols. 11–16. It should be noted that a Jewish quarter was also established in the Tsarist Empire proper, in Vilna. A copy of the decree in Yiddish and Polish, expelling Jews from houses, stores, and market stalls on five principal streets, is found in the Dubnow Papers in the YIVO archive, New York, RG 87, folder 940 II.23.
49. Compasses were established in fifteen of forty such royal towns; in one out of thirty such clergy-owned towns; and in eight of twenty such noble-owned towns.
50. The Bishop of Płock protested this state affairs, fearing that local Catholics might vandalize those portions that lay too close to a church or were fastened to poles originally used for altars, provoking Jews to profane the sacrament in revenge. KRSW, CWW 1410, pp. 67–69; Eleonora Bergman, "The *Rewir* or Jewish District and the *Eyruv*," *Studia Judaica* 5, nos. 1–2 (2002): 91. The following towns planned and mapped Jewish quarters during this period but did

not enforce them: Augustów, Biała Podlaska, Bolimów, Chorzele, Ciechanów, Czyżew, Janowo, Kielce, Krasnystaw, Kuczbork, Łosice, Płońsk, Węgrów, Wyszków, and Wyszogród. In addition, the towns Wschowa and Maków do not seem to have been able to reinstate their Jewish quarters after 1821. See Maria Łodyńska-Kosińska, ed., *Katalog rysunków architektonicznych z Akt Komisji Rządowej Spraw Wewnętrznych w Archiwum Głównym Akt Dawnych w Warszawie* (Warsaw: Państw. Wydawn. Naukowe, 1974). On the successful Jewish resistance to their implementation in Ciechanów, see Bartoszewicz, "Pojekty rewirów," 113, and Janusz Szczepański, *Społeczność żydowska Mazowsza w XIX–XX wieku* (Pułtusk, Poland: WSH, 2005), 53.

51. KRSW 188, fols. 223–26. See also fol. 98 and KRSW 6632, p. 68. These statistics, compiled by Zarządzający Wydziałem Administracyjnym Radca Stanu Biernacki, confirm the low end of Bergman's estimate that Jewish quarters existed in between 12 and 15 percent of towns in the kingdom. Bergman, "The *Rewir* or Jewish District," 86.
52. Mahler, *Hasidism and the Jewish Enlightenment*, 172.
53. 83,915 Jews resided in towns with formal Jewish quarters; another 70,694 Jews lived in towns with *de non tolerandis Judaeis* privileges or clergy-owned towns with similar residential restrictions. See KRSW 6632, p. 68.
54. Border towns lay within three miles of one of those borders. Decree issued on May 29, 1834, published in *Dziennik Praw* 16 (1834). A list of those towns is provided in KRSW 188, which, however, states the date of the decree as 1836. See also KRSW 6632, pp. 64–65 for official figures and explanations.
55. See Artur Markowski, "The *Shtetl* Space in the 19th Century: A Sociological Approach," in Šiaučiunaitė-Verbickiene and Lempertienė, *Jewish Space*, 55. See also Olga Goldberg-Mulkiewicz, "Księga pamięci ('memorbuecher') a mit żydowskiega miasteczka," *Etnografia Polska* 35, no. 2 (1991): 187–99.
56. Montefiore-St. Petersburg Archives (Sergei's batch), Privy Councilor Turkul', Document 14, pp. 226–65. Translated by Svetlana Rukhelman. Many thanks to Abigail Green for sharing these documents with me.
57. KRSW 4287, pp. 63–68.
58. Akta Administracyi Generalney Dóbr i Interessów JW Alexandry z Xiazat Lubomirskich Hrabiny Potockiey 62, p. 2.
59. AG Wil. Adm. Dobr. Wilanowski 73, pp. 3–5, 19.
60. AG Wil. Adm. Dobr. Wilanowski 73, pp. 3–5, 19.
61. WCPL 1830–31, 331, pp. 14–22.
62. Mirosław Pająk, "Spór o propinację Pińczowską: Przyczynek do charakterystyki Aleksandra Wielopolskiego," *Kieleckie Studia Historyczne* 13 (1995): 157.
63. KRSW 6744, pp. 1–12.
64. Arch. Wil. Administracja Generalna Dóbr i Interesów Aleksandry Potockiej 62, p. 10; KRSW 6744, 82, np. (tavern lease from 1832).
65. KRSW 6714, pp. 59–67.
66. KRSW 6714, pp. 3–4, 11–20. Certain urban Jewish tavernkeepers were improperly expelled after the 1840 ban on rural roadside taverns. See KRSW 6637, fol. 6 and fols. 19–20. On the special status of Chelm Jews, see Murphy, "Burghers versus Bureaucrats," 390.
67. KRSW 202, p. 155.
68. KRSW 202, p. 155.
69. KRSW 202, p. 155.
70. KRSW 202, p. 45.

71. Massalski, *Pan Podstolic*, 7–12, 98–100, 165–67.
72. KRSW 202, p. 184.
73. KRSW 6704, fols. 206–22. This was an attempt to enforce the caps on taverns stipulated in 1844, noted earlier.
74. KRSW 6704, fols. 206–222, 224–26.
75. KRSW 6704, fol. 224 (832 taverns) and fol. 300 (821 taverns).
76. KRSW 6704, fols. 206–26.
77. On state attempts to accomplish "legibility" by getting a handle on their subjects' numbers, wealth, land ownership, and so on, see James C. Scott, *Seeing Like a State: How Certain Schemes to Improve the Human Condition Have Failed* (New Haven, CT: Yale University Press, 1998), introduction. For the Jewish case in tsarist Russia, see Eugene Avrutin, *Jews and the Imperial State: Identification Politics in Tsarist Russia* (Ithaca, NY: Cornell University Press, 2010).
78. KRSW 6704, fol. 204. See also fols. 93, 97, 104.
79. For latest recent example, see Israel Bartal and David Assaf, "Shtadlanut ve-ortodoksiyah: Tsadike Polin be-mifgash im ha-zemanim ha-ḥadashim," in Rachel Elior, Israel Bartal, and Chone Shmeruk, eds., *Tsadikim ve-anshe ma'aseh: Meḥkarim be-ḥasidut Polin* (Jerusalem: Mosad Bialik, 1994), 65–90.
80. Kandel, "Nowosilców a żydzi," 142; Frenk, "Meḥiat mekhirat mashkim"; Askenazy, "Z dziejów żydów polskich," 8–9.
81. Printed in full in Mahler, "A Jewish Memorandum."
82. KRSW 6600, fols. 229–43.
83. Kandel, "Petycya 1857 r."
84. KRSW 6704, fols. 304–5.
85. B. Alexandrowicz, "Stanowisko i zasady z jakich rozważanem jest u nas oczynszowanie i gorzelnictwo," *Korespondent Handlowy Przemysłowy i Rolniczy*, 1844, nos. 24–34. Quoted in Rożenowa, *Produkcja wódki*, 151.
86. O. O., "O pijaństwie i gorzelniach pod względem gospodarstwa i moralności," *Korespondent Handlowy, Przemysłowy i Rolniczy*, 1844 no. 41, p. 3.
87. O. O., "O pijaństwie i gorzelniach.
88. F., "Odpowiedź na O. O.," *Korespondent Handlowy, Przemysłowy i Rolniczy*, 1844 no. 49, p. 3.
89. On Montefiore's humanitarian ventures in Russia and Poland, see Abigail Green, *Moses Montefiore: Jewish Liberator, Imperial Hero* (Belknap Press of Harvard University Press, 2010), 174–98, and Bartal and Assaf, "Shtadlanut ve-ortodoksiyah."
90. Montefiore-St. Petersburg archives (Sergei's batch), Privy Councilor Turkul', Document 14, pp. 226–65. In the margins, it was noted that special concessions were currently not required of Jews who ran urban taverns in other parts of the Tsarist Empire, another inconsistency.
91. KRSW 6632, pp. 82 and 90.
92. Rożenowa, *Produkcja wódki*, 243. See also article 252 in *Dziennik Praw* 65 (1866), pp. 80–81, according to which "Jews are permitted . . . to sell alcoholic drinks everywhere, in both cities and small towns, and, in the case of villages, only in those where exclusively Jews reside."

CHAPTER 4

1. Chaim Aronson, *A Jewish Life under the Tsars: The Autobiography of Chaim Aronson, 1825–1888*, tr. Norman Marsden (Totowa, NJ: Allanheld, Osmun, 1983), 21–22.

2. Aronson, *Jewish Life under the Tsars*, 21–22.
3. Aronson, *Jewish Life under the Tsars*, 19.
4. Aronson, *Jewish Life under the Tsars*, 20–21.
5. *L'exposition des abus qui se sont glisses dans l'administration de toutes les fonctions publiques, avec les moyens d'y remedier*, quoted in Wacław Tokarz, "Miscellanea: Z dziejów sprawy żydowskiej za Księstwa Warszawskiego," *Kwartalnik Historyczny* 16 (1902): 272–73. The memo may have been composed by the Polish author Julian Niemcewicz (1758–1841), a highly influential author, historian, and anti-Jewish polemicist.
6. Abraham Duker, "The Polish 'Great Emigration' and the Jews" (PhD diss., Columbia University, 1956), 41.
7. Małgorzata Karpińska, "Policje tajne w Królestwie Kongresowym," *Przegląd Historyczny* 76, no. 4 (1985): 702–3. See also Duker, "Great Emigration," 140–41. The charge is also implied by Jewish author (and maskil) Lev Levanda in his novel *Goriachee vremia* (1872). See Magdalena Opalski and Israel Bartal, *Poles and Jews: A Failed Brotherhood* (Hanover, NH: Brandeis University Press, 1992), 92. In a letter to Elye Tsherikover from September 25, 1932, the historian Emanuel Ringelblum argues, in response to Ignacy Schiper's claim that there are more important things to write about than Jewish spies, that fear of anti-Semitism must not prevent Jewish historians from addressing the role of Jews during the uprisings. Nor does the subject of Jewish spies deserve a separate chapter, which would give "a false picture of the role of the Jews" during the uprising. See Samuel Kassow, "Historiography," in Gershon Hundert, ed., *The YIVO Encyclopedia of Jews in Eastern Europe*, available online at http://www.yivo-encyclopedia.org/article.aspx/Historiography/An_Overview, accessed March 15, 2013.
8. Archiwum gminy żyd. w Warsawie (no longer extant), reprinted in Ignacy Schiper, "Z instytutu badań spraw narodowości," *Sprawy Narodowościowe* 5–6 (1930): 696. Among those murdered were Zalman Nowina and his wife, whose orphaned daughter Rebecca was later raised by Antoni Eisenbaum, director of the Warsaw Rabbinical School (in Schiper, "Z instytutu badań spraw narodowości").
9. R. F. Leslie, *Polish Politics and the Revolution of November, 1830* (Westport, CT: Greenwood, 1969).
10. Henryk Bogdański, "Pamiętnik Henryka Bogdańskiego," in Tomasz Rayski, ed., *Zbiór pamiętników do historyi powstania polskiego roku 1830–31* (Lviv, 1882), 138–39. Also quoted in Leslie, *Polish Politics*, 228.
11. Ignacy Schiper, *Żydzi Królestwa Polskiego w dobie powstania listopadowego* (Warsaw: Hoesick, 1932), 121–24; Jacob Shatzky, "Yidn un der poylisher oyfshtand fun 1831," *Historishe Shriftn* 2 (1937): 355–89. See also Abraham Duker, "Jewish Participants in the Polish November (1830–31) Insurrection: A List of 17 Names Hitherto not Recorded," in *The Abraham Weiss Jubilee Volume: Studies in His Honor Presented by His Colleagues and Disciples on the Occasion of His Completing Four Decades of Pioneering Scholarship* (New York: Abraham Weiss Jubilee Committee, 1964), 81–87.
12. KRSW 7927, pp. 12–14, lists four Jews out of forty-six suspects. There is also a list of eighteen prisoners of war that contains one Jew on p. 96.
13. Wojciech Saltera, "Żydzi wobec powstania listopadowego 1830–1831 roku- na przykładzie wojewòdztw krakowskiego i sandomierskiego," in Jacka Wijaczki and Grzegorza Miernika, eds., *Z przeszłości żydów polskich: Polityka, gospodarka,*

kultura, społeczeństwo (Krakow: Societas Vistulana, 2005), 101. See also Schiper, *Żydzi Królestwa Polskiego*,which claims that Jews in provincial towns like Hrubieszòw refused to fight in the insurrection because they were "led by certain dark tzaddikim" (p. 130), a claim that distorts a letter by Jan Czynski, in *Israel en Pologne: lettres adressées aux Archives* (Paris, 1861), 33. More moderate assessments are found in Hanna Węgrzynek, "Ludność żydowska wobec powstania listopadowego," in Jerzy Tomaszewski, ed., *Żydzi w obronie Rzeczypospolitej* (Warsaw: Cyklady, 1996), 31–42, and Jan Skarbek, "Żydzi Lublina podczas powstania listopadowego 1830–1831," in Tadeusz Radzik, ed., *Żydzi w Lublinie*, vol. 2 (Lublin: Uniwersytet Marii Curie-Skłodowskiej, 1998), 129–53. An interesting variation on this theme is found in Emanuel Ringelblum, *Żydzi w powstaniu Kościuszkowskiem* (Warsaw: Księgarnia Popularna, 1938), 34–39. Ringelblum argues that the Jewish masses (as opposed to the plutocrats) were supportive because of their hatred of the Russians. Another variation is the claim that Jews from the Tsarist Empire proper were pro-Polish during the 1830 uprising owing to their harsh experience under direct tsarist rule, while Jews in the Kingdom of Poland, who did not have reason to hate tsarist rule, were indifferent or hostile to the Polish cause. See Dawid Kandel, "Żydzi w Królestwie Polskiem po 1831 r.," *Kwartalnik Poświęcony Badaniom Przeszłości Żydów w Polsce* 2 (1913): 183–84.

14. Israel Bartal implicitly contests this view of the 1830 uprising in "Giborim o muge lev," in Israel Bartal and Israel Gutman, eds., *Kiyum ve-shever: Yehude Polin le-dorotehem* (Jerusalem: Shazar, 1997), 1:361.
15. Jacob Tugendhold, *Dumania Izraelity na warcie w pierwszych dniach grudnia 1830 roku* (Warsaw, 1831), 4.
16. Anon., "Tzy chwile z mego życia," pp. 542–43. YIVO Institute, Shatzky archive, no pagination in file.
17. KRSW 6603, 128–46. Bernard Gordon and Solomon Abramson requested a liquor monopoly concession or exemption from concession fees for their "services" during the uprising; however, their cultural profile is less certain. See KRSW 6603, 3 and 53.
18. KRSW 6603, 159.
19. KRSW 6603, 260–61.
20. Archiwum gminy żyd. w Warsawie (no longer extant), reprinted in Schiper, "Z instytutu badań spraw narodowości,," 696.
21. KRSW 7687. Two other Jews also received gold medals; three received silver medals.
22. KRSW 6603, 105–13.
23. WCPL 1830–31, 484, pp. 3–116, esp. 111–15. Also reprinted in N. M. Gelber, "Di yidn in Kalish un der oyfshtand in yanuar 1830–1831," *Lodzher Visnshaftlekhe Shriftn* 1 (1938): 261–63. Similarly, in Hrubieszòw a delegation of Jews led by a "venerable rabbi" explained to a Polish commander interested in Jewish recruits that their religion forbade them to shed blood, but promised to commit "their entire fortune" to the insurrection instead. See Czynski, *Israel en Pologne*, 33. Most Synagogue Councils offered to pay double the recruitment tax; however, it was eventually quadrupled. See also Schiper, *Żydzi Królestwa Polskiego*, 107–27, and A. N. Frenk, *Di familye Davidjohn* (Warsaw: Freyd, 1924), 27–30 and appendix II.
24. Jacob Lipschitz, *Zikhron Ya'akov* (Kaunas, n.p., 1924), 30–31. See also Israel Bartal, "Loyalty to the Crown or Polish Patriotism? The Metamorphoses of an Anti-Polish Story of the 1863 Insurrection," *Polin* 1 (2004): 81–95. For more

indications of anti-Polish sentiment among Jews in the Pale during the 1830–31 uprising, see S. Stanislawski, "From the History of the Polish Revolt in 1831" [R], *Evreiskaia Starina* 3 (1910), 419–21.

25. Memoir of Jacob ha-Levi Levin, in N. M. Gelber, *Ha-yehudim ve-ha-mered ha-polani* (Jerusalem: Bialik, 1953), 49–54, 141–42. It is estimated that a little over three hundred Jews enlisted in the national guard, while around 1,400 formed a Civil Guard. See Polonsky, *Jews in Poland and Russia*, 298.
26. Memoir of Jacob ha-Levi Levin.
27. Gelber, *Ha-yehudim ve-ha-mered ha-polani*, appendix.
28. Bogdański, "Pamiętnik Henryka Bogdanskiego," 91.
29. Jacob Glatstein, *The Glatstein Chronicles*, ed. Ruth Wisse, tr. Maier Deshell and Norbert Guterman (New Haven, CT: Yale University Press, 2010), 54. Ezekiel Kotik relates the same tradition. See *Journey to a Nineteenth-Century Shtetl*, 344.
30. M. Bereban, "Geshikhte fun Gerer Hoyf," *Undzer Ekspres*, January 13, 1933; Yitshak Alfasi, *Gur* (Tel Aviv: Sinai, 1978), 88; Dawid Kandel, "Kariera rabiniczna cadyka Icie-Majera," *Kwartalnik Poświęcony Badaniu Przeszłości Żydów w Polsce* 1, no. 2 (1912): 131–36. See also Menasheh Unger, *Pshiskhe un Kotsk* (Buenos Aires: Tsentral-Farband fun Poylishe Yidn in Argentine, 1949), 173–212.
31. Eleazar ha-Kohen, "Ets avot," in *Ḥidushe Maharaḥ* (Warsaw, 1898), 9.
32. Kandel, "Kariera rabiniczna cadyka Icie-Majera.".
33. A. Y. Bromberg, *Mi-gedole ha-ḥasidut*, vol. 18, *Bet koznits* (Jerusalem: Makhon le-Ḥasidut, 1962),104–5; Moyshe Faynkind, *Gute yidn in Poyln* (Warsaw, 1926), 255.
34. Jacob Shatzky, "Warsaw Jews in Polish Cultural Life," *YIVO Annual of Jewish Social Science* 5 (1950): 41–54.
35. On the Jews of Kotzk, see Gen. Samuel Rozycki, *Zdanie sprawy narodowi, z czynności w roku 1831* (Bourges, 1832). Quoted in Duker, *The Polish Great Emigration and the Jews*, 31. On Israel the Polish Hasid, see Kotik, *Journey to a Nineteenth-Century Shtetl*, ch. 5.
36. On R. Samuel Abba, see Efrayim Me'ir Gad Zikhlinski, *Lahav esh* (Piotrków, Poland, 1928), 230–31, 236–37.The Hasidic editor attributes this pro-Polish behavior to the tzaddik's hatred of tsarist recruitment and cantonist policies and his anger over tsarist persecution of the Ukrainian tzaddik Israel of Ruzhin. But compulsory military service in the Kingdom of Poland, introduced in September, 1843, did not involve cantonism, while Israel of Ruzhin was only arrested six years after the 1830 uprising and had purchased a palatial residence in then-Habsburg Sadhora by this time.
37. See Leslie, *Reform and Insurrection in Russian Poland*, 65–66.
38. Zikhlinski, *Lahav esh*, 237.
39. Zikhlinski, *Lahav esh*, 242.
40. See Ernest Łuniński, *Berek Joselewicz i jego syn: Zarys historyczny* (Warsaw: Orgelbrand, 1909), 58–62.
41. Adam Szymanski, "Srul of Lubartów" (1885), in Harold B. Segel, ed., *Stranger in Our Midst: Images of the Jew in Polish Literature* (Ithaca, NY: Cornell University Press, 1996), 190–97.
42. Leon Hollaenderski, *Les Israélites de Pologne* (Paris, 1846), translated by H. A. Henry in the *Jewish Chronicle*, June 23, 1863.
43. KRSW 6603, 204–8. On his sons' service in the Polish army during the rebellion, see "Miscellenea," *Kwartalnik Poświęcony Badaniu Przeszłości Żydów w Polsce* 1, no. 3:1912-13.

44. Bogdański, "Pamiętnik Henryka Bogdańskiego," 181.
45. W. B. Podlewski, "Diaryusz Waleryana Bogoryi Podlewskiego z czasów wojny narodowej z Moskwa w r. 1831," in Rayski, Zbiór Pamiętników, 486.
46. See O żydach, in appendix to Abraham Duker, "Prince Czartoryski on the Jewish Problem," in Abraham Berger, Lawrence Marwick, and Isidore S. Meyer, eds., *The Joshua Bloch Memorial Volume: Studies in Booklore and History* (New York: New York Public Library, 1960), 170.
47. Maurycy Mochnacki, "Powstania narodu polskiego w r. 1830–1," in *Dziela* (Poznań, 1863), 2:50, 66–67.
48. Ostrowski, *Pomysły o potrzebie reformy*, 82.
49. WCPL 1830–31, 221b, p. 1; WCPL 1830–31 557a, pp. 186–88; WCPL 1830–31 557b, pp. 170, 175.
50. WCPL 1830–31 557a, pp. 233–34. Szlama Szmulowicz was acquitted for lack of evidence (WCPL 1830–31 557b, p. 229). WCPL 1830–31 221a, p. 102, lists the following acquitted individuals along with their age and religious affiliation: Bonawentura Dembinski, 34, Catholic; Leopold Rosen, 20, Jew; Józef Dyderski, 45, Catholic; Michał Lindauer, 17, Jew; Józef Ritterstein, 27, Catholic; Izydor Zacharowicz, 42, Catholic; Zaley Weinberg, 45, Jew; Jakob Dobrowolski, 23, Jew; Andrzej Krauze, 51, Catholic; Andrzej Opentkowski, 27, Catholic; Herman Grafs, 16, Jew; Jan Jastrzebski, 20, Catholic; Franciszek Imijewski, 37, Catholic; Jozef Lachowicz, Catholic; Erazm Lastowiecki, 39, Catholic; Jan Skuski, 37, Catholic; Henryk Samuel Horwitz, 30, convert to Evangelicalism (Lutheranism); Daniel Rorciszewski, 52, Catholic; Jozef Lipert; Maryan Raymund Sliwowski, 36, Catholic; Leopold Zeydlitz, 30, Jew. In addition, the Jew Hersz Berkowicz Krozenberg and Józef Friedman, a Jewish convert to Catholicism, were released by secret police (WCPL 1830–31 221a, pp. 341 and 358).
51. WCPL 1830–31 221a, pp. 57–58.
52. WCPL 1830–31 557a, pp. 52–53.
53. KRSW 6603, 243–44, 248–49.
54. WCPL 1830–31 221a, 170–71.
55. WCPL 1830–31 221b, pp. 3 and 13; 557b, p. 12. Other agents included the Jews Majer Matys Harstblum, Hersz Krakowski, Leon Liberstein, Baruch Fiszel Michelsohn, and Abraham Sztarkmann.
56. Ostrowski, *Pomysły o potrzebie reformy*, 82–83; Hollaenderski, *Les Israélites de Pologne*. See also Schiper's discussion, in *Żydzi Królestwa Polskiego*, 136–37.
57. The Interior Ministry agreed he should receive compensation, but the uprising may have been suppressed before it happened. WCPL 1830–31, 274 (apparently no longer extant), printed in the appendix to Gelber, *Ha-yehudim ve-ha-mered ha-polani*, 134–49, and Jacob ha-Levi Levin's memoir, printed in that volume.
58. WCPL 1830–31, 221a, pp. 326, 340. WCPL 1830–31 557a, p. 170.
59. AGAD, KRPiS 2363, 8.
60. KRPiS 2363, 24.
61. WCPL 1830–31, 183. Report from July and August 1831.
62. WCPL 1830–31, 221a, pp. 57–58, 326, 340. WCPL 1830–31 557a, p. 170. The Jews' names were Mosiek Milszteyn and Layzer Szychta.
63. WCPL 1830–31 557b, pp. 202–8; WCPL 1830–31, 221a, pp. 57–58, 326, 340; WCPL 1830–31 557a, p. 170.
64. KRPiS 2364, 98.
65. WCPL 1830–31 114, pp. 10, 11, 13, 20, 57.

66. AGAD, KRPiS 2364, 38 and 103.
67. KRPiS 2364, 105.
68. KRPiS 2364, 94–6.
69. KRPiS 2364, 111.
70. KRPiS 2364, 162. Each person listed had a Polish name and a German alias.
71. KRPiS 2364, 192.
72. KRSW 6632, 64. Decree issued on May 29, 1834, published in *Dziennik Praw* 16 and listed in KRSW 188 (which, however, states the date of the decree as 1836).
73. WCPL 1830–31, 342, 13. See additional cases, pp. 10, 15–17, and 20.
74. AGAD, Lubomirsk z Małej Wsi 1378 (IA/72), 1–24.
75. Lubomirsk z Małej Wsi 1378 (IA/72), 1–24.
76. Lubomirsk z Małej Wsi 1378 (IA/72), 23.
77. Lubomirsk z Małej Wsi 1378 (IA/72), 24.
78. Zarząd Generał Policmajstra w Królestwie Polskim 47, 272.
79. KRSW 6637, 227–29.
80. KRSW 6637, 227–31.
81. KRSW 6637, 247–50; KRSW 6638, 18.
82. KRSW 6637, 251–55.
83. KRSW 6637, 255–58; KRSW 6638, 10 and 16.
84. Lukin, "A Russian Bureaucratic Approach," 120–21.
85. KRSW 6582, 39.
86. Józef Ignacy Kraszewski, *Para czerwona: Obrazek współczesny narysowany z natury* (Krakow: Nowej Reformy, 1905), 79–80.
87. Eisenbach, *Emancipation of the Jews in Poland*, 433–39; Abraham Duker, "Jewish Participants in the Polish Insurrection of 1863," in George Alexander Kohut, ed., *Studies and Essays in Honor of Abraham A. Neuman* (Philadelphia: E. J. Brill, 1962), 144–53; N. M. Gelber, "Onteyl fun yidn in oyfshtand fun 1863," *Lodzher Visnshaftlekhe Shriftn* 1 (1938): 264–66. On the cultural reverberations of Jewish participation, see Opalski and Bartal, *Poles and Jews: A Failed Brotherhood*, esp. 103, and Bartal, *The Jews of Eastern Europe*, 87. See also the documents in A. Eisenbach, D. Fajnhauz, and A. Wein, eds., *Żydzi a powstanie styczniowe: Materiały i dokumenty* (Warsaw: PWN, 1963); Zofia Borzymińska, *Dzieje żydów w Polsce: wybòr tekstòw żrodłowych XIX wiek* (Warsaw: Żydowski Instytut Historyczny, 1994), 113–24; and the appendix to Shatzky, *Geshikhte fun yidn in Varshe*, vol. 2.
88. Zarząd Generał Policmajstra w Królestwie Polskim 48, 768–69.
89. Zarząd Generał Policmajstra w Królestwie Polskim 48, 768–69.
90. Zarząd Generał Policmajstra w Królestwie Polskim 47, 63–64a.
91. Zarząd Generał Policmajstra w Królestwie Polskim 47, 216a. Three out of five Jews making such requests were awarded liquor concessions for the town of their choice: Abram Klejbeg, Benedykt Serwaker, and Szmul Frajlich. But Salomon Senator and Abram Lubelski had never run a tavern in a town, i.e., legally, so they were denied a concession.
92. Zarząd Generał Policmajstra w Królestwie Polskim 47, 137–38a.
93. Zarząd Generał Policmajstra w Królestwie Polskim 47, 137–38a.
94. Zarząd Generał Policmajstra w Królestwie Polskim 47, 259a–260a.
95. Zarząd Generał Policmajstra w Królestwie Polskim 47, 259a–260a.
96. Zarząd Generał Policmajstra w Królestwie Polskim 47, 628–30.
97. Zarząd Generał Policmajstra w Królestwie Polskim 48, 649–50.
98. Zarząd Generał Policmajstra w Królestwie Polskim 47, 225.

99. Zarząd Generał Policmajstra w Królestwie Polskim 47, 81–84.
100. Zarząd Generał Policmajstra w Królestwie Polskim 48, 259–60.
101. Zarząd Generał Policmajstra w Królestwie Polskim 47, 57–58.
102. Zarząd Generał Policmajstra w Królestwie Polskim 48, 508–11.
103. Zarząd Generał Policmajstra w Królestwie Polskim 48, 508–11.
104. Zarząd Generał Policmajstra w Królestwie Polskim 47, 317–19.
105. Zarząd Generał Policmajstra w Królestwie Polskim 47, 324–25a.
106. Peasants were hanged on suspicion of supporting the Russians, who had made efforts to win them over. See Leslie, *Reform and Insurrection in Russian Poland*, 217.
107. Zarząd Generał Policmajstra w Królestwie Polskim 47, 324–25a.
108. Zarząd Generał Policmajstra w Królestwie Polskim 47, 324–25a.
109. Shlomo ha-Kohen of Radomsko, *Ateret Shelomoh* (Piotrków, Poland, 1926), 85–86.
110. Zarząd Generał Policmajstra w Królestwie Polskim 48, 790–91.
111. Eisenbach, Fajnhauz, and Wein, *Żydzi a powstanie styczniowe*, 30, document no. 15. This fraternization between the Polish nobility and Jews was illustrated in a noble-inspired appeal by Jewish notables to rural Jews on March 25, 1861. Jews residing in villages, i.e., tavernkeepers, were, according to Eisenbach, "called upon to explain to the peasants that the landowners had already started fixing the rents." See Eisenbach, *Emancipation of the Jews in Poland*, 444.
112. N. M. Gelber, "A Jewess' Memoirs of the Polish Uprising of 1863," *YIVO Annual of Social Science* 13 (1965): 251 and 256.
113. H. Sutherland Edwards, *The Private History of a Polish Insurrection: From Official and Unofficial Sources*, (London, 1865), 2:20. Quoted in Leslie, *Reform and Insurrection in Russian Poland*, 215.

CHAPTER 5

1. YIVO, Guttmacher Collection, RG 27, 330, Żuromin (mislabeled "Zwromin"). Note that numerous place-names are mislabeled in the archival index; however, the mislabeled renderings are preferred here for practical purposes.
2. Guttmacher, RG 27, 330, "Zwromin."
3. On Hildesheimer and his critics, see Michael K. Silber, "The Emergence of Ultra-Orthodoxy: The Invention of a Tradition," in Jack Wertheimer, ed., *The Uses of Tradition: Jewish Continuity in the Modern Era* (New York: Jewish Theological Seminary of America, 1999), 31–37.
4. Letter excerpted in Victor Hillel Reinstein, "By the Merit of a Tzadik" (PhD dissertation, Hebrew Union College, 1978), 40. On a similarly paradoxical figure, see Joshua Shanes, "Ahron Marcus: Portrait of a Zionist Hasid," *Jewish Social Studies* 16, no. 3 (Spring/Summer 2010): 116–60.
5. YIVO, Guttmacher, RG 27.
6. *Ha-Magid* 12, March 17, 1874, 107–8.
7. A portion of the collection was brought to the Hebrew University in Jerusalem by 1939, where it remains today.
8. Operational Staff Rosenberg, an organization established by Alfred Rosenberg for the systematic plunder of the art and cultural objects belonging to Jews in Europe.
9. A small sample of correspondence (not *kvitlekh*) related to American Jewish immigrant life was published and analyzed by Zalman Reisen, in "Briv fun Amerike tsum Greyditser tsadik," *YIVO Bleter, Yorbukh fun Amopteyl* 2 (1939),

191–218. At the beginning of this project, I was helped by a fruitful collaboration with Natan Meir, who has also begun using this archive.
10. Bolesław Prus, *Placówka* (Wrocław, Poland: Siedmioróg 2000); Henry Sienkiewicz *Charcoal Sketches and Other Tales*, tr. Adam Zamoyski (London: Angel, 1990).
11. Abramovitsh, *Wishing Ring*, 164.
12. Zilberman's letter is printed in Avraham Yitzhak Bromberg, *Mi-gedole ha-ḥasidut*, vol. 24, *Ha-rav Eliyahu Gutmakher: Ha-'tsadik mi-Graidits* (Jerusalem: Makhon le-Ḥasidut, 1969), 150.
13. Elijah Guttmacher, *Tsofnat pa'neaḥ* (Brody, 1875), ch. 9, pp. 16a–17b.
14. See Bromberg, *Ha-rav Eliyahu Gutmakher*, 129–30.
15. On Eiger, see Avraham Duber Mendelsohn, *Toldot ḥemdat Shelomoh* (1922; repr. Jerusalem: Yisra'el Avraham Grinboim, 1996), 19–23.
16. Yaakov Dov Mandelboym, *Sefer ha-zikaron le-rabi Mosheh Lipshits, z"l* (New York: Hotsa'at Almanato, 1997), 867.
17. Yom-Tov Lewinsky, *Sefer zikaron le-kehilat Lomzah* (Israel: Hotsa'at Irgun Ole Lomzah be-Yisra'el l, 1952), 341. See also the Gwyneth Paltrow episode of the NBC show *Who Do You Think You Are*, Episode 207 (2011), chapter 5.
18. YIVO Archives, Guttmacher Collection, RG 27, 1873 (no location), petition by Israel Jacob ben Feiga. For the Chernobyl testimony, see Yehuda Leib ha-Kohen Fishman, *Sare ha-me'ah* (Jerusalem: Mosad Ha-Rav Kuk, 1947), 258. Quoted in Reinstein, "By the Merit of a Tzadik," 54–55. For more reports on Guttmacher's thousands of pilgrims, see Jody Elizabeth Myers, "Zevi Hirsch Kalischer and the Origins of Religious Zionism," in Francis Milano and David Sorkin, eds., *Profiles in Diversity: Jews in a Changing Europe* (Detroit: Wayne State University Press, 1998), 282 n33 (one report alleges that he received about ten thousand pilgrims over the course of a few months). See also Marcin Wodziński, *Hasidism and Haskalah in the Kingdom of Poland: A History of Conflict* (London: Littman Library of Jewish Civilization, 2005), 210 and 219.
19. Eisenbach, *Emancipation of the Jews of Poland*, 477.
20. Moses Rischin, *The Promised City: New York's Jews, 1870–1914* (1962; repr. Cambridge, MA: Harvard University Press, 1967), 23. See also Samuel Ettinger, "Demutah ha-yishuvit ve-ha-kalkalit shel yahadut Rusyah be-sof ha-me'ah ha-19," in *Ben Polin le-Rusyah*, 259 and 269.
21. Arcadius Kahan, "The Impact of Industrialization on the Jews in Tsarist Russia," in Kahan, *Essays in Jewish Social and Economic History* (Chicago: University of Chicago, 1986), 26–34. Kahan is usually careful to restrict his observations to the situation in 1897. See also Bohdan Wasiutyński, "Rola ekonomiczna żydów w Królestwie Polskiem," *Przegląd Narodowy* 4, no. 10 (October 1911): 383–414.
22. Eli Lederhendler, *Jewish Immigrants and American Capitalism, 1880–1920: From Caste to Class* (Cambridge, UK: Cambridge University Press, 2009), 21.
23. Frenk, "Di tsol yidn un zeyere basheftikungen,": 187, table 2.
24. Burszta, *Społeczeństwo i karczma*, 27 and 164.
25. Łukasiewicz, "O strukturze agrarnej Królestwa Polskiego," 296–314, esp. 302. In addition, land ownership among nonnoble townspeople, including perhaps Jews, rose by 3.5 percent, while public-owned land rose by over 1 percent. On losses incurred among the nobility see Rychlikowa, "Ziemiaństwo Polskie 1772–1944," 3–23. Rychlikowa concedes that nonnoble land ownership remained only about 15 percent of noble land ownership down to 1887, and that the most dramatic decline in noble landownership occurred only during the early twentieth century. See also Groniowski, *Kwestia agrarna w Królestwie Polskim*, 60–61 and 76–79.

26. After 1898, a government liquor monopoly was established. For details, see Yehuda Leib ben Yisra'el Lipkind, *Ha-shtiah ke-da'at* (Warsaw, 1898). Many thanks to Shaul Stampfer for bringing this work to my attention.
27. Grain exports rose in value from 4.5 million rubles in 1866 to 14 million rubles in 1871. The grain price index rose from 160 in the 1860s to 170 in the 1870s. See Jezierski, *Problemy rozwoju gospodarczego ziem Polskich*, 232–33. Łukasiewicz's price index figures seem lower; however, he only provides figures beginning in the 1870s. His figures on grain exports do show a rise throughout the 1870s despite temporary drop in 1874–76. See Łukasiewicz, *Krzyzys agrarny na ziemiach Polskich*, 59. On increases in farmed land and grain stocks, see 89–96; on the Land Credit Society and lumber prices, see 104–5.
28. Joseph Opatoshu, *In Polish Woods*, tr. Isaac Goldberg (Philadelphia: Jewish Publication Society of America, 1938), 27. Yiddish writer I. L. Peretz, whose father was one of those lumber merchants, recalls, "Whenever the wind carried the echo of the ax blows from the woods, it made me shudder." See "My Memoirs," in *The I. L. Peretz Reader*, 329.
29. Peretz, "Impressions of a Journey," 23.
30. Between 1877 and 1901, the percentage of land in the hands of large-scale landowners in the Kingdom of Poland dropped from 44.7 percent to 36.3 percent. See Łukasiewicz, *Krzyzys agrarny*, 192. On other aspects of the crisis mentioned here, see 18–24, 60, 103, 110, 128–31, 145, and ch. 5. However, urban residents, it should be noted, did benefit from lower food prices. See Łukasiewicz, *Krzyzys agrarny*, 51 and 70.
31. Peretz, "Impressions of a Journey," 20.
32. Kotik, *Journey to a Nineteenth-Century Shtetl*, 341 and 351–52.
33. Peretz, "My Memoirs," 308.
34. Guttmacher, RG 27, 628, "Piszczac."
35. Guttmacher, RG 27, 8, Uniejow.
36. Guttmacher, RG 27, 54, "Osjakow."
37. Guttmacher, RG 27, 582, "Poddebice, Russian Poland." Many renderings of village names are guesswork, based on an attempt to change renderings in the Hebrew alphabet into Polish equivalents with the aid of gazetteers. More than a few such villages seem to no longer exist.
38. Guttmacher, RG 27, 582, "Poddebice."
39. Guttmacher, RG 27, 330, "Zwromin."
40. Guttmacher, RG 27, 529, "Stawiszyn."
41. Guttmacher, RG 27, 847, "Sieradz."
42. See Cornelia Aust, "Commercial Cosmopolitans: Networks of Jewish Merchants between Warsaw and Amsterdam, 1750–1820" (Ph.D. diss., University of Pennsylvania, 2010), 240.
43. The indemnification to landowners was paid in "liquidation bonds," whose interest and amortization would be paid out of the land tax imposed on the peasants. See Kieniewicz, *Emancipation of the Polish Peasantry*, 172.
44. Łukasiewicz, *Kryzys agrarny*, 195–97. On the situation in Galicia, see Stauter-Halstead, *Nation in the Village*, 134–35.
45. For example, Jacob Katz writes that "it appears that old-style moneylending by Jews gradually declined in importance vis-à-vis the Middle Ages in both relative and absolute terms." *Tradition and Crisis: Jewish Society at the End of the Middle Ages*, tr. Bernard Dov Cooperman (Syracuse, NY: Syracuse University Press, 2000), 42. Hillel Levine is perhaps correct that "moneylending may have

been less central to the economics of Polish Jews than it had been to that of their German Jewish ancestors"; however, it remained a more important side pursuit than most historians have acknowledged. See Levine, *Economic Origins of Antisemitism*, 129–30. On the resilient image of Jews as moneylenders throughout Europe during this period, see Jerry Muller, *Capitalism and the Jews* (Princeton, NJ: Princeton University Press, 2010), esp. 27.

46. Guttmacher, RG 27, 196, "Dwarta." See also "Abraham Isaac ben Feigele, to place in the heart of the *landrot* and the nobleman [the desire] to give him a tavern concession"; and "Jacob ben Zosha Esther, to attain a concession on a tavern, for this will be their livelihood." RG 27, 451, "Village Laski near Kepno," and RG 27, 737, "Huta Krolewska."
47. Guttmacher, RG 27, 253, "Włocławek."
48. Guttmacher, RG 27, 878, no location.
49. Guttmacher, RG 27, 771, "Krepice" (two petitions); 772, "Krepice"; 799, "Rachiaz"; 780, "Radomsko"; 781, "Radomsko 2"; 822, "Rypin"; 779, "Rodolrowicz village, near Plesz"; 743, "Konskie"; 670, "Kozienice"; 644, 454, "Modrzew, Russian Poland"; "Przedborz"; 624. "Piotrkow" (two petitions); 612, "Piaseczno"; 573, "Olkusz" (two petitions); 589, "Poczynow" 528, "Stawnica"; 449, "Lora Huta village"; 377, "Turek"; 360 (Meir b. Nisel and b. ha-Rav Mo. Joseph Yoska of Lissa, *av bet din* of the holy community of Kleczów. "Chęciny"; 856, "Sielerka village"; 631, "Plawno."
50. Guttmacher, RG 27, 781, "Radomsko 2."
51. Guttmacher, RG 27, 628, "Piszczac."
52. Guttmacher, RG 27, 760, "Kramsk village, near Konin."
53. Guttmacher, RG 27, 856, "Sielerka village."
54. Guttmacher, RG 27, 471, "Miodzina village."
55. Guttmacher, RG 27, 592, "Polkow village, near Wegrow."
56. Guttmacher, RG 27, 232, "Wislica."
57. Guttmacher, RG 27, 528, "Stawnica, land of Poland."
58. Guttmacher, RG 27, 528, "Stawnica, land of Poland."
59. Guttmacher, RG 27, 498, "Nieszawa"; 275, "Wola; 343. Zloczow."
60. Guttmacher, RG 27, 513., "Sampolna, Russian Poland."
61. Guttmacher, RG 27, 613, "Piaseczno, near Warsaw."
62. Guttmacher, RG 27, 421, "Lodz 2."
63. Guttmacher, RG 27, 736, "Kajowka village, near Makow."
64. Guttmacher, RG 27, 408, "Jaworzno village."
65. Guttmacher, RG 27, 854, "Siedlimowo village."
66. Guttmacher, RG 27, 72, "Badkowo village, near Nieszawa," two nearly identical petitions.
67. Guttmacher, RG 27, 247, "Village Wieprzszow."
68. Guttmacher, RG 27, 436, "Lowicz."
69. Guttmacher, RG 27, 436, "Lowicz."
70. Guttmacher, RG 27, 727, "Kutno (Kutna) 2." Moses ben Sarna was in a bind because the owner of the house he was renting did not want him running a tavern there anymore, possibly out of moral repugnance. 847, "Sieradz."
71. Guttmacher, RG 27, 673, "Kazimierz."
72. Guttmacher, RG 27, 463. "Morwice village, near Cracow." On the temperance movement and its clash with Jewish tavernkeeping, see Himka, "Ukrainian-Jewish Antagonism," and Stauter-Halstead, *Nation in the Village*, 50.

73. Katz, *Tradition and Crisis*, 49–50, and notes on page 278. Katz traces the earliest monopolistic (*ḥazakah*) ordinance back to 1596, in the minutes of the Lithuanian Council. "Lest money fall into Jewish hands" is a stock phrase, in this instance attributed to R. Solomon Luria.
74. Guttmacher, RG 27, 378, "Turka."
75. Guttmacher, RG 27, 582, "Poddebice."
76. Guttmacher, RG 27, 810, "Russocice."
77. Guttmacher, RG 27, 396, "Czechowice." See also Abraham ben Rebekah's petition in 571, "Ligota."
78. Guttmacher, RG 27, 833, "Szopienice."
79. Guttmacher, RG 27, 609, "Pultusk."
80. Guttmacher, RG 27, 800, "Rawa Mazowiecka, near Warsaw." A tavernkeeper from Warta's entire livelihood was imperiled when his gentile creditor threatened to foreclose on his house, which contained his tavern. See Guttmacher, RG 27, 270, "Warta."
81. Guttmacher, RG 27, 179, "Dobra."
82. Guttmacher, RG 27, 638; Box 17, Misc. "Płock." One petitioner asked the tzaddik to pray that the judge order the nobles to compensate him for "drinks that they took from him for the past four years." A Jewish tavern sublessee who was not permitted to use the tavern's cellar by the nobleman who owned it admitted that he had already signed the contract. (Guttmacher, RG 27, 343, "Zloczow"). Others realized they did not have a case, and sought only a miracle.
83. For a case of a Jew's tavern lease made available after a fire, see Moses ben Sarah, in Guttmacher, RG 27, 847, "Sieradz." For Nathan Nata of Bielany village's encroachment case, see Guttmacher, RG 27, folder 92.
84. Guttmacher, RG 27, 503, "Nechlyn village."
85. Guttmacher, RG 27, 745, "Klobucko 1."
86. Guttmacher, RG 27, 745, "Klobucko 1"; 746, "Klobucko 2." These are actually two petitions, possibly reflecting two separate pilgrimages.
87. He also asked the tzaddik to pray for the health of his wife, Mindel, and their daughter Leah, and asked that "God bring a suitable match for her quickly and a long life, for she has been widowed a second time and she is thirty-two years old and has small children." Finally, for the sake of the prospective groom's room and board (*kest*), Moses needed to collect about 150 rubles from a local nobleman—"may God give us the ability to collect it quickly in order to redeem the jewelry of his widowed daughter, may she live." Guttmacher, RG 27, 800, "Rawa Mazowiecka, near Warsaw."
88. Guttmacher, RG 27, 832, "Szomierki" (possibly Szombierki Bytom, near Częstochowa).
89. Guttmacher, RG 27, 404, "Częstochowa 4." In Bochlacz, a town in Galicia, a tavernkeeper named Isaiah Moses ben Rebekah was informed on by an "evil gentile," and his tavern was taken away (66, "Bochlacz").
90. Guttmacher, RG 27, 3, "Golin/Golina."
91. Guttmacher, RG 27, 3, "Golin/Golina." For more on Jewish informers, see Ruth Wisse, "The Jewish Informer as Extortionist and Idealist," in Richard L. Cohen, Jonathan Frankel, Stefani Hoffman, eds., *Insiders and Outsiders: Dilemmas of East European Jewry* (Oxford: Littman Library of Jewish Civilization, 2010), ch. 11.
92. Guttmacher, RG 27, 543, "Strykow." The term *admor* is an acronym for *Adonenu, Morenu, ve-Rabbenu*, meaning "our lord, teacher, and rabbi." It is commonly used to refer to Hasidic leaders.

93. See Moshe Rosman, *Founder of Hasidism: A Quest for the Historical Ba'al Shem Tov* (Berkeley: University of California, 1996), 71, and Rosman, "History of Jewish Women in Early Modern Poland."
94. Guttmacher, RG 27, 339, "Zwolen"; 454, "Modrzew, Russian Poland"; 612, "Piaseczno."
95. Guttmacher, RG 27, 456, "Modrzejow, near Myslowice."
96. Guttmacher, RG 27, 879, no location given.
97. Guttmacher, RG 27, 875, no location given.
98. Guttmacher, RG 27, 696, "Kaluszn."
99. Guttmacher, RG 27, 772, "Krzepice."
100. Guttmacher, RG 27, 772, "Krzepice 2."
101. Guttmacher, RG 27, 780, "Radomsko."
102. S. Y. Abramovitsh, "The Brief Travels of Benjamin the Third," in Abramovitsh, *Tales of Mendele the Book Peddler*, 306.
103. *The Complete Works of Isaac Babel*, ed. Nathalie Babel, trans. Peter Constantine (New York: Norton, 2002), 51.
104. Burszta, *Społeczeństwo i karczma*, 200–201, quoting *Pregląd Tygodniowy* 10 (1872).
105. Smoleński, *Stan i sprawa żydów polskich*, 13.
106. Guttmacher, RG 27, 868, "Srodula village/Sosnowiece vicinity."

CHAPTER 6

1. Ostrowski, *Pomysły o potrzebie reformy*, 75–76; 168–69.
2. Alina Cala, *The Image of the Jew in Polish Folk Culture* (Jerusalem: Magnes, 1995), 24.
3. Eisenbach, *Emancipation of the Jews*, 1.
4. For a summary of publicist proposals, see Gelber, "She'elat ha-yehudim be-Polin"; Eisenbach, *Emancipation of the Jews in Poland*, 181–96; and Levine, *Economic Origins of Antisemitism*, 191–231. On the failure of artisan schools, see Eisenbach, ibid., 265–66.
5. Węgrzynek, "Zajęcia rolnicze," 87–103.
6. For an overview of colonization initiatives, see Shatzky, "An Attempt at Jewish Colonization." On similar projects in the early twentieth century, involving a surprising degree of coordination between the Soviet regime and the American Joint Distribution Committee, see Jonathan Dekel-Chen, *Farming the Red Land: Jewish Agricultural Colonization and Local Soviet Power, 1924–1941* (New Haven, CT: Yale University Press, 2005). On the agricultural efforts of proto- and early Zionists, see Israel Oppenheim, *The Struggle of Jewish Youth for Productivization: The Zionist Youth Movement in Poland* (Boulder, CO: East European Monographs, 1989).
7. AGAD, CWW 1419, 2–5. Decreed by Tsar Alexander I on March 12, 1823. Jews were also allowed to become artisans.
8. Wodziński, "Clerks, Jews, and Farmers," *Jewish History* 21:3/4 (2007), 290.
9. CWW 1419, 12–39.
10. Eisenbach, *Emancipation of the Jews of Poland*, 267 and 303.
11. KRSW 6632, 93.
12. Jacob Tugendhold, *Skazówki prawdy i zgody* (Warsaw, 1844), 91–92, with an approbation by the chief rabbi of Warsaw, Ḥayyim Davidsohn.

13. Decree printed in full in the appendix to Frenk, *Di familye Davidzohn*, xi–xx. For a discussion of a similar appeal in Germany during this period, see Penslar, *Shylock's Children*, esp. 86–88. But note that its main proponent, Ludwig Philippson, only issued his proclamations about the need for a Jewish return to the soil in 1848, several years after his coreligionists in Eastern Europe had done so.
14. AGAD, PRAKP 5, p. 165; 14, pp. 153, 195–96; 15, pp. 393, 679; 16, pp. 10–11.
15. KRSW 6596, 138; PRAKP 15, p. 679; Shatzky, "An Attempt At Jewish Colonization," 49.
16. Calculations based on estimates by Julian Bartyś, "Stan ilościowy i struktura żydowskiego osadnictwa rolniczego w Królestwie Polskim w okresie przeduwłaszczeniowym," *Biuletyn ŻIH* 43–44 (1962):18–40. These numbers, based on official compilations, contradict those cited by Eisenbach in *Emancipation of the Jews of Poland*, 268, table 1, based allegedly on the same data (for some reason, Eisenbach only counts 2,275 colonists). See also, with equal caution, Shatzky, "An Attempt at Jewish Colonization," 44–50.
17. KRSW 202, 165–88.
18. KRSW 202, 165–88.
19. Montefiore-St. Petersburg archives, Document 2, pp. 6–32. Trans. Svetlana Rukhelman.
20. Glucksberg, *Rzut oka*, 15–23.
21. KRSW 6600, 255–56.
22. KRSW 6597, 67a–71a, 87a.
23. KRSW 6597, 138b.
24. KRPiS 1972, 37–8, 73.
25. Bartyś, "Stan ilościowy," 29.
26. KRPiS 1972, 37–38, 73.
27. KRSW 6597 242a–285b.
28. KRSW 6597 208a–229a.
29. Julian Ursyn Niemcewicz, "The Year 3333, or An Incredible Dream," in Segel, *Stranger in Our Midst*, 66.
30. Prus, *Placówka*, 96–97.
31. Rychlikowa, "Ziemiaństwo Polskie 1772–1944," 12.
32. Guttmacher, RG 27, 363, "Village Chrystos near Widawa."
33. Guttmacher, RG 27, 763, "Klodawa, Poland." The term *admor shelita* is an acronym for *adoneinu, moreinu, ve-rabbeinu she-yehiyeh li-yomim tovim arukhim*, meaning "our lord, teacher, and rabbi, may he live long."
34. Guttmacher, RG 27, 519, "Sobkow."
35. Guttmacher, RG 27, 462, "Village of Morower."
36. Guttmacher, RG 27, 455, "Modrzew."
37. Guttmacher, RG 27, 727, "Kutno (Kutna)2."
38. Guttmacher, RG 27, 648, "Cofter, n. Wieruszow."
39. Guttmacher, RG 27, 802, "Rozprza (Poland)."
40. KRSW 202, 166–89.
41. Guttmacher, RG 27, 243, "Wychoszki, near Sieradz."
42. Guttmacher, RG 27, 873, "Kobsichen."
43. Guttmacher, RG 27, 708, "Konin"; 701, "Kamiensk/Kaminsk."
44. Guttmacher, RG 27, 375, "Village Tom, n. Łęczycza."
45. Guttmacher, RG27, 313, "Zagórów."

46. Guttmacher, RG27, 196, "Dwarta." See also 626, "Piotrkow (Kujawski?)"; and 782, "Radomsko 3."
47. Guttmacher, RG27, 446. "Lask 2" (Nehemia David ben Sharna).
48. Guttmacher, RG27, 829, "Szczakowa village, near Cracow." Mendel ben Leah had already spent a good deal paying off informers. See 685, "Kalisz 2."
49. Simḥa Bunem ben Golda Feiga claimed he had to smuggle because three competitors had set up a store near his and were cutting into his profits. Moses Mordecai ben Sarah had no means of support other than tobacco that was "considered treyf" (not kosher, i.e., illegal). Isaiah ben Sarah had "orphans who depend on him." Guttmacher, RG27, 428, "Lodz 2"; 452. "Lubicz or Lowicz"; 731, "Kolo" 2.
50. Guttmacher, RG27, 626, "Piotrkow (Kujawski?)"; 787, "Radzewo/Radziejow."
51. Guttmacher, RG27, 688. "Kalisz 5." Solomon Tzevi ben Kreindel was currently imprisoned in Vienna on smuggling charges. 873, no location.
52. Guttmacher, RG 27, 317, "Zawoja near Makow Podhalanski."
53. Guttmacher, RG 27, 317, "Zawoja near Makow Podhalanski."
54. Quoted in Kandel, "Nowosilców a żydzi," 152–54.
55. There is some dispute over the date of the decree in the secondary literature, but the most accurate source, *Dziennik Praw* 33 (1843), p. 55, cites the tsar's decree as dated December 24, 1843. On the recruitment process itself, see Polonsky, *Jews in Poland and Russia*, 301; François Guesnet, *Polnische Juden im 19. Jahrhundert* (Cologne: Böhlau, 1998), 183; and Yohanan Petrovsky-Shtern, *Jews in the Russian Army, 1827–1917* (Cambridge, UK: Cambridge University Press, 2009), esp. 28–29. The Jewish community's quota of new recruits was set at 950 as of 1845.
56. KRSW 5911, fols. 54–56.
57. KRSW 5911, fols. 75–76. After 1848, Jewish veterans were at least allowed to settle in any Jewish quarter in the kingdom. See KRSW 6632, p. 71.
58. See Polonsky, *Jews in Poland and Russia*, 301; Guesnet, *Polnische Juden im 19. Jahrhundert*, 183; and Petrovsky-Shtern, *Jews in the Russian Army*, esp. 28–29. On the reverberations in Jewish literature, see Olga Litvak, *Conscription and the Search for Modern Russian Jewry* (Bloomington: Indiana University Press, 2006). Pioneering conceptual work on the episode was done by Michael Stanislawski, in *Tsar Nicholas I and the Jews*.
59. KRSW 6630, fol. 84–89, dated June 5, 1845. Also cited in Shatzky, "An Attempt at Jewish Colonization," 51, albeit without documentation. For a sketch of the Polish recruitment laws, see Jakób Kirszrot, *Prawa żydów w Królestwie Polskiem* (Warsaw: Nakład Zarządu Warszawskiej gminy Starozakonnych, 1917), 138–47.
60. See for example Guttmacher, RG 27, 233, "Wielun": Isaac Meir ben Pesa "to go free from the hands of the soldiers, for I already escaped abroad but returned to my country because I wanted to be a Jew." See also the petition by Elkhanan Abraham ben Gitel: "May God help him, for he escaped from Poland because of the army people, and his wife and children are in Poland." Guttmacher, RG 27,, 405, "Częstochowa 3."
61. Guttmacher, RG 27, 270, "Wehert/Warta."
62. Guttmacher, RG 27, 746,"Klobuck 2."
63. Guttmacher, RG 27, 270, "Wehert/Warta," Gitel bat Shayna and Abraham ben Esther.
64. Guttmacher, RG 27, 831, "Szyszyno."
65. Guttmacher, RG 27, 233, "Wielun."

66. Guttmacher, RG 27, 11 "Ozarkow.".
67. Guttmacher, RG 27, 771, "Krzepice."
68. Guttmacher, RG 27, 199, "Warta 3."
69. Guttmacher, RG 27, 432, "Lodz"; 253, "Włocławek"; 256, "Węgrow"; 303, "Warsaw 12"; 405; "Częstochowa 3"; 432, "Lodz."
70. Guttmacher, RG 27, 8, "Uniejow." See also 253, "Włocławek," where Jacob ben Feiga, a horse trader, complains "I was a soldier in the Russian army for fifteen years, and now I am having no success."
71. Guttmacher, RG 27, 718, "Kvioli/ Kowal 1."
72. Guttmacher, RG 27, 848, "Sieradz 2."
73. Guttmacher, RG 27, 405, "Częstochowa 3."
74. Guttmacher, RG 27, 763, "Klodawa, Poland."
75. Guttmacher, RG 27, 269, "Wola Forest."
76. Guttmacher, RG 27, 411, "Janow."
77. Zarząd Generał Policmajstra w KP 48, pp. 376–78.
78. Aleksander Świętochowski, "Żyd w karczmie i żyd w szkole," *Prawda*, November 26, 1881, 565–66. For more on Świętochowski's admittedly complex views on Jews, see Theodore Weeks, *From Assimilation to Antisemitism: The "Jewish Question" in Poland, 1850–1914* (DeKalb: Northern Illinois University Press, 2006), 82.
79. Klemens Junosza, "Our Jews in Towns and Villages," in Segel, *Stranger in Our Midst*, 188–89.
80. On educational projects for Jews in the kingdom, see most recently Polonsky, *Jews in Poland and Russia*, 291–99. See also Shatzky, *Yidishe bildungs-politik in Poyln*, esp. 13–48. On the differences between reform initiatives in the Russian and Polish cases, see Petrovsky-Shtern, *Jews in the Russian Army*, 26–27.
81. Jewish enrollment in the kingdom's three elementary public schools for Jewish boys in 1820 amounted to three hundred students. There were five elementary public schools for Jews by 1825 with a total enrollment of 432 students, which remained stagnant for the next fifteen years. Several private Jewish elementary schools were set up in Warsaw, Częstochowa, and Lublin. Jews also attended Polish private elementary schools, with Jewish enrollment reaching eighty-one by 1839. See Eisenbach, *Emancipation of the Jews of Poland*, 242–44, and Sabina Levin, "Bate sefer li-vne dat Mosheh be-Varshah be-1818–1830," *Gal-Ed* 1 (1973): 63–100. See also Zofia Borzymińska, *Szkolnictwo żydowskie w Warszawie, 1831–1870* (Warsaw: Żydowski Instytut Historyczny, 1994).
82. Eisenbach, *Emancipation of the Jews of Poland*, 242–44.
83. Shmuel Feiner, "The Pseudo-Enlightenment and the Question of Jewish Modernization," *Jewish Social Studies*, n.s., 3, no. 1 (1996): 62–88; Feiner, "Towards a Historical Definition of Haskalah," in Shmuel Feiner and David Sorkin, eds., *New Perspectives on the Haskalah* (London: Littman, 2001), 185; Michael Stanislawski, *For Whom Do I Toil? Judah Leib Gordon and the Crisis of Russian Jewry* (New York: Oxford University Press, 1988), 4.
84. M. Stanislawski, *For Whom Do I Toil?*, 4.
85. Levin, "Bate sefer," 88. Levin speculates that Tugendhold did not want to step on the toes of traditional Jewish elementary school teachers (*melamdim*). Nathan Glucksberg, another integrationist, supported this decision (89–90).
86. El'azar Tahlgrin, *Tokhaḥat musar: Hu sefer tehilim* (Warsaw, 1854), 9; 28.
87. KRSW 6630, fols. 84–89.
88. KRSW 6630, fols. 84–89.

89. Shatzky, *Yidishe bildungs-politik in Poyln*, 236, document 6.
90. Examples of vocal Hasidic opponents of secular education include R. Isaac of Warka, R. Israel of Ruzhin, and R. Yerahmiel Israel Isaac of Aleksander. On opposition to integrationists, see Bergman, "The Synagogue as a House of Elections," 72. Elyakim accused them of rigging elections to the Warsaw Synagogue Council. On Winawer, see H. M. Winawer, *The Winawer Saga* (London: H. M. Winawer, 1994), 14–26. Winawer was accorded a special privilege for selling liquor wherever he resided, meaning on restricted streets, in 1839. He owned houses at 1091 and 1092 Twarda Street, 2645 and 2646 Mariensztadt Street, 1798 Franciszkańska Street, and at 247 Mostowa Street, the former Hospital of Św. Łazarz. For a contemporary attempt to equate secularization with Christianization, see Talal Assad, *Formations of the Secular: Christianity, Islam, Modernity* (Stanford, CA: Stanford University Press, 2003). For an attempt to equate the aims of Polish reformers with Christianization, see Marcin Wodzinski, "'Civil Christians': Debates on the Reform of the Jews in Poland, 1789-1830, tr. By Claire Rosenson, in Ben Nathans and Gabriella Safran, eds., *Culture Front: Representing Jews in Eastern Europe* (PA: University of Pennsylvania Press, 2008), 46-76.
91. On these institutions, see Wodziński, *Hasidism and Haskalah in the Kingdom of Poland*. However, I must disagree with Wodziński's application of the label "maskil" to figures like Tugendhold. For more on Polish Jewish integrationists, see most recently Michał Galas, *Rabin Markus Jastrow i jego wizja reformy judaizmu. Studium z dziejów judaizmu w XIX wieku* (Kraków, 2007); and Agnieszka Jagodzińska, *Pomiędzy. Akulturacja Żydów Warszawy w drugiej połowie XIX wieku* (Wrocław 2008). For reports from specific communities, see esp. *Jutrzenka* 7 (1861):52–53; *Jutrzenka* 9 (1861): 68–69; *Jutrzenka* 25 (1862): 196.
92. *Jutrzenka* 13 (1862): 100.
93. See, for example, *Jutrzenka* 23 (1861): 184.
94. Guttmacher, RG 27, 232, "Wislica."
95. Guttmacher, RG 27, 726, "Kutno (Kutna)."
96. For an example of hostile attitudes toward state-sponsored schools in the Pale of Settlement, see Sholem Aleichem, *From the Fair*, 79–84.
97. KRSW 5914, 55.
98. KRSW 6603, 128–46.

CONCLUSION

1. Quoted in Burszta, *Społeczeństwo i karczma*, 229–30.
2. Marian Piechal, "Yankel's Last Concert," tr. Segal, in Segel, *Stranger in Our Midst*, 383.

BIBLIOGRAPHY

ARCHIVAL COLLECTIONS

Archiwum Główne Akt Dawnych (AGAD), Komisji Rządowej Spraw Wewnętrznych (KRSW): 187, 188, 202, 4287, 5752, 5910, 5911, 5914, 6582, 6596, 6597, 6600, 6603, 6630, 6632, 6634, 6635, 6637, 6638, 6700, 6704, 6714, 6744, 7687, 7927.

AGAD KRSW/KRPiS: 1849, 1972, 2363, 2364.

AGAD, Akta Kancerlaria Senatora Nowosilcowa: 206.

AGAD, Arch. Wil. Administracja Generalna Dóbr i Interesów Aleksandry Potockiej: 62, 82.

AGAD, Archiwum Gospodarcze Wilanowe, Administracja Dóbr Opatówskich: I/83.

AGAD, Rada Ministów Księstwa Warszawskiego: 165.

AGAD, Protokoły Rady Administracyjnej Królestwa Polskiego (PRAKP): vols. 11–16.

AGAD, Zarząd Generał Policmajstra w Królestwie Polskim: 47, 48

AGAD, AG Wil. Administracja Dóbr Wilanowskich: 62.

AGAD, Centralne Władze Wyznaniowe (CWW): 1871, 1433,1419,1409,1410.

AGAD, Lubomirsk z Malej Wsi: 1348, 1352, 1378, 1405

AGAD, Władze Centralne Powstanie Listopadego 1830–31 (WCPL 1830–31): 557a–b, 229, 221a–b, 341, 358, 114.

YIVO Archives, Eliyahu Guttmacher Collection, RG 27: file nos. 628, 8, 54, 582, 847, 330, 253, 878, 771, 781, 628, 760, 856, 471, 592, 232, 528, 498, 275, 343, 513, 421, 736, 408, 854, 72, 247, 436, 727, 847, 673, 463, 378, 582, 609, 810, 396, 571, 800, 270,179, 638, 343; folders 92, 503, 745, 746, 800, 833, 832, 404, 3, 339, 454, 612, 456, 879, 875, 696, 772, 772, 780, 198, 435, 625, 314, 624, 726, 766, 685, 880, 847, 824, 774, 877, 363,763, 519, 462, 455, 727, 648, 802, 243, 873, 708, 701. 375, 313, 196, 626, 782, 446, 829, 685, 428, 452, 731, 626, 787, 688, 873, 317, 317, 233, 405, 270, 746, 270, 831, 233, 11, 771, 199, 432, 253, 256, 303, 405, 432, 8, 253, 718, 848, 405, 763, 269, 411, 232, 726, 543, 196.

YIVO Archives, Simon Dubnow Collection: II:7.

YIVO Archives, Simon Dubnow Collection: RG 87, I. 18, II.23.

YIVO Archives, Shatzky Collection, np.

Montefiore-St. Petersburg Archives (Sergei's batch), Privy Councilor Turkul': documents 2 and 14. Translated by Svetlana Rukhelman.

PERIODICALS (PRE-WORLD WAR II)

Biblioteka Warszawska
Dziennik Praw
Izraelita
Jutrzenka

Ha-Magid
Prawda
Ha-Tsefirah
Undzer Ekspres

PUBLISHED WORKS

Abramovitsh, S. Y. "Of Bygone Days." Translated by Raymond Sheindlin. In *A Shtetl and Other Yiddish Novellas*, ed. Ruth Wisse, 249–358. Detroit: Wayne State University Press, 1986.

Abramovitsh, S. Y. *Tales of Mendele the Book Peddler: Fishke the Lame and Benjamin the Third*. Edited by Dan Miron and Ken Freiden. Translated by Ted Gorelick and Hillel Halkin. New York: Schocken, 1996.

Abramovitsh, S. Y. *The Wishing Ring*. Translated by by Michael Wex. Syracuse, NY: Syracuse University Press, 2003.

Abramowicz, Hirsz. *Profiles of a Lost World: Memoirs of East European Jewish Life before World War II*. Translated by Eva Zeitlin Dobkin. Detroit: Wayne State Universtiy Press and YIVO, 1999..

Alfasi,Yitshak. *Gur*. Tel Aviv: Sinai, 1978.

Allen, Douglas. *The Institutional Revolution: Measurement and the Economic Emergence of the Modern World*. Chicago: University of Chicago Press, 2012.

Alperin, Aron. *Żydzi w Łódzi: Początki gminy żydowskiej, 1780–1822*. Lodz, Poland: Wydawnictwo Archiwun Akt Dawnych M. Łódzi, 1928.

Anczyc, Władysław. *Pijaństwo: Zguba i nędza włościan*. Warsaw, 1867.

Aronson, Chaim. *A Jewish Life under the Tsars: The Autobiography of Chaim Aronson, 1825–1888*. Translated by Norman Marsden. Totowa, NJ: Allanheld, Osmun, 1983.

Askenazy, Szymon. "Z dziejów żydów polskich w dobie Księstwa Warszawskiego." *Kwartalnik Poświęcony Badaniu Przeszłości żydów w Polsce* 1, no. 1 (1912): 8–9.

Assaf, David, Israel Bartal, and Elchanan Reiner, eds. *Within Hasidic Circles: Studies in Hasidism in Memory of Mordecai Wilensky*. Jerusalem: Bialik Institute, 1999.

Aust, Cornelia. "Commercial Cosmopolitans: Networks of Jewish Merchants between Warsaw and Amsterdam, 1750–1820." PhD diss., University of Pennsylvania, 2010.

Avrutin, Eugene. *Jews and the Imperial State: Identification Politics in Tsarist Russia*. Ithaca, NY: Cornell University Press, 2010.

Ayerst, W. *The Jews of the Nineteenth Century: A Collection of Essays, Reviews, and Historical Notices*. London, 1847.

Babel, Isaac. *The Complete Works of Isaac Babel*. Edited by Nathalie Babel. Translated by Peter Constantine. New York: Norton, 2002.

Bakhtin, Mikhail. *Rabelais and His World*. Translated by Helene Iswolsky. Cambridge, MA: MIT Press, 1968.

Bałaban, Majer. *Dzieje żydów w Galicyi*. Lviv: Nakł. Księgarni Polskiej B. Połonieckiego, 1914.

Baranowski, Bohdan. *Polska karczma, restauracja, kawiarnia*. Wrocław, Poland: Zakład Narodowy im. Ossolińskich, 1979.

Barnai, Ya'akov. *Igrot ḥasidim me-Erets Yisra'el*. Jerusalem: Yad Yitshak Ben-Tsvi, 1980.

Bartal, Israel. "Giborim o muge lev." In *Kiyum ve-shever: Yehude Polin le-dorotehem*, edited by in Israel Bartal and Israel Gutman, 1:353–67. Jerusalem: Shazar, 1997.

Bartal, Israel. *The Jews of Eastern Europe, 1772–1881*. Translated by Chaya Naor. Philadelphia: University of Pennsylvania Press, 2005.

Bartal, Israel. "Loyalty to the Crown or Polish Patriotism? The Metamorphoses of an Anti-Polish Story of the 1863 Insurrection." *Polin* 1 (2004): 81–95.
Bartal, Israel, and David Assaf, "Shtadlanut ve-ortodoksiyah: Tsadike Polin be-mifgash im ha-zemanim ha-ḥadashim." *Tsadikim ve-anshe ma'aseh: Meḥkarim be-ḥasidut Polin*, edited by Rachel Elior, Israel Bartal, and Chone Shmeruk, 65–90. Jerusalem: Mosad Bialik, 1994.
Bartoszewicz, Henryk. "Projekty rewirów dla ludnośći żydowskiej w miastach mazowieckich 1807–1830." *Rocznik Mazowiecki* 18 (2006): 104–20.
Bartoszewski, Władysław T., and Antony Polonsky, eds. *The Jews in Warsaw: A History*. Oxford: Blackwell, 1991.
Bartyś, Julian. "Stan ilościowy i struktura żydowskiego osadnictwa rolniczego w Królestwie Polskim w okresie przeduwłaszczeniowym." *Biuletyn ŻIH* 43–44(1962):18–40.
Beilin, S. "From the Historical Journals: Awaiting the King's Mercy, 1816-1818" [R], *Evreiskaia Starina V* (1912), 340-1.
Ben-Sasson, Haim Hillel. "Takanot isure shabat shel Polin u-mashma'utan ha-ḥevratit ve-ha-kalkalit." *Zion* 21 (1956): 183–206.
Bentham, Jeremy. *The Correspondence of Jeremy Bentham*. Edited by Ian R. Christie. 10 vols. London: Athlone, 1971.
Bergman, Eleonora. *"Nie masz bóżnicy powszechnej": Synagogi i domy modlitwy w Warszawie od końca XVIII do początku XIX wieku*. Warsaw: Wydaw. DIG, 2007.
Bergman, Eleonora. "The *Rewir* or Jewish District and the *Eyruv*." *Studia Judaica* 5, nos. 1–2 (2002): 85–97.
Bergman, Eleonora."The Synagogue as a House of Elections." In *Jewish Space in Central and Eastern Europe Day-to-Day History*, edited by Jurgita Šiaučiunaitė-Verbickiene and Larisa Lempertienė, 67–73. Newcastle, UK: Cambridge Scholars, 2007.
Beri'ah, Moses Elyakim. *Be'er Mosheh*. Józefów, Poland, 1858.
Bezalel ben Solomon. *Korban shabat*. Warsaw, 1873.
Birkenthal, Dov-Ber. *The Memoirs of Ber of Bolechow, 1723–1805*. Translated by M. Vishnitzer. Oxford: Oxford University Press, 1922.
Birkenthal, Dov-Ber. *Zikhronot R. Dov mi-Boliḥov (483–565)*. Edited by M. Wischnitzer. Jerusalem: n.p., 1968.
Birnbaum, Pierre, and Ira Katznelson, eds. *Paths to Emancipation: Jews, States, and Citizenship*. Princeton, NJ: Princeton University Press, 1995.
Bloch, Jan. *Finanse Kr. Polskiego za cały czas istnienia skarbu Królestwa od d. 1 czerwca 1815 do 31 grudnia 1866 r.* Warsaw, 1883.
Blum, Jerome. *The End of the Old Order in Rural Europe*. Princeton, NJ: Princeton University Press, 1978.
Bogdański, Henryk. "Pamiętnik Henryka Bogdańskiego." In *Zbiór pamiętników do historyi powstania polskiego roku 1830–1831*, edited by Tomasz Rayski. Lviv, 1882, 138-39.
Borzymińska, Zofia. ed., *Dzieje żydów w polsce: Wybór tekstów źródłowych XIX wiek*. Warsaw: Żydowski Instytut Historyczny, 1994.
Borzymińska, Zofia. *Szkolnictwo żydowskie w Warszawie, 1831–1870*. Warsaw: Żydowski Instytut Historyczny, 1994.
Botticini, Maristella, and Zvi Eckstein. *The Chosen Few: How Education Shaped Jewish History, 70–1492*. Princeton, NJ: Princeton University Press, 2012.
Boyarin, Daniel. *Unheroic Conduct: The Rise of Heterosexuality and the Invention of the Jewish Man*. Berkeley: University of California, 1997.
Braver, Mikha'el. *Tsevi le-tsadik*. Vienna: Toibesh, 1931.

Brawer, Avraham Yaakov. *Galitsyah vi-yehudeha: Meḥkarim ba-toldot Galitsyah ba-me'ah ha-18*. Jerusalem: Mosad Bialik, 1956.
Breyfogle, Nicholas. "The Religious World of Russian Sabbatarians (*Subbotniks*)." In *Holy Dissent: Jewish and Christian Mystics in Eastern Europe*, edited by Glenn Dynner, 359-92. Detroit: Wayne State University Press, 2011.
Brody, Seth. "Open Up to Me the Gates of Righteousness." *Jewish Quarterly Review* 89, no. 1/2 (July–October 1998): 3–44.
Bromberg, A. Y. *Mi-gedole ha-ḥasidut*. Vol. 18, *Bet Koznits*. Jerusalem: Makhon le-Ḥasidut, 1962.
Bromberg, A. Y. *Mi-gedole ha-ḥasidut*. Vol. 24, *Ha-rav Eliyahu Gutmakher: Ha 'tsadik mi-Graidits'*. Jerusalem: Makhon le-Ḥasidut, 1969.
Burnett, George. *View of the Present State of Poland*. London, 1807.
Burszta, Józef. *Społeczeństwo i karczma: Propinacja, karczma, i sprawa alkoholizmu w społeczeństwie polskim XIX wieku*. Warsaw: LSW, 1951.
Burszta, Józef. *Wieś i karczma: Rola karczmy w życiu wsi pańszczyźnianej*. Warsaw: Ludowa Społdzielnia Wydawnicza, 1950.
Cala, Alina. *The Image of the Jew in Polish Folk Culture*. Jerusalem: Magnes, 1995.
Certeau, Michel de. *The Practice of Everyday Life*. Translated by Steven Rendall. Berkeley: University of California Press, 1984.
Chełminski, Maxymilian. *Wspomnienia gospodarskie z pięćdziesięciodniowej podróży po kraju tutejszym, odbytej w roku 1842*. Warsaw, 1843.
Cuffel, Alexandra. *Gendering Disgust in Medieval Religious Literature* (IN: Notre Dame University Press, 2007).
Dan, Joseph, and Klaus Herrmann, eds. *Studies in Jewish Manuscripts*. Tübingen, Germany: Mohr Siebeck, 1999.
Davidson, Israel. *Parody in Jewish Literature*. New York: Columbia University Press, 1907.
Davis, Marni. *Jews and Booze: Becoming American in the Age of Prohibition*. New York: New York University Press, 2012.
Dearborn, Henry Alexander Scammell. *A Memoir on the Commerce and Navigation of the Black Sea and the Trade and Maritime Geography of Turkey and Egypt*, vol. 2. Boston, 1819.
Deinard, Ephraim. *Zikhronot bat ami*, vol. 2. New Orleans: n.p., 1920.
Dekel-Chen, Jonathan. *Farming the Red Land: Jewish Agricultural Colonization and Local Soviet Power, 1924–1941*. New Haven, CT: Yale University Press, 2005.
Dov Baer ben Samuel. *In Praise of the Baal Shem Tov*. Translated and edited by Dan Ben Amos and Jerome Mintz. Northvale, NJ: Jason Aronson, 1994.
Drimer, Solomon, of Skole. *Bet Shelomoh*. Lviv, 1855.
Dubin, Lois C. *The Port Jews of Habsburg Trieste: Absolutist Politics and Enlightenment Culture*. Stanford, CA: Stanford University Press, 1999.
Dubnow, Simon. *History of the Jews in Russia and Poland: From the Earliest Times Until the Present Day*, tr. Israel Friedlaender, 3 volumes (Philadelphia: The Jewish Publication Society, 1918).
Dubnow, Simon, ed., *Pinkas ha-medinah, o Pinkas va'ad ha-kehilot ha-rashiyot be-medinat Lita*. Berlin: Ayanot, 1925.
Duker, Abraham. "Jewish Participants in the Polish Insurrection of 1863." In *Studies and Essays in Honor of Abraham A. Neuman*, edited by in George Alexander Kohut, 144–53. Philadelphia: E. J. Brill, 1962.
Duker, Abraham. "Jewish Participants in the Polish November (1830–31) Insurrection: A List of 17 Names Hitherto not Recorded." In *The Abraham Weiss*

Jubilee Volume: Studies in His Honor Presented by His Colleagues and Disciples on the Occasion of His Completing Four Decades of Pioneering Scholarship, 81–87. New York: Abraham Weiss Jubilee Committee, 1964.

Duker, Abraham. "The Polish 'Great Emigration' and the Jews." PhD diss., Columbia University, 1956.

Duker, Abraham. "Prince Czartoryski on the Jewish Problem." In *The Joshua Bloch Memorial Volume: Studies in Booklore and History*, edited by in Abraham Berger, Lawrence Marwick, and Isidore S. Meyer, 165-79. New York: New York Public Library, 1960.

Dynner, Glenn. "Hasidism and Habitat: Managing the Jewish-Christian Encounter in the Kingdom of Poland." In *Holy Dissent: Jewish and Christian Mystics in Eastern Europe*, edited by Glenn Dynner, 104–30. Detroit: Wayne State University Press, 2011.

Dynner, Glenn. "How Many *Hasidim* Were There Really in Congress Poland? A Response to Marcin Wodziński." *Gal-Ed* 20 (2005): 91–104.

Dynner, Glenn. *Men of Silk: The Hasidic Conquest of Polish Jewish Society*. New York: Oxford University Press, 2006.

Dzierzkowski, Józef. *Śliska do przepaści droga*, in *Powieści Józefa Dzierzkowskiego w pierwszem zupełnem wydaniu*, edited by A. J. O. Rogosza, 2:289–330. Lviv, 1875.

Edwards, H. Sutherland. *The Private History of a Polish Insurrection: From Official and Unofficial Sources*. 2 vols. London, 1865.

Ehrmann, Dob Baer. *Devarim arevim*. 1903; repr. Tel Aviv: n.p., 1963, two volumes.

Eisenbach, Artur. *The Emancipation of the Jews in Poland, 1780–1870*. Edited by Antony Polonsky. Translated by Janina Dorosz. London: Blackwell, 1988.

Eisenbach, Artur. "Memoriał o położeniu ludności żydowskiej w dobie konstytucyjnej Królestwa Kongresowego." *Teki Archiwalne* 21(1989): 177–215.

Eisenbach, Artur. "Mobilność terytorialna ludności żydowskiej w Królestwie Polskim," in *Społeczeństwo Królestwa Polskiego*, edited by Witold Kula and Janina Leskiewiczowa, 2:179–316. Warsaw: PWN, 1966.

Eisenbach, Artur. "Di tsentrale reprezentants-organen fun di yidn in varshaver firstntum (1807–1815)." *Bleter far Geshikhte* 2 (1938): 33–88.

Eisenbach, A., D. Fajnhauz, and A. Wein, eds. *Żydzi a powstanie styczniowe: Materiały i dokumenty*. Warsaw: PWN, 1963.

Eleazar ha-Kohen. *Ḥidushe Maharaḥ*. Warsaw, 1898.

Emeliantseva, Ekaterina. "The House on the Corner: Frankists and Other Warsovians in the Struggle for Spatial Benefits in Late 18th-century Warsaw (1789–92)." In *Jewish Space in Central and Eastern Europe Day-to-Day History*, edited by Jurgita Šiaučiunaitė-Verbickiene and Larisa Lempertienė, 91–113. Newcastle, UK: Cambridge Scholars, 2007.

Epstein, Jehiel Michael. *Arukh ha-shulḥan* [S.l.: s.n., 199-?].

Ettinger, Samuel. *Ben Polin le-Rusyah*. Jerusalem: Zalman Shazar, 1994.

Fajnhauz, Dawid. "Dwór i karczma żydowska na Litwie w połowie 19 w." In *Studies in Jewish History: Presented to Professor Raphael Mahler on His Seventy-Fifth Birthday*, edited by Shmuel Yeivin, 62–76. Merḥavia, Israel: Sifriyut Po'alim, 1974.

Faynkind, Moyshe. *Gute yidn in Poyln* (Warsaw, 1926).

Feiner, Shmuel. "The Pseudo-Enlightenment and the Question of Jewish Modernization." *Jewish Social Studies*, n.s., 3, no. 1 (1996): 62–88.

Feiner, Shmuel. "Towards a Historical Definition of Haskalah." In *New Perspectives on the Haskalah*, edited by Shmuel Feiner and David Sorkin, 184–219. London: Littman, 2001.

Fisch, Harold. "Reading and Carnival: On the Semiotics of Purim." *Poetics Today* 15, no. 1 (Spring 1994): 55–74.
Fischelsohn, Ephraim. "Teater fun khsidim." *Historishe Shriftn fun YIVO* 1 (1929): 649-93.
Fishman, Yehuda Leib ha-Kohen. *Sare ha-me'ah*. Jerusalem: Mosad Ha-Rav Kuk, 1947.
Fram, Edward. *Ideals Face Reality: Jewish Law and Life in Poland, 1550–1655*. Cincinnati, OH: Hebrew Union College Press, 1997.
Fram, Edward. "Percepetion and Reception of Repentant Apostates in Medieval Ashkenaz and Premodern Poland." *AJS Review* 21, no. 2 (1996): 299–340.
Frank, Michael. "Satan's Servant or Authorities' Agent? Publicans in Eighteenth-Century Germany." In *The World of the Tavern: Public Houses in Early Modern Europe*, edited by Beat Kumin and B. Ann Tlusty, 12–43. Burlington, VT: Ashgate, 2002.
Frankel, Avraham Ḥayim ben Naftali Tsevi. *Shabat bet Ropshits*. Jerusalem: A. Ḥ Frankel, 1994.
Frankel, Jonathan. *Prophecy and Politics: Socialism, Nationalism, and Russia's Jews, 1862–1917*. Cambridge, UK: Cambridge University Press, 1984.
Freeze, ChaeRan. "When Chava Left Home: Gender, Conversion, and the Jewish Family in Tsarist Russia." In "Jewish Women in Eastern Europe," edited by ChaeRan Freeze, Paula Hyman, and Antony Polonsky. Special issue, *Polin* 18 (2005): 153–88.
Frenk, A. N. *Di familye Davidzohn*. Warsaw: Freyd, 1924.
Frenk, A. N. "Meḥiat mekhirat mashkim." *Ha-Tsefirah* 179, August 21, 1921.
Frenk, A. N. "Di tsol yidn un zeyere basheftikungen in di shtet un derfer fun Kenigraykh Poyln in 1843tn yor." *Bleter far Yidishe Demografye, Statistik un Ekonomik* 3 (1923): 184–93.
Friedlander, S. Y. *Sefer ha-tikun*. Czernowitz, 1881.
Galas, Michał. *Rabin Markus Jastrow i jego wizja reformy judaizmu. Studium z dziejów judaizmu w XIX wieku* (Kraków, 2007).
Garczyński, Stefan. *Anatomia rzeczypospolitey-polskiey*. 1754; repr. Whitefish, MT: Kessinger, 2009.
Garncarska-Kadary, Bina. *Ḥelkam shel ha-yehudim be-hitpatḥut ha-ta'asiyah shel Varshah ba-shanim 1816/20–1914*. Tel Aviv: Tel Aviv University, 1985.
Gelber, N. M. "A Jewess' Memoirs of the Polish Uprising of 1863." *YIVO Annual of Social Science* 13 (1965): 243–63.
Gelber, N. M. "Korot ha-yehudim be-Polin mi-reshit halukatah ve-ad milhemet ha-olam hashniyah." In *Bet Yisra'el be-Polin*, edited by Israel Halpern, 110–27. Jerusalem: Ha-Maḥlaḳah le-Inyene ha-Noʻar shel ha-Histadrut ha-Tsiyonit, 1948.
Gelber, N. M. "Onteyl fun yidn in oyfshtand fun 1863." *Lodzher Visnshaftlekhe Shriftn* 1 (1938): 264–66.
Gelber, N. M. "She'elat ha-yehudim be-Polin bi-shnat 1815–30." *Zion* 13–14 (1949): 106–43.
Gelber, N. M. *Ha-yehudim ve-ha-mered ha-polani*. Jerusalem: Bialik, 1953.
Gelber, N. M. "Di yidn in Kalish un der oyfshtand in yanuar 1830–1831." *Lodzher Visnshaftlekhe Shriftn* 1 (1938): 261–63.
Glatstein, Jacob. *The Glatstein Chronicles*. Edited by Ruth Wisse. Translated by Maier Deshell and Norbert Guterman. New Haven, CT: Yale University Press, 2010.
Glucksberg, Jan (attr.). *Rzut oka na stan izraelitów w Polsce*. Warsaw, 1831.
Goldberg, Jacob. "Poles and Jews in the 17th and 18th Centuries: Rejection or Acceptance." *Jahrbücher für Geschichte Osteuropas* 22 (1974): 261–68.

Goldberg, Jacob. "Tavernkeeping." In *The YIVO Encyclopedia of Jews in Eastern Europe*, available online at http://www.yivoencyclopedia.org/article.aspx/ Tavernkeeping. Accessed February 6, 2011.

Goldberg, Jacob. "Ha-yehudi ve-ha-pundak ha-ironi ba-ezor Podlasiyah." In *Ha-ḥevrah ha-yehudit be-mamlekhet Polin-Lita*, 232–247. Jerusalem: Merkaz Zalman Shazar, 1999.

Goldberg-Mulkiewicz, Olga. "Księga pamięci ('memorbuecher') a mit żydowskiega miasteczka." *Etnografia Polska* 35, no. 2 (1991): 187–99.

Goldberg-Mulkiewicz, Olga. "The Stereotype of the Jew in Polish Folklore." In *Studies in Aggadah and Jewish Folklore*, edited by Issachar Ben-Ami and Joseph Dan, 83–94. Jerusalem: Magnes, 1983.

Gorizontow, Leonid. "Aparat urzędniczy Królestwa Polskiego w okresie rządów Paskiewicza." *Przegląd Historyczny* 85, nos. 1–2 (1994): 45–58.

Green, Abigail. *Moses Montefiore: Jewish Liberator, Imperial Hero*. Cambridge, MA: Belknap Press of Harvard University Press, 2010.

Groniowski, Krzysztof. *Kwestia agrarna w Królestwie Polskim, 1871–1914*. Warsaw: PWN, 1966.

Grossman, Henryk. "Struktura społeczna i zawodowa Ks. Warszawskiego." *Kwartalnik Statystyczny* (1924) 2: 1–108.

Guesnet, François. *Polnische Juden im 19. Jahrhundert*. Cologne: Böhlau, 1998.

Guttmacher, Elijah. *Tsofnat pa'neaḥ*. Brody, 1875.

Haber, Adolf. "Ha-pundaka'im ha-yehudiim be-publitsistikah ha-polanit shel 'Ha-sem ha-gadol' (1788–1792)." *Gal-Ed* 2 (1975): 1–24.

Halpern, Israel, ed. *Pinkas va'ad arba aratsot: Likute takanot, ketavim u-reshumot*. Jerusalem: Mosad Byalik, 1989.

Harring, Harro. *Poland under the Dominion of Russia*. Boston, 1834.

Hensel, Jürgen. "Polnische Adelsnation und Judische Vermittler 1814–1830." In *Forschungen zur osteuropäischen Geschichte*, edited by Jürgen Hensel and Heinz-Dietrich Löwe, 71–93. Wiesbaden, Germany: Otto Harrassowitz, 1983.

Hensel, Jürgen. "Żydowski arendarz i jego karczma: Uwagi na marginesie usunięcia żydowskich arendarzy ze wsi w Królestwie Polskim w latach 20. XIX wieku." In *Kultura żydów polskich XIX–XX wieku*, edited by Ryszard Kołodziejczyk and Regina Renz, 83–99. Kielce, Poland: Kieleckie Tow. Nauk., 1992.

Heschel of Apta, Abraham Joshua, Isaac Meir Heschel, and Meshullam Zusya Heschel. *Igrot ha-"Ohev Yisra'el": Kevutsat igrot, mismakhim ve-haskamot ha-muva'im bi-sefarim ve-kitve yad*. Jerusalem: Mekhon Sifte Tsadikim She'a, 1999.

Himka, John-Paul. "Ukrainian-Jewish Antagonism." In *Jewish-Ukrainian Relations in Historical Perspective*, edited by Howard Aster, Peter J. Potichnyj, 111–58. Edmonton, AB: Canadian Institute of Ukrainian Studies, 1988.

Hollaenderski, Leon. *Les Israélites de Pologne*. Paris, 1846.

Horowitz, Isaiah. *Shne luḥot ha-brit*. Amsterdam, 1649; repr. Jerusalem: n.p., n.d.

Hundert, Gershon. "The Introduction to *Divre binah* by Dov Ber of Bolechów: An Unexamined Source for the History of Jews in the Lwów Region in the Second Half of the Eighteenth Century." *AJS Review* 33 (2009): 225–69.

Hundert, Gershon. *Jews in a Polish Private Town: The Case of Opatów in the Eighteenth Century*. Baltmore: Johns Hopkins University Press, 1992.

Hundert, Gershon. *Jews in Poland-Lithuania: A Genealogy of Modernity*. Berkeley: University of California, 2005.

Hurwitz, Israel. *Ma'asiyot me-ha-gedolim ve-ha-tsadikim*. Warsaw: n.p., 1924.

Hyman, Paula. *Gender and Assimilation in Modern Jewish History: The Roles and Representation of Women.* Seattle: University of Washington Press, 1995.

Idel, Moshe. "R. Israel Ba'al Shem Tov 'In the State of Walachia': Widening the Besht's Cultural Panorama." In *Holy Dissent: Jewish and Christian Mystics in Eastern Europe,* edited by in Glenn Dynner, 69–103. Detroit: Wayne State University Press, 2011.

Jaakov Joseph of Polonoye. *Toldot Ya'akov Yosef.* Jerusalem: Agudat Bet Vialipoli, 1973.

Jacob, William. *Report on the Trade in Foreign Corn: And on the Agriculture of the North of Europe.* London, 1826.

Jagodzińska, Agnieszka. *Pomiędzy. Akulturacja Żydów Warszawy w drugiej połowie XIX wieku* (Wrocław 2008).

Jezierski, Andrzej. *Problemy rozwoju gospodarczego ziem polskich w XIX i XX wieku.* Warsaw: Książka i Wiedza, 1984.

Kadish, Yo'ets Kayim. *Siaḥ sarfe kodesh.* 5 vols. Przytyk, Poland: n.p., 1923.

Kahan, Arcadius. *Essays in Jewish Social and Economic History.* Chicago: University of Chicago, 1986.

Kaidanover, Zevi Hirsch. *Kav ha-yashar.* Frankfurt, 1705.

Kamelhar, Gershon. *Mevaser tov.* Podgórze, Poland, 1900.

Kandel, Dawid. "Kariera rabiniczna cadyka Icie-Majera." *Kwartalnik Poświęcony Badaniu Przeszłości Żydów w Polsce* 1/2 (1912): 131–36.

Kandel, Dawid. "Nowosilców a żydzi." *Biblioteka Warszawska* 2 (1911): 142–54.

Kandel, Dawid. "Petycya 1857 r." *Kwartalnik Poświęcony Badaniu Przeszłości żydów w Polsce* 3 (1913): 154–55.

Kandel, Dawid. "Żydzi w Królestwie Polskiem po 1831 r." *Kwartalnik Poświęcony Badaniom Przeszłości Żydów w Polsce* 2 (1913): 183–84.

Karniel, Josef. "Das Toleranzpatent Kaiser Josephs II für die Juden Galiziens und Lodomeriens." *Jahrbuch des Instituts für Deutsche Geschichte* 11 (1982): 58–89.

Karp, Jonathan. *The Politics of Jewish Commerce: Economic Thought and Emancipation in Europe, 1638–1848.* New York: Cambridge University Press, 2008.

Karpińska, Małgorzata. "Policje tajne w Królestwie Kongresowym." *Przegląd Historyczny* 76, no. 4 (1985): 679–709.

Katz, Jacob. *The "Shabbes Goy": A Study in Halakhic Flexibility.* Translated by Yoel Lerner. Philadelphia: Jewish Publication Society of America, 1989.

Katz, Jacob. *Tradition and Crisis: Jewish Society at the End of the Middle Ages.* Translated by Bernard Dov Cooperman. Syracuse, NY: Syracuse University Press, 2000.

Kaźmierczyk, Adam, ed. *Żydzi polscy: 1648–1772; Źródła.* Krakow: Uniwersytet Jagielloński, Katedra Judaistyki, 2001.

Kieniewicz, Stefan. *The Emancipation of the Polish Peasantry.* Chicago: University of Chicago Press, 1969.

Kirszrot, Jakób. *Prawa żydów w Królestwie Polskiem.* Warsaw: Nakład Zarządu Warszawskiej gminy Starozakonnych, 1917.

Klainman, Mosheh Ḥayim. *Or Yesharim.* 1924; repr. Jerusalem: n.p., 1967.

Klein, Menashe. *Mishnah halakhot.* Brooklyn, 1960.

Klier, John. *Russia Gathers Her Jews: The Origins of the "Jewish Question" in Russia, 1772–1825.* DeKalb: Northern Illinois University Press, 1986.

Kłodzinski, Adam. *Żyd polski, czyli Każdy ma swoje przebiegi.* In "Miscellanea z doby oświecenia," ed. Z. Golinski. Special issue, *Archiwum Literackie* 25 (1982): 280–327.

Kochanowicz, Jacek. *Backwardness and Modernization: Poland and Eastern Europe in the 16th–20th Centuries.* Burlington, VT: Ashgate, 2006.

Kolberg, Oskar. *Dzieła wyszystkie.* 67 vols. Wrocław, Poland: Polskie Towarzystwo Ludoznawcze, 1961–62).
Kotik, Yekhezkel. *Journey to a Nineteenth-Century Shtetl: The Memoirs of Yekhezkel Kotik.* Edited by David Assaf. Detroit: Wayne State University Press, 2002.
Koźmian, Kajetan. *Pamiętniki.* 3 vols. 1858; repr. Wrocław, Poland: Zakład Narodowy im. Ossolińskich, 1972.
Kraszewski, Józef Ignacy. *Para czerwona: Obrazek współczesny narysowany z natury.* Krakow: Nowej Reformy, 1905.
Kraszewski, Józef Ignacy. *Wspomnienia Polesia Wołynia i Litwy.* Rev. ed. Vilnius, 1861.
Kula, Witold. *An Economic Theory of the Feudal System: Towards a Model of the Polish Economy, 1500–1800.* Translated by Lawrence Garner. London: Humanities, 1976.
Kumin, Beat, and B. Ann Tlusty, eds. *The World of the Tavern: Public Houses in Early Modern Europe.* Burlington, VT: Ashgate, 2002.
Lederhendler, Eli. *Jewish Immigrants and American Capitalism, 1880–1920: From Caste to Class.* Cambridge, UK: Cambridge University Press, 2009.
LeDonne, John. "Indirect Taxes in Catherine's Russia, II. The Liquor Monopoly." *Jahrbücher für Geschichte Osteuropas* 24 (1976): 173–207.
Leiner, Mordecai. *Me ha-shiloaḥ.* 1860; repr. New York: Lainer, 1984.
Leskiewicz, Janina, and Jerzy Michalski, eds. *Supliki chłopskie xviii wieku.* Warsaw: Książka i Wiedza, 1954.
Leslie, R. F. *Polish Politics and the Revolution of November, 1830.* Westport, CT: Greenwood, 1969.
Leslie, R. F. *Reform and Insurrection in Russian Poland, 1856–1865.* London: Athlone, 1963.
Lestschinsky, Jacob. "Die Umsiedlung und Umschichtung des jüdischen Volkes im Laufe des letzten Jahrhunderts." *Weltwirtschaftliches Archiv* 30 (1929): 123–56.
Leszczyński, Anatol. "Karczmarze i szynkarze żydowscy ziemi Bielskiej od drugiej połowy xvii w. do 1795 r." *Biuletyn ŻIH* 102, no. 2 (1977): 77–85.
Levin, Sabina. "Bate sefer li-vne dat Mosheh be-Varshah be-1818–1830." *Gal-Ed* 1 (1973): 63–100.
Levine, Hillel. *Economic Origins of Antisemitism: Poland and Its Jews in the Early Modern Period.* New Haven, CT: Yale University Press, 1991.
Lewinsky, Yom-Tov. *Sefer zikaron le-kehilat Lomzah.* Israel: Hotsa'at Irgun Ole Lomzah be-Yisra'el, 1952.
Light, Ivan H., and Steven J. Gold, *Ethnic Economies.* San Diego, CA: Academic Press, 1999.
Lipkind, Yehuda Leib ben Yisra'el. *Ha-shtiah ke-da'at.* Warsaw, 1898.
Lipschitz, Jacob. *Zikhron Ya'akov.* Kaunas: n.p., 1924.
Lipschitz, Solomon Zalman. *Hemdat Shelomoh: Drushim ve-ḥidushim.* Warsaw, 1890.
Lipschitz, Solomon Zalman, and Isaac of Warka. *Likute shoshanim.* Edited by Ḥayim Yesha'yah ha-Kohen. Lublin, 1883.
Listy z zagranicy z powodu kwestii chłopskiéj poruszonéj w Cesarstwie Rossyjskiém, mianowicie w prowinciach dawnéj Polski i w Królestwie. Paris, 1858.
Litvak, Olga. *Conscription and the Search for Modern Russian Jewry.* Bloomington: Indiana University Press, 2006.
Łodyńska-Kosińska, Maria, ed. *Katalog rysunków architektonicznych z Akt Komisji Rządowej Spraw Wewnętrznych w Archiwum Głównym Akt Dawnych w Warszawie.* Warsaw: Państw. Wydawn. Naukowe, 1974.
Loewenthal, Naftali. *Communicating the Infinite: The Emergence of the Habad School.* Chicago: University of Chicago Press, 1990.

Loewenthal, Naftali. "Rabbi Shneur Zalman of Liadi's *Kitzur Likkutei Amarim*: British Library Or. 10456." In *Studies in Jewish Manuscripts*, edited by Joseph Dan and Klaus Herrmann, 89–138. Tübingen, Germany: Mohr Siebeck, 1999.

Lowe, Heinz-Dietrich. *The Tsars and the Jews: Reform, Reaction, and Anti-Semitism in Imperial Russia, 1772–1917*. Reading, UK: Harwood Academic, 1993.

Łukasiewicz, Juliusz. *Krzyzys agrarny na ziemiach polskich w końcu XIX wieku*. Warsaw: PWN, 1968.

Łukasiewicz, Juliusz. "O strukturze agrarnej Królestwa Polskiego po uwłaszczeniu." *Przegląd Historyczny* 1 (1971) 296–314.

Łukasinski, Walerian. *Pamiętnik*. Edited by Rafał Gerber. 1818, repr. Warsaw, 1860.

Lukin, Benyamin. "A Russian Bureaucratic Approach to the Economic Role of Malorossian Jews, 1830." *Jews in Russia and Eastern Europe* 57, no. 2 (2006): 111–31.

Lukowski, Jerzy. *Disorderly Liberty: The Political Culture of the Polish-Lithuanian Commonwealth in the Eighteenth Century*. London: Continuum, 2010.

Łuniński, Ernest. *Berek Joselewicz i jego syn: Zarys historyczny*. Warsaw: Orgelbrand, 1909.

Lupovitch, Howard. *Jews at the Crossroads: Tradition and Accommodation during the Golden Age of the Hungarian Nobility, 1729–1878*. Budapest: Central European University Press, 2007.

Luria, Ilyah. *Edah u-medinah: Ha- ḥasidut ḥabad ba-imperyah ha-rusit, 588–643*. Jerusalem: Magnes, 2006.

Mączyński, Józef. *Włościanie*. Krakow: 1858.

Mahler, Raphael. *Divre yeme Yisra'el: Dorot aḥaronim*. 6 vols. Merhavia, Israel: Sifriyat Po'alim, 1952–1976.

Mahler, Raphael. *Hasidism and the Jewish Enlightenment: Their Confrontation in Galicia and Poland in the First Half of the Nineteenth Century*. Translated by Eugene Orenstein, Aaron Klein, and Jenny Machlowitz Klein. Philadelphia: Jewish Publication Society of America, 1985.

Mahler, Raphael. *A History of Modern Jewry, 1780–1815*. London: Vallentine, Mitchell, 1971.

Mahler, Raphael. "A Jewish Memorandum to the Viceroy of the Kingdom of Poland, Paskiewicz." *Salo Wittmayer Baron Jubilee Volume on the Occasion of his Eightieth Birthday*, edited by in Saul Lieberman, 2:669–96. Jerusalem: American Academy for Jewish Research, 1974.

Mahler, Raphael. "Statistik fun yidn in der Lubliner Voyevodstva." *Yunger Historiker* 2 (1929): 67–108.

Mahler, Raphael. *Yidn in amolikn Poyln in likht fun tsifern*. Warsaw: Yidish Bukh, 1958.

Maimon, Solomon. *Solomon Maimon: An Autobiography*. Translated by J. Clark Murray. Urbana: University of Illinois Press, 2001.

Mandelboym, Yaakov Dov. *Sefer ha-zikaron le-rabi Mosheh Lipshits, z"l*. New York: Hotsa'at Almanato, 1997.

Manekin, Rachel. "The Lost Generation: Education and Female Conversion in Fin-de-Siécle Kraków." In "Jewish Women in Eastern Europe," edited by ChaeRan Freeze, Paula Hyman, and Antony Polonsky. Special issue, *Polin* 18 (2005): 189–219.

Margoshes, Joseph. *A World Apart: A Memoir of Jewish Life in Nineteenth Century Galicia*. Boston: Academic Studies Press, 2008.

Markowski, Artur. "The *Shtetl* Space in the 19th Century: A Sociological Approach." In *Jewish Space in Central and Eastern Europe Day-to-Day History*, edited by Jurgita Šiaučiunaitė-Verbickiene and larisa Lempertienė, 51–66. Newcastle, UK: Cambridge Scholars, 2007.

Massalski, E. T. *Pan Podstolic albo czem jesteśmy czem być mozemy: Romans administracijny.* St. Petersburg, 1833.
Mayer, Arno J. *The Persistence of the Old Regime: Europe to the Great War.* New York: Pantheon, 1981.
McCaul, Alexander. *Sketches of Judaism and the Jews.* London, 1838.
Mendelzohn, Avraham Duber. *Toldot ḥemdat Shelomoh.* 1922; repr. Jerusalem: Yisra'el Avraham Grinboim, 1996.
Mendes-Flohr, Paul R., and Jehuda Reinharz, comps. and eds. *The Jew in the Modern World: A Documentary History.* 3rd ed. New York: Oxford University Press, 2011.
Merunowicz, Teofil. *Żydzi.* Lviv, 1879.
Mickiewicz, Adam. *Pan Tadeusz.* 1834; repr. London: Polska Fundacja Kulturalna, 1990.
Mieszczankowski, Mieczysław. *Struktura agrarna Polski międzywojennej.* Warsaw: PWN, 1960.
Mikhalzohn, Avraham Ḥayim Simḥah Bunem. *Ohel Naftali.* Lviv, 1911.
Mikhalzohn, Avraham Ḥayim Simḥah Bunem. *Ateret Menaḥem.* Biłgoraj, Poland: N. N. Kranenberg, 1910.
Mikoszewski, Karol. *Kazania o pijaństwie.* Warsaw, 1862.
Mochnacki, Maurycy. *Dziela.* Poznań, 1863.
Muller, Jerry. *Capitalism and the Jews.* Princeton, NJ: Princeton University Press, 2010.
Murphy, Curtis G. "Burghers versus Bureaucrats: Enlightened Centralism, the Royal Towns, and the Case of the *Propinacja* Law in Poland-Lithuania, 1776–1793." *Slavic Review* 71, no. 2 (2012): 389–409.
Myers, David. "Between Diaspora and Zion: History, Memory, and Jerusalem Scholars." In David Myers and David Ruderman, eds., *The Jewish Past Revisited: Reflections on Modern Jewish Historians.* New Haven, CT: Yale University Press, 1998, 88–102.
Myers, Jody Elizabeth. "Zevi Hirsch Kalischer and the Origins of Religious Zionism." *Profiles in Diversity: Jews in a Changing Europe*, edited by in Francis Milano and David Sorkin, 267–94. Detroit: Wayne State University Press, 1998.
Myovich, Samuel T. "Josephism at Its Boundaries: Nobles, Peasants, Priests, and Jews in Galicia, 1772–1790." Ph.D. diss., Indiana University, 1994.
Nadler, Allan. "Holy Kugel: The Sanctification of Ashkenazic Ethnic Food in Hasidism." In *Food and Judaism*, edited by Leonard Greenspoon, 193–211. Omaha, NE: Creighton University Press, 2005.
Naḥman of Bratslav. *Likute etsot.* Lviv, 1858.
Nathans, Benjamin. *Beyond the Pale: The Jewish Encounter with Late Imperial Russia.* Berkeley: University of California, 2002.
Neale, Adam. *Travels through Some Parts of Germany, Poland, Moldavia, and Turkey.* London, 1818.
Niemcewicz, Julian Ursyn. "The Year 3333, or An Incredible Dream." In *Stranger in Our Midst: Images of the Jew in Polish Literature*, edited by Harold B. Segel, 61–70. Ithaca, NY: Cornell University Press, 1996.
Oberlander, Barukh. "Ha-yerushalmi le-seder kodashim ve-ha-mo"l shelo." *Or Yisra'el* 3, no. 16 (1999): 174–75.
Ochs, Michael Jerry. "St. Petersburg and the Jews of Russian Poland, 1862–1905." PhD diss., Harvard University, 1986.
Oisteanu, Andrei. *Inventing the Jew: Antisemitic Stereotypes in Romanian and Other Central-East European Cultures.* Translated by Mirela Adascalitei. Lincoln: University of Nebraska Press and the Vidal Sassoon International Center for the Study of Antisemitism, 2009.

Oniszczuk, Aleksandra. "Jews in the Duchy of Warsaw: The Question of Equality in Administrative Theory and Practice." In Glenn Dynner, Antony Polonsky, and Marcin Wodziński. Special issue, *Polin* 27: *Jews in the Kingdom of Poland* (forthcoming, 2014).

Opalski, Magdalena. *The Jewish Tavern-Keeper and His Tavern in Nineteenth-Century Polish Literature*. Jerusalem: Zalman Shazar, 1986.

Opalski, Magdalena, and Israel Bartal. *Poles and Jews: A Failed Brotherhood*. Hanover, NH: Brandeis University Press, 1992.

Opatoshu, Joseph. *In Polish Woods*. Translated by Isaac Goldberg. Philadelphia: Jewish Publication Society of America, 1938.

Oppenheim, Israel. *The Struggle of Jewish Youth for Productivization: The Zionist Youth Movement in Poland*. Boulder, CO: East European Monographs, 1989.

Ostrowski, Antoni. *Pomysły o potrzebie reformy towarzyskiéy w ogólności, a mianowiciéy, co do Izraelitów w Polszcze przez założyciela miasta Tomaszowa Mazowieckiego*. Paris, 1834.

Pająk, Mirosław. "Spór o propinację Pińczowską: Przyczynek do charakterystyki Aleksandra Wielopolskiego." *Kielckie Studia Historyczne* 13 (1995): 153–65.

Palache, Ḥayyim. *Lev Ḥayim*. Salonika, 1823.

Parush, Iris. *Reading Jewish Women: Marginality and Modernization in Nineteenth-Century Eastern European Jewish Society*. Translated by Saadya Sternberg. Waltham, MA: Brandeis University Press, 2004.

Pawlikowski, Józef, and Dawid Pilchowski. *O poddanych polskich*. [Kraków]: 1788.

Penslar, Derek. *Shylock's Children: Economics and Jewish Identity in Modern Europe*. Berkeley: University of California Press, 2001.

Peretz, I. L. *The I. L. Peretz Reader*. Edited by Ruth Wisse. New York: Schocken, 1990.

Perl, Joseph. *Revealer of Secrets*. Translated by Dov Taylor. Oxford: Westview, 1997.

Petrovsky-Shtern, Yohanan. *Jews in the Russian Army, 1827–1917*. Cambridge, UK: Cambridge University Press, 2009.

Pintner, Walter McKenzie. *Russian Economic Policy under Nicholas I*. Ithaca, NY: Cornell, 1967.

Piotrowski, Wiator. *Wybór kazań niedzielnych, świątecznych i przygodnych*. Warsaw, 1840.

Piwek, Jerzy. "Rola żydów w gospodarce wielkiej własności ziemskiej między Wisłą a Pilicą w latach 1815–1864." In *Żydzi w Małopolsce*, edited by Feliks Kiryk, 165–70. Przemyśl, Poland: Południowo-Wschodni Instytut Naukowy w Przemyślu, 1991.

Podlewski, W. B. "Diaryusz Waleryana Bogoryi Podlewskiego z czasów wojny narodowej z Moskwą w r. 1831." In *Zbiór Pamiętników do historyi powstania polskiego*, edited by Tomasz Rayski, 481-93. Lviv, 1882.

Polonsky, Antony. *The Jews in Poland and Russia*. 3 vols. Oxford: Littman Library of Jewish Civilization, 2010.

Porter-Szucs, Brian. *Faith and Fatherland: Catholicism, Modernity, and Poland*. New York: Oxford University Press, 2011.

Prus, Bolesław. *Placówka*. Wrocław, Poland: Siedmioróg, 2000.

Quint, Alyssa. "The Currency of Yiddish: Ettinger's *Serkele* and the Reinvention of Shylock." *Prooftexts* 24, no. 1 (2004): 99–115.

Reinstein, Victor Hillel. "By the Merit of a Tzadik." PhD diss., Hebrew Union College, 1978.

Reisen, Zalman. "Briv fun Amerike tsum Greyditser tsadik." *YIVO Bleter, Yorbukh fun Amopteyl* 2 1939, 191–218.

Ringelblum, Emanuel. *Kapitlen geshikhte fun amolikn yidishn lebn in Poyln*. Buenos Aires: Tsentral-Farband fun Poylishe Yidn in Argentine, 1953.

Ringelblum, Emanuel. *Żydzi w powstaniu kościuszkowskiem*. Warsaw: Księgarnia Popularna, 1938.

Rischin, Moses. *The Promised City: New York's Jews, 1870–1914*. 1962; repr. Cambridge, MA: Harvard University Press, 1967.

Rosman, Moshe. *Founder of Hasidism: A Quest for the Historical Ba'al Shem Tov*. Berkeley: University of California Press, 1996.

Rosman, Moshe. "The History of Jewish Women in Early Modern Poland." *Polin* 18 (2008): 25–56.

Rosman, Moshe. *The Lords' Jews: Magnate-Jewish Relations in the Polish-Lithuanian Commonwealth during the 18th Century*. Cambridge, MA: Harvard University Press, 1990.

Roth, Joseph. *The Radetzky March*. Translated by Joachim Neugroschel. Woodstock, NY: Overlook, 2002.

Rothstein, Bob. "Geyt a yid in shenkl arayn: Yiddish Songs of Drunkenness," in The Field of Yiddish: Studies in Language, Folklore, and Literature, Fifth Collection, ed. David Goldberg (Evanston, IL: Northwestern University Press and New York: YIVO Institute for Jewish Research, 1993), 243-62.

Rożenowa, Halina. *Produkcja wódki i sprawa pijaństwa w Królestwie Polskim 1815–1863*. Warsaw: PWN, 1961.

Rozental, Shlomo Gabriel. *Hitgalut ha-tsadikim*. Edited by Gedalyah Nigal. Jerusalem: Hotsa'at Karmel, 1996.

Rubin, Ruth. *Voices of a People: The Story of Yiddish Folksong*. New York: McGraw-Hill, 1979.

Rutkowski, Jan. *Historia gospodarcza Polski*. 2 vols. Poznań, Poland: Księgarnia Akademicka, 1947–1950.

Rychlikowa, Irena. "Ziemiaństwo Polskie 1772–1944: Dzieje degradacji klasy." *Dzieje Najnowsze, Rocznik XVII* 2 (1985): 3–23.

Saltera, Wojciech. "Żydzi wobec powstania listopadowego 1830–1831 roku: Na przykładzie wojewòdztw krakowskiego i sandomierskiego." In Z przeszłości żydów polskich: Polityka, gospodarka, kultura, społeczeństwo, edited by Jacka Wijaczki and Grzegorza Miernika, 87–102. Krakow: Societas Vistulana, 2005.

Schiper, Ignacy. *Przyczynki do dziejów chasydyzmu w Polsce*. Edited by Zbigniew Targielski. Warsaw: PWN, 1992.

Schiper, Ignacy. *Żydzi Królestwa Polskiego w dobie powstania listopadowego*. Warsaw: Hoesick, 1932.

Schiper, Ignacy. "Z instytutu badań spraw narodowości." *Sprawy Narodowościowe* 5–6 (1930): 696.

Scott, James C. *Seeing Like a State: How Certain Schemes to Improve the Human Condition Have Failed*. New Haven, CT: Yale University Press, 1998.

Segel, Harold B., ed. *Stranger in Our Midst: Images of the Jew in Polish Literature*. Ithaca, NY: Cornell, 1996.

Shanes, Joshua. "Ahron Marcus: Portrait of a Zionist Hasid." *Jewish Social Studies* 16, No. 3 (Spring/Summer 2010): 116–60.

Shapira, Ḥayim El'azar. *Sefer nimuke oraḥ ḥayyim*. 1930; repr. Brooklyn, NY: Emes, 2004.

Shatzky, Jacob. "An Attempt at Jewish Colonization in the Kingdom of Poland." *YIVO Annual of Jewish Social Science* 1 (1946): 44–63.

Shatzky, Jacob. *Geshikhte fun yidn in Varshe*. 3 vols. New York: YIVO Institute, 1947–1953.

Shatzky, Jacob. "Warsaw Jews in Polish Cultural Life." *YIVO Annual of Jewish Social Science* 5 (1950): 41–54.

Shatzky, Jacob. *Yidishe bildungs-politik in Poyln fun 1806 biz 1866*. New York: YIVO, 1943.

Shatzky, Jacob. "Yidn un der poylisher oyfshtand fun 1831." *Historishe Shriftn* 2 (1937): 355–89.
Sherwin, Byron. *Sparks amid the Ashes: The Spiritual Legacy of Polish Jewry*. New York: Oxford University Press, 1997.
Shlomo ha-Kohen of Radomsko. *Ateret Shelomoh*. Piotrków, Poland, 1926.
Sholem Aleichem. *From the Fair: The Autobiography of Sholom Aleichem*. Translated and edited by by Curt Leviant. New York: Viking, 1985.
Shugarov, Mikhail T., ed. "Doklad o Evreiakh imperatoru Aleksandru Pavlovichu." *Russkii Arkhiv* 41 (February 1903): 258–64.
Sienkiewicz, Henryk. *Charcoal Sketches and Other Tales*. Translated by Adam Zamoyski. London: Angel, 1990.
Silber, Michael K. "The Emergence of Ultra-Orthodoxy: The Invention of a Tradition." In *The Uses of Tradition: Jewish Continuity in the Modern Era*, edited by in Jack Wertheimer, 23–84. New York: Jewish Theological Seminary of America, 1999.
Skarbek, Jan. "Żydzi Lublina podczas powstania listopadowego 1830–1831." In *Żydzi w Lublinie*, vol. 2, edited by Tadeusz Radzik, 129–53. Lublin: Uniwersytet Marii Curie-Skłodowskiej, 1998.
Skowronek, J. "Tadeusz Mostowski." *Polski Słownik Biograficzny* 22 (1977): 73–78.
Slezkine, Yuri. *The Jewish Century*. Princeton, NJ: Princeton University Press, 2004.
Slobin, Mark. *Tenement Songs: The Popular Music of the Jewish Immigrants*. Urbana, IL: University of Illinois Press, 1996.
Slomka, Jan. *From Serfdom to Self-Government: Memoirs of a Polish Village Mayor, 1842–1927*. Translated by William John Rose. London: Minerva, 1941.
Smith, R. E. F., and David Christian, *Bread and Salt: A Social and Economic History of Food and Drink in Russia*. Cambridge, UK: Cambridge University Press, 1984.
Smoleński, Władysław. *Stan i sprawa żydów polskich w XVIII wieku*. Warsaw, 1876.
Soloveitchik, Haym. "Can Halakhic Texts Talk History?" *AJS Review* 3 (1978): 153–96.
Soloveitchik, Haym. *Ha-yayin bi-yeme ha-benayim: Perek be-toldot ha-halakhah be-Ashkenaz*. Jerusalem: Zalman Shazar, 2008.
Sperling, Abraham Isaac. *Sefer ta'ame ha-minhagim*. Lviv: David Roth, 1928.
Stanislawski, Michael. *For Whom Do I Toil? Judah Leib Gordon and the Crisis of Russian Jewry*. New York: Oxford University Press, 1988.
Stanislawski, Michael. *Tsar Nicholas I and the Jews: The Transformation of Jewish Society in Russia, 1825–1855*. Philadelphia: Jewish Publication Society of America, 1983.
Stanislawski, S. "From the History of the Polish Revolt in 1831 [R]." *Evreiskaia Starina* 3 (1910): 419–21.
Stanley, John. "The Politics of the Jewish Question in the Duchy of Warsaw, 1807–1813." *Jewish Social Studies* 44 (1982): 47–62.
Stauter-Halsted, Keely. "Jews as Middleman Minorities in Rural Poland: Understanding the Galician Pogroms of 1898." In *Antisemitism and Its Opponents in Modern Poland*, edited by Robert Blobaum, 39–59. Ithaca, NY: Cornell University Press, 2005.
Stauter-Halsted, Keely. *The Nation in the Village: The Genesis of Peasant National Identity in Austrian Poland, 1848–1914*. Ithaca, NY: Cornell University Press, 2001.
Stawiski, E. "Kronika pewnej wioski." *Biblioteka Warszawska* 4 (1843): 665.
Stern, Eliyahu. *The Genius: Elijah of Vilna and the Making of Modern Judaism*. New Haven, CT: Yale University Press, 2013.
Stern, Moshe. *Shut be'er Mosheh*, vol. 6. Jerusalem, 1984.
Stone, Daniel. *The Polish-Lithuanian State, 1386–1795*. Seattle: University of Washington Press, 2001.
Świętochowski, Aleksander. "Żyd w karczmie i żyd w szkole." *Prawda*, November 26, 1881, 565–66.

Szczepaniak, Marian. *Karczma, wieś, dwór: Rola propinacji na wsi wielkopolskiej od połowy XVII do schyłku XVIII wieku*. Warsaw: LSW, 1977.
Szczepański, Janusz. *Społeczność żydowska Mazowsza w XIX–XX wieku*. Pułtusk, Poland: WSH, 2005.
Szczypiorski, Adam. *Ćwierć wieku Warszawy, 1806–1830*. Wrocław, Poland: Zakład Narodowy im. Ossolińskich, 1964.
Szymanski, Adam. "Srul of Lubartów." In *Stranger in Our Midst: Images of the Jew in Polish Literature*, edited by Harold B. Segel, 190–97. Ithaca, NY: Cornell University Press, 1996.
Tahlgrin, El'azar. *Tokhahat musar: Hu sefer tehilim*. Warsaw, 1854.
Teller, Adam. *Kesef, koah ve-hashpa'ah*. Jerusalem: Zalman Shazar, 2006.
Teter, Magda. *Sinners on Trial*. Cambridge, MA: Harvard University Press, 2011.
Tlusty, B. Ann. *Bacchus and Civil Order: The Culture of Drink in Early Modern Germany*. Charlottesville: University of Virginia Press, 2001.
Tokarska-Bakir, Joanna. "Żydzi u Kolbergu." In *Rzeczy mgliste: Eseje i studia*, 49–72. Sejny, Poland: Fundacja Pogranicze, 2004.
Tokarz, Wacław. "Miscellanea: Z dziejów sprawy żydowskiej za Księstwa Warszawskiego." *Kwartalnik Historyczny* 16 (1902): 272–73.
Topolski, Jerzy. "Uwagi o strukturze gospodarczo-społecznej Wielkopolski w XVIII wieku czyli dlaczego na jej terenie nie było żydowskich karczmarzy?" In *Żydzi w Wielkopolsce na przestrzeni dziejów*, edited by Jerzy Topolski and K. Modelski, 71–82. 2nd ed. Poznań, Poland: Wydawn. Poznańskie, 1999.
Trunk, Yehiel Yeshaia. *Poyln: My Life within Jewish Life in Poland; Sketches and Images*. Translated by Anna Clarke. Edited by Piotr Wróbel and Robert M. Shapiro. Toronto: University of Toronto Press, 2007.
Tugendhold, Jacob. *Dumania Izraelity na warcie w pierwszych dniach grudnia 1830 roku*. Warsaw, 1831.
Tugendhold, Jacob. *Skazówki prawdy i zgody*. Warsaw, 1844.
Tuwim, Julian, ed. *Polski słownik pijacki i antologia bachiczna*. Warsaw: Czytelnik, 1959.
Unger, Menasheh. *Pshiskhe un Kotsk*. Buenos Aires: Tsentral-Farband fun Poylishe Yidn in Argentine, 1949.
Walden, Moshe Menachem Mendel. *Nifla'ot ha-rabi*. Biłgoraj, Poland, 1911.
Wasiutyński, Bohdan. *Ludność żydowska w Polsce w wiekach XIX i XX*. Warsaw: Wydawn. Kasy im. Mianowskiego, Inst. Popierania Nauki, 1930.
Wasiutyński, Bohdan. "Rola ekonomiczna żydów w Królestwie Polskiem." *Przegląd Narodowy* 4, no. 10 (October 1911): 383–414.
Wassercug, Moshe. "Korot Moshe Vasertsug ve-nedivat lev aviv ha-manoah R. Isserel z"l." Edited by Heinrich Loewe. *Jahrbuch der Jüdisch-Literarischen Gesellschaft* 8 (1910): 108–13.
Weeks, Theodore. *From Assimilation to Antisemitism: The "Jewish Question" in Poland, 1850–1914*. DeKalb: Northern Illinois University Press, 2006.
Węgrzynek, Hanna. "Ludność żydowska wobec powstania listopadowego." In *Żydzi w obronie Rzeczypospolitej*, edited by Jerzy Tomaszewski, 31–42. Warsaw: Cyklady, 1996.
Węgrzynek, Hanna. "*Shvartze khasene*: Black Weddings among Polish Jews." In *Holy Dissent: Jewish and Christian Mystics in Eastern Europe*, edited by Glenn Dynner, 55–68. Detroit: Wayne State University Press, 2011.
Węgrzynek, Hanna. "Zajęcia rolnicze żydów w Rzeczypospolitej w XVI–XVIII wieku." In *Małżeństwo z rozsądku? Żydzi w społeczeństwie dawnej Rzeczypospolitej*, edited by Anna Michałowska-Mycielska and Marcin Wodziński, 87–103. Wrocław, Poland: Wydawnictwo Uniwersytetu Wrocławskiego, 2007.

Wein, Adam. "Żydzi poza rewirem żydowskim w Warszawie (1809–1862)." *Biuletyn ŻIH* 41 (1962): 45–70.

Wengeroff, Pauline. *Rememberings: The World of a Russian Jewish Woman in the Nineteenth Century.* Translated by by Henny Wenkart. Bethesda: University Press of Maryland, 2000.

Wertheim, Aaron. *Law and Custom in Hasidism.* Translated by Shmuel Himelstein. Hoboken, NJ: Ktav, 1992.

Wilensky, Mordecai. *Ḥasidim u-mitnagdim.* 2nd ed. 2 vols. Jerusalem: Mosad Bialik, 1990.

Winawer, H. M. *The Winawer Saga.* London: H. M. Winawer, 1994.

Wischnitzer, Mark. "Proekty reformy evreyskago byta." *Perezhytoe* 1 (1908): 170–71.

Wisse, Ruth. "The Jewish Informer as Extortionist and Idealist." In *Insiders and Outsiders: Dilemmas of East European Jewry*, edited by in Richard L. Cohen, Jonathan Frankel, Stefani Hoffman, 188–204. Oxford: Littman Library of Jewish Civilization, 2010.

Wodziński, Marcin. "Clerks, Jews, and Farmers: Projects of Jewish Agricultural Settlement in Poland." *Jewish History* 21, no. 3/4 (2007): 279–303.

Wodziński, Marcin. *Hasidism and Haskalah in the Kingdom of Poland: A History of Conflict.* London: Littman Library of Jewish Civilization, 2005.

Wodziński, Marcin. "How Many *Hasidim* were there in Congress Poland? On the Demographics of the Hasidic Movement in Poland during the First Half of the Nineteenth Century." *Gal-Ed* 19 (2004): 13–49.

Wodziński, Marcin. "'Civil Christians': Debates on the Reform of the Jews in Poland, 1789-1830, tr. By Claire Rosenson, in Ben Nathans and Gabriella Safran, eds., *Culture Front: Representing Jews in Eastern Europe* (PA: University of Pennsylvania Press, 2008), 46-76.

Wolff, Larry. *The Idea of Galicia: History and Fantasy in Habsburg Political Culture.* Stanford, CA: Stanford University Press, 2010.

Wolfson, Elliot. "Lying on the Path: Translation and the Transport of Sacred Texts." *AJS Perspectives* 3 (2001): 8–13.

Wolfson, Elliot. *Open Secret: Postmessianic Messianism and the Mystical Revision of Menaḥem Mendel Schneerson.* New York: Columbia University Press, 2009.

Yeḥiel ben Abraham. *Ḥesed le-Avraham.* Czernowitz, 1884.

Yerushalmi, Yosef. *Zakhor: Jewish History and Jewish Memory.* Seattle: University of Washington Press, 1982.

Zikhlinski, Efrayim Me'ir Gad. *Lahav esh.* Piotrków, Poland, 1928.

Zinberg, Israel. *A History of Jewish Literature.* Translated and edited by Bernard Martin. 12 vols. Cleveland: Press of Case Western Reserve University, 1972–78.

Zipperstein, Steven. *The Jews of Odessa: A Cultural History, 1794–1881.* Stanford, CA: Stanford University Press, 1985.

INDEX

1862 liberalization decree, 32, 81, 94, 99, 101, 135, 160, 182 n20, 183 n5, 189
Abraham Joshua Heschel of Apt (Opatów) *see also* Hasidism, 55
Abramovitsh, S. Y. (Mendele), 3, 10, 23, 133, 151, 177
acculturation, 5, 87, 102, 165, 193 n152
Advisory Committee (Jewish), 58, 198 n49
agricultural colony, Jewish, 81, 101, 113, 135, 153–157, 166, 174, 177
agunah (grass widow), 149, 150
Aharon of Chernobyl *see also* Hasidism, 134
alcohol *see also* tavern, 139, 176
   wine, 20, 37–41, 43–45, 58, 73, 185 n25, 192 n128
   liquor, 1–14, 15–47, 48–82, 83–103, 104–31, 132–53, 154–79, 182 n19
   legislation, 9, 17, 49, 54, 57, 62, 79–81, 92, 152, 194 n13, 197 n37, 198 n47, 205 n11
   distillery, 17, 26, 77, 79, 82, 140, 144, 158–59, 203 n123
   distilling process, 25, 61, 66
   rye (vodka), 10, 20, 25
   Christian consumption of, 1–14, 15–47, 48–82
   Jewish consumption of, 35, 43, 45
   Hasidism and, 35–45
   monopoly (*propinacja*), 3, 20, 54, 64, 74–76, 78, 79, 83, 89, 94, 96, 104, 117, 131, 139, 143–44, 146–47, 173, 176, 186 n51, 194 n13, 197 n35, 198 n45, 201 n90, 203 n128, 211 n17, 217 n26
   excise tax 10, 20, 55, 67,74
   concession (*konsens*), 74–76, 80–81, 84–86, 89–92, 95–96, 98–101, 104, 119–29, 131, 142, 143, 145, 148–50, 158, 173–75, 177, 198 n46, 200 n71, 203 n128, n135, 206 n26, 209 n90, 211 n17, 214 n91, 218 n46
   beer, 25–26, 50–51, 63–65, 67, 73, 100, 125, 187 n57, 188 n68, 189 n80, 201 n90
   mead, 25, 39, 42, 44, 65, 73, 77–78, 118, 201 n90
   plum brandy (*tslivovits*), 39
   arak, 40, 116
   vodka, 18, 20, 22, 26–30, 48–51, 61–64, 73, 75, 77, 100–101, 118, 151, 169, 189 n80, 192 n128, 201 n95, 203 n132
Aleichem, Sholom (Sholem Rabinovich), 11, 177, 182
Alexander, Michael Solomon (Anglican Bishop of Jerusalem), 19
Alter, Isaac Meir of Ger (Góra Kalwaria) *see also* Hasidism, 108, 135, 156
Alter, Judah Aryeh, the "Sefat Emet" *see also* Hasidism, 135
America, 3–4, 45, 134, 138–39
Anczyc, Władysław, 73, 186 n50, 203 n130
anti-Semitism, 1, 4, 6, 60, 210 n7
arenda (non-agricultural lease) *see also* tavern, toll collection, dairy lease, 6, 16, 22, 66, 70, 180 n12, 182 n3, 195 n20,
   contract, 28, 49, 53, 67–68, 71, 75–76, 80, 154, 203 n135, 219 n82
   encroachment, 50, 146, 147, 148, 219 n83

(241)

arendarz (leaseholder/tavernkeeper), 3, 16, 22, 58, 78, 160, 162, 176
Aronson, Chaim, 103–04
Aryeh Leib, the "Shpoler Zeyde" *see also* Hasidism, 39
assignacja (assignation), 15, 51
Augustów, 2, 71, 168
Austria *see* Habsburg Empire

ba'al shem, 133, 191
Babel, Isaac, 151, 220
Badeni, Ignacy, 61, 155
Barszcz [borsht], 21, 44
Będzin, 108
Belweder Palace, 105
Bełżyce, 120, 125
Bentham, Jeremy, 22, 185 n32, 204 n155
Berkowicz, Józef, 59, 106, 110
Betzalel Darshan of Przemyśl, 66
Biała Góra village, 141
Bialik, Hayyim Nahman, 23–4
Biały, 63
Bielany village, 147
Bielsko-Biala, ix
Biłgoraj, 95
Birkenthal, Dov Ber, 31
black market *see* smuggling
blood libel *see* ritual murder accusation
Blumrozen Affair, 48–52, 65, 70, 80
bootlegging (liquor), 74, 117
Bracław Palatinate, 52
brewery, 82, 107, 154, 159, 201
Brody, 108
Buczacz, 67
Bund *see also* Jewish Socialism, x
Burgher *see* Christian townspeople
Burnett, George, 21
Byelorussia, 55, 69, 196

cameralism, 53, 60, 61, 80, 84, 87, 102, 175, 184 n. 15
cantonist, 110, 165, 212 n. 36
caravansary, 18
Census of 1897, 136–37
Center for Jewish History, ix
Chagall, Marc, x
Chęciny, 115
Chelm, 96, 208 n66

Chernigov *see also* expulsions, 55, 196 n32
Chinów village, 126
Chmielnicki massacres, 66
Chodel, 97
Chopin, Friedrich, 105
Chorzele, 94
Christian townspeople, 5, 6, 15, 83–84, 86, 87, 88–89, 90, 92, 93, 94, 95, 96, 97, 98, 100–101, 106, 112, 116, 118, 124, 125, 127, 157, 158, 194 n13
Christianity *see also* church, clergy, temperance movement, 19, 35, 70, 145, 224 n90
  Catholicism, 70, 93, 189, 213 n50
  Lutheranism, 213 n50
  holidays, 10, 29, 42, 73, 143
Chrusty village 160
Church, 14, 19–23, 29, 32, 48, 77, 86, 92, 155, 185 n19, 189 n80
Ciechanów 208 n50 *see also* Kahana, Abraham Isaac of Ciechanów
circumcision ceremony (*bris*), 44, 162, 190 n102
city, x, 6–7, 39, 82–84, 86–93, 98, 125, 167
Civic Guard (Polish), 105, 108
clergy, Christian, 16, 33, 45, 52, 67, 72, 145
clothing decrees, 11
Cminski, 77
Cohn, Abraham Simon, 158
Cohn, Matthias, 74–76, 90, 156
commerce, 3–6, 7, 8, 17, 18, 20, 50, 58, 72, 95, 97, 116, 120, 143, 167, 157, 176
Commission for the Peasants, 154
Communism, 9
"compass" (*obręb*), 93, 133, 207 n.49
Congress Kingdom of Poland *see* Kingdom of Poland
Constantine, Pavlovich (Grand Duke), 104–06, 164, 206 n17
contraband, 8, 18, 54, 115–16, 119, 163
converts, conversion *see also* Frankists, 19, 35, 69–70, 114, 163, 199 n.63, 202 n.103, 213 n.50
Corn Laws (1825–45), British, 25
Council of Four Lands, 200

crafts, 10, 26, 53, 60, 100, 101, 117, 135, 136–37, 140, 154, 162, 170, 186, 220 no. 4
Cricheff (Krichev), 22
Crimean War, 99
criminalization, 8, 52, 70, 81
Cyprynus (pseud., Polish memoirist), 164
Czarnów village, 141
Czartoryski, Adam, xi, 95, 111, 154, 199 n64
Czechowice, 146
Częstochowa, 2, 172

Dąbrowiecka, 89
dairy lease, 51, 157, 161–62, 163, 180 no. 12, 194 no. 10
Davidsohn, Hayyim, Rabbi of Warsaw, 156, 220 n12
de non tolerandis Judaeis, 93
De Witt, (governor of Warsaw), 100, 114
death anniversary (*yortsayt*), 36, 39, 43
*dina de'malkhuta dina,*103
divorce, 34, 37, 133, 150, 168
Domanowo village, 141
dowry, 140, 145, 150
drinking *see also* liquor, 43–45, 55, 61, 72, 79, 96, 100–01, 145, 150, 174, 176, 192 n133, n137
   drunkenness, 8, 9, 16, 24, 26, 32–35, 42–46, 72, 97, 100–01, 175, 186 n46, 188 n77, 190 n.102, 192 n133, 193 n154
   sobriety, 6, 16, 31–32, 36, 39, 42, 45, 72
   temperance movement, 45, 72, 145–46, 193 no. 154, 218 no. 72
   songs, 20, 22, 29, 30, 40, 42, 72, 106, 127, 191 n126
   myths, vii, 11–45
drinking vouchers (*kwitki*), 72
Duchy of Warsaw, 1, 2, 10, 55–57, 86, 88, 99
Dyneburg, 165
Dzierzkowski, Józef, 48, 193

East Central Europe, 3
Eastern Europe, ix, 3–8, 45, 85, 132, 134, 171

education, 4, 10,87, 102, 106, 153–54, 169–78, 223 n81
   university, 12
   state-sponsored schools, 152, 154, 169, 173,-74, 223 n81
   Warsaw Rabbinical School, 106
   *heder,*169–74
   melamed, 172
Eiger, Akiva of Poznań, 132, 134
Einsatzstab Rosenberg, 132
Eisenbaum, Antoni, 170–71, 210 n8
Emancipation, vii, 3, 5, 78, 131, 135–42, 175, 179
   of peasantry, 12, 78, 129, 131, 135–42, 176
   of Jews, 81, 101, 110, 135–42, 153, 159, 160, 174, 177
Emeliantseva, Ekaterina, 93
Epstein, Jacob, 156
eruv (Sabbath/festival boundary), 93
escort fee (*geleitzoll*), 88
espionage, 12, 78, 104–05, 108, 111–14, 115, 119, 121–30
ethnic economy, 16
ethnography, 28, 188 no. 69, 191 n126
expulsions, 9, 40, 53, 99, 196 n32
   from countryside, 3, 11, 18, 24, 55–56, 61, 67, 70, 73–74, 80–81, 85, 99, 196 n32
   from border towns, 117
   from mining towns, 93
   from Chernigov and Pultava (Russian Empire), 55, 196 n32
   from main rural roads, 49, 70, 85
   from principal urban streets, 89, 94
exymowany (restricted), 87
Ezekiel (Yehezkel) Kotik, 36, 55, 109, 139, 190 n102

factor (for nobility), 3, 5, 111, 135, 140
farming, Jewish *see* agricultural colony
fertility, 143
folk forms, 15, 30, 32, 48, 151
   dances, 29, 192 n137 (Hasidic)
   idioms, 28, 32, 46, 154
   songs, 20, 22, 29–30, 40, 42, 72, 106, 127
   healing, 134
Forefathers, holiday, 29, 39, 106

fornication, 18–19, 24
"Four-year Sejm" (1788–92), 24, 53
France, 20, 61
Frank, Jacob, 70, 93, 202 no. 104
Frederick August, the Duke of
    Warsaw, 87
Frederick Wilhelm, King of Prussia, 54
Friedlander, S.Y., 37, 190 n110

Galicia, 21–22, 43–44, 53–55, 57, 67, 69,
    107, 145–46, 165, 176, 179 n6, 183
    n8, 187 n66, 195 n21, 217 n44
Garczyński, Stefan, 1, 3, 178
garkuchnia (cheap restaurant), 50–52, 71,
    119–20, 161
Gdańsk (Danzig), 2, 6, 25
genealogy, ix,
gentile *see also* goy, 4, 11, 16, 24, 29, 31,
    38–42, 45, 65–70, 140–48, 162–63,
    168–68, 172
German (ethnic), 4, 6, 31, 106, 109, 111,
    115, 128, 134, 138, 171, 173
Germanization, 179 n6
Germany, 109,138, 179n7
ghetto, 87–88, 132
Glodnow village, 160
Gluchowce village, 115
Glucksberg, Jan, 91, 157
Glucksohn, Raphael, 75–76, 156
Glukl of Hameln, 207 n40
Gombiner, Abraham Abele ("The Magen
    Avraham"), 43–44
goy, 45, 131, 141, 143, 163, 166–67
Grabowski, W., 30
grain trade, 25, 63, 138
Grätz (Grodzisk Wielkopolski), 131–32,
    135
Great Emigration, 104
Great Sabbath (Shabbat ha-gadol), 143
Gródek, 116
Gudel village (Augustów District), 71
Guttmacher, Elijah (Eliyahu) of Grätz
    (Grodzisk Wielkopolski), 12, 33–35,
    131–35, 137, 140–41, 143, 146–49,
    151–52, 160–63, 166–68, 172

halakha (Jewish ritual law), xi, 5
Ha-magid,132, 133
Harring, Harro, 83, 116
Hasidism *see also* drinking, 7, 35–40

Hasid, 35–45, 55, 69–70, 104–110,
    126–27, 129, 132–35,
    171, 178
worship through corporeality, 191
tzaddik, 35–36, 38–45, 52, 55, 69,
    108–10, 126, 131–35, 140–51, 156,
    160–63, 166–68, 173
Stolin, 38
shtibl (prayer house), 38–39, 42, 69
Kotzker, 109, 193 n154
Lubavitch, 37, 40–41, 104,
    192 n132
songs, 40–42, 192 n137
dance, 39, 42, 192 n137
Haskalah, 5, 129, 171, 224 n91
Halberstam, Hayyim of Sanz *see also*
    Hasidism, 44, 193 n.149
Hebrew, xi, 23, 31, 37, 39, 58, 132, 156,
    170–71
ḥemer medinah, 20, 43
Hildesheimer, Esriel, 132, 172
Hollaenderski, Leon, 110
Horowitz, Isaiah, 43
Horowitz, Jacob Isaac, the "Seer of
    Lublin," 36, 44
Hrubieszòw, 211 n23
Hungary, 43–44, 195 n23
Hyman, Paula, 5

illness, 139, 143, 149, 150, 172–73
industrialization, 5, 7, 9, 99, 133, 142,
    177
factories and 59, 87, 89, 113, 117,
    135, 139, 158
informer, 47, 49,133–34, 144, 146, 148,
    151, 163, 219 n91
inn *see* tavern
insurrection *see* uprising
integration, 4–5, 16, 85, 90, 102, 106,
    156, 165, 170–72
Interior Ministry, 48–49, 58–61, 71, 76,
    86, 106, 157, 170
Iron Curtain, 9
Ivan Paskevich (Viceroy), 57–58, 64, 70,
    72, 88, 99, 154–55
Izraelita, 172

Jakubowicz, Judyta, 156
Jerozolimski, Moses, 166, 170–71
Jerusalem, 1, 19 60, 169

Jewish Committee, 55, 58, 60–62, 101, 155, 199 n64, 202 n.106
Jewish quarter *see rewir*
Jewish Socialism, 5
Jewish-Christian relations, 4–8, 24–33, 79, 88, 129
   economic protectionism 16, 146–7
Joselewicz, Berek (Col.), 110
Joseph II, Emperor, 53
Junosza, Klemens, 169
Jutrzenka, 171–72

Kabbalah, 37, 132, 164
kahal, 59, 66
Kahana, Abraham Isaac of Ciechanów *see also* Hasidism, 127
Kaidanover, Tzevi Hirsch, 24, 33
Kalish, Isaac of Warka (Vurke), 43, 156, 224 n90
Kapulye (Kapyl, Belarus), 4
Karo, Joseph Hayim (Rabbi of Włocławek), 128
Kazimierz Dolny, 145
Kielce 75, 114, 123
Kiev, 52, 85
Kingdom of Poland, vii, 1–2, 11, 15, 22, 24–28, 35–36, 46–51, 55–63, 68–73, 84–88,94, 104, 107–09, 131, 134–36, 139, 142, 146, 153, 164, 167–68, 171, 177–78
Kinskaia gang, 121
Kisielnice, 49–51
Kisielnicki, Franciszek, 49–52, 70, 80
Kłodzinski, Adam, 193, 47–49
Kobylin, 49–51
Kock (Kotzk) *See also* Hasidism, 98, 108–09
Koleński, A., 178
Kolno, 64
Konary, 125
Końskowola, 95–96
Konstantyn, 116
Koźmian, Kajetan, 57
Krakow, 2, 35, 65–66, 78, 86, 107, 195 n.23
Krantz, Jacob, the "Dubno Maggid," 134
Kraszewski, Józef Ignacy, 22–23, 121–22
Królewska Street (Warsaw), 91
Kuchary, 113
kvass, 22, 44

kvitlekh (petitions), xi, 9, 12–13, 25, 33, 57, 75, 78, 84–86, 91–92, 96, 102, 106, 132

Labiau, 165
Lachowicze, 184 n11
Land Credit Society, 138, 141
land ownership, Jewish, 59, 140, 158–60
Landau, Israel Yona, 134
Landy, Michał, 122
leaseholding *see arenda*
Leipzig *see also* trade fair, 58, 90, 116
Lejbowicz, Mordecai, of Grodno, 164
Leslie, R.F., 105
Levashov, Vasili, 55
Levi Isaac of Berdichev (Berdyczów), 35
Lipschitz, Jacob, 107
Lipschitz, Solomon Zalman, 68
Lithuania (historic) 1, 3, 6, 7–11, 14, 20, 24, 43, 52, 56, 61, 66, 83, 96, 103, 175, 202 n107
Lithuanian Council, 219 n73
Liubarskii, Iosel, 121
Lodz, 3, 89, 106, 109, 145, 158
Łomza (district), 2, 49, 50, 52, 116, 121, 155, 158
lord-Jew relationship (*see also arenda*), 16, 71, 80, 71–2, 80–1, 152, 183 n9 and n10
lottery, 33, 112, 143, 148, 166
Lubavitcher Hasidism *see* Hasidism
Lublin, 2, 36, 44, 70, 71, 83, 98, 107, 115, 119, 120
Ludmir (Włodzimierz/Volodymyr-Volyn'skyi), 66
lumber, 137–40, 163, 217 n28

Mączyński, Józef, 22, 185
Maimon, Solomon, 7, 23–25, 30, 31–33
marriage, 16, 37, 46, 133, 149–50
Marymont district (Warsaw), 59
maskil, x, 35–36, 85, 169–73, 190, 195, 224 n91
Massalski, E.T., 80, 97
matchmaking, 28, 133, 143
Mayer, Arno, 3
Mazovia, 63–64, 88–89, 200, n80, 203 n130
Medzowiec village, 125
Meisels, Rabbi Dov Ber, 99, 122, 127

Menachem Mendel of Kotzk *see also* Hasidism *and* Kock, 108, 193 no. 150, 202 no. 105
Menaḥem Mendel of Rymanów *see also* Hasidism, 69
Menaḥem Mendel of Vitebsk *see also* Hasidism, 52, 69
Mendele *see* Abramovitsh, S.Y.
Mennonites, 121
merchant, 4–8, 17, 20, 31, 50, 55, 58, 69, 72, 74, 87, 95, 97, 112–113, 116, 119–20, 127–28, 135, 140, 143, 156, 167, 176
Meshullam Phoebus of Krakow, 65
Mickiewicz, Adam, 3, 14–15, 24, 45–46, 48, 105–06, 174
Międzyrzecz , 76, 116
migration, 3, 22, 56, 73, 98, 104, 133, 136, 139
Miklos village, 120
Mikoszewski, Karol, 32
military conscription, Jewish, 12, 153, 155, 164–68
military suppliers, 7, 105, 114
mining, 77, 93, 161
miracle working, 133–34
Mirowski army barracks, 92
missionaries, 19, 42
mitnagdim ("opponents"), 35, 38
Mochnacki, Maurice, 111
Mogielnica, 54, 109, 118
Mokotowska Street (Warsaw), 90
moneylending, 8, 133, 138, 140–42, 217 n42 and n45
Montefiore, Moses, xi, 101, 157
Mohrer, Fruma, xi
Moses Elyakim Beriyah of Kozienice *see also* Hasidism, 69, 196 n.33
Mostowski, Tadeusz, 57, 60, 88, 199 n60
Muszkat, J. M., Rabbi of Praga, 156
Muszyński, Matteusz, 61–62

Naftali Tzevi of Ropczyce *see also* Hasidism, 69
Nahman of Bratslav *see also* Hasidism, 41
Napęków village, 123
Napoleon, 1–2, 55–56, 82–83, 86, 88, 95, 104, 111, 198 n54
National Guard (Polish), 105–06, 108, 110–11, 212 n25

Neale, Adam, 21
Nechlyn village, 147
New York City, 132
Niemcewicz, Julian Ursyn, 159
nobility, 3, 6–7, 10, 17, 21, 23, 25, 50, 52–53, 58, 61, 84, 93, 100, 102, 127, 130, 135–41, 148, 175–76, 199 n68
Norwid, Cyprian Kamil, 122
Novosiltsev, Nicholas, 57, 88, 99, 164, 197 n43
Nowy Świat Street (Warsaw), 90–91
NSDAP Institut zur Erforschung der Judenfrage (Institute for Investigating the Jewish Question), 132

Odessa, 85
Olszowni village, 123
Opatoshu, Joseph, 138
Opatów, 16, 18, 90, 94–95, 98, 123
Organic Statute (1832), 91
orphan, 66, 113, 125, 147, 149, 171
Osjaków village, 140
Ostrowno village, 140
Ostrowski, Antoni, 31–32, 111–13, 153

Pale of Settlement, 55, 110
Palestine (Land of Israel), 132, 139
Paltrowitz, Tzvi Hirsch of Nowogród, 134
Pan Tadeusz (1834), 3, 14, 174
Paniszczów village, 141
partitions of Poland, 7–8, 9, 11, 17, 53–4, 83–4
Passek, P. B., 55
Passover, 49, 70, 104, 143–44
Pawlikowice, 158–59
peasant *see also* emancipation *and* serfs, vii, 3, 5–8, 12, 14–18, 20, 21–32, 45–46, 48–52, 54–57, 61, 69, 72–79, 97–101, 105, 126, 129, 131, 135–43, 151, 158–59, 162, 169, 174–77, 188 n.76
Peasant Bank of the Kingdom of Poland, 142
peddler, 6, 18
Peretz, I. L., 27, 80, 138–39, 145, 177
Perl, Joseph, 189–91, 205, 208
Piaker village, 147

Piaski (Lublin District), 71
Piechal, Marian, 178
Pietrów village, 141
Pilatti, Gustaw, 29–30
Pińczów, 95
Piotrków, 160
pirogy, 21
Pistorius liquor still *see also* distilling, 25, 187 n55
Płock, 2, 62–63, 82, 115
pogrom, 4, 138, 176
Poland-Lithuania *see* Polish-Lithuanian Commonwealth
Polek village, 141
Polesia, 22
Polish-Jewish relations *see* Jewish-Christian relations, 1, 106
Polish-Lithuanian Commonwealth, 1, 6–9, 11, 14, 20, 24, 43, 61, 96, 175, 178
pollution (spiritual), 11, 20, 22
Poltava *see also* expulsions, 55, 196 n32
Poryte, 49–51
positivism, 9, 151, 169
Posner, Solomon Marcus, 108, 113
potato *see also* alcohol, 25–26, 77
Potocki, Stanisław, 89–90, 94–95
Praga, 100, 106, 156
Prawda, 169
Prince Nicholas Repnin, 55, 79
propinacja (propination) *see* liquor monopoly
Prus, Boleslaw, 133, 159
Prussia, 1–2, 8, 19, 25, 54, 93, 116–17, 131–32, 135, 146, 176
Przymja village, 160–61
Psary village, 141
publicists (Polish), 56–57, 80, 194 n17
Puławy, 95

R. Israel Ba'al Shem Tov, the Besht, 133, 191 n121 *see also* Hasidism
Radi, 23
Radom (District), 2, 123, 126
Radziwiłł, Karol, 23, 25
Radzyn, 76, 120
rape, 18–19, 138
Raszyn, 165
recruitment tax, 107, 169
Redlich, Joseph, 156

Reform Judaism, 5
reincarnation, 38
rewir (Jewish quarter), 88, 89, 93–99, 205 n11, 207–08 n.50
Ringelblum, Emanuel, 184 n.14, 210 n.7, 211 n.13
ritual murder accusation, 30–31, 121, 128
rivi'it, 44, 193 n.144
Robert-Fleury, Tony, 122
Rokeaḥ, Shalom of Belz, 44 *see also* Hasidism
Rosen, Isaac, 156
Rosman, Moshe, 9, 13, 16, 183 n.9
Roth, Joseph, x
Rozniszew village (Radom District), 126, 123
Rozycki, Samuel (Gen.), 109
Russia *see also* Tsarist Empire, 1–4, 46, 55, 61, 71, 75, 78, 95–96, 103–199, 123–128, 138–39
Russian Poland *see* Kingdom of Poland
Ryki, 119–21

Sabbateanism, 19
Sabbath, 21, 33, 36, 38–39, 43–50, 65–69, 72, 80–81, 110, 119, 124, 142–43, 149, 162
Salcstein, Gecl, 109
Samogitia District (historical Lithuania), 103–05
Samsonów, 74, 76–77, 79
Samuel Abba of Żychlin *see also* Hasidism, 109–10, 212 n36
Sandomierz, 2, 165
Schneur Zalman of Lyady *see also* Hasidism, 40, 44, 196 n30
schools, secular *see* education (state-sanctioned)
Ściegienny, Piotr, 109
secularization, 5, 133, 171–72, 178
Segal, David ha-Levi ("The TaZ"), 43
Sejm (Polish parliament), 24, 52–53
seminary, 132, 170, 172
serf *see also* peasant, 135, 139, 157, 176, 183 n.10
Shapira, Ḥayim Me'ir Yeḥi'el of Mogielnica *see also* Hasidism, 109
Shapira, Hayyim Eleazar, 43–44

Shiker iz der goy (The gentile [*goy*] is drunk), 45
shtetl, x, 3, 94, 133, 136
Shulḥan Arukh ("Set Table"), 37
Siedlce, 2, 109, 127
Siekierek, 115
Simchat Torah, 38–39
Slomka, Jan, 22, 27, 32, 69
Słowacinek, 76
Słowacki, Juliusz, 105
smuggling, 8, 12, 15, 48, 92, 93, 114–21, 128, 137, 163
Sobolewski, Ignacy, 56–57, 86–87
sojourner's tax (*billet*), 88
Sokołów, 60, 115
soldiers, vii, 12, 18, 78, 92, 94, 103, 105, 110, 114,116, 127, 137, 153, 164–73
Solomon Drimer of Skole, 67
Solomon of Radomsko *see also* Hasidism, 40
Sombart, Werner, 146
Sonnenberg-Bergson, Temerel, 156
spying *see* espionage
St. Alexander's Church, 32
Stanisława (County), 63
Stanislawski, Michael, 170
starosta, 7, 181, 194 n13
Stary village, 118–19
Starzek village, 141
Staszic, Stanisław, 24
Stawiski, 49, 117
Stern, Abraham, 36, 169–70
Stryków, 149
Stueckgold, Cecilia, 127
supliki (petitions to landowners), 84
Suwałki, 81
Synagogue Council, 59, 171
  Warsaw, 99–100, 156–57, 166, 171
  Lublin, 107
Szydłowiec, 123
Świętochowski, Aleksander, 169

Tahlgrin, El'azar, 170–71
takanot (rabbinic decrees), 12, 65
Talmud, the 38–40, 103, 156, 169–70
tariff, 8, 25
Tarnobrzeg, 22
tavern, ix-x, 1–7, 10–14, 16–33, 39–42, 47–51, 52–58, 60–79, 81–101, 104–111, 117–126, 131, 138–152, 156–161, 169, 175–78
Teller, Adam, 12, 16
theft *see also* contraband, 54, 113, 117, 119–21
  bandits, 119, 121, 128, 144
  "fences," 72
tikun (cosmic repair), 37, 41
Tlusty, B. Ann, 36
Toeplitz, Theodore, 156
toll collection, 67
Tomaszów, 124
Tomaszów Mazowiecki, 153
Torah, 23–24, 35, 37–39, 66, 68, 91, 109, 143, 145, 163, 167
town *see also* expulsions *and* revir, xi, 1–37, 49, 52–54, 69–72, 79–85, 88–101, 108–09, 115–24, 134–57, 168–69
  market *see* shtetl,
  private, 6–7, 10, 59, 94, 96, 160, 181, 184
  royal/state-owned, 7, 96, 181, 194, 207
  clergy-owned, 207 n.49
trade fair, 6, 47, 49, 90, 97, 116 *see also* Leipzig
trade *see* commerce
traditionalism, 5, 35, 88, 94, 107–08, 178
translation, xi
travelers, 3, 6, 10, 21, 49–52, 63–64, 71, 120
Treasury (Polish), 58, 60–65, 71, 74, 76–79, 107, 115, 124
Trunk, Y.Y., 36, 69
Tsar Alexander I, 94
Tsar Alexander II, 78, 99
Tugendhold, Jacob, 110, 156, 169–71
Turkul, H.E., 58, 94, 101, 174

Ukraine, the, 67, 121
Uniejowice, 140
Uprising, 1830–1, vii, 8, 12, 46, 62, 64, 71–81, 85, 89–90, 95, 99, 104–19, 158, 165, 171
Uprising, 1863–4, 3, 12, 36, 46, 106–10, 121–30

village, x, 1–10, 15–20, 22–29, 32–33, 42, 48–66, 69–86, 93–104, 113–116, 123–26, 135, 139–44, 147–48, 157–61, 177
Vilna, 85, 132, 189, 207 n48
violence, 1, 28, 65, 67
Vistula river, 6, 115, 119
Volhynia, 23

Walachia, 191 n121
Walencen village, 144
War of 1812 (Napoleonic), 55, 95, 104, 111, 165, 196 no. 31
Warka, 36, 43, 112, 156
Warsaw, xi-7, 10, 12, 32, 43, 49, 55–59, 64, 68, 74–75, 80–88, 91–106, 108–115, 119–124, 155–57, 165–66, 205 n13, 206 n21
Wassercug, Moses, 33, 82–84
Western Europe, 4–5, 134
widow, 34, 37, 64, 91, 95, 125, 140, 147, 149–50, 161–62, 167, 207 n.38
Wielopolski, Margrave Aleksander, 78
Wieluń, 172
Wierszek village, 141
Wilanowski estate, 89
Winawer, Abraham, 64, 171

Włocławek, 128, 172
Wola Magnuszeska village, 126
Wolfson, Elliot, xi, 13
women, Jewish, 91–2
Wraxall, William, 21
Wyspiański, Stanisław, 54, 89, 94

Yankel (Jankiel) the Tavernkeeper, 3, 14–15, 24, 46, 48, 174, 178
Yerushalmi, Yosef, 179 n.2
Yiddish, 3, 5, 11, 23, 27, 30, 37, 40, 45, 47, 133, 138, 143, 177
YIVO Institute for Jewish Research, 12–13, 132
Yom Kippur, 38, 69

Zajączek, Józef, 57–59, 88, 155
Zakroczym, 93
Zamość, 2, 98, 106, 124, 134, 165, 173
Zamoyski family, 25, 26
Zastowski, 89
Zbytki, 89
Zhitomir, ix
Zilberman, Eliezer Lipman, 133
Zionism, 5, 132
Złoczek village, 141
Zohar, Book of, 37

www.ingramcontent.com/pod-product-compliance
Ingram Content Group UK Ltd.
Pitfield, Milton Keynes, MK11 3LW, UK
UKHW042006230426
12048UKWH00009B/581